key
MARKETING
SKILLS

key
MARKETING
SKILLS

2nd edition

**strategies,
tools and
techniques
for marketing
success**

peter cheverton

**KOGAN
PAGE**

London and Sterling, VA

Publisher's note

Every possible effort has been made to ensure that the information contained in this book is accurate at the time of going to press, and the publishers and authors cannot accept responsibility for any errors or omissions, however caused. No responsibility for loss or damage occasioned to any person acting, or refraining from action, as a result of the material in this publication can be accepted by the editor, the publisher or any of the authors.

First published in Great Britain and the United States in 2000 by Kogan Page Limited
Second edition 2004

120 Pentonville Road
London N1 9JN
United Kingdom
www.kogan-page.co.uk

22883 Quicksilver Drive
Sterling VA 20166–2012
USA

© Peter Cheverton, 2000, 2004

ISBN 0 7494 4298 0

British Library Cataloguing-in-Publication Data

A CIP record for this book is available from the British Library.

Library of Congress Cataloging-in-Publication Data

Cheverton, Peter
    Key marketing skills : turning marketing strategy into marketing reality, a complete action kit of strategies, tools and techniques for marketing success / Peter Cheverton – 2nd ed.
    Includes index.
    ISBN 0-7494-4298-0
    1. Marketing. 2. Strategic planning. I. Title.
HF5415.C52254 2004
658.8—dc22
                                2004017032

Typeset by Saxon Graphics Ltd, Derby
Printed and bound in Great Britain by Scotprint

Contents

Foreword to the first edition

Why does the world need another book on the principles and practice of marketing?

Well, for one thing, marketing by its very nature must keep pace with the changing business practices of the real world, and perhaps it is now more than at any other time in the last 30 years that these changes promise to alter the shape of the marketer's vision. That is the up side.

If misunderstood, these new practices also threaten to disrupt the poorly informed marketer's equilibrium, sending them back into the dark age of a secondary support function.

What are these changes? They include the so-called 'new economy' heralded by the *e-revolution* – does it change the rules of marketing? Another is the increasing focus on *Key Account Management* – does that move the responsibility for marketing elsewhere? And a third, looking beyond the hype that almost threatens to engulf and suffocate *Customer Relationship Management* – is there genuine value for the marketer?

In answering these questions this book shows how the marketer's vision can indeed be reshaped, but perhaps the more important contribution to the practice of marketing lies in the stress given to the continued importance of a disciplined approach, without hyperbole or false expectations. The sad truth behind many of today's marketing failures is the false belief that fundamentals such as understanding the market, segmentation, positioning, marketing planning and management of the marketing mix are no longer relevant.

Twenty years ago companies were too often guilty of investing millions in advertising campaigns with little or no understanding of their true impact, or sometimes even of their purpose. This book certainly shows how to avoid such mistakes, and lays down the warning not to repeat the malpractice with today's 'new toys'.

The fundamentals still apply, but it isn't just about 'sticking to your knitting'. The new concepts provide opportunities for these fundamental tools of marketing to be used and envisioned in radically different ways. The Internet certainly changes the face of the marketing mix, Customer Relationship Management offers approaches to segmentation that would previously have been extremely difficult or expensive, whilst Key Account Management provides the opportunity to build barriers to entry and achieve sustainable competitive advantage through integrated relationships.

The second reason that this book is needed (and any marketer knows that needs are what drive the market) is that professional marketers are crying out for help with the practical application of marketing tools and concepts. This book's approach is throughout a practical one. Written by a practitioner, for practitioners, it uses real case studies in abundance to illustrate what could otherwise sometimes seem rather abstract concepts. As such, the book is a mine of inspiration, and of timely warnings.

Case studies, particularly those that are still running their course, are always dangerous territory for the author. This author chooses his with an eye first and foremost on whether they instruct and illuminate. If posterity sees some of them turn the 'wrong way' then so be it – the emphasis here is on learning, not prediction.

My third reason for welcoming this new book to the distinguished list of marketing texts is perhaps a more depressing one. The role of marketing in guiding and directing business strategy is a vital and fundamental one, yet for many companies it is still their 'weak link'. All too often marketing is seen as the promotional arm of an organization rather than the function that informs all other functions what their contribution should be to creating customer value.

This book is intended to help raise the profile of marketing as a crucial element of corporate strategy. It offers help to experienced marketers through a disciplined focus on what the activity really means. By stripping away some of the trees we have a welcome re-sighting of the wood. Newcomers will benefit from the hugely efficient explanation of key tools and concepts, while those from the so-called 'non-marketing functions' will appreciate the wealth of cases that bring the activity to life, rather than shrouding it in abstruse and academic models.

If you are interested in marketing, whether in pursuit of a professional qualification, or in order to make an effective contribution to your own company's marketing activity, or simply to better understand and work with your marketing colleagues, please be assured that reading this book will be a rewarding experience.

Professor Malcolm McDonald
September 2000

Preface to the second edition

Key Marketing Skills was well received as an addition to the practical end of the marketing bookshelf; it was seized on by those who actually have to do marketing for a living. The many letters and e-mails from readers have been a great delight – compliments are always appreciated – but there was a theme: make it even more practical!

This second edition is an attempt to do just that. It is a significant rewrite of the first edition, with several new chapters and plenty of new or revised case studies. It centres around a brand new model for marketing planning, developed through the real-world experience of helping clients implement their own marketing plans. 'Too academic', they said of the old model; so out it went.

With practicality the key theme, it was important to look again at the standard marketing toolkit. How many of these tools were there just for the sake of it; to make marketers look as if they knew what they were doing? That wasn't good enough, of course, and so each tool in this new edition has been *vetted* for its merits in practical application. In working through the text, I was often reminded of an old TV advert for Corona fizzy drinks (anyone else remembering this ad, and indeed the product, should let me know; it's good to discuss old times…), where the cartoon character Top Cat declared, *'Every bubble's passed its fizzical.'*

I'm sure you will let me know if any duds have made it through…

Preface to the first edition

This book is designed as a practical guide to the concepts, processes and *application* of professional marketing practice. Its intention is to provide the reader with the skills and knowledge required for professional application in their own business, and market circumstances. The tools and processes discussed are applicable to consumer goods, retail, industrial, business to business, and service environments.

A short comment on examples and case studies: Wherever possible I have used real examples, often as up to date as the moment of writing. The advantage of this is a topicality and immediacy that I hope is welcomed, but the down sides are obvious, and potentially embarrassing! I trust that not too many of my 'success stories' have gone bust by the time the book reaches the bookstore, and that events have not so overtaken any questions or predictions as to render them the mutterings of an imbecile.

As the first edition went to press, e-retailers were falling out of the sky, and as the second edition makes its way, so the world is fast becoming a more uncertain place for much wider-ranging reasons. Times change, and so do fortunes; such is the challenge before today's marketing professional.

Acknowledgements

My thanks as ever to my colleagues in INSIGHT Marketing and People Ltd. Their knowledge and experience have added greatly to the relevance and practicality of this book.

Professor Malcolm McDonald, Emeritus Professor at Cranfield University School of Management, and Chairman of INSIGHT, has been his usual generous self in providing encouragement for my ideas as well as allowing me to use a number of his own.

In particular I would like to thank Mats Engström and Per Resvik from the IHM Business School in Stockholm and Gothenburg for helping to inject into this book an even more practical approach than even I thought was possible!

Peter Cheverton
September 2004

Part I

Definitions, purpose and process

What is marketing?

WHAT THE PUBLIC THINKS…

Ask a sample of people in the pub or standing at a bus queue, 'what does marketing mean to you?' and the chances are you will get responses not so very far removed from these:

Making people buy things they don't really want

or

Producing expensive adverts

or even

Dressing up ordinary products as something special.

It's not a good start, and unfortunately it gets worse. A recent opinion poll in the United Kingdom found that marketing folk were rated at only one rung above politicians and tabloid journalists on the ladder of 'respectable' careers… but if you want to hear *real* cynicism, try asking businesspeople what they make of their marketing colleagues. *'Slippery'* is a common description, *'unaccountable'* another, with *'unprofessional'* another regular criticism. Compared to the rigour of an accountant or an engineer or a research scientist, it seems that non-marketers have a hard time seeing any formal process or discipline in the marketer's activities.

So why all this contempt, and how is it that marketers have marketed *themselves* so badly?

The media delight, of course, in 'outing' the latest marketing farragos, and it has to be said that the outings are often well deserved.

Just a drop in the ocean?

When Coca-Cola launched its Dasini brand of bottled water in the United Kingdom, it was with undisguised glee that the press announced the product's source: the exact same tap water that supplied the local community. It wasn't denied, and a spokesperson for Dasini went on to say that it was Coca-Cola's unique processing that fully justified the premium charged over the locally available brew: £1.90 against £0.06 a litre. The spokesperson couldn't understand the fuss, as if taking the water from the tap was entirely normal practice, adding that when you thought about it, all water came from the same source in the first place… Whatever the marketing capability displayed, Dasini certainly confirmed that Coca-Cola's grasp of PR was even worse. A scare over a possible chemical contamination just a few weeks later was enough to see the launch abandoned.

Such high-profile disasters are bound to give the marketing profession a bad name, and saying that this particular story represents only a tiny, tiny fraction of the great mass of marketing activity is hardly going to change the public's perception, although it may at least reassure those of us involved in the profession that we are not a bunch of charlatans. Hopefully we knew that already.

What the Dasini story raises is the issue of public scrutiny – a relatively new issue for the professional marketer. Today's consumers are increasingly interested in aspects of the products they buy that were of little or no concern to previous generations: where they are made, how they are made, and the working conditions of the people who made them. This has inevitably put many companies under the spotlight, with accusations ranging from despoiling the environment to exploitation of workers, or poor standards of health and safety. Marketers must of course take account of this; such issues have become part of their products, and quite rightly so. A brilliantly branded pair of trainers cannot hope to succeed if it is founded on a sweatshop business model, any more than a trendy coffee shop can be founded on subsistence-level prices for the growers. Indeed, the whole notion of branding is changing such that 'sweatshop' and 'brilliantly branded' could scarcely appear in the same sentence any longer. Of course, marketing professionals must go further than just 'taking account': they must take an active role in ensuring proper standards throughout the supply chain of their products – an opportunity for them to gain competitive advantage, and perhaps to regain some of the respect they appear to have lost.

Naomi Klein has done much to raise the importance of this issue in her excellent book *No Logo*, and will have done much to improve the integrity of the marketing activity as a result, but her book will also have added to the wider sense that marketing is somehow less than moral, if not exactly immoral. This is unfortunate, as for the most part marketing is an activity that aims to create genuine value for customers from responsibly managed resources.

There is one final problem with the public's view of marketing, but this time one that also bedevils the business community's proper understanding of what it is all about. This is the idea that marketing simply equals advertising. Many a marketing department, in many a large company, _is_ in fact just the place they make the glossy brochures. That's promotion, and a very important task, but it isn't marketing.

Much more than promotion...

SO WHAT DO _YOU_ THINK?

Which of the following six statements do you feel give the best definitions of what marketing is all about? Perhaps none of them matches your own understanding, but which come closest? Try to identify the three that you feel are the best, or, if none of them appeals very much, then at least the three least bad!

Marketing is:

1. selling everything that you make;
2. making our customers prosperous;
3. making the best-quality product;
4. making whatever quality the customer wants;
5. getting out of unprofitable lines;
6. looking for future needs.

I confess that none of these statements is meant to be an adequate definition. The point of the exercise is to establish whether you have any current bias in your understanding – are you a _'left-sider'_ or a _'right-sider'_ (see Figure 1.1)?

Are you a 'left-sider' or a 'right-sider'

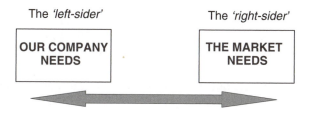

Figure 1.1   _The attitude spectrum_

Perhaps you can identify a commonality between statements 1, 3 and 5, and another between 2, 4 and 6? Definitions 1, 3 and 5 are the 'left-sider' views: a concern with internal issues – achieving sales targets (or efficient use of production capacity), an emphasis on the product and a focus on the present. Numbers 2, 4 and 6 are the 'right-sider' views; right-siders' focus is external: the customer, and a concern for the future.

Is one side any better than the other? Let's debate the 'left-siders':

- *Marketing is selling everything that you make.* So what if the market doesn't want what you make? What if it prefers someone else's product or service? In such a situation your only option may be to drop the price and have a clearance sale. Is that good marketing?
- *Marketing is making the best-quality product.* So what if people feel they can do with something less than a Rolls-Royce? How do you force a cordon bleu meal on someone determined on eating a Big Mac? Indeed, why should you try?
- *Marketing is getting out of unprofitable lines.* So what if you supply stationery items direct to local offices, and most of your lines are profitable, but not envelopes. Do you drop envelopes from the range and make the customers go elsewhere? How would they feel about you, and what if they get to like where they go for their envelopes?

There are clearly some significant limitations to defining marketing solely in this 'left-sider' way. So, let's debate the 'right-siders':

- *Marketing is making our customers prosperous.* Sounds good – prosperous customers will return – but there are some obvious limitations to this idea. The easiest way to make customers prosperous might be to supply them with top-quality product, with top-quality service, free of charge… But the concept sounded right. Perhaps it was that comment about the *easiest* way to make a customer prosperous that should worry us; perhaps there are *better* ways…?
- *Marketing is making whatever quality the customer wants.* Makes sense – but what if we can't do it competitively? Let's say we make fabric dyes – top-quality fabric dyes. Perhaps there is a demand for a low-quality, low-price dye for some applications, but we can't hope to compete with low-price imports. Do we supply at a loss, as an act of goodwill?
- *Marketing is looking for future needs.* Of course, to argue with that would be dull, but how far ahead do we look before it becomes 'wild blue yondering' and a potential distraction from the real needs of *today*?

Acts of faith…

So, which side do you fall on? The left-side definitions are dangerously narrow and self-interested, but perhaps you feel that the right-side definitions are just too vague, almost becoming acts of faith rather than practical definitions?

…or states of mind?

Rather than 'acts of faith', I would prefer to represent them as a 'state of mind', and a very valuable state of mind: the professional marketer's state of mind. The notion that getting it right for the customer, now and in the future, will result in our own success is a simple enough one, but is not always shared across a typical multi-function business.

Other mindsets will be found: success will result from cost reduction (the accountant's mindset?); success will result from better products (the R&D mindset?); success will result from supply-chain efficiencies (the Operations mindset?). Are they all right? Is business success inevitably a compromise between apparently conflicting functional notions? The answer to that is a resounding _no_, and it is marketing that provides the solution to this apparent dilemma – or at least, it will do if it follows the guidance given by the _Marketing Model_, discussed in the next chapter.

2

The Marketing Model

The six possible definitions of marketing given in Chapter 1 were certainly not intended as the final word on the matter. They expressed two apparently conflicting thought processes: the left-sider's concern with 'reality' and the right-sider's desire to enquire and understand.

Let's consider another definition, this time from the United Kingdom's Chartered Institute of Marketing:

Marketing is anticipating, identifying and satisfying customers' needs, profitably.

This is good in that it stresses the future: marketing is a proactive task; it is about *anticipating*. It sees marketing as an inquisitive pursuit, not simply the result of what we know and do already; it is about *identifying*. It gives marketing a fundamental goal – *satisfying customers' needs* – and it provides a 'real-world' test – that this should be done *profitably*.

But there are still some problems, or things lacking. I might identify three:

1. In the real world, none of this happens in a vacuum. There are competitors struggling just like you to anticipate, identify and satisfy. This has an implication for *how* you will go about the task: finding ways to do it better than the competition. At its core, marketing must be about seeking such *competitive advantage*.
2. As well as the *competitive environment*, there is also your own environment: your own businesses capabilities. The real world again – resources, money, time, people and skills: factors that will impact on your ability to anticipate, identify and satisfy, profitably.

3. Something often lacking in written definitions of marketing is what we
    might call 'the spur to action'. You read the definition under discussion
    only a few seconds ago, but do you remember it? Does it *live* in your
    mind? Will it make you want to do anything new or different about
    your business?

In relation to point 3, how about this one for an absolute 'howler' of the
kind:

> *Marketing is the process of: (1) identifying customer needs; (2) conceptualizing*
> *these needs in terms of the organization's capacity to produce; (3) communicating*
> *that conceptualization to the appropriate focus of power in the organization; (4)*
> *conceptualizing the consequent output in terms of customer needs earlier iden-*
> *tified; (5) communicating that conceptualization to the customer.*

If you could be bothered to fathom its meaning, there *is* actually something
there, but frankly, who would be bothered to find it?

The Marketing Model proposes a pictorial definition, as shown in Figure
2.1.

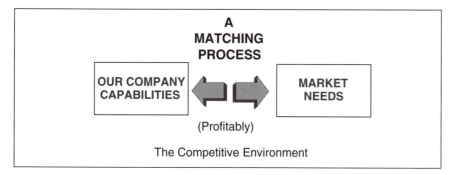

Figure 2.1   *The INSIGHT Marketing Model: a definition*

This describes marketing as a matching process between our capabilities
and the market needs – a matching process that has as its goal a profitable
competitive advantage. It aims to combine the left- and the right-sider's
views without allowing either dominance over the other, or losing the
marketer's mindset in a fudged compromise.

The search for this match happens, of course, in a competitive environment. Assuming that your competitors understand something about
marketing (and I can't promise that they won't be reading this book!), then
they will be pursuing much the same goal. Given that this is the case, your
ambition must be to find some form of advantage over them, preferably
through some element of uniqueness in your match. That edge, that source
of *competitive advantage*, should be robust and sustainable. It is of little
advantage, or profit, to find a match that your competitors can copy, and
perhaps ultimately achieve at lower costs than you.

The search for this unique match also happens in a complex time-frame: coping with today's demands while anticipating tomorrow's, and planning for the future beyond tomorrow. Marketing is not static. Above all else, it must concern itself with the future: seeking to anticipate needs, even to create them, and seeking to mould capabilities in order to meet those needs. The exact time-frame will depend on the industry and the market. In the world of high fashion, clothes designers must always be looking a season ahead, for the manufacturer of military aircraft the future is a decade or more away, and in the world of IT, it could be only weeks. Figure 2.2 adds this element to the model.

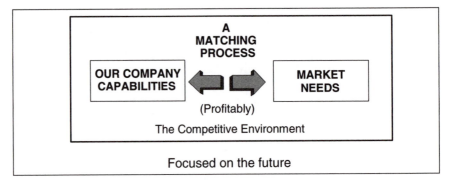

Figure 2.2   *The INSIGHT Marketing Model: an anticipatory definition*

TESTING THE MODEL

The real test of any such model or definition has to be: does it make any difference to how decisions are made, strategies are set, or how resources are applied? Would an understanding of this model have helped any of those businesses that have failed because of poor marketing?

The fall and rise of Triumph

The decline and fall of the British motorcycle industry in the 1960s and 1970s can be understood within the bounds of this model – in the omission rather than the commission of its strictures. Japanese manufacturers had understood the needs of the market better than had the UK operators, and they had a capability to provide the solutions. British manufacturers had failed to look ahead, failed to anticipate, and when at last they saw that the time had come for change, they were not able to transform their capabilities at sufficient speed to keep up. Looking ahead means just that: looking for how things will be different, not planning the future based on the past. This is never easy for a business that glories in a successful past, and none more so than Triumph in the motorcycle industry.

Triumph had a great brand name with tremendous customer loyalty, but let it slip away as it tried to move into the future by incremental steps based on the past. New features such as electronic starters and disc brakes were added to old designs, and all this was done on old equipment that dated from the 1930s. Moreover, as it chased down the road of cost reduction and improved productivity, it fell yet shorter of the new standards set by market expectations – expectations that were being stimulated by the new entrants. The vicious circle of decline is not uncommon for companies that fail to understand what marketing is all about.

Could things have been different? Of course. There was no fundamental British inability to manufacture good motorcycles, only a deadening slowness to recognize that selling those bikes required marketing skills that had not yet been properly developed – or, in some cases, even been seen as necessary. The '*marketing is for wimps*' school of thought is not an attractive one in a boardroom.

The story has a happy ending, with the rebirth of Triumph in the 1990s. The rebirth didn't just resurrect the brand name; it was realized that alongside, there was a need to meet new needs, internally and externally. There was to be a new and unique match between needs and capabilities. The new Triumphs were not retrospectives of the glory days, but totally new designs made with totally different, computer-aided production techniques. Where reliability and quality had been sapped away in pursuit of reduced costs in the 1970s, the new drive was for top quality and top reliability delivered by a workforce of passionate motorcycle enthusiasts. Now the Japanese come to Britain to see how to build motorcycles, and Triumph builds more bikes than BMW, with its greatest success in Germany!

The death of a brilliant product: the slide rule

Back in the 1950s and 60s we might imagine a manufacturer of slide rules, just south of Munich, making excellent profits because it made excellent slide rules.

For those too young to remember, the slide rule was an instrument for calculating: multiplication and division, and for expert users a good deal more. It worked on the principle of logarithmic scales (don't worry, we don't need to know!) printed with great precision on something about the size of a ruler with a central slider that moved in and out to facilitate the calculations. All we need to know perhaps is that schoolchildren hated them.

The company had a match: it was good at making a tool that met a need – portable calculation. Unfortunately, the company didn't understand its activity in this way. It thought it made good slide rules, full stop. Its efforts and resources were devoted to making a better slide rule, a cheaper slide rule, a fancier slide rule – but in all cases, a slide rule.

Of course, the moment someone launched the electronic pocket calculator, the slide rule's days were numbered. No level of price discounting would reverse the decline; nor would any advertising campaign or upmarket packaging. The idea was dead.

So how might the Marketing Model have helped? First, the company might have understood the basis of its success: a match of capabilities and needs, not simply a good product.

Second, it might have spent some time defining just what need it was meeting. It wasn't a need for a slide rule; it was a need for portable calculation, and that could be met in a number of different ways, including new technology.

Third, it might have identified more accurately the nature of its own capabilities: not merely making good slide rules, but the ability to make precision instruments generally.

Armed with that understanding, the company would have had some choices that might have provided the basis for a long-term future:

1. investigate new needs for its capability: the manufacturing of precision instruments;

2. develop a capability to provide better means of portable calculation (a real need – remember how much schoolchildren hated slide rules!).

In other words, the company could have looked for a new kind of match, either by accepting its main capability and seeking new applications (a 'left-sider' bias), or by seeking to change its capabilities in pursuit of a better solution to the market's needs (a 'right-sider' bias).

At this point the time-frame would have become important. Once the first electronic calculator was on the market, it would already have been too late to start trying to change capabilities. A slide rule manufacturer cannot become an electronics manufacturer overnight. The 'right-siders' focused on market needs would have needed to start work on their 'left-side' capabilities years in advance. To repeat an earlier comment, *marketing is not static*. Above all else, it must concern itself with the future: seeking to anticipate needs, to define needs, even to create needs, while at the same time moulding capabilities in order to meet those needs.

3

Issues raised by the Marketing Model

What the slide rule manufacturer really needed was an understanding of *what business it was in*. If we had asked its executives, doubtless the answer would have been 'the slide rule business, of course!'. Such an answer would have betrayed their lack of understanding and application of marketing. For them, we might guess, marketing meant designing the packaging and making sure the sales team had a good product brochure. The marketing department (if it existed at all) would have been about short-term tactical activities.

So what business *was* it in, if not the slide rule business? This is just one of several issues raised by the model, and perhaps I should list them first and then deal with each in turn.

1. What business are you in? Are you product led or market led?
2. Should your activities be for the benefit of your own business, the customer, or the market? Is it market growth or market share you should strive for and promote?
3. Which side should you be working on: changing capabilities or influencing needs?
4. Should fast-moving consumer goods (fmcg) marketers be more concerned with the right side, and B2B marketers with the left?
5. Is it market needs or consumer needs?
6. Is profitability the automatic consequence of a good match?
7. How far ahead must you be looking?

WHAT BUSINESS ARE YOU IN? ARE YOU PRODUCT LED OR MARKET LED?

It's not what you do, or even how you do it...

The problem that our slide rule manufacturer had was that it defined its business by the product it made. This might sound an obvious enough thing to do, but it misses the point of the model. It is such a common mistake, made by businesses that are not marketing orientated, that it deserves a lot of attention. It betrays a left-sider's mindset: valuing tangible things (such as products) above intangible concepts (such as needs and customer perceptions). It is a typical statement of a *product-led* business.

...it's who you do it for...

How about defining the company's business not by what it made, but by what it did for its customers? Let's say it was in the portable calculation business. This is a *market-led* position.

This is one of those defining moments in our understanding of the marketer's mindset. If this definition of the manufacturer's business as 'portable calculation' seems only a matter of semantics to you, then you are not yet thinking like a marketer. The important test is: what might this market-led definition have done for the company?

As a *product-led* business (defining itself by the product it made: slide rules), it would spend money and energy on improving that product. Marketing would have been a function devoted to better packaging and sales drives, while R&D and production would have been the main forces in the business. Great, so long as the industry technology remained non-electronic, but terminal once that change occurred – like the paraffin salesman fighting against the advent of electric light.

As a *market-led* business (defining itself by the solutions it brought to the market: portable calculation), it might have spent more of its money and energy on developing alternative solutions: better means of portable calculation, attending to the hatred of its product by all those schoolchildren! This way might have led to a long-term position in the market.

So, should it have invented the electronic pocket calculator? Unlikely, you say, unreasonable to expect it, even impossible? So what about seeking to work with a partner? Why not team up with Texas Instruments or Commodore and offer to wed their technical capability with its own experience in the marketplace?

And if none of this was realistic or practical, at least it should then have been aware of its limitations in the portable calculation business, an awareness that would only have come from understanding the business it was really in. Accepting its limitations, the company might have started looking for alternative applications for its technology and that technology's capabilities. This might have found it defining its business not by the product it made, nor by the solution it brought, but by the expertise it possessed: the precision instrument business.

Is this second definition simply another kind of 'product-led' approach, replacing the product with a technology or an expertise? It could be, if the business were not using the Marketing Model. By using the model it will understand that once it finds a market for its expertise, it will be the needs of that new market that drive it, not the features of its current technology. Above all else, it should remember the phrase drummed into salespeople at their basic training: *people buy solutions, not products*.

An interesting aspect of this product- or market-led debate is the way that it highlights the competitive environment. Table 3.1 illustrates the comparison between product-led and market-led approaches, indicating the likely 'business we are in' definition and the resultant understanding of where the competition might lie.

Table 3.1 *Product or market led? The competitive environment*

Product Led	Competition	Market Led	Competition
Slide rule	Other manufacturers	Portable calculation	Electronics
¼-inch drill	Other manufacturers	¼-inch holes	Lasers, adhesives
The hover lawn mower	Other manufacturers	Garden control	Chemicals, concrete
Heavy-roller lawn mower	Other manufacturers	Garden aesthetics	Gravel or pebble gardens
Make-up	Other manufacturers	Hope!	Nature!
Hats	Other manufacturers	Fashionable appearance	Hairdressers
Exterior gloss paint	Other manufacturers	Durability	Plastic windows
Three-piece suite of furniture	Other manufacturers	Lifestyle	Holidays…

The product-led company will see itself as largely fighting against fellow manufacturers; market share will be the goal. The market-led company has the luxury of a broader view, realizing that there are alternative solutions to its own. I have said enough about slide rules; let's consider lawn mowers. The product-led manufacturer of a hover mower might see the roller mower as a competitor. Hardly the case in reality: they exist in two different markets, performing two different roles, namely garden control and garden aesthetics. The true competition comes from alternative means of achieving those same ends: concrete or gravel!

Charles Revlon once said that other firms made cosmetics, but Revlon sold hope! The point was well made, and cosmetic manufacturers have always striven to convince their customers of their need – nature cannot be allowed to win; even the natural look needs make-up.

The manufacturer of exterior gloss paint knows that plastic window frames have been much bigger competition than any other paint manufacturer. Not painting is an attractive option for the consumer.

The implication of this must be clear to marketers: there are competing sources for the money they hope to get from their customers. Some of those sources are competing manufacturers, but there are other sources apparently outside their market (as viewed by the product-led business!). A typical family might have the choice of a new three-piece suite or a summer holiday. The truly successful furniture manufacturer is the one that not only makes its offer better than that of the other makers of chairs and settees, but also manages to make it more attractive than the prospect of lying in the sun for two weeks!

This leads us into the second issue arising from the marketing model…

SHOULD YOUR ACTIVITIES BE FOR THE BENEFIT OF YOUR OWN BUSINESS, THE CUSTOMER, OR THE MARKET?

Is it market growth or market share you should strive for and promote?

If the furniture manufacturer is in reality in competition with holiday firms, then it must devote much of its marketing activity to enhancing the value and attractiveness of furniture – anyone's, not just its own. Silentnight, a major bed manufacturer based in the United Kingdom, has long realized that the route to riches is more about getting people to change beds more often than it is about simply insisting they buy a Silentnight bed when the time comes. It seems that many of us keep our beds for over 20 years, with all the attendant risks of bad backs. If only we would spend some of the money we spend on healthy living – food, exercise and relaxation – on a new bed a few years earlier, then Silentnight's directors and staff would be very happy people, as would their fellow bed manufacturers, their competitors.

The decline in the hat industry from the dizzy heights of the 1920s and 30s was partly due to the war years, partly to the more informal approach to dress, but also very significantly due to the increase in hairdressing and hair washing. There was a time when even the most meticulous would wash their hair only once or twice a week, and visits to the hairdresser were infrequent. As it became easier to wash hair at home more often and the number of hairdressing salons (not barber shops!) increased, so one of the uses of hats declined. Today's hat maker works in a different environment where the hat is no longer a utilitarian item of clothing designed to hide a bad hair day, but an additional adornment to an already pampered head. I heard a director of a hat firm complain recently that people don't wear hats properly: 'We make them to fit round the broadest part of the head and they want to wear them perched on the back, to show off their faces I suppose.' I couldn't help feeling that the firm was missing not only the point, but also an opportunity for a hat revival!

So which is right: looking after your own interests, or those of the market as a whole?

Fruit of the loom?

Consider the case of a UK carpet manufacturer. In the space of only 30 years, the market share of genuinely loom-woven carpets, as opposed to those made by cheaper manufacturing styles, has fallen from some 80 per cent to less than 5 per cent. This particular manufacturer is the UK market leader in loom-woven carpets, a big fish in a shrinking pond. The reason for the decline is money. Until recently, loom-weaving technology had not changed significantly in a hundred years; it took as long to make a loom-woven carpet in 1990 as it did before the First World War. This made the loom-woven carpet very expensive and, compared to the new 'tufted' carpets, positively exorbitant. But help is at hand in the form of a new loom that promises to increase the speed of manufacture fourfold. The result is that the yawning gap between the price of woven and non-woven carpets could close significantly.

The carpet manufacturer has a choice. Should it keep the new loom for its own use, so boosting its own market share, or license the technology to other woven carpet manufacturers, so raising the total market share of woven carpets?

The answer to such a question lies in the manufacturer's definition of its business, and hence its perception of the competition. If it sees its competition as other uses for the consumer's money, then licensing the technology and making woven carpets more attractive in general would have much merit as a strategy. If it is certain, however, that its competition is only other woven carpet manufacturers, then selfishness is the best policy.

Ask any retailer where they would rather be: on a bustling high street in a thriving town with consumers spending lots of money in all the shops *including* their competitors', or the only shop on a quiet road in a run-down town, and you might guess the answer. Of course, the costs of being on the high street will be much higher, and the retailer's ability to compete will be more thoroughly tested. This brings us in part to the next issue raised by the model…

WHICH SIDE SHOULD YOU BE WORKING ON: CHANGING CAPABILITIES OR INFLUENCING NEEDS?

Changing capabilities

Can a company change its capabilities? Can an independent food retailer used to trading from a corner shop hope to take on the big boys by moving to the shopping centre? Or should it stay where it is and concentrate on what it is good at doing, in its own way?

The answer has to be, yes of course capabilities can be changed, with the application of sufficient resource and skill, but an equally important question is, for what purpose *should* they change? An awareness that the market's needs are changing, or will change, is certainly one of the best incentives; this could be about survival. The problem is that a successful past can be a huge obstacle to change. How easy is it for the successful manufacturer of main-frame computers to see the implications of PCs, or the busy corner shop to see the significance of the new mall, or the thriving, but traditional, training firm to see the opportunities of training via the Internet? And even if they do, is it possible for them to change capabilities built up over years?

The greater the complexity of the technology, or the more entrenched the business is in its mode of operation, the harder it will be to change. Recognizing that reality will be of value, not a reason for despair. If your existing capabilities really are the heart of your business then perhaps there is more sense in finding new applications for your expertise. The corner grocer could become a delicatessen rather than a supermarket; the training company could provide its materials and expertise to an expert Internet operator. But perhaps the mainframe manufacturer just has to make the change…

Being led by your capabilities: good or bad news?

Once a business gets to be good at something, that capability tends to affect its view of the world; it becomes the secret of its success. So long as the capa-bility is relevant to customer needs then there is no problem (for the present – but see the IBM story below), but this raises one of the difficulties for conglomerates operating in a diverse range of market environments: can one capability be applied to all?

When the pen is not mightier than the razor…

Gillette has forged a unique 'match' in the shaving market by applying 'high-tech' capa-bilities to its global brand. It was an approach that it found hard to replicate in some of its other businesses, such as its three stationery brands: Parker Pens, Papermate and Waterman. With no significant technological breakthroughs in these businesses, the alternative was a tough fight for market share in a very mature market – a situation that Gillette found 'uncomfortable' when compared to its success in the shaving market. The result? The pen businesses were put up for sale.

We hear much talk about 'core capabilities', particularly when a business is considering outsourcing some activity *not* considered to be core. Great care should be taken that core capabilities are defined by reference to the needs of the market, and are not simply those things that you happen to be good at.

IBM and the small outfit from Seattle…

IBM's core capabilities in the 1970s were in the manufacture of computer hardware. When it went into the PC business (coming from behind), it chose to outsource two 'non-core activities': the microprocessor to Intel, and the operating system to a small software outfit based in Seattle… What business was IBM in – metal boxes, or solutions? If the former, then it was right to do as it did, but if the latter, then the operating system was vital, a truly core capability and not something to be outsourced.

Buying new capabilities

One of the most common ways for a business to change its capabilities is to buy them through acquisition. This seems to be straightforward enough: if you are a pharmaceutical company with plenty of money but no pipeline of new drugs, then buy a competitor that has such a capability. Such has been one of the biggest motivations behind the bewildering number of acquisitions and mergers in this market over recent years. All is not so simple, however, and sometimes it can take years to bring together the different cultural and business values of two such one-time competitors. Suppliers to the huge business GlaxoSmithKline say, even now, that depending on what site you are dealing with, you can still feel the spirit of Glaxo-Wellcome or SmithKline Beecham…

Perhaps retailers should buy Internet companies (and they have done) as a means of jumping on the e-retailing boat? A good idea, so long as they understand the challenges involved – I am reminded of a front cover of *Time* magazine depicting the head of Sears in an appropriately serious suit and the head of Sears's burgeoning e-commerce business in appropriately casual bags and sneakers. Nice picture, but wouldn't you love to be a fly on the wall of that particular boardroom?

Unilever – set to clean up?

It was no surprise to hear of the setting up of Myhome, a company offering home cleaning services to those cash-rich but time-poor households we hear so much about, except that it was set up by Unilever. Can a multinational manufacturer of soap powder, ice cream, butter *et al* turn itself into a service provider? Unilever approached its new venture with care. First came a pilot: it bought an existing company, Mrs McMopp. Then Myhome was created out of this as an independent organization. But why the move in the first place? Tight margins in manufacturing operations often make the idea of moving into services appealing, yet the change often ends in disaster when it is realized just how different the challenges are. But Unilever was also chasing another goal: knowledge. Myhome was set up, in part, to provide it with a vehicle for understanding the real needs that its product and service propositions must meet, particularly in the 'cash-rich, time-poor' segment. What business is Unilever in: cleaning materials, or clean homes? If the latter, then Myhome makes a good deal of sense. And if the former? Well, can you hope to be successful in the cleaning materials business if you don't fully understand the use to which your products are put?

Influencing needs

Can a company create needs? How many of us knew that we wanted a Mars Bar ice cream, or a Post-it note, or alcoholic lemonade, or Natural White paint – before, that is, it was offered to us? Marketers thrive on what they call 'latent needs' – the sort we all have, but haven't realized it yet. The Mars Bar ice cream created a whole new market sector out of nothing: the branded confectionery bar ice cream. We hadn't been clamouring for it, but there was clearly an opportunity. Interestingly, it is arguably Nestlé that has gained most from the new sector, having followed up the Mars idea with a host of its own confectionery brand names. Mars had the idea, but perhaps Nestlé had the wider capability: its broad range of branded confectionery lines.

Some markets are more conservative than others: the opportunities for influencing and creating needs are perhaps greater in the beer market than in the wine market, for instance. Widgets in cans of beer came to stay, and we suddenly realized that what we wanted was draught beer in a can. Wine in a box, while equally innovative, didn't create the same shift in our idea of what we wanted from the product.

Sometimes, however, revolutions do occur, and in the most conservative markets. Health care in the United Kingdom before the Second World War was a complex but static mix of private provision, charity, self-help and 'just put up with it'. The National Health Service changed all that, and within a generation people were demanding treatments for ailments they had not even heard of only a few years before. A new capability in the market created new needs such that we now have a health service strained to the limits – fertile ground for new providers to offer alternative solutions, hence the rise of private health insurance and at the same time the growth in alternative medicines and treatments from acupuncture to faith healing.

Business itself has always been one of the most conservative markets to influence. B2B marketers have always had a hard time getting new needs established for their clever ideas. Spare a thought for Alexander Graham Bell and his telephone. A revolution for business communications, he said, and, to one doubting businessman in particular, 'Just think, with one of these you can talk to a customer three hundred miles away.' The doubting businessman's reply expressed precisely the inertia in the business market: 'But Mr Bell, I don't have any customers three hundred miles away…'

Developing products and then hoping for needs to arise is a risky path to take. The Post-it note, developed by 3M by accident (as the story goes), is often raised as an example of the success of such an approach; but take care before using it as a role model. The path is too littered with failures, and expensive ones at that, for it to be right to encourage anyone to develop products in the hope that if they are clever enough they will be able to create a need after the event.

Of course, *creating* needs is the most dramatic end of the marketing model's spectrum – far right. *Influencing* needs will be as important, and often a lot easier. We all need petrol for our cars, but the oil company that convinces us that its petrol will be less damaging to the environment, or kinder to our car, or the most economical, will win a lot of customers by pushing at a need that is already there. This is the role of branding: helping customers make their mind up by influencing the way they think about their needs.

SHOULD FMCG MARKETERS BE MORE CONCERNED WITH THE RIGHT SIDE, AND B2B MARKETERS WITH THE LEFT?

In a word, no. The problem with this stereotypical thinking is the way it keeps people in their comfort zones – being good at what they are good at. In truth, it is rare that any business will not need to work on both sides of the model. It may seem that B2B marketers will spend more of their time concerned with changing capabilities within their own organization, while fmcg marketers are busy influencing needs through promotion and branding. This might be the case in the grand scheme of things, but consider the following outcomes of such a one-sided approach.

While Mars did a brilliant job of understanding and exploiting our latent desire for a Mars Bar ice cream, it slipped up famously by asking retailers to put the new product in their existing refrigerators, owned by Walls or Lyons Maid! It lacked a capability, and, though the mistake was soon put right, it was an embarrassment and an expensive error.	**Mars and the cold shoulder**

ICI did a brilliant job in the 1990s in creating an alternative for CFCs (chemicals used in refrigerants, air conditioning and aerosols, said to contribute to the erosion of the ozone layer), which were soon to be banned by international agreement. Its capability as an inventive chemical company was seen at its best, and there was much enthusiasm for the new product. Its reading of the market dynamics was less inspired. It failed to see how many aerosol-dependent manufacturers would prefer to change to roll-on or pump-spray applications rather than use the new CFC replacement. It also underestimated the speed with which competitors would be able to bring their own CFC alternatives to the market. This misreading of supply and demand caused a mismatch between ICI's excellent capabilities and the true needs of the market – an expensive mistake. Confidence in ICI's technical capability and an insufficient understanding of the dynamics of the market (a common syndrome in large and 'clever' companies) led to a significant over-investment in capacity. Now that CFCs have finally been banned, the demand for such alternatives is increasing and there is a need to consider new capacity. As is so often the case in marketing, timing can be everything.	**Misreading the opportunity**

These two examples highlight the bear trap waiting for the one-sided marketer, a bear trap made all the more dangerous by the way this one-sidedness can become the culture of the company, and can result in undue dominance by certain functions. Find a company with a left-side bias and you will very often find a company driven by R&D or production, or operations. The right-side bias finds us in the realm of the sales-driven business. Neither has to be a bad thing, until it becomes unthinking, or until it becomes polarized. The task of marketing is to bring both sides together and to remember that brilliance on one side or the other is not enough: *it is the quality of the match that matters*.

The greatest challenge for many fmcg marketers is managing change within their own organization. Often they see this as an unnecessary burden, with other departments as obstacles to be knocked down, and consequently they go about it badly. Equally, the greatest challenge for many B2B marketers will be understanding the dynamics of a market in which they may be but a small player, and this leads us to the next issue from the marketing model.

IS IT MARKET NEEDS OR CONSUMER NEEDS? THE CONCEPT OF THE MARKET CHAIN

When we turn to the all-important subject of market segmentation (Chapter 15) we will be reminded of a good piece of advice: *a market never bought anything; people do that*. When we speak of market needs, then, we should always remember to identify clearly who we mean by 'the market' – but it isn't always that easy.

It may seem straightforward enough for the fmcg marketer: the customers are the consumers… But what about the retailers that sell their products to the consumers – are they not customers too? For many years, fmcg businesses tended towards two separate marketing teams: one for the consumer and one for 'the trade', a position that often led to more confusion than was necessary, and a lack of clarity between *market* and *consumer*.

And if that was difficult, how about the company that sells electrical wire to manufacturers of televisions, or sulphuric acid as a raw material in a product that is in turn a raw material for another that may even end up in the electrical wire that goes into that television? What market are they in: acid, wire, television, electronics or something else?

All businesses that sell to an intermediary before the final consumer are in a market chain. Those closest to the consumer tend to receive the greatest rewards, as it is usually at that end of the chain that the most 'apparent' value is put in. I use the word 'apparent' as it is usually a matter of perception. Farmers have often complained that supermarkets make too much money selling their products and that the farmer receives too small a share of the final consumer price. So why does it happen? For many consumers, the final display of ripe apples cosseted in tissue paper in a spotlessly clean, air-conditioned superstore would convey more apparent value than thinking of the months the apples had spent hanging on trees in all weathers. Farmers may complain, but whatever the truth of the matter, when it comes to expressing what is of value, it is the consumer's perceptions that matter.

Perhaps farmers have not done much of a job of marketing their produce to the final consumer? French supermarkets are now obliged to display how much they have paid for some fruit and vegetables in order to assure consumers that farmers are not being abused, and to allow consumers to make their own minds up about added value. This is a government-inspired attempt to regulate the flow of value and reward in the market chain, but sometimes those suppliers at the head of the chain will take matters into their own hands.

The growth of farmers' markets in recent years, where consumers can meet face to face with the producer and select their own apples from reassuringly rural baskets (rather than tissue paper), or pick potatoes from the very soil in which they grew (rather than finding them ready peeled and washed), demonstrates not only an attempt by farmers to capture the value from the chain, but also the continuing truth that value is in the eye of the beholder.

The challenge for marketers is: in aiming to meet the needs of the market, how far down the chain should they be looking? Since most value tends to be added closest to the final consumer, the first question to ask is: does our product or service contribute to value as perceived by the consumer? In the case of the agrochemical company selling pesticides to farmers, there is a very close relationship between its product and consumer value (see Figure 3.1), but it is a relationship not always seen in a positive light.

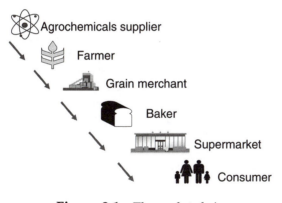

Figure 3.1 *The market chain*

On the one hand, pesticides add value by helping to improve the quality of the final product, says one lobby. On the other hand, many people feel that pesticides are harmful in the food chain and that a proper definition of a high-quality product would be a pesticide-free one. Whichever case is supported, there is little doubt that the agrochemical supplier needs to be very aware of the needs and perceptions at the consumer end of this market chain.

Understanding the farmer's needs goes beyond the interface between agrochemical supplier and farmer; it is necessary to understand the farmer's market chain. Not long ago, yield was the all-important measure of value; it determined the farmer's profits and the prices down the chain. In such an environment was born the focus on genetically modified (GM) crops. Many of the problems that have beset the suppliers of such products in recent years could be said to result from a poor understanding of how consumers in Europe feel about their GM products, exacerbated by the suppliers' continued focus on yield as the measure of value. Times change.

Concern about food safety among consumers, spurred on by the press, pressure groups, and supermarkets staking a claim to a point of competitive advantage, and fuelled by a run of food scares from benzene in Perrier, salmonella in eggs, and dioxins in Coca-Cola and Belgian chickens, has entirely changed that measure of value in the chain. Safety is now the watchword. Supermarkets demand 'food passports' from their suppliers, demonstrating where and how the food was produced. The food manufacturers demand in their turn complete transparency from their suppliers – no more secret ingredients. The farmers' main concern now is 'will I be able to sell my product?', not 'how much can I grow?' – and the challenge for the agrochemical supplier is a very different one.

The market environment is always changing, and those businesses that focus only on their own part of the market chain are less likely to see the changes that will determine their future. In the early 1990s it was organic farmers who struggled to keep their head above water, but they were looking forward, not planning their future on the successes of the past. Now they are enjoying the rewards of that 'investment'. Farmers who find their livelihoods under threat through changing food fads or fashions make, like deserted mining villages, poignant stories for TV documentaries, and show just how hard it is for some businesses to work within the marketing model. They also show the dangers of working outside the model.

Working within the model and understanding the idea of the market chain is one thing; ensuring that a fair reward is gained for your efforts is another. The further you are from the end consumer, the harder it is to secure a large piece of the action – and remember, the goal of marketing is profit. Producers of raw materials might appear to be at the mercy of manufacturers who take their products and turn them into added value – branded goods – but some raw material suppliers have found a way to secure their share of the reward.

Brands within brands...

Du Pont has successfully branded Teflon® and Lycra®, in each case a very small proportion of the finished product, whether it be non-stick frying pan or sportswear, to represent the key ingredient in those products. A personal computer without an 'intel inside'® sticker would seem to be lacking something, and Nutrasweet® gives a badge of credibility to diet drinks.

These brands aim to secure ownership of the market chain, as viewed by the end consumer, for the supplier. The concept of ownership in this sense is an important one. Ownership brings power and security, and, for wise marketers, the ability to change with the times. Teflon® is no longer simply about non-stick frying pans; it is an important ingredient in paint, clothing and building materials, to name just three. Its success rests on its inherent qualities, but also on its ability to match up to consumers' needs and perceptions – not a bad definition for a successful brand.

IS PROFITABILITY THE AUTOMATIC CONSEQUENCE OF A GOOD MATCH?

Much stress has been laid in this chapter on the importance of finding a good match between capabilities and needs, but is that all that is required to make profits?

It is certainly the case that profitability, over the long term, is hard to achieve without a good match. Cases abound of businesses that touched a nerve in the market and shot to stardom but declined, or even failed in the end, through some lack of capability; very often a financial capability: Dicky Dirts, the trail-blazing jeans retailer, Laker and Skytrain, Pineapple Studios, Sinclair, De Lorean – and the list goes on.

Philips, the Dutch conglomerate, has trail-blazed more innovations in hi-fi and electronic gadgetry than seems credible from one company, an amazing fertility of ideas. Yet when it comes to commercial success, the way is littered with tales of failure and losing out to competitors from the Far East. Its ability to identify with the market needs of the moment seems to lag behind its ability to invent and develop new products.

So, matching is important, but is it all that is required?

A match made in hell?

The rise of 'alcopops' is an interesting case in this regard. Manufacturers of beer and cider in the United Kingdom were concerned to see trends away from consumption of their products by the younger generation in the early 1990s. It seemed that youth had different (though no more creditable!) outlets for their money. The answer was a stream of alcoholic lemonades, fruit juices and other previously virtuous soft drinks. They hit a nerve and sales boomed. Here was a good match: manufacturers with spare capacity and all the right channels to market, and a latent consumer need that could be developed through advertising and, more importantly, through the 'jungle drum' media of youth culture.

So far so good, except that these new products needed huge marketing support – much bigger budgets than some of their more humble cider and beer predecessors demanded. Not only that, but the sales boom brought in competitors like moths to a candle, resulting in a price war at the retailer, the club and the public house. Profit and loss accounts actually dipped as a result of such success, but it was the sort of success that demanded more, sucking manufacturers in further. In such an environment even more promotion was required, starting to raise the concerns of parents that their children were being led down a worrying path – and this from the makers of good, wholesome, traditional cider! Marketers should never forget that their activities, however brilliant, take place in a competitive environment, and the demands of that environment can take a good idea and make it seem bad.

In the end (and the jury is still out), the rebranding of cider – the Red Rocks and the Two Dogs *et al* – might appear to be a more successful strategy, and certainly one with lower risks.

What the environment does in fact is expose any shortcomings in the match. The low-cost, low-price airline has been a feature of the travel market ever since Laker, but there have been more failures, often spectacular ones, than successes. And yet the idea seems such an obvious one. It's a good premise, taking a leaf out of Henry Ford's book. Ford reckoned that if he could get the price of a car down below $500 he would be able to sell millions, a rather different premise from the idea that if he could sell enough cars the price would come down. The answer for Ford was mass production and any colour you liked so long as it was black. For the low-price airline, the idea is that if it costs less than £50 to fly from the United Kingdom to Amsterdam then more people will fly, and the way to make this work is through low costs. The theory is fine, but it takes *genuinely* low costs to make it work in practice. Airlines that pretend to low costs but actually support the same infrastructures as the 'full-price' airlines are doomed to failure. The mismatch is exposed and profits drain away or never materialize.

Moral of the story? If you want to make money, it has to be a *genuine* match, not a piece of wishful thinking based on a 'good idea'.

HOW FAR AHEAD MUST YOU BE LOOKING?

This is the ultimate 'how long is a piece of string' question. Each industry, each market, even each business has its own relevant horizons. There is the trading period, the mid term, the long term and the wild blue yonder. Each needs attention from the marketer. I have heard it said that the marketer's job is to predict the future. It is tougher than that: it is to *manage* the future.

Figure 3.2 *Managing the future*

Managing the future requires a balance of three things (see Figure 3.2): your objectives, your resources and the market opportunity. Hockey-stick graphs of wild objectives with no foundation in opportunities or resources are not about managing the future. No more are extravagant investments in assets with no clear direction for their use. And guess what: brilliant market research studies without the money to exploit the knowledge gained will not manage the future any more successfully.

Of these three, the market opportunity is the hardest to control but the most important to understand, which is why I devote the whole of Part II of this book to the challenge. Of course, in the end it takes all three, in balance, and achieving that balance takes discipline – the discipline of the marketing process (see Chapter 5).

A final thought to close this chapter: I have heard it said that marketing is a good place for new graduates to start in business because 'they can't do much harm there'. OK, engineers can build factories that fall down, and R&D folk can design products that don't work, but marketers can do worse: they can wreck the future.

4

In search of *'good* marketing'

If marketing is a true profession and not just, as some suggest, a shady practice carried out by those with insufficient qualifications to do anything else, then it should be possible to identify with clarity what constitutes *good marketing*. There must be some standards – mustn't there? It can be done for other professions: for lawyers and for doctors and architects – can't it?

But what makes a good doctor? Is it the number of ill patients made better? Or is it the amount of illness prevented? Or is it, as many people on the receiving end will inevitably judge, the doctor's bedside manner?

What makes a good lawyer? Is it the number of clients vindicated, or criminals sent down? Many observers (and not a few juries) might be swayed just as much by the way the lawyer spoke in court and the ingenuity of his or her arguments.

Judging a good architect has always been a tough one. Is it the number of buildings still standing and in use after a hundred years? What about their influence on other architects, or ability to break new ground in design or technology? Or is it just a matter of taste?

Judging marketers presents us with similar problems. While there are some obvious hard measures – brand share, profitability, growth and the like (the equivalents perhaps of the healthy patient, the victorious case and the long-standing building) – some observers might argue that there is more to good marketing than results.

Now just hang on a minute – more to marketing than results?! Isn't this the sort of idea that sees people handing out awards for 'Best TV ad of the year' for an ad supporting a product that nobody remembers and nobody buys? Well, no it isn't, and before I justify the comment, let's just challenge the notion of results being the acid test.

Not all business success stories are down to good marketing. Some, if only the winners were honest enough to admit it, are down to the marketing ineptitude of the losing competitors. Decidedly average marketing has been known to win when facing resolutely incompetent marketing!

And then there are those little 'acts of God'. Who is the better marketer: the one who achieves 20 per cent growth and a record brand share – and all because their main competitor went out of business after a fire in their factory – or the one who hangs on to share in an increasingly competitive marketplace with new players entering by the coachload?

Then there are the high-profile, not to say flashy, 'seat-of-the-pants' marketers who get lucky, and just for long enough to ensure that they get promoted well out of range of the fallout that follows in their wake. Compare them to the sound-thinking and methodical type, the one who doesn't depend on luck yet usually manages to succeed against the odds. We know who gets the praise, but who would you prefer on your team?

Judging the outcome is not enough; we must also judge the quality and the discipline of the approach. Good marketing is about following a good marketing process, because in truth it is the discipline of that process that ensures, in by far the majority of cases, a good outcome. Chapter 5 will discuss the elements of that process, but in the meantime let's look a little more closely at what constitutes good marketing, perhaps by first considering some examples of where it went wrong…

First, there is the peril of 'surface gloss': the pretty packaging, the clever slogan. 'This is the age of the train' was a 'clever' slogan for British Rail, but to admire it would be rather like admiring the doctor for their bedside manner and forgiving them for the death of the patient.

Second, there is the peril of the high-profile product that might make for good PR, but not always marketing success. The launch of Clive Sinclair's now notorious C5 'car-cum-oversized roller skate' was impressively high profile and the product was certainly novel, but very few were ever sold (if you have one, hang on to it; there will be museums keen to get hold of them one day).

Third, there is the peril of arrogance – a condition common among so-called market leaders. When Mr Dyson invented his bagless vacuum cleaner based on the cyclone system, he took it first to Hoover. They rejected it. What attraction could such an invention have for them when such a large proportion of their income and profits came from selling bags? So Dyson launched it himself and redefined the whole market within a year. His offer was appropriate to the needs of consumers because he understood their predicament: poor suction as bags filled, and messy disposal once they were full. He knew his offer would work, but Hoover couldn't or wouldn't see it; they were of course the number one brand: big, successful and very superior. Similarly, the tale of how IBM missed, ignored or wilfully denied the opportunity to develop the market for personal computers is so often told as to need no retelling, other than to point out the danger of being the biggest, the most successful, the most complacent and the least observant.

Being bad at marketing can be OK, provided your competitors are worse!

Good marketing doesn't have to be flashy; it is often routine and repetitive. It doesn't even have to be novel, and it doesn't need the backing of huge advertising budgets. It has been argued that one benefit of a small marketing budget is the responsibility it puts on the marketer to be intelligent, and humble – but don't let your Chief Financial Officer hear that one!

GOOD MARKETING AND READING THE SIGNALS

Good marketing is about reading the signals. There are clues aplenty if you are prepared to look, and if you know where to look. Then come the choices. Marketing is about making decisions – where, what, how and when; these will be ever-present questions – and the answers are to be looked for in the signals. The trouble is, signals can be misread…

The tale of the shoes

The old stories are often the best, and there is still a wonderful debate to be had over one of the oldest in the marketing textbooks: the shoe salesman in darkest Africa (it is an old story, so salespeople are still men and Africa is still dark…). Picture the scene as the salesman steps off the plane at some remote jungle airport, and looks, as is his instinct, at the feet of those come to greet him: no shoes.

What would be a 'good marketing response'? Get on the next flight home, or regard this as a wonderful opportunity? Markets can be made, just as much as they must be responded to, so what's the choice?

The best market research is the sort that helps you make the right decisions (shouldn't that be the only kind?)

The answer has to be – more information. Investing millions on this one 'signal' would be unwise, not to say reckless. But what sort of information? Well, the slick answer to that is: the kind of information that will help you make the right decision. That isn't quite as trite as it may sound. Too much time is spent on gathering market 'data', the main purpose of which seems to be to fill out a dozen or so appendices to the marketing plan. If your market research budget is tight then focus on the information that helps to make decisions. How about starting with: *why no shoes?* Obvious, of course, but so often there is something that makes us resist asking such questions, a certainty that they should, and will, wear shoes – if only you can get the promotion right. It is an arrogance that comes with being big and successful, or, worse, with feeling superior.

The uncertainty principle

Humble (and successful) marketers will observe the uncertainty principle – that they don't always know the answer. They will never take anything for granted. They will always ask questions – *'why?'* being a good one. And the bigger and more successful they are, the more watchful they will be for signs of arrogance. Benjamin Franklin could easily have had the likes of Hoover and IBM in mind when he advised, 'Learn to doubt a little your own certainties.'

The need to deal with uncertainty, yet seek answers to pressing questions, is undoubtedly what makes marketing such a challenge, and, for many, the fun that it undoubtedly is – the best fun you can have with your clothes on, I have heard it said by one professor of marketing. The uncertainties of marketing give it some of its intellectual challenge, but an ivory tower is no place to pursue certainty. The best tip I was given when I took on my first marketing role for an fmcg company was: think like our customers, read the newspapers they read, watch the television programmes they watch, and talk to them whenever you can. That way there's a better chance that what you do will be relevant to them and their needs. A better chance – good marketing isn't about certainty, but it certainly is about improving the odds.

The marketing process

The 'tale of the shoes' shows us the importance of discipline in marketing – the discipline of knowing when to ask questions and when to make decisions (usually in that order!). This is where the marketing process comes in. The marketing process will stop us making decisions based on inadequate knowledge – the result of insufficient questioning. But, and just as importantly, it will also stop us collecting data just for the sake of it. Data is for a reason: it will help us to make a decision.

Chapter 5 will lay out a map for working through the marketing process, from information through to application, and will highlight the key stopping points in between: the decisions required. This is the starting point of good professional marketing, and also provides us with a format for one of the most important tools and indicators of good and professional marketing: the _marketing plan_ (see Chapter 6).

GOOD MARKETING AND PROVIDING VALUE

Put yourself in the shoes of each of the following three customers and ask yourself, 'Why might I be doing this?'

1.   You are the buyer for a large building firm and one of your regular orders is for paint, thousands of litres at a time. You always use the same supplier and the sales reps from rival manufacturers have a problem getting appointments with you even though you know you are paying as much as a 5 per cent premium for a product with no appreciable difference in quality.
2.   You are doing the weekly supermarket shop, and more out of interest than economy you are comparing prices of products that make it into your trolley. It intrigues you to note that you are paying more for a small (but attractive) glass bottle of still mineral water with a _twist_ of peach (or was it a _hint_ of loganberry?) than for a plastic bottle of orange

3. You are the marketing manager of a small software house based in Cheltenham – small in turnover but big in ambition. You are hiring a company to deliver marketing training to all the staff in your business, and you have a choice between a large London-based company with an impressive client list and a long track record, and a smaller local company just making its way in the business. Cost is not the issue: the London firm has a surprisingly low price as it has put a junior partner on the job, and the local company is at its top whack because you're getting the MD. You choose the smaller company.

What is it that makes us choose one product or supplier over another? In each of these cases, if we assume that the customer is behaving with good and rational reason, and if we also assume that the successful supplier understands that reason, then the answer to that question is, marketing.

Customers seek value for money – a phrase that can mean a hundred and one things from the cheapest to the longest lasting, the most convenient to the most fitting for the purpose; it all depends on the customer. Good marketing is about providing value-for-money solutions to customers' problems and desires – or perhaps good marketing is about finding the customers who regard your particular offer as good value for their money? Either will do, provided there is a good match… (see Chapters 2 and 3).

1. The building company's paint buyer puts more importance on speed of delivery than anything else. She reckons that if they can have a delivery within 24 hours rather than the industry standard 72 hours (and their favoured supplier manages 24 hours every time), then that is worth the premium. They have very little storage space, and the little they have, they prefer to use for things that can take months to deliver. Fast delivery means low stocks, and that equals value for money.

2. As you push your trolley around the aisles, you remind yourself that money isn't a big issue with you, but time and convenience count for a lot. You work hard, and when it comes to relaxing you want to treat yourself. Novelty is always fun, and it helps you feel that all your hard work is worth it. The mineral water company has had your aspirations in its sights for some time, and the problem with squash is that with the water in your area it's sometimes more like rust than orange, and you always have to run the tap for three minutes before it starts to come out even remotely cool…

3. The trouble with big companies, it seems to you, as you consider the ideal training supplier, is that they speak big-company language. That's OK if your staff are wielding advertising budgets of millions and are launching new products in global markets, but if your biggest concern is satisfying local customers for whom you can design bespoke

packages to meet their needs, then maybe a company that speaks your language and shares your challenges might be more appropriate – better value for money.

GOING BEYOND 'GOOD MARKETING'

If good marketing is about providing value then we might go one step further and define _excellent marketing_ as inventing a 'new currency' for value, a currency uniquely suited to your offer, so gaining yourself true market leadership. The multiplex cinema has redefined the experience of going to the pictures and raised a new standard of value expected from a good night out. Despite predictions of the death of the cinema at the hands of the video, the multiplex idea has seen cinema attendance reach levels not seen since the boom years before there was a television in every home. And then along comes the man from easyJet and proposes another currency: the no frills cinema, with the possibility of buying tickets in advance for as little as 20p. It's too early to judge the success or otherwise of this spin-off from the original no-frills airline idea – but if it works then it will be because a successful match has been forged between a capability (assuming the economics work!) and a need, latent or existing – and that will be good marketing.

The cinema is dead, long live the cinema

Let's take an entirely fictitious bank and suppose that it has just completed a study on the cost to it of processing cheques. Its managers were expecting a big number but are staggered by the huge scale of the cost when all its implications are considered. Clearly something must be done. Somebody suggests that they simply announce a long-term plan to remove cheques as a service in line with the natural increase in electronic payments in the market. Someone else suggests that they should levy a charge for using cheques, first to non-customers of the bank but eventually even to their own customers. The next person attempts to soften this by suggesting that they offer a discount to those people who use methods other than cheques. This isn't marketing. This isn't about reading the signals, and it certainly isn't about providing value. This is a fixation with the bank's own issues.

Do banks do marketing?

   Yes, there is a benefit to the bank in no longer processing cheques, and if it is a big enough benefit then they had best find a way of promoting a faster move towards electronic payments. They would need to understand people's perceptions about using cheques as against electronic transfers and how questions of trust, confidence and security weigh against issues such as cost and convenience. And by 'people' I don't just mean the bank's customers; I mean everyone out there who makes or receives payments – the marketplace. If the bank's managers were able to truly understand the concerns of the market in this way, they might find a way to make the no-cheque offer a value offer by removing the fears and sharing their own benefits with the market. That way lies competitive advantage for their own bank, while securing all the internal benefits of reducing cheque processing. We might call this marketing.

CONSUMER, BUSINESS TO BUSINESS, OR SERVICE?

Is what comprises *good marketing* different depending on whether you sell products to end consumers or products to other manufacturers (business to business, B2B), or sell services rather than products? Put very simply: no. That there are differences in the application of marketing in these different environments is clear – the tactics will vary, and we will look closely at this in the sections devoted to marketing tactics – but the overall process is very much the same, as are the discipline and rigour demanded, as are the decisions required, as are the tools used. Many marketing books draw thick lines between these three 'types' of marketing, a kind of market segmentation that allows the writer and publisher to release three variants on the one book. Some might call that good marketing, but I'm not sure that it makes for a helpful guide on how to do it.

Above all else, this book is intended as a practical guide to how to do it, and as such it will not impose arbitrary distinctions that can obscure the simplicity of the essential foundation of good marketing: a good *marketing process*.

5

The marketing process

Beware of textbooks that portray the marketing process as a straight line. It often goes like this: the market audit (information and analysis) – the marketing plan – the implementation. Beware, because it is of course something of an ivory tower approach, and, in a complex world of change, competitive pressures and the super-abundance of data, a dangerously narrow-minded one.

The problem with the straight-line approach is that it reckons the world to be the marketer's oyster, with barely a thought for customer reaction, still less for competitor reaction, and none at all for the possibility of getting things wrong. And only in the world of marketing textbooks is there the luxury of starting from scratch. Most businesses are already deep into the implementation stage long before any formal audit process takes place – such is the real world.

We might improve on the straight-line idea with a circular process that revolves around the reality of today's implementation (see Figure 5.1).

In the real world the clock doesn't stop to give you a period of reflection; planning happens in the midst of current activity, and the marketer has to respond to its realities, thus changing the nature of the implementation. It is what managers delight in calling an iterative process – properly meaning, a series of actions and reactions that build on each other, but all too often improperly confused with the 'suck-it-and-see' approach...

There is a discipline involved in this process that requires anticipation as well as reaction, and a studied analysis that belies the myth that marketing is something best practised by flamboyant imagineers. The ratio between perspiration and inspiration suggested by Mark Twain for writers (95:5) holds equally true for the marketing profession.

Inspiration or perspiration?

Figure 5.1 *The marketing process*

The circular process recognizes that most marketers are pitched into a maelstrom of short-term pressures and reactions, and aims to ensure that those pressures don't get in the way of planning for tomorrow – the marketer's ultimate purpose. It also aims to banish the excuse that 'Change is upon us, so what's the point of planning?'

Planning to avoid the information overload...

In a circular process it might be supposed that there is no real starting point, or, if there is, then surely it is with the gathering of information... both suppositions would be wrong. The starting point has to be the plan. But hang on, you say, how can you plan without information? Quite right, but equally, how do you know what information you need if you don't know what you are trying to plan? It is a bit like collecting holiday brochures before you even know whether you will be taking a holiday this year. Sure, it might inspire you to book a two-week cruise, and it might also just tempt you to spend a lot more than you can afford.

More than likely, your pile of brochures will simply cause you to suffer from information overload and a long period of procrastination, a situation not uncommon with modern marketers. I stress, *modern* marketers. It is not so many years ago that the problem was lack of information, and the result was a good deal of guesswork, inspired or otherwise. This was before the world of the Internet and the other technologies that put more and more information at our fingertips – indeed, a super-abundance. Put simply, there is so much information available that the real-world marketer will often be hard pressed to make sense of it all.

Take the marketing manager of a retail grocery chain. The combination of point-of-sale scanners and customer loyalty cards means that it is entirely possible for that manager to know exactly how many people buy bacon, at two o'clock in the afternoon, in Hull, and even what type of people they are (or at least, what they are interested in – a conclusion culled from how they spend their loyalty card points). And how many people buy boiled sweets, in Exeter, at ten in the morning... and so on, and on. Potentially this information is incredibly valuable, but only if it can be distilled into some cogent conclusions.

There are so many questions that _can_ be asked that marketers are caught between two equally dangerous temptations: ask them all, and disappear up the jungle paths of analysis paralysis, or ask only those to which they already know the answers – which makes for a happy but terminally myopic marketer.

What is needed is a means of focusing the enquiry, and what better focus than the _marketing plan_? Why not reckon to ask the questions (and we will call this questioning process the _market audit_) that will help complete that plan? It is the marketing plan that will either turn your data and analysis into real-world implementation, or else leave you in the limbo of theory.

...planning to know what you need to know

Marketing plans that are simply repositories for information are likely to land you in trouble. If you allow the market audit to take on its own life, separate from the need of a plan, then what tends to occur is a plan filled with data that obscures rather than facilitates decision making. Successful implementation demands a _market plan_ made up of decisions, not data. Frame the market audit around the data required for you to make those decisions, and you are staring practical marketing in the face.

THE MARKETING PLAN

The marketing plan can be divided into three clear sections, each made up of a series of decisions and actions, as shown in Figure 5.2.

These three sections are:

1. _strategic positioning_ – which includes the big issues of how we wish to be, how we wish to appear to our customers, and how we will succeed;
2. _delivering the value_ – which turns to the essence of what our value proposition will be in our target markets and segments;
3. _tactical application_ – which is the (relatively) short-term set of activities designed to make the plan happen.

Chapter 6 will discuss the planning process itself, and each individual element of the plan will be covered in the chapters noted below against each of the three main sections:

1. Strategic positioning:
    – vision and objectives (Chapter 11);
    – how will we grow? (Chapter 12);
    – how will we compete? (Chapter 13);
    – what will drive us? (Chapter 14);
    – who will we serve? (Chapter 15);
    – branding (Chapter 16).

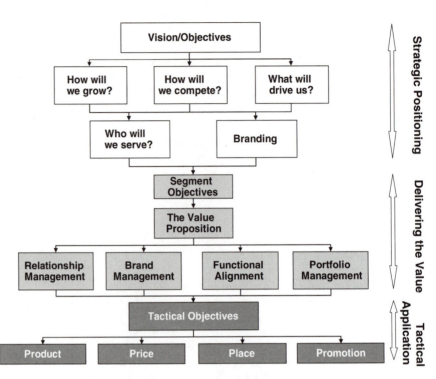

Figure 5.2   *The sections of the marketing plan*

2.   Delivering the value:
     – the value proposition (Chapter 18);
     –   relationship management (Chapter 19);
     –   brand management (Chapter 20);
     –   functional alignment (Chapter 21);
     –   portfolio management (Chapter 22).
3.   Tactical application:
     –   the tactical audit (Chapter 23);
     –   product (Chapter 25);
     –   place (Chapter 26);
     –   promotion (Chapter 27);
     –   price (Chapter 28).

The decisions made in the plan are the result of questions asked and information gathered during a parallel process: the *market audit* (see Chapters 7 to 10 in Part II). It is these two parallel activities that form the heart of the marketing process: the audit facilitates the plan, and the requirements of the plan drive the questions asked in the audit.

The relationship between plan and audit (or, as we will see, audits) is shown in Figure 5.3, as well as the detail of which tools and models are used at each stage of the process.

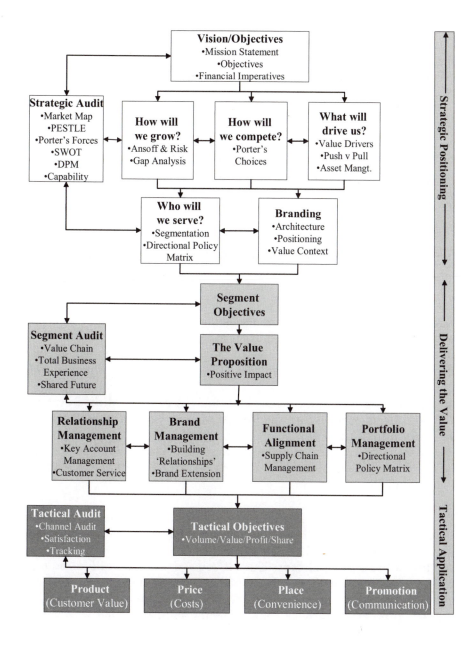

Figure 5.3 _Plan and audit: the marketing process_

THE MARKET AUDIT:
INFORMATION AND ANALYSIS

Part II of this book will explore in depth the necessary ingredients, and the methodology for conducting the strategic market audit. Suffice it to say here that this should of course be a continual process, not a one-off exercise, nor even an annual event. Understanding develops over time, and change is constant.

There are in fact three separate audits, each with its own clear purpose:

1. The *strategic audit* – helping to take the top-level decisions: how we will grow, how we will compete, what will drive us, whom we will serve, and the role of branding.
2. The *segment audit* – this helps us to develop the plan for each market segment, looking at issues such as our value proposition, relationship management, key account management, brand management, functional alignment and portfolio management.
3. The *tactical audit* – providing the understanding required to prepare the detailed plan for the marketing mix: the famous four P's, namely product, place, promotion and price.

Each audit comes in two parts: the gathering of information, and the analysis. The information comes from market research, both quantitative (data) and qualitative (judgements). The analysis is focused through a range of tools, including:

*   in the *strategic audit*: the market map, PESTLE analysis, Michael Porter's five-forces analysis and the SWOT analysis (strengths, weaknesses, opportunities, threats);
*   in the *segment audit*: value chain analysis and the shared future analysis;
*   in the *tactical audit*: market share data, satisfaction ratings and tracking studies.

Good discipline at this stage of the marketing process is vital; it is all too easy to replace rigour with assumption, and to deny conclusions that don't suit preconceived ideas. The purpose of the audit is to help take decisions, not to justify decisions already taken. If you ever find yourself forced into the latter course (usually by a boss in a hurry), you may as well tell them that you can save the business a good deal of money, and speed their decision process yet further, by scrapping the audit altogether… Or better, stand your ground and explain what an audit is for: to ensure you make the *right* decisions.

THE SANITY CHECK

Just as the audit was driven by the decisions required in the plan, so now the analysis from the audit fuels that plan. In such an iterative circumstance, where a degree of momentum can develop and things can even take on a life of their own, it is necessary to step back on occasions and take stock. We will call this process the _sanity check_.

There is another reason for pausing to check. The data you have based your decisions on is already history by the time you get round to implementation, and in some fast-changing markets that could be a serious issue.

When flying by the seat-of-the-pants causes rushes of blood to the head...

It is perhaps this stage in the process that most distinguishes the professional marketer from the seat-of-the-pants variety. It asks a series of questions that recognizes how the real world involves change, the unexpected and the unknown. It also aims to protect the business (and the marketer!) from the consequences of over-excited rushes of blood to the head:

- Are we being realistic?
- Can we trust the data?
- Are there things we don't know?
- Can we find out?
- Might the unknown have an impact?
- How will our competitors react?
- What if a new player enters the market, particularly if they enter with a radically different value proposition (the man from easyJet opening a no-frills cinema next to your gleaming multiplex...)?
- Should we have contingency plans?
- Are we still headed in the direction we set out for?
- Are we being consistent?
- Has the plan won the support of those who will implement it?
- Will our customers support it?
- Is it worth the effort?
- Do we have the capability (the _capability audit_).

The capability audit

Part of the sanity check is what we might call the capability audit. Chapter 2 described the marketing model as a matching process between the needs existing in the market and our company capabilities – our ability to meet those needs.

The sanity check is an opportunity to ask ourselves whether we have the capabilities required by our plans. This is obviously a question to be asked from the outset, but not _only_ at the outset. We are back to that business of momentum in the iterative process. You may have started out with a plan that was well within your capabilities, but the series of responses and reactions to market realities might have raised new demands. Are your modified plans realistic, or must you develop new capabilities?

We will return to this issue in Chapter 21, seeking the alignment of all relevant functions behind the plan.

IMPLEMENTATION AND REVIEW

The implementation stage is in reality less a stage and more a continuum. Nor is it a separate entity from the stages that went before and led up to it: research, analysis and planning. Implementation feeds the next round of research, analysis and planning, through the process of reviewing its effectiveness. This review is not a one-off assessment at the end of the year or end of the campaign period, but a continuous monitoring of progress measured against the objectives and performance standards established in the original plan. Disciplined monitoring and review are the oil that allows the marketing process to proceed as a continuous flow rather than a series of lurches forward (the new plan) and staggers backward (the realization that another new plan is needed).

THE 'THREE-STAGE' PROCESS

We have seen from the discussion of the marketing plan and the marketing audits that the marketing process actually comes in three stages. These are shown in Figure 5.4 as circles within circles – which is precisely how in reality it happens.

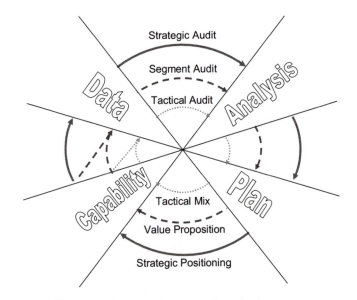

Figure 5.4 *The 'three-stage' marketing process*

All stages are active at once, with the time horizon shrinking as we move towards the centre. The 'strategic positioning' stage will take a time horizon of perhaps three to five years, while segment plans will need perhaps one to three years, while 'tactical application' probably involves looking at the current year.

6

Writing the marketing plan

'The business was founded in Bolton in 1927…' – so started a plan I was once asked to critique, and it didn't get any better.

The marketing plan should be a logical sequence of decisions and actions, not a record of the company history, nor even a record of the analysis that brought you to the decisions. Such matters, if required at all, should be kept to the appendices.

Nobody should be impressed by plans the thickness of telephone directories

The same plan that opened with the laying of the foundation stone in Bolton went on for some 65 pages, most of which was taken up with four-box matrix after four-box matrix. This is a sure sign that the writer is out to impress someone – look at me, I've swallowed a marketing textbook – rather than laying out a series of decisions and actions. It was full of data, very obviously the result of a great deal of time, effort and money, but it was very short on actionable conclusions. It was rather like one of those flow charts with intricate connections and backward loops that all boil down to the final box, wherein are found the words: *'and then a miracle occurs'*.

And to compound all those sins, it was stamped *'Company Secret'*; the stamp might just as well have read *'not to be read by **anyone**'*, which was almost certainly its actual fate.

WHY WRITE A PLAN?

There are plenty of reasons, and I have listed just 10 below, but perhaps the most important is illustrated in Figure 6.1 (yes, a four-box matrix, but a good one!).

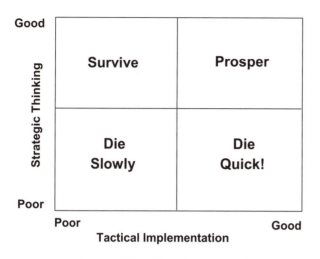

Figure 6.1 *Why plans matter*

The marketing plan turns strategy into tactics, bridging the gap between ambitions and actions, and ensuring that the business prospers. Both sides are important to that prosperity. A business that has good direction based on sound thinking (strategy) will survive even though its application in practice (tactics) is poor. It's not to be recommended, but it survives nonetheless. Businesses die when direction is poor and application is poor – that goes without saying – but the businesses that die the fastest are those with poor direction but enthusiastically applied tactics. Think of it as a person, a sales representative, and instead of referring to good or poor application we describe the person as lazy or hard-working. The lazy but well-directed rep will always survive, but the last thing any company wants is a hard-working but misdirected sales rep; such people just make trouble for all concerned! Making the wrong decisions and then applying resources with energy and enthusiasm is a terrible way to go…

Ten reasons to write a marketing plan

1. to ensure that we have asked the right questions and taken all the necessary decisions;
2. to make coherent sense of what will have been a complex set of decisions;
3. to transform our thinking (strategy) into action (tactics);
4. to align the whole business with the marketing strategy, and to allow the supporting functions to develop the capabilities required for implementation;
5. to demonstrate to our stakeholders (customers, owners, investors, staff and suppliers) that we are a sound, responsible and professionally managed business with a clear vision and coherent direction;

6. to enable us to measure progress towards our objectives, and the success of our activities;
7. to remove the tendency to drift – a dangerous malaise that afflicts businesses that take their eye off the future;
8. to provide a mechanism for prioritizing and allocating resources;
9. to focus the collective mind on change;
10. to maximize the chances of success.

THE PLANNING CASCADE

Much has been said about the plan existing within the context of reaction and change, but it also exists in another context: the long-term ambitions of the business as a whole.

As well as the Marketing Plan there will be a Business Plan, and in a large company perhaps a Corporate Plan ahead of that. Figure 6.2 illustrates a typical 'cascade' of such plans.

Figure 6.2 *The planning cascade*

Several issues are raised by the idea of the cascade. There is clearly a need for consistency between the various plans; no man is an island, least of all in the marketing department. This can be ensured if each plan follows the preceding one, but is it as simple as a series of mother–daughter relationships? When people speak of 'marketing-led' businesses there is a suggestion that the marketing plan is expected to drive the business; and so drives to some significant extent the business plan. Even if the business isn't described as 'marketing led', there still must be a certain amount of two-way traffic between plans. As in life, sometimes the child can influence the parent.

If the marketing plan concludes that the best route to competitive advantage is a lowest cost one (see Chapter 13 and Porter's choices), then it will be in trouble from the start if the business plan has chosen to invest heavily in a new R&D capability to develop differentiated products. So which do you change?

Business plan or marketing plan?

This debate over which plan comes first raises the final issue with the cascade: what is actually the difference between a business and a marketing plan?

A common response is that a marketing plan is a business plan without the financials – but I would worry a good deal if I read a marketing plan that took no concern over issues such as revenue, investment and profitability.

Another response is that the marketing plan represents a functional view, while the business plan is cross-functional, but that's another worrying scenario – an island mentality.

A third definition has it that the business plan is about resources and the marketing plan about the opportunity, but that polarizes marketing towards a right-sider mentality, and we have seen enough by now to know that marketing must bring the two sides together.

Perhaps a really good marketing plan *is* the business plan? Each company must make its own definitions such as suit the nature and realities of its business, but in doing so it must avoid artificial lines of demarcation. Remember the idea of the two-way street and don't get hung up about the relative merits of top-down or bottom-up approaches.

THE PLANNING HORIZON

Every industry, market, business has its own 'natural' planning horizon. This might be considered the period in which it is reasonable to assume that things will stay the same, at least sufficiently so for plans to be developed and implemented. For some, like an aircraft manufacturer, this might be as long as 10–20 years. For an IT service provider we may be talking of months. This is not to say that the IT service provider should not plan for more than six months ahead, rather that it will have a hierarchy of plans from long-term strategic plans to short-term tactical implementation. A typical manufacturing business might have a long-term plan of 10 years, a medium-term plan of 2–3 years (reflecting the 'natural' planning horizon) and an annual plan for tactical implementation. The certainty of the outcome should of course increase the shorter the time horizon considered, as should the detail of the contents. The annual plan will deal in the realm of prices, promotional spend and new-product launch dates. The medium-term plan will focus more on the analysis of the market opportunity, the choice of market segments and the allocation of resources. The long-term plan will be considering the forces and the trends that will shape the market in the future and the capabilities required for success in that future.

The only valid assumption is to assume that none of your assumptions is reliable…

And, of course, all this comes with a giant health warning. The phrase 'reasonable to assume that things will stay the same' is so full of danger as almost to need no further elaboration. Marketers must learn to assume change. It may even be wise to put into your plan the assumptions on which it has been made – such as 'no new competitor will enter the market' – just to act as a trigger to review the plan when the unexpected happens.

THE TEMPLATE

Using someone else's template for your marketing plan is not usually a good idea. It leads to the box-ticking approach: 'I've done that four-box matrix, so it must be a good plan.' Well, perhaps that particular four-box matrix was of no relevance to your own circumstances…

So, it is with much trepidation that I provide a PowerPoint template on the CD ROM attached to this book. It is only a suggested list of contents, and a logical flow, but feel free to change it, as radically as you like, to fit your own requirements.

TEN TIPS ON WRITING THE MARKETING PLAN

1. Involve a wide (and possibly cross-functional) team in preparing the plan. This is not a solo endeavour of personal creativity.
2. Don't write *War and Peace*. Use a format that will help to keep it tight and concise. Bullet points are fine – this is an action plan, not an exercise in purple prose. PowerPoint is ideal, avoiding the two sins of 'wordiness' and 'spreadsheet overload'. Excel-based plans turn out to be 'the budget', which is not the same thing at all. Most importantly, PowerPoint is ideal for presenting the plan to others. (If you do use PowerPoint, don't cheat, as one of my clients once did, by using font size 2…)
3. Focus on conclusions and actions. Keep the analysis to a minimum, or put it into an appendix for those who want to see how you got to where you got to.
4. Start with a one-slide executive summary, distilling the plan down to its essence. Preparing this précis is a valuable exercise in itself, ensuring that you have clarity of direction and are not wandering down too many sidelines.
5. Avoid jargon and marketing-speak. Marketing-speak has its place, as a shorthand among professionals, but don't expect the rest of the world to warm to it; they'll just think you're being lazy, or showing off.

Get it read

6. Don't stamp it 'company secret' – aim to have it widely read and understood. Present it far and wide.

7. Put confidential data into appendices that can have restricted access (if you really must!).
8. Take the plan right down to the level of actions and tactics, and ensure that this is done at the level of market segments or customer groupings.
9. Focus on the future. The past may be glorious, but it is no guarantee of future success (as they say in the small print…).
10. Avoid unsubstantiated hype. Hockey-stick graphs need full justification; it is not good enough to say, 'I have written the plan, therefore from now on all will be well…'

Part II

The strategic market audit

7

Market research

Rupert Murdoch doesn't believe in market research – or rather, he prefers to rely on his own instincts rather than PowerPoint presentations of numbers and statistics. He seems to do all right.

The Sony Walkman was launched in the face of some highly adverse market research comments. Sony went ahead with the launch because its founder, Akio Morita, felt that market research couldn't ask the right questions in such new territory. He said, 'I do not believe that any amount of market research could have told us that it would have been successful. The public does not know what is possible. We do.' It seems to have done all right.

So what is the big noise about doing market research? Is it just research agencies justifying their existence (and their not insubstantial fees)?

I remember the day that the final degree results were announced at my university. I went with a friend to look at them posted on the wall, with some trepidation, as I feared the worst, not helped by my friend's absolute confidence in his having got a first.

Instinct… or facts?

The place was crowded when we got there and we had to look over two rows of shoulders to find our results. They were posted in groups, by the class of degree: first, two-one, two-two, and too bad to think about. I found mine pretty quickly – the advantage of an unusual name – and sighed with relief at my more than welcome two-one. My friend scanned the first-class list and twitched visibly as he failed to find his name, and then looked down the two-one list – nothing there, at which point he let out a whoop of delight and turned to me with a mile-wide grin: 'I knew it, a first.' It was two whole days later that he discovered to his horror that he had in fact got a two-two.

That's the problem with some very intelligent people: they know the answers already and strongly resist any evidence to the contrary. When my friend couldn't find his name in the two-one list, the only possible explanation, to his overbearingly confident mind, was that he had in fact got a first but just hadn't been able to spot his name through the crowd.

This is also the problem with some very clever companies. The amount of brain power and ability that goes into developing new products and services can often convince a company that what it is doing just must be right. At best this is wishful thinking, but at worst it is sheer arrogance.

Often, market research is commissioned with the intent of proving one's convictions to be right rather than as a serious test of trends or opinions. It is as David Ogilvy (guru and pioneer of the advertising industry) complained: market research is too often used as a drunk uses a lamp-post: for support rather than illumination. Such an intention makes it very easy to ignore or reinterpret bad news.

Some companies don't feel the need to peer into the unknown, doubting the speculative nature of market research and finding ample support for their case in the facts of the past. But the evidence of the past is a poor guide in today's fast-changing business environment. Even the very recent past can mislead.

Star struck

In May 1999 the new Star Wars movie *Star Wars Episode One* led to a boom in sales of Star Wars books for the publisher Dorling Kindersley. 'On that basis, judgements were made about investing further in stock, believing that this could be a Star Wars Christmas,' said Peter Kindersley, executive chairman in January 2000 after the disaster had hit and a £25m pre-tax loss for the second half of 1999 was on the cards.

It wasn't a Star Wars Christmas and Dorling Kindersley found itself with 10 million books left in stock from 13 million printed in anticipation of the rush. Some hot things can go cold very quickly. It also spelt the end of Dorling Kindersley as an independent concern. It was bought up by Penguin, part of the Pearson empire.

'Past performance should not be taken as a guarantee of future success,' warn the investment adverts; and it is useful advice for marketeers. Marks & Spencer suffered a significant slip in its sales and profits in 1999 largely from a misjudgement of clothing fashions. 'Leggings and tunics lasted as the thing to wear for so long that we took our eye off the ball,' said Peter Salsbury, the M&S chief executive, his words serving perhaps as a microcosm of the company's wider problem.

Companies that use the past as a guide are perhaps less to be blamed than those that actually do the research into future needs and then ignore the results. This is such a common scenario around new product launches that it deserves its very own name – I call it the 'Akio Morita syndrome'.

A company invests heavily in developing a new product; let's say a paint company develops a clever new system that allows consumers to mix their own colour in-store, by themselves, using a self-service machine. The market research says that people won't use the new system because of what the researchers call 'techno-fear': they don't want the embarrassment of breaking the machine, or spilling paint, or any of a hundred other accidents waiting to happen. The launch team ignore techno-fear, quoting in their defence the words of Akio Morita: 'The public does not know what is possible. We do.' The product fails. Not only does it fail, but it also costs the company significantly in lost credibility. This is what happened to the Dulux brand in the late 1980s with a system called Colour Options. For some time afterwards, retailers were more wary of accepting 'good ideas' from a brand that had enjoyed success after success over the previous 10 years.

A case of the blues

The launch of the Sony Walkman was a great success, but it was not the norm. The fact that it is still quoted and discussed shows that, and while Akio Morita was clearly right in this case, we should take care in following his bold example.

And so the debate rages on: instinct versus statistics, the momentum of product launches versus the caution of researchers.

Of course, research can get it wrong too.

Hoover UK ran a consumer promotion in the early 1990s offering free airline flights to customers who spent £100 or more on its products. Research suggested a modest take-up, based on previous experience, but this promotion hit a spot and Hoover was inundated. At first, it couldn't handle the demand, and people waited weeks and weeks for tickets. When the dust had settled, Hoover faced a bill for some £20 million, and a reputation for naivety.

Flights of fancy

Blind tests for a new-formula Coca-Cola in 1984 suggested that the company was on to a winner. Rarely had research been so compelling, yet the subsequent launch in 1985 brought howls of protest, and after only three months the original Coke was back – Classic Coke was born. Cynics might say that this was a grand trick to effect a relaunch of an old product and give it a whole new life cycle. The redundant executives scattered around Atlanta, Georgia, might argue otherwise.

The real thing: statistics or emotions?

What all this argues, I think, is that research has an important place, but must be used with care. It shouldn't command, but nor should it be ignored. The real skill, of course, is not in interpreting the answers, but in framing the questions in the first place. This is a genuine skill, and, like advertising, should be left to the professionals. I have seen research surveys prepared by keen but innocent managers, including gems ranging from the naively simple 'Is our product too expensive?' ('Gosh no, please put your price up!') to the impossible vastness of 'What do you want?'

The value of facts and figures depends not just on the accuracy of the study, but very much on the choice of questions that created them. Suppose a car manufacturer had taken its clipboards on to the street 10 years ago to test the prospects for a new range of four-wheel-drive off-road vehicles. The researchers might have asked, 'How often do you drive your car off-road?' or, even more directly, 'How often would you like to drive your car off-road?' The resultant statistics would have shown very small percentages in both cases. Had they used those facts and figures alone to determine their future strategy for off-road vehicles, they would have almost certainly missed the growth phenomenon of the 1990s in the European car market. This was a task that called for more subtlety in questioning; attitudes and the realm of latent needs are rarely uncovered by such a direct approach – the very problem that Akio Morita observed.

RESEARCH AND DECISIONS

Let's remind ourselves, and do so continually, that research is for a purpose: to help us make decisions. First, the big ones:

- How will we grow?
- How should we aim to compete?
- What will drive us?
- Who should we sell to?

And then the more tactical ones:

- What price?
- What quality?
- How much to make?
- How to get the product to the customer?
- How to promote?

This focus will help us keep control over what can become a massive and never-ending search for data.

Here's a useful rule of thumb on what constitutes 'enough data'. When you have enough data to enable you to make these decisions, and sleep at nights, then that's enough data!

TYPES OF RESEARCH

Perhaps we should distinguish some types of research. The first distinction is between quantitative (facts and figures) and qualitative (ideas, attitudes and opinions).

Quantitative research

Quantitative research includes such things as demographics (numbers of households, population aged 25–40, etc), market size, brand shares and price points. This is the realm of hard facts, though the famous dictum 'lies, damned lies and statistics' should be a warning to us all. The problems usually lie in the definitions and interpretations.

What is the size of the market for snack foods? Define a snack.

What is the market share of brand A? Do we mean by volume or by value? How do we define the total market in which brand A has a share? (See the question above.)

When companies ask, 'what is the size of the market?' they must take care not to limit their horizons. So many restrict their view by taking current customers as the basis for defining the market. Those with real growth aspirations take a different kind of view.

I once heard a senior executive from Coca-Cola ask an audience what Coke's global brand share was, with replies ranging from 20 to 50 per cent. He stunned us momentarily by telling us that it was a little less than 3 per cent, and then explained that he was measuring Coca-Cola's share of all purchased liquids consumed, including tea, beer, wine, coffee… (The point was that Coca-Cola still had a long way to go: the important goal was an increasing 'share of stomach'.) This is an important notion when defining market sizes and measuring shares: are you looking at direct competitors (those with similar products) or at competing outlets for the customer's money? Coca-Cola's view – that it was in competition with tea, beer, wine, coffee and the rest – indicates a much greater ambition than simply looking at Pepsi, and its market information requirements are that much broader as a result.

Share of what? How about share of stomach?

A valuable quantitative data bank for fmcg marketers is what is sometimes known as the 'consumer diary'. A group of consumers is asked to keep a daily diary of purchases – everything from soap powder (with brands noted) to three-piece suites (with price and retailer). Over a period of time these diaries provide valuable trend information as well as indicating short-term responses to factors such as seasonality, weather and promotional campaigns. Maintaining your own study is an onerous task, but it is possible to buy into such diaries maintained by firms such as ACNielsen.

As well as facts about the past (quantitative data by their very nature tend to be history), we might also use quantified studies to assess our current effectiveness. A typical example would be the use of *tracking studies* to measure the effectiveness of promotional campaigns. After all, if you are spending £5 million on an advertising campaign, perhaps it is worth £50,000 to test how well it worked? (See Chapter 23.)

Research and forecasting

As well as 'hard' facts there are also those studies that deal with such things as market forecasts or intentions to buy. It is important to remember that many such 'predictions' are extrapolated from past and current data and so are of course subject to the changing times. Benz is famed for having carried out one of the first predictive research studies into the UK car market as early as the birth of the 20th century. It predicted that the market would not exceed 1,000 cars, owing to the shortage of chauffeurs.

The forecasting of demand based on trend analysis is never straight-forward, not least because of the way it is influenced by the current strategy of the company seeking the insight.

Airbus or Boeing – who's got the future sized up?

Airbus, the European aircraft manufacturer, is set to launch the A380 super-jumbo (with a staggering 555 seats) in early 2006. Back in the late 1990s it was forecasting that there would be a demand for some 1,500 of these aircraft over the next 20 years, a forecast that was four times greater than that of its main rival and existing jumbo supremo, Boeing. As we get closer, so the number starts to fall, as 'issues' arise. Virgin has delayed its first delivery of the plane, owing to concerns that some airports will not be able to cope with the logistics surrounding the arrival of 555 people in one go.

So, did the Airbus forecast consider such things? How much was it based simply on the company's decision to build the aircraft, itself the result of having the technical capability, or the offer of government funding (and excellent job prospects), is open to debate, as indeed is Boeing's much smaller forecast, based perhaps on its own strategy to stick to more conventional jumbos. Some people say forecasting is too difficult to attempt for the long term, but perhaps there is an equal peril: when it is as easy as predicting what you have decided to do already!

Qualitative research

Qualitative statements deal with preferences, opinions, latent wants and needs. Such comments are often prompted by the much-vaunted and oft-maligned focus group. A group of customers, carefully chosen to represent the target market, are encouraged to discuss the merits or otherwise of anything from chocolate bars to television programmes. How much reliance can be put on the remarks of half a dozen such guinea pigs is open to much debate – but what a great way to have your ideas challenged or tested. Many a successful consumer product has been aired, modified and launched on the back of such focus groups, with sample sizes as low as 12 or 18 people. The real requirement is not so much large numbers as expert facilitation – another job for the experts, not an over-enthusiastic sales or marketing manager who pushes the group to accept the product.

Qualitative studies are of great value to marketers seeking to understand and segment their marketplace. Chapter 15 ('Who will we serve?') will describe a market segment as a group of customers with similar needs, attitudes and perceptions. Quantifiable surveys might shed light on the size of such groups, but the qualitative data from studies such as focus groups will be of vital importance to understanding the softer aspects of their attitudes and perceptions.

Expert opinion is often accepted as valid qualitative research, and can be hugely valuable where the experts are the intended customers. Customer surveys are most useful in this regard, but, as ever, the questioning requires expertise and subtlety. Sending the sales force out to canvas opinion is not the ideal way to conduct such research, especially if it is customers' opinions of the sales force! Trade shows provide excellent opportunities to gauge customer opinion, provided they are planned to include that purpose. The questioning must be disciplined and consistent, and the answers assessed with equal discipline and rigour, else the danger is of ending up with a loose list of anecdotal stories that become folklore. Some businesses will attempt to set up 'advisory panels' of key opinion leaders in their market. This practice is particularly common in the pharmaceutical industry, where specialists abound and interest and pressure groups prosper.

The expert pundit is another matter altogether, more fruitful ground for embarrassment than for serious guidance. An 'expert' reporting on the unveiling of television at a 1930s New York trade fair foresaw a dim future for the invention, as it involved the family sitting still in a darkened room and not talking to each other. Barry Norman, the BBC's top film critic, safely predicted the decline of the cinema as a result of the video, and was later honest enough to confess his mistake, and his failure to foresee the rise of the luxury multiplex.

A new source of market information

There is one hugely significant new source of data for the marketer, one supplying both quantitative and, with a little bit of effort, qualitative information: the business's own information systems. The wealth of data captured by systems ranging from the large-scale operational systems such as SAP, to those such as customer relationship management (CRM – see Chapter 19), allows for a whole new level of analysis and understanding. Without having to call in the 'clipboard brigade', you already have access to detail on sales rates, customer preferences, seasonality, price elasticity (see Chapter 28) and plenty more. But be warned not to rely solely on this new wealth, mind-boggling though it is, for it has one significant downside: it is based on you – your activities, your sales, your view of the world. Take care not to be too dazzled by its brilliance, and keep looking outside at how customers behave away from your presence, and in the presence of competitors. The marketer still needs the clipboard brigade.

FOCUSING YOUR DATA NEEDS

Here is a fine irony: there is more information available to the marketer than ever before, yet many marketers feel worse off than their 'less well informed' predecessors. The huge amounts of data can be daunting, bringing on brain overload rather than true knowledge. The urgent need is to slim things down a little:

1. What data do you need to make those all-important decisions already listed (see above), and so write the marketing plan?
2. What data do you need to run your own business – realistically?

For the second of these, if you are a four-person company making widgets for sale in Devon and Cornwall, what use is it for you to know the world market size for widgets? Even if it's easily available information, what does it matter to you? You will probably be much better served by a survey of local opinion and satisfaction that highlights a need for improved delivery times than by an inch-thick document of statistics on the global sale of widgets. Of course, the big picture might highlight trends that will affect the local picture, and in this respect trends and forecasts are probably of more value than the 'hard' facts.

There are perhaps some specific issues that might slip through the two-point 'sieve' noted above, such as data to present to customers, perhaps as evidence of our capability, or data to monitor performance towards goals, or data with which to assess the impact of a particular activity (ie brand image and recognition studies). These are quite specific studies, but first, a checklist for the 'big-canvas' questions.

A checklist: the big canvas

1. How do we define the market?
   - Segments:
     - size and value;
     - market shares.
2. Trends and forecasts:
   - volumes and values;
   - opportunities and threats.
3. What are the routes to market?
   - size and share by channel;
   - market shares.
4. Who are the customers?
   - current customers?
   - potential customers?
5. What share of their business do we, and the competition, have?
6. What are their needs, attitudes, behaviours and aspirations?
   - usage and attitude (U&A) studies.
7. How well do we perform, in the customers' eyes?
   - by their standards;
   - compared to the competition.
8. What capabilities are required, now and in the future?

Some of these are big questions indeed. Item 6 alone is a massive under-taking if it is to be done properly. Some of the above will be available through desk research; other questions will require commissioned surveys and other research exercises.

Four health warnings

1. Data available to desk research is, almost by definition, out of date.
2. Official statistics are bedevilled by problems of definition.
3. Commercially available reports, while useful, very often leave you wishing they had broken it down by just one level more: from the national to the regional, from the market to the segment, from the macro to the micro.
4. Your own sales statistics are very poor sources of information in this regard; there is no better way to limit your horizons!

These 'problems' should of course be the starting point for commissioning your own research.

COMMISSIONING YOUR OWN RESEARCH

The following eight-step process will help you through the maze:

1. Prepare the research brief, detailing:
   - Purpose of research. (The outcome desired. Be sure you know why you are going to all this effort – what decisions are you hoping to be able to make, what sort of actions are you wanting to test? You might ask, as a general 'test of value' at this point, 'If we are not going to do anything as a result of this research, why are we bothering?')
   - Scope of research (market/segment/customer).
   - Timetable for results.
   - Budget (and aim to stick to it!).
2. Shortlist the agencies using the following criteria:
   - What experience do they have in this field (the market and the methodology)?
   - Are there any issues of confidentiality? A good agency will be able to work with your competitors, with all the benefits that brings of general awareness, and still maintain confidentiality, but you will need to be specific regarding your demands. (For really sensitive issues such as product launch testing, you should look for exclusivity.)
   - Are they able to respond to your timetable?
   - Will they work within your budget? A good agency should be able to suggest alternative approaches to help work within a tight budget.

3. Brief the agency:
   - Ask for a presentation that demonstrates an understanding of the task, the agency's capability, the proposed methodology, proposed sample size (where appropriate), timetable and logistics, and costs.
   - Be very clear if you require the agency to make recommendations or choices rather than simply gather information. This is very important to avoid any disputes post-research.
4. Select the agency:
   - Issue a more detailed brief if necessary.
   - Be clear what involvement you want (if any) in the research: attending focus groups, etc.
   - Reconfirm timetables (particularly debriefings) and budgets (not because agencies are slack, simply because such things suffer from the 'ooze syndrome').
5. Fieldwork:
   - Where possible, it is almost always advantageous to attend some sessions such as focus teams, provided that you let the agency get on with what it does best, without hindrance or undue direction from you. A good agency will welcome your presence, and the best agencies will manage you to perfection!
6. Results debrief:
   - The research will have cost a lot both in time and money; aim to maximize its value by involving as many people as appropriate. The debrief process itself can be as illuminating as the facts and figures presented.
   - Ensure that the aims of the research are restated at the outset. This will allow you to judge the effectiveness of the agency in its work.
   - Take care to listen to the agency's feedback before being tempted to put your own spin on the results.
   - Be clear on conclusions and recommendations.
   - Ask for a written report if required.
   - Commission new research as required.
7. Action plans:
   - Integrate results, conclusions and recommendations into your plans.
8. Re-evaluate:
   - Research data grows old; have plans to stay up to date.

A final tip: make sure that the research is kept available for use, and that its aims and circumstances are carefully documented. Corporate memories are notoriously short!

Budgets

The age-old question, and one more prone to short-termism than any other in marketing, is how much to spend on market research. It is so easy *not* to spend money on research and nothing suffers, for the present. The professional marketer on the other hand might like to declare the research budget inviolate: a long-term investment and not something that is done only in good times when money is flush. Should you perhaps spend a percentage of sales turnover on market research, in the same way some businesses aim to spend a percentage on R&D? Such an approach has one great advantage: there will be a budget! Unfortunately, market research is often a last-minute thought and there is no budget allocated. The result is either no research, or research on a shoestring that is of questionable value. The percentage of turnover approach also demonstrates a commitment to understanding the market environment – particularly important in a fast-changing market.

The 'percentage of turnover' approach may even result in the mainte-nance of a full-time in-house market research department. The pros and cons of this are lengthy on both sides, including overhead cost and possibly restricted expertise on the downside and the possibility of selling data to others on the up. The overwhelming plus is the development over time of some very deep knowledge that can be of benefit to you and to your customers. This can represent significant competitive advantage. Perhaps the biggest concern is that horizons can be limited by the 'that's how we see things around here' school of thought.

In the end, perhaps the best approach is to spend by need and retain a good slice of common sense. Consider how much money is invested in the development and launch of a new product. If the figure is in the millions of pounds, then surely it is worth spending the tens of thousands on research to enhance the success of that launch? Chapter 23 will look at two examples of such research that perhaps fit best within the tactical audit: customer satisfaction surveys, and tracking of advertising effectiveness.

ACT OF FAITH?

So is it all worth the effort? Much time and certainly much money will be required, and a precise cost–benefit analysis is not always possible. For some, it is an act of faith; for others, it seems more like health insurance: so long as you're healthy it seems a dreadful waste, but when your heart starts to flutter or your legs to wobble it seems the smartest move you ever made!

My company runs a marketing training event where delegates take part in a computer-based business simulation involving them in the investment of £500 million in plant and equipment for a new venture. It is frightening, but not uncommon, to see them balk at the idea of spending just a few hundred thousand pounds on research in order to understand the market for which this huge investment is intended.

Of course, some research (and perhaps the most important, if Rupert Murdoch is to be believed) can be done for little or no cost.

Christian Rucker, founder of The White Company, a mail-order business specializing in household linens, towels, dressing gowns, bedspreads and the like – all, of course, in

Getting it white

white – was spurred into action by hearing her sister-in-law remark that she couldn't find the right kind of white linen. 'I had to do it by mail order. I went away and couldn't sleep I was so excited.'

If money is an issue, perhaps the focus should be on enhancing your qualitative understanding of market and customer perceptions and needs. Listen to people, ask questions everywhere you go, involve everyone in the company in the thirst for knowledge, perhaps even conduct a few focus groups.

The next chapter, a short detour into the world of fiction, may help to galvanize your determination to know more.

8

Chakravati's piano, or, why you need market research...

(For those who might need further convincing of the need for market research, or identifying the right data, this chapter provides a brief respite from the author's assertions, and calls instead on the help of the maestro...)

After a day of near-broiling heat in the big city, the cool of the evening wafts us across the greenery of Hyde Park and into the magnificent auditorium of the Albert Hall. London's traffic continues its roar just yards from the doors, but inside all is hushed. We have taken our seats, shared pleasantries with our neighbours, cleared our throats, and now the house lights are going down. A single spot picks out the elderly man seated at the concert grand; he is alone on stage. He flexes his fingers, closes his eyes and hangs his hands over the keys.

V K Chakravati, after 10 years in retirement, is back on the concert circuit and filling the halls as if he had never been away. We are part of a special audience this evening, here by special invitation for more than a piano recital: we are here to learn the mysteries of Chakravati's piano.

Our senses flex as the great man's hands come down with a huge fortissimo to strike the opening chord of Chakravati's Second Piano Concerto – only there is nothing, or rather just a single note, a lone tone of pathetic smallness; hardly enough for the grand emotion of his physical effort.

His hands are moving quickly and there are more sporadic notes and the occasional remnant of a chord, but they are a surprisingly poor output for the frantic activity on stage. They form no recognizable melody or harmony, just isolated sounds that confuse the audience into an uncomfortable shuffling of feet.

On stage, Chakravati seems oblivious to the confusion his performance is causing. Already there are beads of sweat on his forehead as he thunders on into his performance. Occasionally a recognizable snatch of music holds us for a moment, but then the mime show takes hold again and we frown and tilt our heads.

It is not long before we lean towards our neighbours: 'Is it just me or do you think his piano's not working?' 'Maybe it's the microphone?' 'Maybe it's the acoustics where we're sitting?' 'Maybe he's gone avant-garde in the last 10 years?' We cough, we tut, somebody at the front is on their feet, and all of a sudden Chakravati stops. He comes to the front of the stage and the single spot follows him down. He speaks: 'And that, ladies and gentlemen, was the opening of my Second Piano Concerto, played with a very special arrangement – I call it my business variation.' He smiles at us, just to confirm that he means the comment to sting. 'It takes just as much effort as the normal arrangement, only the final outcome is a little disappointing, I think you will agree? I have spent the last 10 years, what some people have called my retirement, watching people like you. You are all businesspeople here tonight, and I have the greatest pity for you.'

The audience is not taking this explanation well. First he performs three minutes of incoherent nonsense, and then he starts to insult us. At least, we think he is insulting us; nothing is clear about Chakravati. He continues unabashed: 'I am a musician and as such the last few minutes have been terrible for me – far more terrible than for you. And why? Because I know what you should have been hearing. Most of you do not; you only know that you didn't hear very much at all. And why do I say I pity you? Perhaps you think me very rude?'

The same smile, only this time a little more engaging. 'As I said, I have been watching you for the last 10 years, watching your struggles and your frustrations – and wincing at your blind ignorance.'

No smile could engage us after that, but he carried on, as oblivious to our mounting annoyance as before. 'You spend your business lives like poor Chakravati's piano. My piano has 94 notes divided into 8 octaves, each of 12 notes – yet just now you only heard 12, one octave.'

He breaks off seemingly concerned for the first time at something he has said. 'I must be confusing you; an octave with 12 notes. Perhaps you were expecting 8 – octagons, octopuses, octogenarians, like me, and the rest of those octs. Well, there are seven white keys and five black, and eight tonal progressions, but perhaps I should say no more of that; it is unimportant, like sales statistics.'

A finger seemed to come out from Chakravati and poke a thousand eyes. 'Most of you, I suspect, think I was not doing my job up here just now, short-changing you, but I promise you I put every effort into every moment – I always do. I have practised this piece for weeks, for months, every day.

Practice is important: if I miss a week, my audiences notice; if I miss a day, I notice.'

He seemed to relax at that thought and leant towards us a little more kindly. 'No, it was not I, Chakravati, that let you down; it was my piano, poor Chakravati's piano. You see, only the middle octave, only 12 notes, work. They are all you heard, and yet in only three minutes I had covered most of the keyboard. And that is how you spend your business lives, hearing only the same 12 notes, while you scatter your hands all over the keyboard.'

He walks back to the piano and sits as before, hands hanging over the keys, only this time, as he brings them down, we leap from our seats, struck by the volume, the force and the complexity of the sound – every key was working now. Chakravati turns on his seat and looks at us, it has to be said, with very evident pity. 'Do you remember how you heard that the first time?' and he takes a finger and lazily hits a single key. 'That is how you heard it and how you hear in your business lives. I hope for your own sakes it is not a disability that clouds your private life. You have only your middle octave working and you miss so much; perhaps you miss the whole point.'

We murmur, though more in complaint than through any sense of self-realization. 'You are displeased with poor old Chakravati. You think he goes too far, but you forget, I have been watching you. That single note, that is your sales statistics, isolated numbers, and history, quickly gone and faster forgotten, almost pointless. You have already forgotten my one puny note,' and he struck it once more to remind us, 'but you will perhaps never forget that first mighty chord' – and we leap a second time as he twists like a snake to strike that huge sound once again.

'You know what the rest of those notes are, in your business lives of course? Perhaps you don't; Chakravati forgets himself, blind ignorance cannot be overcome in a moment.' The monumental cheek of the man bites into us, but at the same time, perhaps we are beginning to see the point, slowly and reluctantly. 'If the middle octave is the past, sales history expressed in volumes and values, then go one octave down and we are already exploring much richer territory. This is where rhythm resides, the beat of your business – your customers. Here we find what your customers think of you, the spoken and the unspoken – the realm of their perceptions. Let me show you.'

He plays a simple melody in the middle octave, the sort that a child would pick out with two fingers; we guess that is what he thinks of sales history! Then comes the surprise: the same simple melody but with the addition of rich, complex harmonies and rhythm, just one octave below. The transformation is amazing, and the point is made. 'Go further down the scale and we find those foundation notes: the needs of the market, the real needs, and I mean real, not just the ones you chose to hear because they suit you. Further down again and we are in those profound bass notes of the unspoken needs, perhaps as yet unimagined.'

Chakravati plays the same melody again, this time with a progression of deep bass notes, and we have to admit that the addition does indeed sound 'profound'. 'If we come back to the middle and start moving up the octaves, we are in the realms of the potential future, a fascinating place that should interest us a great deal more than the plodding present. See how more interesting a small addition can be.' Again the same simple melody but with just a few unexpected leaps into the next octave – just a few notes, but a step change of sophistication. 'In these treble octaves we find excitement and melody. At first we hear the potential that lies already in your own capabilities, the genius of your people, the brilliance of your technology. Moving up the octaves, we find new capabilities hungering to be used.'

We are treated to a rush of melody that makes us feel the future at our fingertips, and then Chakravati stops abruptly and turns on us. 'So why don't you hear these things? Why the fascination with history, that dull middle octave, when the rest of the keyboard is the rhythm of your market, and the melody of your future?'

Put that way, we begin to wonder. At first it is quiet contemplation, but soon the whispered asides turn to a chattering, and then a bubbling torrent that fills the hall. And just above this building hubbub, we can hear Chakravati speaking slowly and quietly: 'And if you want to hear the sound of your market, the rhythm of your business, and to hear the melodies of your future, then you must expand your consciousness, octave by octave, up to the trillest treble and down to the deepest base. You cannot listen to notes; you must listen to the music, the whole thing. Let's start this very evening. Let's explore the music out there, and start by learning the secrets of Chakravati's piano.'

We were well entertained that evening, with more from Chakravati's Second Piano Concerto, slower and quieter passages, as well as more thunder and lightning. His piano was most remarkable, expanding and shrinking its playing range at his command. He was able to show how the addition of each octave let us appreciate more and understand more of the music, but the most interesting demonstration was this.

He played a melody, a new one backed by the whole piano, and then subtracted a few of the lower octaves. The melody was still clear, but the end result was not nearly as satisfying. He asked our opinion on the matter, and we all agreed: the full piano was better.

'Why?' he asked, and the best we could come up with, a thousand opinions, was that it just sounded right.

'In that case, I am satisfied, your opinion is good enough for me, and the answer is – it just is. But your bosses might want a better explanation. How would they react if your explanation for launching product X were that it just felt right? Would they sanction that million-pound spend to make it happen?

'Perhaps you, a true musician with the instinct of a maestro, perhaps you can just tell, but others? They need the proof and the evidence. They want someone to say to them, "We've tried this out on a lot of folk, they say it's good, they've even helped us improve it – we've researched it." And you know what, even a maestro like me, even I need that too. Feedback, it sometimes hurts, but you're almost always the better for it.

'Let's say I want to know how well my comeback is going down. I could wait for the royalty cheques from the CD companies. Accurate, but a little late if I'm a flop. I could measure how fast I manage to play a piece and compare that to how fast I was 10 years ago to see if I'm likely to be more successful. You think I'm crazy? What about seeing if I could take some of the notes out, Bach without all those time-consuming semi-quavers – so much more efficient.' And Chakravati entertained us with the fastest and undoubtedly the most efficient Bach's Toccata and Fugue ever played – a comic rendition of great application, but a musical monstrosity.

'Crazier still? You're right, who'd want it? Of course, I shouldn't count seconds or engineer out semi-quavers just in the pursuit of efficiency; I should do research.

Of course, there is research and research. There is measuring and knowing stupid things, because you can – how many notes, how fast – and there is ignoring the really important stuff, because you don't know how to get to it – what people think.

'If I were brave, and I am not – most artists are scared silly of feedback – but if I were brave, I would go out and ask people. I might ask their opinion, their advice even. I would listen to the other music that was going on around me, my competition you might say, and I would try to understand what inspired it, what made it work. I would try to understand what people wanted, and who was giving it to them. I would do research.

'So how about you? Do you do research, or do you just improve things by playing it faster or taking out the semi-quavers?

'Let's say you want to improve your service to customers, and you start with some easy stuff, like answering the phone. Someone suggests you should answer it within three rings, and you can measure that, so you're happy. Is that it?'

He waited, clearly expecting one of us to answer, but a thousand people sitting around you is a daunting thing – we said nothing.

'Do you know the worst thing about such measurements? It is that they become the only important thing; they become the truth, the whole truth, and nothing else matters, so help you God. Consider. Because you can measure something, this doesn't always make it important. You could measure how many watts of electrical energy go down the line during a call – does that matter? Does anyone care how many number eights are in the numbers you dial? – but you could measure that if you wanted. Such data is not important.

'There is worse to come. Because you can't measure something, that doesn't mean it isn't important. Let's suppose you measure two aspects of all calls received: the number of rings before the call is answered, and the length of calls. Let's also suppose that both the number of rings and the length of calls have been reducing, and you conclude that customer service is both improving and growing more efficient. Does anybody want to hear my rendition of Bach again?'

We laughed, but only to relieve our discomfort at what we were being told. 'How would it be then if, at the same time, your staff were growing ever ruder to customers, to get them off the line so that they could answer the next call promptly, and the shortness of calls was due to their not knowing the answers to customers' questions, or not caring enough to find out – what then?

'If you asked customers which they valued more in customer service, the speed with which calls are handled or the manner in which they are handled, you might get an answer that would upset your peace of mind, and the appropriateness of your data measurements.'

We were uneasy in our seats; this seemed like a trick, and someone, a brave soul given the domineering presence of the maestro on stage, stood up and asked in a clear, loud voice, 'But Maestro, surely we could measure whether people liked Bach fast or Bach slow, and that would be worth knowing, and then we could start asking why. And surely we could ask our customers what they thought of our telephone service; we could even ask them to rank in order of importance things like availability versus helpfulness, versus politeness?'

'My dear sir, you are quite right, and let me say, your question shows a profound understanding of the secret of Chakravati's piano.' There was a moment of silence, and then a ripple of applause around the hall; we all felt we were getting somewhere.

The strategic audit

The 'S' word – *strategy* – plays a big part in this chapter. It is a word that means so many different things to different people that it can be positively dangerous in communication. There are those who use it to justify anything vague, or poorly thought through, or uncosted: 'It's strategic,' they say, as if to also say, 'Don't ask, it's just going to happen.' Then there are those who use it to block anything they don't understand, or don't like – 'It's not strategic,' they say.

Here I use the word to mean *the big picture*. The strategic audit asks the sorts of questions, and conducts the sort of analysis, that will help us make some big decisions in that big picture.

ANALYTICAL TOOLS AND DECISIONS

Once again, let's remind ourselves that the analysis of information is for a purpose: to help us make decisions. First, the big ones:

- how to grow;
- how to compete;
- what will drive us;
- who to sell to.

And then the more tactical ones:

- what price;
- what quality;

- how much to make;
- where to sell;
- how to promote it.

Without such a focus, some of the tools discussed here can take on a life of their own, and before you know it, you are in box-ticking mode. This is where it is more important to use the tool, and be seen to use the tool, than it is to draw conclusions and make decisions. That isn't marketing, that's just a waste of effort.

Used properly, the tools discussed in this chapter will transform the data discussed in Chapter 7 into decisions that will determine your future. They are important tools, and should be used with the care and discipline described in what follows.

The tools for analysis

We will look at five tools:

- PESTLE analysis;
- the market map;
- Michael Porter's 'five forces' analysis;
- the SWOT analysis;
- the Directional Policy Matrix (DPM).

As we work through them, we subtly shift from understanding towards action, the SWOT and DPM in particular bridging the gap between knowledge and action.

PESTLE ANALYSIS

We start this audit of the big picture with the really big picture: the impact on our market of those large and usually long-term factors: the **P**olitical, **E**conomic, **S**ocial, **T**echnological, **L**egal and **E**nvironmental changes going on around us. The acronym PESTLE has grown out of PEST (before environmental issues were so important), adding legal to become SLEPT and now environmental to become PESTLE, and there will be many more variations. Use whatever you wish, so long as you are looking.

For much of the time, these factors are simply things that we read about in the newspapers, but from time to time they have a dramatic impact on the working dynamics of our own marketplace. The marketer's task is to make sure that this 'time to time' impact doesn't come as a surprise, and, even further, to seek to gain advantage by recognizing and understanding the relevance of these changes, ahead of the competition.

Political change

Political change can bring large-scale revolutions such as the opening up of Eastern Europe after the fall of the Berlin Wall, but the changes need not always be so dramatic. Changes in government can signal shifts in values and priorities in the country (even if they don't cause them). The more caring society heralded when New Labour replaced the Conservatives in 1997 was reflected in the messages and marketing strategies of many consumer products. Red-braced executives became stock jokes rather than role models, and cars became less clearly defined as symbols of power and status, with a consequent rise in values such as safety and environmental impact.

Government intervention is sometimes said (usually by economists and purists) to distort the marketplace, but the political institutions are just as much a part of the fabric of commercial life as are suppliers and customers – they just attract more criticism! One of the debates during the 2000 US presidential election campaign was over whether Internet business should be taxed. Traditional businesses, especially retailers, called foul, while new start-up companies praised the foresight in wanting to nurture a new and vital sector through tax breaks. Whatever your view, there is no doubting the impact on competitiveness of a decision either way.

Deregulation in the European airline industry caused the meteoric rise of the low-cost, low-price operators (sometimes Ryanair's capitalization has been bigger than BA's), so priming a huge increase in passenger traffic in the early years of the current century. It is noteworthy that the majority of the operators fly out of the United Kingdom, and that British travellers represent the largest part of the leap in traffic; it has been the UK government that has led the way in deregulation policies. The same cannot be said of the transatlantic market. There are still limits on the number of airlines allowed to fly out of Heathrow to major US destinations, and the US government prevents foreign airlines from operating in its domestic markets – a combination of policies that put a serious damper on the low-price offers that have swept Europe.	**Flying over uneven playing fields**

On 1 May 2004 the European Union grew by the addition of 10 new members. While the _Daily Mail_ goes into hysterics over supposed mass migrations to the United Kingdom from Eastern Europe, serious marketers must assess the likely impacts: on the one hand, a huge increase in potential markets; on the other, the greater accessibility to lower-cost markets for manufacturing. It would be a brave person to predict anything with certainty, but closing your eyes to it because of the complexity could be terminal.

Perhaps you think the political stage too large, too far away from your concern as a business manager. What, after all, can you do to affect it, beyond voting once in a while? But consider: your own job may depend on your understanding of these kinds of issues. If you sold to the National Health Service (NHS) in the United Kingdom, yet didn't understand the political nature of that particular customer, then you would be lost. And misreading the signs of change can be as serious as not noting them in the first place.

Predicting the unpredictable?

The CEO of Nestor Healthcare resigned when his company, an employment agency specializing in the provision of doctors and nurses, misjudged the requirement for an out-of-hours GP service. Nestor set up two call centres in preparation for a rise in contracts, only to find that the local primary care trusts (an important part of this hugely complex and hugely political decision-making unit) preferred not to outsource the service. Nestor issued a profits warning, and the CEO was on his way.

Economic change

Economic change includes the 'big-picture' cycles of growth and decline that impact so greatly on markets like chemicals or building, with knock-on effect for other businesses such as engineering suppliers or estate agents, but also the more immediate impact of, say, an extra 20p on wine at the Budget. Many businesses put a lot of effort into understanding economic trends and forecasts as an important element in their own planning: when to build new assets, when to expand the workforce, when to batten down the hatches. A squeeze on consumer spending in the high street can impact on a host of businesses far removed from fast-moving consumer goods, including catering, building, decorating, cleaning services, and so on.

Out of the frying pan and into the fire...

May 2004 saw BA announce improved profits – welcome news in a very difficult market – but its shares went down in value as analysts noted the effect of rising oil prices on its future: an additional bill of £150 million. Of course, such things can be mitigated by forward buying, but the shares slipped because BA had forward-purchased significantly less than its main competitors. Such things should be the concern of the marketer. OK, purchasing is the responsibility of the purchasing department, but when it can have such significant impact on the marketing plan, it becomes a shared responsibility.

Hard times don't always hurt everyone, of course. In times of general economic depression when people start to worry about the under-funding of the NHS, there is often a rise in subscribers to private health insurance. I also remember from my days in the paint industry how during the 1984–85 miners' strike there was a mini-boom in sales in mining districts (for the first few months) as stay-at-home miners had brushes and rollers thrust into their hands!

Social change

Social change, such as the increasing number of 'double-income' families, particularly the Dinky (double income, no kids yet) ones, has led to a combination of households that are more prosperous but with less time to enjoy their prosperity! Ready-cooked microwavable meals have enjoyed great success, as have Internet shopping services. The 'double-pension' household is fast on its way in large numbers, and with the addition of time to enjoy this continued prosperity, we might expect an increase in leisure activities designed to *fill* time rather than save it – perhaps even a return to shopping trips?

'Ping' cuisine

A fascinating and rather unexpected impact of social change was the way the rise of TV ownership damaged the bus industry. As people stayed at home more, gazing into their new and highly prized possession, so bus operators suffered. Of course, bus operators or bus manufacturers who defined their business as 'buses' weren't going to see that coming, but those who saw themselves as something larger – perhaps part of the leisure industry – had other ways to turn, the growth of the touring coach industry being one such result.

Any business involved with the food industry will have had to take note in recent times of the Atkins diet. So widespread has the influence been of this particular route to fitness and well-being that it has become a subject for the boardroom at grocery retailers, food manufacturers, and those who supply ingredients and raw materials to food manufacturers. The negative impact on potato growers has been profound, as has the positive impact on those in the meat trade. One of the biggest difficulties with such socially based changes is deciding whether they are here to stay. The manufacturer that makes significant changes to its sourcing policies and production processes, only to find that Atkins was a fad, may regret its move; but not to move, should the influence of Atkins be here to stay, would be a yet more serious error.

Atkins: fad or deep-seated change?

Such social changes can also become political ones, as governments start to take an interest in what we eat and the health of the nation. The campaign to help children to eat more healthily will have significant impact on the marketing policies of the likes of McDonald's and Burger King. Already, new products are appearing on their menu – food bags, salads – and there are subtle changes to promotional messages, such as the removal of special deals on trading up to 'king-' or 'super'-size meals.

No more super-size…

Technological change

Technological change has been the norm of the past hundred years, and perhaps the expectation of change in this area (more so than any other

Remember Y2K?

PESTLE factor) is well integrated into the marketing process. Even so, many businesses are still well behind the pace in responding to the rise of e-commerce. Whether the Internet Luddites will be dead and gone in five years' time, as some predict, only time will tell. We can only observe that there is scarcely a business in existence today, from major corporation to corner shop, that doesn't have a computer sitting somewhere on a table. A whole army of consultants made a thriving trade out of Y2K worries (technological failings can have just as significant an impact as technological successes), and no one would deny that gene technology has opened up huge new vistas for the pharmaceutical and agrochemical industries. Technology used in the marketing process itself promises to shift the boundaries of much marketing practice: speeding the development of new products, giving instant access to information and knowledge, and potentially facilitating entirely new ways of working with customers.

Changing snapshots in time...

Companies entrenched in one technology often find it difficult to see coming what everyone else has observed for some time. Kodak has been associated with high-quality film for decades, and consequently has been slow to make the shifts required by the rise of digital photography. The new technology 'hurts'; it quite possibly even offends some in the business – you can hear them talking in the staff canteen: 'It will never work, have you seen the lousy resolution?' Now Kodak's place in the market is under threat not from competing film manufacturers, but from technology companies such as Sony, Hewlett-Packard and Canon.

Legal changes

Legal changes can have instant impact – the banning of beef on the bone being a dramatic example of the sudden removal of a market opportunity. They can also raise new opportunities – the deregulation of the transport industry, from aeroplanes to buses, being a prime example. Safety is an important issue in the public's mind, and lawmakers are continually tightening the standards for businesses that supply the public. In Germany there is a serious debate over whether to make leather seats mandatory in cars and aircraft, as a fire prevention measure. Makers of fabrics beware; tanneries and cattle farmers rejoice?

Painting the town red

Paint manufacturers love Singapore. The law requires all property owners to repaint the outside of their buildings every year. The consumption of exterior paint products per head is higher in Singapore than anywhere else in the world. If only they would pass a law like that everywhere... which is, of course, a legitimate ambition and interest for any paint manufacturer. Is it a job for marketing? Who else?

Environmental issues

Environmental issues and concerns have demonstrated quite clearly their impact on business, from the banning of lead in petrol to the restrictions on genetically modified (GM) food products. This factor, along with technological change, appears to be the most easily seized on as a means of gaining competitive advantage, whether it be supermarkets declaring the absence of GM foods in their stores or hotels telling us that they won't be washing our towels, in order to avoid pouring more detergents down various drains.

The largest bill in most hospitals is not, as you might guess, the drugs bill, or the surgeons bill, but the laundry. If hospitals were to adopt a similar policy to the hotel trade ('sheets on the floor if you want them changed, sheets on the bed if you're happy to use them another day'), imagine the savings! But seriously, shouldn't detergent manufacturers be talking with hospitals to see what can be done? Shouldn't detergent manufacturers be put under the same pressure as drug companies to come to the aid of the beleaguered health service? Shouldn't environmentalists be marching on their local hospital?

Cleanliness is next to costliness

Making your own luck

It might seem that as so many of these issues are outside the control of the marketing process, surely they cannot be worth worrying about until they happen? Who seriously planned for the fall of the Berlin Wall? Who honestly prepared for the rise in one-parent families? Who anticipated mad cow disease? This is missing the point. Those marketers who keep their senses attuned to such broad-canvas changes will be the ones who are fleetest of foot. Avoiding the pain of unexpected change and gaining from the opportunities presented is not a matter of accident. My own business opened an office in Kuala Lumpur almost on the day when the currencies and economies of the Asian 'tigers' collapsed. We didn't predict it, but we certainly responded (and stayed!), and have emerged from the other side with a lot of credibility and strength in the region.

When the world changes and some companies do well, people call them 'lucky'. Virgin was 'lucky' to be around when the airline industry was deregulating and a whole new generation was looking for a new way to travel the globe. What this tends to ignore is the important truth that the most successful businesses have a way of making their own luck. Virgin's success lies substantially more in the hands of its market researchers and brand managers than it does in those of fortune. It is just as the famous golfer once said when told he was lucky to be so good at golf: 'You know, the more I practise,' he smiled, 'the luckier I seem to get.'

MARKET MAPPING

The next step in the big picture brings us a little closer to home. This is where we start to map out the way the market works. To start with, draw out the route your product takes to the final consumer, through the various channels of supply. There are many reasons for doing this at the analysis stage:

- to gain an understanding of your current routes to market;
- to assess potential new routes to market;
- to establish where your current strengths and weaknesses lie in comparison to those of the competition;
- to highlight opportunities for growth;
- to highlight areas where your position may be at risk;
- to establish the options for segmentation (see Chapter 15).

Note that I am asking you to trace the flow of your product to the *final consumer*. If you are in the fmcg business then this may not seem surprising, but why do it if you are in the B2B business? It is vitally important in all markets, but particularly in B2B ones, to look beyond your current customers. Why? Here are three key reasons:

- to ensure that you understand your immediate customers' challenges, in order to help them meet them;
- to raise awareness of possible new opportunities – too many businesses restrict their view by considering the market to be only those customers who pay them money;
- to ensure that you appreciate your own value to the immediate customer.

A cautionary tale

If you want to know your true value...

I was once asked to help a telephone services supplier identify its true value to the customer, and I came upon some unexpected market research…

I was running a training event one day at a manufacturing plant of another customer, it was the morning break and I wanted to check my e-mails. So, I found an office and asked if I could plug into their wall socket telephone line. Sure, they said, *'but not that one…!'* – but it was too late; I had pulled the existing line from the wall and plunged the site into an hour's worth of telephone silence!

Well, that was the end for me, I thought, only to find at lunchtime that there were people wanting to shake me by the hand: 'So, you're the fellah who shut down our telephones – thanks, we got something done for a change this morning…'

Once I'd recovered from the surprise, I wondered what would have happened had I been working that day not at a factory, but at the head office of the HSBC bank… it makes me shudder to think. Anyway, I went back to the telephone company and asked them if they sold to both banks and factories. Of course, they said. And did they sell at different prices, or terms, or with different packages? Not really, they said. 'But you're so much more valuable to the bank,' I said. 'Shouldn't you be getting a better reward?'

They didn't, and it was almost too late to do anything about it.

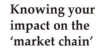

…look at your map

Thinking for your customer

Let's suppose that we sell film material that is used in the consumer goods packaging industry. Our direct customer is the 'converter', the company that takes the film, prints it and manufacturers the final packaging item, whether it be a crisp packet or a 'glossy' box for an upmarket perfume. A summary of the market chain is shown in Figure 9.1.

Knowing your impact on the 'market chain'

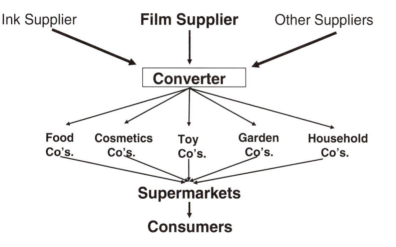

Figure 9.1 *The film/packaging market chain*

Each different end use of the packaging material has its own needs and demands: food companies require high standards of hygiene and safety; cosmetics manufacturers are concerned principally with image and aesthetics; the toy producer will be concerned about safety; the garden chemicals company will want to ensure absolute clarity of instructions, and probably durability (for products that might sit in a garden shed for many months); and the household goods firm will perhaps be interested in costs above all else. So what? What if the film supplier is unaware of all that? The result will be that it is the converter that 'owns' the market, and quite justifiably, because it understands, and presumably satisfies, the different needs. The converter will also, it is to be hoped, be receiving different rewards for the different types of value delivered. The film supplier just gets paid for delivering film…

The film supplier can only be on the defensive, or in 'reactive mode', in such a situation. When opportunities for new products appear, it will be the converter who sees them, drives them and wins the lion's share of the reward. If the film supplier's personnel could only but see the needs and opportunities themselves, then perhaps they could be proactively suggesting new products – thinking for the customer.

Chapters 17 and 18 will explore this issue further, looking at how such understanding of the market map (or value chain, or customer activity cycle) helps us to develop truly value added propositions.

MICHAEL PORTER'S 'FIVE FORCES' ANALYSIS

Porter's 'five forces' analysis is one of the oldest tools in the trade, and still hugely powerful if used correctly. It comes in two stages: first the analysis, and second, the conclusions and actions. It is the second stage that is all-important, bridging the gap between research and the marketing plan, but it is also the second stage that is most often forgotten.

In his book *Competitive Strategy* (Free Press, New York, 1980), Michael E Porter gives us a tool that helps us to understand the different competitive forces that bear down on a business. These are shown in Figure 9.2.

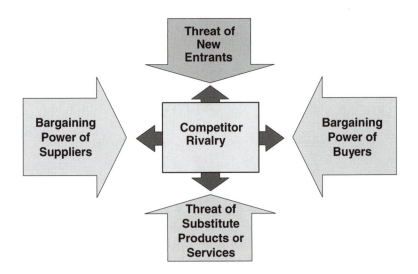

Figure 9.2 *Competitive strategy, according to Michael E Porter*

We see here how a business operates within the ferment and flux of five different competitive forces. As well as making some general comments on each, I will look at the position of the UK food supermarkets in the early 21st century to illustrate the different forces at work.

- *Current competitor rivalry*, each competitor jockeying for position through price, quality or service. There has been an ever more heated 'battle of the giants' between the big players in this market: Tesco, Sainsbury, Asda, Morrisons and the Co-op. The fallout has manifested itself in everything from price wars (baked beans for 2p a can, bread for 5p a loaf) to the race to launch new services from home shopping to ever more generous loyalty cards. This latter service has taken a particularly heavy toll on supermarket margins over recent years.

  Store Wars

  The past decade has been the era of the takeover – Wal-Mart buying Asda, Morrisons buying Safeway – and outside this market it has been the same theme in telecommunications, pharmaceuticals and financial services. Such mergers change the competitive landscape at a stroke. For those merging, the objective is improved security, enhanced capability and higher profits through scale and market presence, but for those left independent, the rules have just changed.

  Industry rivalry increases when there is little difference between players, those players are few, and evenly sized, the market is mature with growth slowing, there are high exit costs (players can't leave, perhaps because they are committed to filling production plants, etc) and there are low switching costs (it's easy for a customer to change from one supplier to another). If that sums up your position, then don't expect an easy ride from the competition.

- *The threat of new entrants*, perhaps attracted by the profitability or growth of this market, or possibly by the failings of the incumbents. New forces are continually hovering, spotting gaps in the market left by the ever-repositioning major players. First there were Aldi and Netto, promising cut-price shopping, and most recently the most dynamic grocery chain in the United States, Wal-Mart, has threatened to bring its 'category-busting' tactics to the United Kingdom through its acquisition of Asda.

  Category busting

  Not all these new entrants are as successful as their aggressive launch plans promise, but their very presence reshapes the competitive dynamics of the market. New entrants come in many guises: Aldi opened new stores, Wal-Mart acquired existing ones. Sometimes they expand the market, and sometimes they just steal share.

  New entrants are most likely when the market is attractive, existing players are weak and entry barriers (and costs) are low.

- *The threat of substitute products or services* replacing your offer, perhaps through new technology or a lower-cost alternative, or perhaps a 'simpler' solution. Will the Internet and home shopping replace the supermarket as we know it? Certainly the supermarkets themselves are spending heavily on ensuring their own salvation through this medium, attempting to be their own substitutes before someone else does it to them.

  Substitutes are most likely when technology takes a leap forward, existing players are weak, or when customers have 'grown tired' of the status quo.

Saving trees...
... losing your
business?

Xerox and 3M have formed an alliance to manufacture and market 'electronic paper', a technology that threatens to replace newsprint. A thin plastic sheet can be 'charged' with words and images, erased, and recharged, allowing the owner to hang on to just one 'page' but have as many newspapers (for instance) as he or she wishes. Newspaper publishers are interested, yet the American Forest and Paper Association hangs on to a prediction of 3 per cent per annum growth of paper usage through to 2010. Is it ignoring the threat of a substitute? Perhaps its prediction is just an example of the sort of broad but unhelpful statistic for the marketer – paper for what use? Newsprint, books, packaging? For suppliers of newsprint, as well as printing machines, inks and a range of other associated products and services, putting their heads in the sand is not an option.

The power of
'walking'

- *The bargaining power of customers*, often reducing in numbers through amalgamation, and consequently increasing their buying power. In the UK retail industry, consumers still have the ability to vote with their wallets, as Marks & Spencer found to its cost in 1999. Food supermarkets working on relatively low margins need steadily growing volume in order to prosper. It is no surprise that there is so much noise about who sits on the number one position and why chief executives find their jobs under threat if they allow their store to slip down the rankings. The customer has genuine power in this regard.

  Consumers find other routes through which to apply their bargaining power, such as pressure groups for more organic produce or campaigns to remove GM food from sale. Of course, the retailers aim to turn such pressures to their own competitive advantage, with high-profile campaigns promising an end to battery-farmed eggs (Marks & Spencer) or a banning of genetically modified food products (Iceland). These are examples of retailers assessing a potential threat and acting to turn it into an opportunity.

  Buyer power increases when buyers are much bigger than sellers, sellers fail to differentiate their offers, the products concerned are of low importance to the customer, and when switching costs are low – 'Cut your price or we walk...'

Being critical...

- *The bargaining power of suppliers*, sometimes through merger and consolidation, often through the provision of increasingly specialist, high-value and unique services. At the other end of the supply chain, major suppliers can wield enormous power, either through brand names (who could envisage a major supermarket without Coca-Cola or Cadbury?) or simply through the scale of their operation: GM food products will be on the shelf simply because of the scale of the suppliers' activities in such a wide range of food areas.

  Suppliers' power increases when they are a critical component in the customer's product (or life), when suppliers are much larger than customers, or when there are high switching costs – suppliers would call this 'lock-in'.

Actions from the analysis

So what? And 'so what?' is the right question to ask after using every tool in the audit stage – what do you do about it? That depends on your starting point.

If you have a well-established position in a market then these forces will appear as threats, and so your response to the analysis should be: how do we build barriers to entry?

If you are seeking to enter a market – you are in fact the *new entrant* – then analysing these forces will be done in search of gaps, or weak spots, that you can take advantage of.

In both cases the objective is to gain competitive advantage. Porter identifies two main options for gaining competitive advantage, and these will be discussed in Chapter 13: a strategy of differentiation, or a strategy of becoming the lowest-cost supplier.

Do Porter's definitions matter? Competitor, new entrant, substitute – aren't they all just competitors? They matter because the purpose of the Porter analysis is to prompt your reaction to help you build an appropriate competitive advantage as a defence or offence.

Let's suppose you are the manufacturer of a leading brand of PCs – the *traditional PC* (that is, the personal computer). You are now faced with the rise of the mobile personal communicator, the 'new PC'. How you define the new PC will in turn help define your reaction.

The PC is dead; long live the PC

Does it represent a new entrant or is it a substitute? If it is a potential substitute threatening to replace the traditional PC then you might have to consider developing your own *new PC* response. If it is a new entrant in the traditional PC's market, does it fight on the same ground for the same customers, or does it redefine the market? If the former, then you will need to argue the superior benefits of your product's approach. If the latter, then perhaps the market will divide into two separate kinds of applications, with room for both new and old PCs. Which do you think it is?

THE SWOT ANALYSIS

Illustrated in Figure 9.3, this is one of the best known of the marketing tools, one of the most used, one of the easiest to comprehend, but unfortunately also one of the most abused!

Typical failings include a tendency to be too general and superficial. For a multinational manufacturing company I could almost write the items that get put into the four boxes here and now:

- strengths: our people, our technology, our experience;
- weaknesses: our speed to respond, flexibility, internal constraints;
- opportunities: the Far East;
- threats: the Far East.

Figure 9.3 *The SWOT analysis*

Traffic lights, that might save your life

Such an analysis will get us nowhere. Stating the purpose of a SWOT analysis will make clear its importance, and hence the rigour with which it should be completed. The SWOT analysis provides a set of traffic lights for our options: go, stop, or more research required – amber. It assesses our capability in seeing off the threats and seizing the opportunities, and it highlights the priorities for enhancing or changing that capability.

Another failing is to use the SWOT analysis at too high a level, typically as a means of assessing the position of the whole company. First of all, a SWOT is not about the company, but about that company's position in the marketplace, and unless it is a one-product, one-market business then that's going to be hard to capture. Second, the value of a SWOT analysis tends to increase as we move from a SWOT of the market down to a SWOT of the segment, and even down to a SWOT of the product or service.

The third main failing is a tendency to see the world through the rose-tinted glasses of our own perception. The strengths and weaknesses highlighted in the SWOT should be based on the market's and the customers' judgement and perception of our capability. I remember once being involved in a top-level SWOT of a business in which at the time I was but a small cog, and seeing, somewhat to my surprise, our global scale (we were the largest in the world) identified as a strength. What that scale meant to my customers in Norfolk and Suffolk I never did discover.

The opportunities and threats should be external factors, not issues within your own direct control. The fact that you have money available to expand your production capacity is not an opportunity; it is a possible strength (if such an expansion is relevant to the market's needs). The opportunity is (if it exists) that the market will stand more capacity, or even demands more capacity. This may sound like pedantry; what does it matter in what box we place something, provided we know what we are good at and what is out there to be grabbed? This is of course the point, going right back to the Marketing Model described in Chapters 2 and 3. The SWOT allows us to assess our capability (strengths and weaknesses) as a match for the market needs (opportunities) in the light of the competitive environment (threats). Precision in completing the SWOT will not only highlight imbalances in the match, but also help us communicate these to all those in our business concerned with securing that match.

SWOT and the Marketing Model

The rigour of a SWOT should go beyond general phrases. We should be trying to measure the scale of strength and weakness, in comparison to our competitors, and the scale of the opportunities and threats, in comparison with each other. This takes us to the last tool of the analysis stage, the Directional Policy Matrix.

THE DIRECTIONAL POLICY MATRIX (DPM)

Chapter 15 (on segmentation) and Chapter 22 (on portfolio management) will revisit this model, and in the latter we will also look at its close cousin, the _Boston Box_. In those contexts it considers the selection of target segments and the management of a product portfolio: what products to give priority and resource to and where to remove resources and manage costs more tightly. It is an excellent tool for considering options where you have a finite resource to apply, hence its use, under subtly different guises, at several stages of the marketing process.

At this stage of the marketing process, the strategic audit, it can be used to consider the broad scale of options in front of you: what countries or territories to work in or chase, or what markets, or what segments? If you are already focused on a particular market then the DPM will help you decide what segments (as used in Chapter 15) to focus on. If you are already focused on a segment then it will help you consider your product portfolio (as used in Chapter 22).

A tool for using at every level of the marketing process

The principle of the DPM is to take the elements of the SWOT analysis and put them to a more rigorous test, quantifying your strengths and weaknesses as seen by the market, and ranking the attractiveness of the different options (or opportunities) before you. The result is a four-box matrix (or nine-box, if you want to indulge a penchant for 'greyness', for the world is rarely black and white...) that will position your markets, territories, segments, customers or products (the choice is yours, and the DPM is a very versatile tool) in a way that helps you to allocate resources, effort and attention. This is shown in Figure 9.4.

The example shown is for a training company considering a choice of possible market segments (defined at a fairly high level). The 'advice' given in the boxes is only that: it is not mandatory, simply a guide to your choice from the options available. The ranking and rating of the vertical axis, attractiveness, is of course in your own hands. There are other training companies, for instance, that would see NVQ training as very attractive on

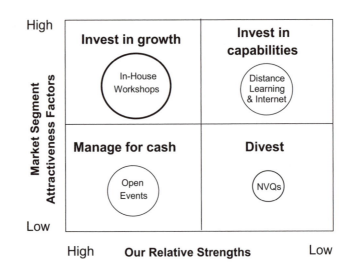

Figure 9.4 *The Directional Policy Matrix*

the basis of their own capabilities and future ambitions. The horizontal axis is in the eyes of the market, and should always be viewed from the perspective of the customers in those markets or segments.

Finding the facts...

The DPM demands data, not guesswork, and so we are back to our market research exercise discussed in Chapter 7. Indeed, the need to complete a DPM analysis is in itself a common spur for carrying out such research. Not a problem, provided you plan to use it not to make you look clever in your marketing plan, but to make some serious decisions: where to focus your valuable and finite resources.

The ability to complete a DPM with confidence (not too many guesses and no wishful thinking) is often the sign that we are ready to proceed to the planning stage – we know enough (in so far as you can ever know enough). The DPM asks us to consider options, and the next step is choices.

10

The CONNECT Inc case study

The purpose of this case study is to allow you to assess the quality of a real audit, and the conclusions that flowed from it. This is a real case; the names are changed to protect the not so innocent...

It is 1992. After two and a half years as Chief Executive, Simon Clark felt satisfied that he had at last begun to get to grips with his marketing problems at CONNECT Inc. He had started work on these problems two years before and had made a series of changes in an effort to secure the future growth of the business into the next millennium. His actions had been undertaken in the context of the business objectives of the parent group, a complex organization based in the United States.

THE COMPANY BACKGROUND

CONNECT is the Canadian subsidiary of an international organization that, while the parent company does not much like the word, is a conglomerate. The parent has some very clear operating principles. Over the past 10 years, and certainly until recently, its profit before tax has grown by 15 per cent per annum despite many difficult situations that have been encountered. As a result, 15 per cent annual growth of profit before tax has become a requirement placed on every operating division and subsidiary in the entire international operation.

The parent operates in many markets, grouping companies into 'sectors'. It is strong in the automotive components sector, timber and pulp, and has an interest in telecommunications. It is also very large in electronic components – CONNECT is a part of that sector. It is well represented in the service industries, owning a major car hire company, an international hotel group and a number of life and fire insurance companies.

CONNECT itself has its headquarters in Toronto. It has a manufacturing operation in Montreal, with smaller ones in the United States, the United Kingdom and France, and marketing operations in Toronto, Los Angeles, London and Paris. There are small sales operations in Italy and Germany, while the rest of its world markets are covered by a variety of long-established agents and representatives.

The greatest strength of CONNECT, indeed its core capability throughout the 1970s and 1980s, has been its ability to manufacture high-specification electrical connectors sold to the aerospace industry. The connectors range in price from $500 to as high as $7,500. At the upper price bracket these connectors are made to very low tolerances for use in critical applications such as flameproof bulkheads and aircraft engines. Such connectors are of course critical to aircraft safety.

In common with other major suppliers to the aerospace industry, CONNECT has suffered from the major cutbacks in purchases that have taken place in recent years because of defence programme reductions. After a decade of growth in the 1970s, the more difficult trading environment of the 1980s presented CONNECT with severe problems in achieving the parent's 15 per cent growth target. Put quite simply, they couldn't do it any more. The collapse of the Berlin Wall seemed to signal the demise of CONNECT's own business.

Most projections for the future of the aerospace and defence industries were gloomy. The best that could be hoped for, and that was somewhat wishful thinking, was a static volume requirement for connectors. Clark believed that CONNECT could hold its own in the current market, but even an increasing market share would probably mean overall decline. Growth as demanded by HQ would require some big changes.

SALES ORGANIZATION

One of Simon Clark's first tasks had been a close look at the sales force, and the part it played in CONNECT's marketing mix. The North American sales force, to take an example, had consisted of 20 field salespeople with a back-up staff of nearly 75. This large 'HQ' number was required because of the technical nature of the product. Technical Service was a major department, with both pre-sale and after-sales service being a key part of the CONNECT approach. There was also a large inside sales operation, because of the number of inquiries to be answered by letter and telephone. Individual inquiries required individual quotations because CONNECT products were usually tailor-made and there were no standard price lists.

It was clear to Clark that he had a superbly well-qualified team, from a technical standpoint. The North American field sales force was organized on a traditional basis, with a VP Sales and three Area Sales Managers – for Canada, the eastern United States and the western United States respectively – each with a team of representatives. They were experts in their market, having developed close relationships with key customers over a number of years.

THE NEW MARKET

Very early in his time with CONNECT, Clark had decided that they should enter a new market for electrical connectors – commercial and industrial. He wanted to attack this market vigorously.

This 'new' market was composed of companies in areas such as automation equipment, process control equipment and consumer durables: washing machines, refrigerators and televisions. CONNECT was also interested in entering the automobile market.

Clark was aware that this new market highlighted a big weakness in his sales team: their call rates. Call frequencies were less than one call per day. This had not been a problem in the old days, but the decision to go for a new market put it into a new context.

The connectors required by the customers in this new market were very different from those that CONNECT had designed and manufactured for the aerospace industry. They were low-tech, standard items, made to what seemed to CONNECT's staff enormously broad tolerance specifications, and they were required in huge numbers.

CONNECT had to undergo a number of changes to manufacture these new connectors, starting with Engineering. Clark engaged a new team of design engineers knowledgeable in commercial connectors. After that, he began the changes necessary in the manufacturing operation. The main impact was the construction of a new building on the Montreal site, housing the manufacturing plant for all CONNECT's commercial connectors.

THE NEW SALES TEAM

Now CONNECT had to find some sales, and this was where the call rate problem arose. It was clear to Clark that if one were trying to sell connectors at $2 a time rather than $500, or even $5,000, then volume was vital, and the sales activity needed to get that volume was very different from that in the aerospace market. For a start, CONNECT's sales representatives would have to call on a much wider range of customers. When Clark looked at the market opportunity, he was impressed by the huge number of potential customers compared to the small number in the aerospace market. If they could make an impression on only a small number, they would still be achieving big sales volumes.

Clark's corporate targets prevented him from increasing the size of the sales force to any great degree, so the answer was to increase call rates to at least five per day. This brought him to a more knotty problem: psychology.

The CONNECT salespeople knew their market and their customers well. They enjoyed high prestige with their customers, owing to the significance of their products and their own technical knowledge, and they were used to dealing at senior levels. This was the root of the 'psychological' problem. Put quite simply, many of the representatives were neither willing nor able to change their style of working. As they said at team meeting after team meeting, it was a hard thing to do – selling to the VP of Development at a major aircraft company before lunch, and then fitting in three calls to junior buyers in the household goods business in the afternoon.

More than this, many of CONNECT's employees were apathetic about this new market. They did not see why CONNECT needed it, when after all it was still the industry leader in its traditional market, and, while that market was not buoyant, customers like McDonnell Douglas were not about to go away.

Clark's solution was to split the sales force into two, appointing a new VP Sales and Marketing for the commercial connectors market with a team of 24 sales representatives. VP Sales and *Marketing* was a new title in CONNECT, a company that had seen marketing as something that was done by soap powder manufacturers. The challenge for this side of the business was clear: it was an almost unknown market.

The VP Sales and Marketing for the aerospace market also had a new challenge (and the same new title, which made him smile – a cynical kind of smile). His sales force was now only six, to cover the same list of customers.

THE 'UNKNOWN' MARKET

One of the first jobs for the new VP Sales and Marketing Commercial Connectors was to commission some market research. The range of opportunities was huge, and they needed to target some key ones.

A not insignificant problem was that CONNECT had relatively few products to sell. The new design engineers had been slower than anticipated in getting new products off the drawing board and into production, and so CONNECT found itself contracting out a number of products to other manufacturers. The sales force referred to these products as their 'imports'. Though actually manufactured in Canada or the United States, they were regarded as inferior to CONNECT's own manufacture. The label soon developed into a reality as CONNECT turned to the UK manufacturing plant to help with production. The UK plant had specialized in the highest-spec products, but it had a lot of spare capacity as a result of the market's downturn, and working on the new connectors would help it to cover its costs.

There were now several reasons why the sales team began to lose their enthusiasm for the new task. They felt that some of the products were inferior, both to their own and to those of the competition. There was a lack of in-house expertise about these products. There was an ever-present doubt about security of supply. And not least, there was the problem of transfer pricing: the UK people would regularly want to charge more than the local contract suppliers – they had some very high costs to cover.

Against that background, the VP Sales and Marketing had the task of deciding who to sell to, and how to sell to them. The inside sales team and the technical service people were available to him, but he didn't know what use he could make of them. Indeed, he didn't yet know what platform of customer service would give CONNECT competitive advantage.

TARGETS AND FORECASTS

The VP Sales and Marketing had been given very clear volume targets by Clark. These were based on some calculations of market size, and a goal of 20 per cent market share within three years. Clark had talked of a penetration strategy based on CONNECT's core strengths and a dose of new blood. A small number of the new sales team came from outside CONNECT, from the commercial market, while the majority were from the original aerospace sales team.

High volume targets brought a relatively new issue to CONNECT's attention: the need for accurate long-range forecasts. The new connectors were not 'custom made'; they were made for stock. Many of the customer sectors in this market were cyclical, responding to changes in consumer spending and buying behaviour. Good forecasts were vital if CONNECT were to avoid major over-stocks, or worse, no stock at all in the middle of a consumer spending boom.

CONNECT had to develop a new system fast. They established a system based on historical usage, added inputs from the field sales team, and overlaid this with the new market research data. Clark demanded six-month forecasts minimum, with trends two years out.

THE BUSINESS IN 1992

The sales forecasting system has become the operational core of the CONNECT business. The company is now manufacturing for stock, in a way it had never done in the aerospace market, where nearly every order was unique. It now has a price list; that one change had been quite something, and the people in the quotations department had resisted it for months. As Clark explained to them, it was simply a question of customer needs.

In the aerospace business, customers normally know a year ahead of time what their requirements are, and CONNECT still builds more or less to order. A delivery time of eight weeks or more is quite acceptable, and price is something that is negotiated contract by contract.

In the commercial sector, customers demand delivery within 24 hours, with tough just-in-time (JIT) and on-time-in-full (OTIF) targets. Customers do not normally declare their requirements very far ahead of time, and they require up-to-date price lists to allow them to shop around in a market that is very price sensitive.

A similar transformation has also taken place in the field of promotional activity. The aerospace market remains one of personal contacts and long-standing reputation. In the commercial market there is a need for broader promotional activity. CONNECT's presence is still not that great (they have fallen well short of the 20 per cent market share target), and there is a need both to amend, and indeed to establish, its image. An agency has been approached to help with this work. The agency's challenge is to take a company with a strong image as a manufacturer of specialized high-performance connectors and reposition it as a mass-market supplier of low-cost connectors, and to do so without damaging its image in the aerospace market.

Because of that potential dilemma, and because of the high costs involved in promotion, Clark has retained control over the promotional budget for both markets. If all else should fail, this budget remains a useful 'escape hatch' in order to meet the parent company's profit targets.

CONNECT is at last able to manufacture most of its products for the North American market in Montreal. Using the UK operation was only ever a temporary solution. An unfortunate side effect of that had been a number of problems on the UK site, which is now refocused on repairing its reputation in the aerospace market.

Distribution has become an important factor in the new business. High volumes have put a strain on the existing set-up, and Clark has considered the possibility of working through a network of independent distributors. He would like to feed the smaller customers through those channels, keeping the major customers direct. This and the promotion issue are his next main challenges.

THE MARKETING REVIEW

Progress has not been as good as hoped, and there are big concerns that future targets will not be met. Clark has ordered a full marketing review of activities, with an emphasis on cost reduction and increased sales volumes.

Clark himself has not yet begun to panic, although some of his lieutenants are getting worried.

CASE STUDY QUESTIONS

1. Assess CONNECT's original plan to enter the new market. How good was its assessment of the opportunities, and of its own capabilities?

2. If you had been employed as a marketing consultant, how would you have advised Clark when he first considered this new venture?
3. How do you rate CONNECT's actions and progress to date?
4. How do you rate the company's chances of success in the future, as it is currently set up?
5. If you were now employed as a marketing consultant to help with the CONNECT marketing review, how would you advise Clark to proceed:
   – in the new market?
   – in the aerospace market?
   – in any other way?

If you would like to e-mail your answers or any other comments on this case study to INSIGHT at Customer.service@insight-mp.com, we will gladly critique your report and send you our own thoughts.

Part III

Strategic positioning

11

Vision and objectives

Marketing is about the future, so it must have a vision and it must have objectives. The difference? Vision is the big picture: where we want to be – often summed up in a mission statement. Objectives are more specific, and must conform to the acronym SMART: specific, measurable, achievable, realistic and time bound.

We will look at these two tools in a moment, but first let us just consider the challenge of 'managing the future', introduced in Chapter 3 and briefly re-examined here.

MANAGING THE FUTURE

We saw in Chapter 3 how managing the future was about finding the balance between three things, as shown again in Figure 11.1.

The *business objectives* are what you want your business to achieve in the future. The *market opportunity* is the net sum of the forces that will help you or hinder you: customers and competitors. The *business resources* are those things that will support or constrain your progress: your own capabilities, production capacity, R&D, logistics, money and, not least, your people.

Simple in theory. The challenge in practice is that the balance keeps shifting as the world changes. At one time, banks aimed to grow their market share (objectives) by opening new branches. The winners were those who sat on the most property (resources). The opportunity was there, and developments in IT provided the capability (resources) to manage large chains. The objective was realistic and the strategy was workable, until

Figure 11.1 *Managing the future*

times changed. Market share is still the objective, but the opportunity and the resources deployed have changed. Now, instead of more branches it is home banking and call centres, or new virtual brands.

Strategic inertia

Of course, the banks should be congratulated on making the change – no easy task when a strategy has been successful for some time, and has become entrenched; a part of the culture. What tends to happen in reality is a certain amount of overlap between old and new strategy – with the senior managers creating the new strategy while the middle management are still implementing the old. Doubtless there were banks still opening new branches while the board was girding its loins to go into home banking. In a similar vein, there were grocery supermarket chains selling off their smaller high street stores just at the moment that their strategists were deciding to re-establish themselves there with convenience store concepts.

Large businesses are not unlike ocean-going oil tankers in this respect: they take a good deal of turning, and it is the marketer's job to ensure that turn they do. And it isn't only the large concerns that have the problems. Many a small business finds it hard to take the time to look into the future, let alone manage it.

The 'resource elevator' and the perils of missing the bus

Working in an under-resourced business is no fun: everything is strained to the limit, including you. The reasons for under-resourcing are many; here are three common ones:

- lack of investment – because of insufficient funds, or perhaps because of insufficient vision;
- the inevitable time lag between a new opportunity appearing and the organization getting its act together;
- the desire to use available resources as efficiently as possible – the 'lean and mean' school that takes things to the limit, and sometimes beyond.

Whatever the reason, in a growth market the result is the same; a period of stress, and then time for bold action and an injection of resource sometimes beyond the immediate need. This is particularly common in the service industries, where the prime resource is people. You may only need half a new person but you have to take on a whole one!

We might call this situation the 'resource escalator', and it is illustrated in Figure 11.2 with its characteristic pattern of feast and famine, with only the briefest period of perfect balance in between (statisticians would tell us that, on average, you have the perfect resource – but don't listen to them!).

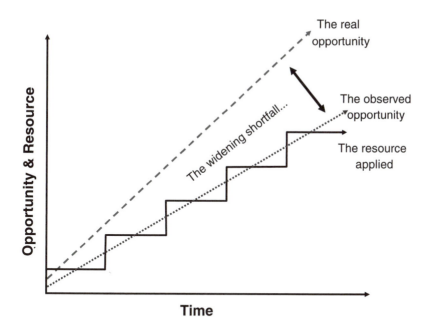

Figure 11.2 _The resource escalator_

If the only problem with this situation was an imbalance of resource to opportunity then that would be one thing, but Figure 11.2 also shows what is perhaps the real problem with the resource escalator. The fixation on finding the right level of resource can easily turn into an internal focus driven by a desire to maximize efficiency. In a growth market this can be seriously bad news. Perhaps the resource escalator keeps reasonable pace with the _observed_ opportunity, but is that the same thing as the real opportunity? When your business is growing, particularly if you feel smart (not to say smug) about how you manage your resource in line with that growth, it is easy to feel satisfied. Satisfaction and complacency are near neighbours, and you can soon be missing the point that the *real* opportunity is much larger and in fact a gulf is appearing between your own performance and that real opportunity.

So what should we conclude? That the marketer must start by understanding the opportunity, then secure the resource required, and then set the appropriate objectives. Don't be bullied by managers setting targets that are beyond the true opportunity, or impossible with the given resource, but neither should you just refuse their requests. The professional marketer must always be ready to challenge targets that come from on high, if they are not realistic, and to say why, and to say what would be required to make them realistic. If you get what is required, then everyone is happy and you can look forward to a well-managed future.

Let's return now to the two tools introduced at the start of the chapter: vision, or the mission statement, and objectives.

VISION: THE MISSION STATEMENT

Are these one-liners mission statements?

- 'Never knowingly undersold.'
- 'Double sales and profits by 2006.'
- 'We try harder.'
- 'To win!'

Or are they just slogans?

The trouble with such pithiness is that in their attempt to be memorable, they can end up giving very little guidance, and leaving too much to the imagination. Is it 'To win!' at any price? How will we double sales and profits? Is never being 'knowingly undersold' (the 'property' of the John Lewis Partnership) a mission for the business or a slogan for the customer? Of course, a good mission statement will be one that *does* mean something to both customers and staff, and to suppliers and stakeholders. For the John Lewis Partnership, the UK department store retailer, it is a policy; for the customer, a promise; and for staff it guides them as to how to behave – how to procure, how to sell, how to watch the competition – and so it works, which is why it has endured for so many years.

A good mission statement must be short, memorable, motivating, challenging, and, above all else, it must guide the organization through the choices that it will have to make. To do this, without leaving too many holes for potential 'misunderstanding', there should perhaps be five key ingredients to a mission statement:

1. What business are you in?
2. What future position do you aspire to?
3. What core competencies will get you there?
4. What segments and customers will help you get there?
5. What measure of success (including financial) will you use?

You will recall from Chapter 3 that the question 'What business are we in?' should, wherever possible, be couched in terms that talk of the benefit gained from our product or service, not the nature of the product itself – selling hope, not cosmetics!

A publisher of business books is certainly not simply in the book market; it is in the market for improving business performance, or developing management capability, or improving personal performance, and there are many more definitions that would help that publisher carve out a unique position. The publisher of this book, Kogan Page, is very much in what it calls the business practitioners' market, seeking to help develop the skills and knowledge of those working in the business environment. This gives its books a practical feel, with tips and techniques, and real-world examples, so that they are easy to read, and hopefully even enjoyable!

There is no need for justification of the elements of a mission statement, no need for statistics to back it up, and no need to pin it down to specifics – a mission statement is a signpost, not the map.

MARKETING OBJECTIVES

If the vision, summed up in the mission statement, is a signpost, then objectives are the specific destinations on that signpost. They should be written in strict accordance to the acronym SMART:

- **S** – specific;
- **M** – measurable;
- **A** – achievable;
- **R** – realistic;
- **T** – timed.

Anyone who has gone through a personal performance appraisal and objectives setting session, has probably come across something very like SMART – and the lessons apply just as much to marketing objectives as to personal ones.

Avoid objectives such as:

- We will successfully enter the market for high-price designer teddy bears.
- We will become the market leader.
- We will launch three new products.

- We will ensure full customer satisfaction.
- We will achieve a return on net assets (RONA) of 25%.

How do you define success, how do you define high price, and by when will 'success' be achieved? What does market leader mean – highest volume, greatest value, best-known brand name? Again, by when? When will the three products be launched, and is launching them the only measure of success? What makes a customer satisfied, and does full satisfaction mean zero complaints, and is that realistic? At least the 25 per cent RONA is specific and measurable; we will have to assume it is achievable and realistic; and if we add a date then at least one out of five objectives passes the SMART test.

The Viking or the 'gently does it' approach

Your marketing objectives will drive your business for the next year, three years, maybe longer, so they deserve a lot of attention both for their content and for their style of presentation. Use them to throw down gauntlets by all means, provided the rest of the plan shows how that challenge will be handled. Most people like to work in an organization that takes on challenges, provided these are not reckless or unrealistic. Your objectives will say a lot about the aspirations of the business, but also much about the level of professionalism involved in managing the business.

We might like to consider two different philosophies of 'making it happen', two extremes that might characterize different approaches to business and marketing objectives. We might label them *Viking* and *Gently does it*.

The *Viking* philosophy argues that you should row on to the enemy shore, disembark your troops and burn your boats. That way, making things work is your only option. Success in such circumstances is bold, daring and the stuff of legend. Failure is brutal and unsung.

The *Gently does it* philosophy argues that you should hold offshore, viewing the enemy through long-range binoculars, looking for signs of weakness, hoping that they might fall into a hole of their own digging, and then creep ashore to take their place. Success is met by praise of your great wisdom and tactical genius. Failure brands you a coward.

THE FINANCIAL IMPERATIVES

Any CEO or CFO (Chief Financial Officer) would worry if your vision did not include some comment on the financial imperatives – where is the money coming from? Figure 11.3 shows just some of the options that will help determine your financial objectives. Those financial objectives are very important here, not least because they are often missing from a marketing

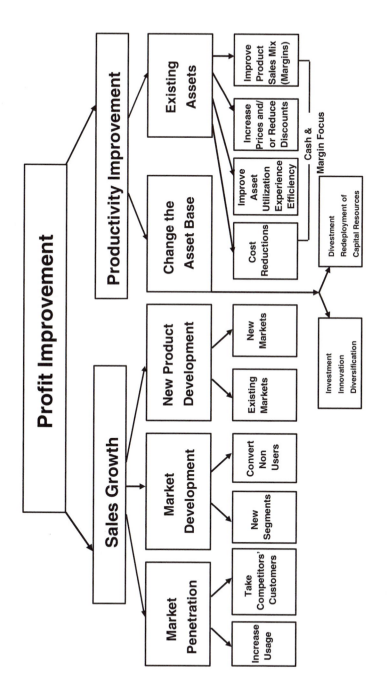

Figure 11.3 *Options and more options...*

Source: Malcolm McDonald, *Marketing Plans*, Butterworth-Heinemann, Oxford, 1999, and after Professor John Saunders, Aston University

plan, particularly in organizations in which marketing is regarded as the 'creative' side of the business.

We face here another of those 'chicken or egg?' questions: do we decide how much money, and how, before we write the plan – so that the plan is designed to achieve the target – or do we allow the planning process to illustrate the possibilities for revenue and profit? The answer has to be, this is two-way traffic – and we should be working from both sides simultaneously.

Figure 11.3 illustrates not only the options, but also the complexity of the choice. Faced with such complexity, it is perhaps not surprising that many businesses choose to 'stick to their knitting', an awful phrase that ably conveys the dullness and despair of carrying on with what you have always done.

It is the very complexity shown here that calls out for the tools we discussed in Part II: 'The market audit'. For the purposes of our vision and objectives, it will suffice to indicate the implications of our plan on revenue, investment, cash flow and profit.

12

How will we grow?

The first of the big 'positioning' questions – *how will we grow?* – takes us to two planning (planning, rather than audit) tools designed to take us through some tough decisions. They are the *Ansoff matrix* and *gap analysis*.

THE ANSOFF MATRIX AND RISK

For any business wishing to grow, there are four choices, based on what it sells and where it sells. These are expressed by the four boxes in the Ansoff matrix, named after its developer, Igor Ansoff of the Boston Consulting Group (Figure 12.1).

The choices are:

- *penetration* – sell more of existing products into existing markets;
- *market extension* – sell existing products into new markets;
- *new product development (NPD)* – sell new products into existing markets;
- *diversification* – sell new products into new markets.

Risk

The percentage figures shown in the boxes are Ansoff's estimation (after analysis of a wide range of different markets) of your likely success rate. Put another way, they also indicate the level of risk: NPD is likely to fail 70 per cent of the time, and diversification 85 per cent of the time.

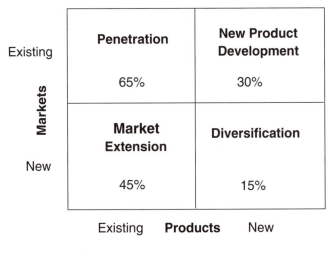

Figure 12.1   *The Ansoff matrix*

As your chosen growth strategy moves around the matrix from *penetration* to *market extension* to *NPD*, or even to *diversification*, the risk of failure increases. With each step away from your existing market and your existing products, you are moving further into the unknown, hence the smaller percentage success rate shown in each successive box. These are of course averages, or 'typical' numbers. Different markets may see higher or lower figures, though the ratio between them tends to stay much the same. An fmcg food manufacturer might be very pleased indeed with an NPD success rate of 30 per cent (the average for its market is in single figures), while a training company like my own would be distraught!

Managing risk

Risk is good...

There are two principal uses of the Ansoff matrix: first, to assess the level of risk in your growth strategy, across a range of products, for a market segment, or across a whole market or business; and second, to prompt you to take the necessary risk-management or risk-reducing actions.

Of course, some level of risk is necessary if you wish to grow, but any sensible business will always seek to manage or contain that risk, as far as it can. There are many things that can be done to manage risk:

... provided it's managed

- market research;
- market testing;
- forming alliances or joint ventures with experienced partners;
- working with expert suppliers (asking them to share the risk);
- working with key customers, developing new ideas together, and perhaps sharing the risks and the rewards;
- taking on experienced staff;

- training existing staff;
- acquisition and merger;
- making use of the 'brand halo' (see Chapter 16).

The key to using the Ansoff matrix is in an honest assessment of which box (or boxes) you are operating in. Too often a business will underestimate the risks involved in its growth plans (partly as a means of gaining sanction) by seeing its activities as 'less than they really are' in Ansoff matrix terms. It is something of a vicious circle: underestimation leads to less homework, fewer risk-management activities, and so an increase in risk – and so it goes on.

Let's consider each box in turn, assessing the nature of risk and the likely means to success.

Penetration

Provided that there is more business to be had in your existing market (ie you do not already 'own' the lion's share), penetration is usually the safest strategy. You already have a presence, you know the requirements, and you can measure your activities with some confidence.

Each circumstance is unique, of course, but penetration becomes less attractive in a declining market, or where your share is so high that further growth is unrealistic. Shifting share from 5 per cent to 10 per cent may sound a huge leap, but compared to moving from 80 per cent to 85 per cent it is often a lot easier. For one thing, customers don't like suppliers to gain such dominance, and will actively favour your competitors to maintain a more open field. It may be that the legal system will stop you: monopolies are not liked as a rule (remember PESTLE from Chapter 9), and there are always competitors who refuse to die whatever you do.

Market extension

Entering new markets with existing products – market extension – is perhaps the most fertile ground for horror stories. So many otherwise successful businesses assume that what works _here_ will work _there_ (when thinking of new markets as new countries). Very few companies are able to sustain a standard offer worldwide – even McDonald's has to call its Quarter-Pounder with Cheese a 'Royale' in France (as any watcher of _Pulp Fiction_ will know!), and Kentucky Fried Chicken had to take the coleslaw out of the package when Colonel Sanders went to the land of the rising sun. Yet time after time corporate ego gets the better of a business and it comes to grief.

Ben & Jerry's ice cream was a phenomenal success in the United States with its quirky mix of showmanship, fun, local referencing, entrepreneurial spirit and social conscience, a formula that meant very little when the product was launched in the United Kingdom. Not only did British consumers care little for the plight of Vermont dairy

Not getting the joke...

farmers (the brand's support of this beleaguered group won it a warm following in the United States), but few Brits got the jokes in ice cream names such as Cherry Garcia (work it out for yourself).

Even brand names can let you down: the Vauxhall Nova flopped in South America, where Nova means 'won't go', and even Coca-Cola (so the folklore has it) can sound like 'lice in the carpets' in some parts of China!

The dog that wouldn't travel

ICI Dulux, for many years predominantly a UK brand, acquired a number of non-UK paint companies in the 1980s, including the largest operators in France (Valentine) and the United States (Glidden). It was some time before its marketers stopped trying to force the famous 'Dulux dog' on to their new colleagues. In France, Valentine finally accepted an animal in its advertising, but a black panther matched its positioning and message better than the dog, and in the United States the use of animals to express brand values never did catch on. One of the ironies of this is that Dulux is a brand that conducts more market research than any other in its market, and is in the top league of research among fmcg companies, yet corporate ego held it back from asking some simple questions when entering, what to Dulux, if not to Valentine and Glidden, were very new markets indeed.

Retailers often make the same mistake: Marks & Spencer struggled with its ventures into North America and continental Europe, Texas Homecare had an expensive flop in Spain (made public by being featured in the parallel flop *Eldorado*, a UK television soap), Aldi and Netto have never captured British hearts and minds in the way they have on the Continent, and Wickes Building Supplies, a leader in profitability in the UK market, ran a chain of poorly performing stores in the Netherlands and Belgium throughout the 1980s; the winning formula did not transfer as easily as it had hoped.

The challenge is bigger than envisaged at the outset. Products that have been carefully honed for their home market may need revision (and more than new labels) for an overseas market. They may need reworking to such an extent that they become new products, and soon the venture teeters closer and closer to diversification. Not that diversification itself is necessarily the problem; Virgin, for one, has shown how it can be done successfully. It is diversifying without ever realizing you are diversifying that leads to tales of disaster!

New product development

There is what we might call a 'double whammy' here. Not only is the risk of failure high, but the development costs involved can often run well beyond budget (particularly when things start to go wrong). This is not a signal to abandon all NPD, far from it. What the Ansoff matrix encourages us to do is proceed with caution, observe a disciplined process for NPD (see Chapter 25), take risk-reducing steps such as test-marketing or working closely with partners (suppliers or customers), and try to focus your efforts on the more certain winners.

3M has long been heralded as an innovative company, with much talk about its policy of allowing employees to devote large chunks of their time, and 3M's money, on developing, well, almost whatever they like! It makes the proud claim that the majority of its profits in only five years' time will come from products not yet launched, or even off the drawing board, and it works, _for 3M_. One of the problems of using such high-profile examples to illustrate winning strategies is that it is easy to forget the circumstances that make that strategy work. A company that plans a high level of NPD needs to ensure it has the capabilities. These might include a well-supported R&D resource, an ability to work collaboratively with partners and suppliers, an ability to get new products to market _fast_, a management structure that both allows and stimulates creativity, an acceptance of failure and an ability to learn from it. It will also need a way to deal with the large numbers of ideas that inevitably get thrown up in such an environment, choosing which should be supported and which should be rejected. We might call it a _stage-gate_ process, and we will look at this more closely in Chapter 25.

In global markets the cost of NPD can be almost prohibitive for any one player, and we see an increasing number of partnerings – alliances and joint ventures – to share the costs, reduce the risks and ensure that the capabilities are in place.

Hewlett-Packard dominates the market for small-sized inkjet printers for the business user. Xerox has a much smaller share, but targets significant growth. Arguably, this is a penetration strategy for Xerox. It has products on the market already, but its share is so small, barely a toehold, that its growth plans will require significant NPD. The scale of the task calls for new capabilities and resources, so it is partnering with Fuji Xerox (its Japanese joint venture) and Sharp of Japan.

Partnering for NPD

Diversification

Mars scored a famous success with its launch of the ice cream Mars Bar in the United Kingdom, creating a whole new market out of nowhere. The launch was diversification: a very novel product for Mars, and a new market, that of ice cream buyers, not confectionery buyers. There was, however, one failing that marred its success, as we have already seen. It turned out that Mars was asking retailers of the new ice cream to put it into their existing freezer cabinets. Unfortunately for Mars, these cabinets were rarely the retailer's own property. More often, they were owned by one of the two big ice cream brands, Walls or Lyons Maid. The response from these manufacturers was fast and litigious. Mars had to react in double-quick time by providing its own cabinets (I always think of that refrigerator supplier; it must have seemed like Christmas!).

Underestimating the risk

Why the mistake? Because, rather than considering the launch as diversification, and determining to take the necessary risk-reducing steps, too many people involved in the launch saw it as NPD, something Mars was good at, and so this one would be a breeze…

In the end, of course, the diversification was hugely successful, not least because of the heavy promotional spend behind the launch, but also, very importantly, because of the strength of the Mars name. Using an existing brand to enter new markets or launch new products can be a very effective way of reducing risk, provided that the values attached to the brand are transferable. In the case of Mars this was apparently so; in the case of Virgin the success is even clearer.

Some say that Virgin breaks all the rules of the Ansoff matrix – that moving from record label to airline to hotelier to cola producer to financial services to rail operator is diversification with a vengeance and that it should have failed more often. The point is that far from breaking the rules, Virgin has observed the most important rule: understand the challenge and the risk, and aim to minimize it when away from home territory. In Virgin's case it is a combination of the brand halo (see Chapter 16), meticulous market research, and its use of expert partners and suppliers that gives it its success.

Diversifying to escape decline

Philip Morris, owner of the Marlboro brand, envisages a slow decline of that brand as a result of increasing restrictions on tobacco advertising. This is not a situation that it is about to take lying down, not least because the brand is one of its most important assets, valued at $23 billion. Plans under consideration include diversification into hotels and leisure, under the Marlboro brand. One way of reducing the risks of diversification is *brand extension*: taking an existing brand and using its 'halo' effect (see Chapter 16) to establish a presence in the new market. But some of the challenges are clear: can the Marlboro brand values be translated to, say, a hotel stay (presumably guests will still be encouraged not to smoke in bed?!), and will the attempt be accepted by the market (the US government, for one, prevents such activities)? Philip Morris must weigh the options, including diversification to keep the brand alive, or perhaps conceding its long-term decline and milking it for funds to invest in penetration strategies for growth brands in the portfolio such as Kraft or Miller brewing.

Growth options in a mature market

If anything other than penetration is so risky, why do it? The answer is that growth is always the objective, and when a business is operating in a mature or declining market, penetration is not always the best route.

Few consumer markets are more mature than that for breakfast cereals in the United States: the big brands have slugged it out consistently for decades on the battleground of market share. General Mills recently scored a victory over Kellogg's by knocking its long-term rival off the number one spot for the first time, but the champagne is flowing less freely than might be expected as these players begin to realize that the battleground needs to change. General Mills is looking at genomic research to design foods for treating or preventing specific illnesses. Quaker, a smaller player in the cereals market, but of equal heritage, partnered with Novartis, forming Altus Foods, in order to escape the price and share demands of this mature market. Altus Foods will pursue opportunities for food as a form of health treatment. 'We need to change food companies to nutrition companies,' says Robert Morrison, Quaker's chief executive. What might sound like NPD is really diversification, and the risks involved and the new capabilities demanded call for such partnerships and alliances. Even then, success is far from assured. The Novartis–Quaker combination launched the Aviva brand in the United Kingdom with a muesli that promised heart benefits, an orange juice drink with bone benefits and a crunchy wholewheat biscuit with digestive benefits. The promises were upfront and the packaging carried a clinically proven badge with the tag line 'Enjoy the taste today – enjoy a healthy tomorrow'. But it flopped. An idea ahead of its time? We'll see.

Kellogg's has chosen a different route; aiming to reduce its dependence on cereals through the growth of successful convenience foods such as Pop-Tarts. Penetration is still an option when a company operates in multiple segments.

GAP ANALYSIS

Ansoff lays out the nature of the risk; gap analysis makes graphic the nature of the whole task of growth (see Figure 12.2).

Few things are certain in marketing, least of all growth, but it is close to certain that doing nothing will end in decline. This is represented in gap analysis as the 'do nothing' scenario. What about just staying as you are? That is one of the hardest things in business, and attempts to stand still usually result in a slow slippage backwards.

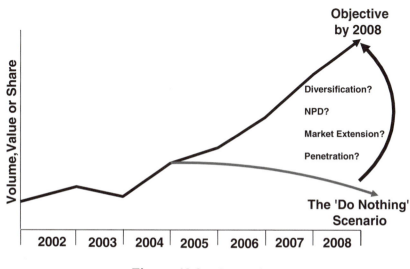

Figure 12.2 _Gap analysis_

Then there is the target handed down from on high by an ambitious board. In the old days there was just one target, and it was tough. Now there are two targets: the tough one, and then the 'stretch target', laid down as if to say, those ordinary targets are too easy for the likes of you. Between 'do nothing' and our target are a range of 'do somethings'. These choices are in fact the choices outlined by the Ansoff matrix.

Using the analysis

Gap analysis is a mini sanity check: is this growth possible? It is also a means of assessing what the task will call for, and, perhaps most valuable of all, a means of presenting back to those who set the targets for your requirements: 'If you want that level of growth, then we will need NPD, and that will take…' Of course, I am describing a fairly old-fashioned approach here: targets from on high. Modern professional marketers will want to set their own targets, based on a disciplined audit and assessment of capabilities, but even then, from time to time, the bosses get ideas…

13

How will we compete?

PORTER'S CHOICES

Chapter 9 discussed Michael E Porter's model of competitive forces that bear on a business and impact on its profitability. We discussed in general the need to build barriers against those forces, and it is in this chapter that we will discuss how, by using Porter's own recommendation. There are two principal ways to respond to those forces, and so gain sustainable competitive advantage:

- be the lowest-cost supplier;
- be a differentiated supplier.

The options may sound simple and rather stark, but the reality is that many businesses fail to make the choice and linger in a never-never land of compromises. What they often lack is the discipline to focus the whole business on whichever route is chosen. A typical outcome is, for instance, a production function devoted to becoming the lowest-cost supplier and a marketing function wishing to offer flexible product ranges. Result: conflict, frustration and mediocrity.

The choices are not about right and wrong; most markets present the possibility of either strategy succeeding as a means to competitive advantage. The airline industry is an excellent example, with both strategies in evidence, and at one time even within the same airline as BA tried to operate Go as a low-cost player taking on the likes of easyJet and Ryanair. They are choices that, as ever, depend on your assessment of the opportunity, your capabilities, and the possibility of a good match between the two.

Don't be fooled into thinking, however, that this means the choice doesn't matter, or that it is easy to be either, or even both at once. In truth, we are looking at two different strategies, two different mindsets and two different business cultures.

Lowest-cost supplier

Being the lowest-cost supplier does not mean being cheap or slipshod. It does not mean that the company will necessarily sell at the lowest price, though it will be able to do this should the need arise, or if indeed this becomes the key to its success. A successful practitioner of this strategy once said to me, 'The trick is to be the lowest-cost supplier, but not let the customer know that you are!'

Where the strategy *is* to sell at the lowest price then the disciplines of such a business must be very tight indeed.

Investing in spending less

easyJet is an example of such an operator, and its success depends on reducing the costs of its operation at every possible point in the supply chain. Starting from the top, the management team occupy a utilitarian open-plan office – part of the strategy, and very much a symbol to the rest of the organization. More importantly, costs are reduced by operating from smaller airports: Luton and Liverpool rather than the likes of Heathrow. Critically, the turnaround time on the ground is shaved to the shortest possible, allowing each plane to make more flights and carry more passengers. This requires close liaison with the airport operators and constant attention to detail. The sales operation must be honed to work efficiently, effectively and at lowest cost. Efficiency comes from use of the Internet: over half of easyJet's bookings come that way. Effectiveness is about ensuring that where seats *can* be sold at higher prices, they are. This ability comes from understanding the demand patterns for each route, forecasting usage, and developing pricing strategies that will fill planes at the optimum price. The sales effort is run at low cost by declining to work through middlemen, the travel agents, so saving commission payments on every transaction. Promotion is a key ingredient, but rather than having heavyweight high-cost TV campaigns, easyJet makes excellent use of price offers through the national press.

Over and above all this, success depends on there being a demand for a low-price, no-frills service, and easyJet has been able to capitalize on just such a demand as more people see air travel as an option to be compared with rail or bus.

None of this means a company that doesn't invest. Don't confuse low-cost operators with cheap-jacks. Where investment will reduce operating costs, such as investing in an Internet ticket-booking capability or in a call centre that allows the airline to cut out travel agents' commission, that investment is made with alacrity.

Differentiation

Just as easyJet and Ryanair aim to meet the needs of those travellers who simply want to get from A to B at the lowest price, so there are airline operators, indeed the majority, who aim to provide more than that, and provide it to a different segment of the market. Segmentation is what allows two such different strategies to succeed in the same market. There is no such thing as an air traveller; there are air travellers who want speed, those who want comfort, those who want fun, those who want to be excited, those who want to be calmed, those who want their egos stroked, those who want to make business deals, those who want a relaxing holiday, those who want to 'fly the flag', those who want to feel safe, and many more besides. The differentiated airline aims to offer a package that appeals to a particular mix of these needs, so hoping to stand out from the competing crowd.

Differentiation can be many things in such a market, but above all it must be seen by the customer to add value. A business-class ticket will have many facets of added value, perceived in a variety of ways depending on the customer and the circumstance. A business traveller needing an earlier flight will perceive huge value in a ticket that allows him or her to make that change, at no extra cost, with priority attention, even if he or she has to travel in an economy seat! On another occasion, say waiting for a delayed flight on a busy Monday morning, the business-class lounge will seem more than enough value for the premium price paid.

To develop a successful differentiated strategy, a business must be able to understand the complex interactions of price and value in its market, and must be able to present offers that meet real needs while distinguishing itself from the competition.

Going global – changing the values

For many years, British Airways made great play of being the nation's airline, 'flying the flag', giving it a unique piece of differentiation. As deregulation in the industry loosened the ties between airlines' routes and airports, so competition grew, and this patriotic positioning became of less value to passengers. Amidst a storm of protest from traditionally minded supporters (including Margaret Thatcher and a handkerchief on one famous occasion), British Airways removed the Union Jack from its tailplanes and took on the mantle of a global airline. Adverts stressed how many Americans travelled by the airline, not how many British, and how many of them were businesspeople, with all the obvious implications. A new positioning, but still a very differentiated one.

Just as we should not mistake the lowest-cost strategy for stinginess, we should not equate differentiation with massive promotional budgets or a spendthrift attitude. Differentiation can of course come from a high-profile advertising presence, but, more significantly, it comes from identifying and providing things that customers value and will pay a premium for. For such things, investment should flow, and for things of no value, the accountant's knife should be sharpened to the full.

Is it *'either–or'*, or is it *'and'*?

Porter advises marketers to make their choice – differentiation or lowest cost – and so avoid the perils of the 'inbetweeny'. But must it always be such a choice? Is it not possible to combine both? Certainly there are examples of companies that, because of their scale, will almost certainly have the lowest costs in the business but are nevertheless highly differentiated – Coca-Cola is one, Microsoft another. The real question is not whether they achieve this position, but how they use it and which of the two gains them their competitive advantage.

When we look at pricing strategies in Chapter 28 we will see how the company that has an opportunity both to reduce costs *and* differentiate is likely to find itself in the role of 'price leader' in the market – an enviable position, but rarely achieved except by large-scale mass-market producers.

The 1980s was a decade when marketers made bold choices (it was definitely *'either–or'*), largely as a reaction to the blur and inertia of the 1970s, but more recently businesses are asking for both differentiation *and* lowest cost (the era of *'and'* is well and truly with us). Let's look at a case study of one business that has managed the combination successfully.

The Accor hotel group operates a range of hotel brands from differentiated upmarket chains such as Sofitel down to the lowest-cost player, Motel 6 in the United States. One of its brands, Formule 1, seems to have achieved the magic double: lowest cost but also differentiated. How so? Figure 13.1 shows what marketers call the value curves for three hotels: a typical one-star, a typical two-star and Formule 1.

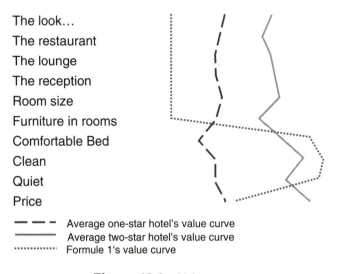

The look…
The restaurant
The lounge
The reception
Room size
Furniture in rooms
Comfortable Bed
Clean
Quiet
Price

— — — Average one-star hotel's value curve
———— Average two-star hotel's value curve
············· Formule 1's value curve

Figure 13.1 *Value curves*

The one-star represents the basic offer across a range of features we expect to find in a hotel. Compared to that, the two-star's enhanced facilities command a price premium because there are customers out there who value those things. This is a differentiated offer, and it is to be hoped that the extra revenue outweighs the extra costs of operating such a hotel.

What Formule 1 does is to strip out a whole range of features (and usually those that cost the most to provide), so ensuring it the lowest-cost status. The features that go are the ones it believes its customers do not really want, need or value. The features that stay – quietness and cleanliness in particular – are the ones that it believes its customers do want, need and value. Not only do these features stay, but Formule 1 aims to make them superior to those found in a typical two-star hotel's offer. This is of course a differentiated offer, but on a very narrow band of features.

The secret to this approach can be summed up in one word: segmentation. By selecting a clearly identified group of target customers who share similar needs, attitudes and behaviours, Formule 1 is able to assess very precisely which features to strip out and which to leave in and enhance. The segment is the frequent business traveller on a tight budget, constantly on the move – out with the client all evening, up with the lark in the morning – and who simply needs a good sleep at night. 'When you're asleep, our rooms look as good as anyone's…' is the motto.

Other hotels have tried to copy aspects of this approach: Ramada International advertises itself as 'everything except excess', with a photograph of a fancy sterling-silver food dome at a $$$$ price next to one of a simple catering plate ring at a $$ price, but this is only a part of the story. The no-frills approach must drive down costs such that customers can see the value of their abstinence reflected in a low price, and they must receive what they really value in spades.

Where less is more

14

What will drive us?

There are three tools or models to be considered in this chapter:

- value drivers;
- push or pull strategies;
- asset management.

These are about determining what makes the business tick – or better, what makes it hum. As ever, they involve some big choices, but ones that need to be made, or else the people who work for the business will be unclear on their purpose, their objectives, and what makes good performance or bad performance. This is of course the importance of getting this right: that the whole business should work as one.

VALUE DRIVERS

A value driver is a set of ideas or notions, a business culture, or a guide map that allows all members of the business to identify with what they should be doing to achieve success.

Treacy and Wiersema, in their book *The Discipline of Market Leaders*, identify three value drivers. All may be present in any successful business, but for a *really* successful business, one or other of these drivers will stand out, distinguishing the business for its staff and its customers, and distinguishing it from its competitors.

Table 14.1 *Value drivers*

Value Driver	Examples
Operational excellence	McDonald's, IKEA, Dell, Wal-Mart
Product leadership	Microsoft, 3M, Pfizer, Intel
Customer intimacy	Kraft, KPMG, Quest, INSIGHT

Operational excellence

Operational excellence is about doing what you do, well. It is about effective processes, smooth mechanics, and the efficiency with which products or services are brought to market. Efficiencies of production, economies of scales, uniformity and conformance, accurate forecasting, slick distribution, fast response – these are the sorts of things that might be important to a business seeking 'operational excellence'. Such 'excellence' can bring significant competitive advantage in a market where reliability is important, or price is competitive. Businesses in the mass market – no frills, low hassle, low price – arena will often be driven by this value.

IKEA achieves huge efficiencies through its logistics chain, from manufacture to store, and in store the 'self-selection, self-collection' formula completes the operational excellence of its supply chain, reflected in excellent value for its customers. International uniformity (Swedish product names like 'Gutvik' and 'Sprallig' make it all the way to Australia), modular ranges and a carefully honed product choice (limited, but it doesn't seem so) are some of the watchwords.

Logistics...

Wal-Mart achieves incredible cost savings through the logistical efficiency of its EPOS (electronic point of sale) based ordering system. As each product goes through the checkout scanner, it is reordered to be back on the shelf within 48 hours. When you consider the scale of Wal-Mart, the number of stores, their geographical spread and the potential complexity of such a business, the efficiency and cost savings driven by this one aspect of Wal-Mart's operational excellence explain its dominant position.

... and more logistics – very much the marketer's concern

Product leadership

Product leadership is about producing the best, leading-edge or market-dominant products. Businesses with high rates of innovation and patent application often have this value at their heart. It is hard to imagine a successful pharmaceuticals company that is not driven by this value. Investment in successful NPD is the key to success: the market for 'nearly there' or 'almost as good as the best one' drugs is rarely good! One of the biggest threats for a business driven by this value is that of falling behind, and it is necessary to continually push the boundaries of performance, and be *seen* to be doing so.

Working at the edge

The pace of innovation achieved by Microsoft is amazing, the downside being that you can sometimes feel out of date as soon as you carry the new product out of the store. The company walks a very difficult tightrope: innovate and risk upsetting customers who feel forced to replace what they saw as perfectly good products, or slow down and be seen as dull. It must also ensure reliability (just witness the publicity when there are doubts over the new version of Windows) and yet keep its foot on the accelerator. Occasional failure is almost inevitable for such a company, yet the costs of failure are huge, financially and perceptually – a difficult tightrope indeed.

Customer intimacy

Customer intimacy is the ability to identify with specific customer needs and match products and services accordingly. What distinguishes the customer-intimate business is its stated determination to develop close customer relationships, and to act on the resultant knowledge at all levels of its operation. Such a company will probably have a wide menu of products and services, and the ability to mix and match these to suit individual customer requirements – or perhaps it will go further than this and offer a totally bespoke service. There is a limit to how many customers this can be done for, and a customer-intimate business will have to think carefully about segmentation and key account identification. Something else that often distinguishes a business driven by customer intimacy is its willingness to share risks with its customers and to expect a concomitant share of the rewards.

So close to the customer you can smell them

Quest International supplies fragrances to the perfume industry. Each of its customers' products is unique, and the fragrance is equally unique – there are few off-the-shelf solutions. The perfumer's art is as much one of black magic as of chemistry, and Quest must be able to identify with this. Customer intimacy is essential for success; it enables an absolute identification with the customer's needs, and focuses the whole organization on meeting them. Many of Quest's customers are themselves driven by product leadership – branding is all – and Quest must be intimate with *that* value driver in order to be regarded as a key supplier. Its success is evidence of a broader observation: truly customer-intimate suppliers must be able to identify with value drivers in their customers that are quite different from their own.

Implications for the business

Once a value driver has been chosen, all parts of the business must fall in line – and that's a tough one to achieve. Certain functions may have natural tendencies towards one or other of the drivers. Production and operations people lean towards operational excellence – it's the way they are measured. R&D folk may favour product leadership – it's what their job is about. Sales and marketing people may find themselves chasing customer intimacy... So who is right? Does it matter? Yes indeed.

A business in which the distribution department adheres to operational excellence, sales to customer intimacy, and R&D to product leadership is a business heading for trouble, both internally and in its market.

I once witnessed an argument (that went on for six full months) between sales and distribution in a large supplier to a manufacturing company. The customer was demanding shorter lead times on deliveries, and the sales people were pressing for these with distribution. It's all about customer intimacy, they said. Distribution dug their heels in and said they wouldn't do it – not because they couldn't, but because the customer was wrong to be asking for this. Their belief was that full and correct deliveries were what the customer wanted and needed, and that took time. Rush the timing and we would end up delivering the wrong things occasionally, they said. Their view came not from their knowledge of the customer, but from their adherence to operational excellence – or at least, their definition of it. Excellent distribution was about getting full deliveries right every time, and that was how they were measured.

The debate was finally resolved in favour of the customer's demands, but only once something very important had happened: the performance measures used in distribution were changed.

You 'are' how you are measured; which provides us with a clue

---

This question of performance measures is vital. If functions are measured against criteria that conflict with the chosen business focus, then there will be trouble, or at least sub-optimal performance. A common misconception is that if, for instance, customer intimacy is the lead driver for the business, then somehow operational excellence no longer matters. Not at all: the task is to identify what makes *appropriate* operational excellence.

Let's say that customer intimacy is indeed the driver, and that this leads to sales professionals encouraging orders for a number of product variants. If the production team is measured on occupacity, and targets are based on running single lines, then there is going to be a problem. Perhaps production should be measured on their flexibility – their ability to switch product lines with speed?

Reverse the case and make the lead driver operational excellence, based on reducing manufacturing complexity; then the sales force must be targeted and measured on their ability to take orders that fit with production schedules.

Value drivers and strategic change

While one driver may lead, the other two are still important. There may in effect be a ranking of importance across the three options. This ranking will form an important part of the marketer's search for that unique match in the marketing model, between capabilities and need.

In any market there will be what we might think of as 'minimum standards' for each of the drivers. We could call those minimum standards the 'givens'. A fast-food chain may well be led by operational excellence (OE), but it cannot ignore the need for innovation (product leadership, PL) or choice (customer intimacy, CI); there are minimum standards required in both those areas. Provided those standards are met, the chain might then choose to excel at the product aspect of the business – the best burger in town – or on the operational aspects of the business, with a slickly efficient supply chain from purchase through to delivery, and the fastest service in town. Table 14.2 represents the result of this analysis and the decision to chase the latter of these two strategic choices.

Table 14.2 *Value drivers and the strategic mix*

Value Driver	Customer Requirement	Strategic Mix
Operational excellence	60	80
Product leadership	30	30
Customer intimacy	10	10

The minimum or 'threshold' customer requirement is shown in the first column of the table. Matching those demands are the 'givens' to operate in this market. The business must now match those thresholds and then decide where it will exceed the requirement, so establishing its particular position in the market and defining its lead value driver. If customer demand is expressed as points out of 100, expressing the strategic mix as points out of 120 allows the marketer to express his or her chosen preference.

This suits today just fine, but will it suit tomorrow? Perhaps the business is identifying an increasing demand for wider menu choice. Perhaps it has established itself as a regular Sunday lunch call for families, and those customers would now like to think they could ring the changes a bit, without going elsewhere. In such a case the attention given to customer intimacy must grow. Table 14.3 shows how a business might represent this strategic shift using this model.

Of course, the numbers are not precise; they are indicators – aids to analysis and strategic thinking. They are intended to show the size of the change required if the new strategy is to be achieved, and so help the business come to some realistic conclusions as to the feasibility of such a strategy, and the nature of the steps required. The choice may be to remain as a business driven by operational excellence while meeting the threshold required for customer intimacy. This is not an unsupportable strategy. A

Table 14.3 _Value drivers and the future strategic mix_

Value Driver	Current Customer Requirement	Current Strategic Mix	Future Customer Requirement (5 years)	Future Strategic Mix (5 years)
Operational excellence	60	80	30	30
Product leadership	30	30	30	30
Customer intimacy	10	10	40	60

business may choose to excel at a driver that is not in fact the most significant in the market, and succeed, provided that it meets the threshold standard for the other drivers. This choice may well mark that business out as special, and if it allows the company to make a genuine, sustainable and unique match between company capabilities and market needs, then it will have every chance of success.

PUSH OR PULL STRATEGIES

More will be said about the choice between a push and a pull strategy in the chapters on segmentation (Chapter 15) and place (Chapter 26). It is a fairly fundamental one. Let's suppose that we sell pens: do we aim to communicate our proposition to the end users in the market, so building up a demand that 'forces' the distributors and retailers to stock our product (pull strategy), or do we intend to persuade those distributors and retailers to take our product and ask them to promote them actively for us (push strategy)?

The pros and cons will be discussed in Chapter 26, but it is clear to see how the choice must relate to our capabilities. For instance, pull strategies might call for expertise in consumer research and promotion, often with significant budgets that must be spent in advance of any sales, while push strategies might call for large sales resources and channel management skills.

Marketers must choose the option that is right for their overall plan and objectives, but they must also take note of how well they are equipped to carry out their strategic choice.

ASSET MANAGEMENT

'Marketers should manage the market and leave the operations people to manage the factory and the distribution.' While that may be very poor advice, it is in truth the normal situation in far too many manufacturing businesses. Why this demarcation between functions? In the main it is because of poor understanding of what is involved. If a marketer doesn't understand how the product is made, then they tend to leave decisions about manufacture to the experts. That this is a mistake should be pretty evident by now!

There is little point in getting it right in the market if the resultant flow of orders cannot be handled by the internal operations. Let's just consider a few disaster stories from the 'growing-pains' days of the 'e' revolution.

Poor logistics?

Toys 'R' Us in the United States saw some of its customers considering legal action when they didn't get their purchases delivered in time for Christmas 1999. The retailer was forced to offer a $100 gift voucher as compensation – an expensive rearguard action, but the cost to the company's reputation and the cost of lost sales were much greater.

Poor systems?

Victoria Secret, the US retailer of lingerie, scored a massive initial success with its pre-1999 Christmas Web site, which was said to be receiving 250,000 hits an hour. With 1.5 per cent of these hits turning into sales, at an average of $80 a time, the prospect was looking good for a very happy Christmas, until the system broke under the load. On these numbers, a three-day crash might have cost the retailer anything up to $7.2 million in lost sales.

Poor IT?

Hershey, the US chocolate manufacturer, issued a profit warning after a disastrous period of trading in the second half of 1999. A new computer system designed to revolutionize customer order processing was blamed. Hershey had seen its market share 'whittled away by its inability to get customers the right amount of chocolate'. The disaster struck at the worst time possible – the Halloween and Christmas boom periods – and the Hershey share price tumbled from $53 to $38.

Each of these cases tells the same story: good marketing drove sales, but poor marketing led to their not being met. Note: poor marketing, not poor logistics, or poor systems, or poor IT. Marketers are responsible for ensuring that the operational capabilities are in place to meet their marketing activities, otherwise their order book may exceed all expectations, but it will also exceed their company's capabilities.

If your business is particularly reliant on volume, if lead times are a vital part of your competitive advantage or if margins are low, then asset management will be even more important. This may sound as if we are turning the principles of marketing on their head, but in such businesses it is important to find markets and customers that suit the nature of the company's assets. This is no more than the Marketing Model described in Chapter 3. A typical chemical manufacturer, by the very nature of chemistry, finds itself making a range of by-products when it makes its primary product. Success or failure will often depend on finding markets for those by-products as well as the primary product. Is this the sin of products chasing markets that marketing is meant to avoid? Not at all. It is, first of all, a recognition of reality, and second, it points out the importance of attending to both sides of the marketing model. Success in this example will go to the company that is able to target the right mix of markets and customers, so generating the right mix of volumes and products, so ensuring the most efficient use of assets, so reducing costs, so ensuring competitive advantage, and so (coming full circle) being able to target the chosen mix of markets and customers…

SUMMARY

In summary of what is a complex range of choices – Treacy and Wiersema's model provides a good guide to one of the fundamental 'what will drive us' choices, but it is not in isolation. Marketers must also consider the preference for push or pull, and the ability to make their choice happen, and they must also consider the need to manage their internal assets effectively. The number of 'chicken or egg' issues surrounding these choices can appear daunting. The secret is to approach these decisions like all others in marketing: with a disciplined process.

15

Who will we serve?

SEGMENTATION

This is a long chapter, but please don't be put off by that; this is perhaps the most important issue in marketing. What makes this one aspect of marketing more important than any other? There are perhaps two answers to that. First, segmentation impacts on all other aspects of the subject. Done well, segmentation is the secret to the matching task within the marketing model, it is the key to developing genuine value propositions, it is vital to any plan for key account management, and it is vital to any proper deployment of the marketer's tactical tools: the four P's. Second, segmentation can secure competitive advantage almost through the intellectual process alone.

That is quite a claim, and raises the question, is segmentation a science or an art? It is both. The process attempts to observe a discipline and rigour that justify the word 'scientific', and yet this is an issue that sees success through moments of inspiration, and through plain trial and error – particularly error! That is to say, it is a game with endless possibilities. Segmentation is often not so much a case of right and wrong choices, but of what you ultimately do with those choices; it is about the rigour and discipline of your application.

What is a segment?

When you are next standing at the soap powder aisle in the supermarket, or marvelling at the choice of restaurants in a busy city centre, just stop to consider why there are so many in each case. Why not one soap powder for all? Why are the people evenly spread across the restaurants instead of all piled into one? The answer is segmentation. Each offer, powder or restaurant is targeted at its own chosen clientele, and, as a result, manages to meet that particular audience's needs better than any other.

This is the start of a definition: a market segment is a group of customers with similar needs. But there is more. If we only looked at needs, we would be limiting our options. We all _need_ food; so on that basis there is only one segment in the food market. Of course there are many more than one, perhaps hundreds, because although we all need food, we display an amazing array of _attitudes_ to the stuff, and exhibit an equally large range of _behaviours_ when buying and using it. It is the combination of needs, attitudes and behaviours that determines a segment: a group of customers who exhibit broadly similar needs, attitudes and behaviours.

Looking at the food market, we can easily identify the following potential segments based on considerations of needs, attitudes and behaviours:

- eating out: restaurants, cafés, fast food, food on the move, vending;
- eating in: breakfast, lunch, dinner, entertaining, barbecues…;
- business: canteens, hotels, institutions, catering, airlines…;
- retail: supermarkets, wholesalers, cash and carry, delicatessens…;
- branding: brands, own brand, no brands…;
- health: low sodium, diet, low fat, high fibre…;
- diet: vegetarian, vegan, organic…;
- ethnic: Indian, Chinese, Italian, Moroccan…;
- family: 2.4 kids, single-parent, retired, single…
- experience: cordon bleu, first-time cooks, professionals…

Add to this list the range of food fads, local tastes, traditions, income levels, time to cook, lifestyles and more, and you can see that the list is huge. Two things become clear at this point. First, the capacity to segment a market is almost endless – but that would leave it as an unmanageable mess. Second, segmenting by all these individual factors would result in a very unrealistic picture of the food market. In reality, these facets of behaviour and attitude overlap each other such that they can be consolidated into larger chunks, or market segments. For instance, people who want to cook their own Chinese food to eat at home, but have little knowledge or experience of how to do so, could be a realistic and manageable segment. So could, for example, hospitals that want to have pre-cooked meals prepared to strict dietary specifications for fast reheating on-site.

In any market there will be many different options for grouping customers. Identifying the possible groupings is perhaps the science of segmentation; choosing the best options is the art.

Art _and_ science

The 'viable' segment

The hospital that wants pre-cooked meals to dietary specifications for reheating on-site – that starts to sound like a segment for which an offer could be developed. What we might call a good or a 'viable' segment is one that meets that test and a few more. When identifying a market segment, it should stand up to these questions:

- Is it large enough to justify focused attention?
- Are the customers' needs, attitudes and behaviours similar enough to be aggregated together?
- Are the needs, attitudes and behaviours specific enough to be distinguishable from those of other segments?
- Is it possible to design an appropriate *marketing mix* (the four P's) for the segment?
- Is the segment *reachable*; can it be identified, measured, analysed, communicated to and sold to, *discretely* from other segments?

Positive answers to these questions will suggest that you are looking at a *viable* segment.

WHY SEGMENT? THE STRATEGIC OPTIONS

There is no rule that says you *must* segment your marketplace, nor, if you choose to, to what degree. There are some clear benefits of segmentation (discussed a little later in this chapter), but also some clear demands on your own business capabilities. Consider the three strategic options shown in Figure 15.1.

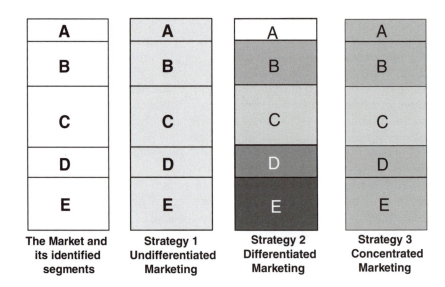

Figure 15.1 *Segmentation: the strategic options*

The market is divided into five potential segments, for which there are three broad strategies, each with its own pros and cons:

- *Strategy 1* ignores the segments, offering a single product to all five (see the 'wonder watch' below). This approach runs the risk of misunderstanding the precise needs of the market, at best forgoing some opportunities, at worst losing competitive advantage to a more tailored approach. On the plus side, if the market will accept a standard offer across all segments there is the potential for economies of scale and lower costs. Many supermarket own labels might appear to follow this strategy, but in fact the supermarket chain itself has targeted specific segments. In the United Kingdom, Waitrose, for instance, is chasing a rather different clientele as compared to Lidl. Very few successful products follow such an undifferentiated approach. Not even supposed commodities such as milk and sugar are untargeted in this way.
- *Strategy 2* recognizes the segments and spreads its risk by participating in all of them. If a business following this strategy is able to manage this many separate offers, it may find itself in a commanding position. If it overstretches its resources, it may find itself losing out to more focused competitors. Kelloggs follows this strategy in the breakfast cereal market (a market with a surprising number of segments identified by the incumbent manufacturers), with a product offer in nearly every segment; from health to fun, kids to energy, traditional to novelty. Its promotional spend is consequently huge (£55 million), but it occupies 8 out of the top 10 positions for breakfast cereals sold in the United Kingdom.
- *Strategy 3* has the strength of focus – expertise, specialism, reputation, etc – but takes the risk of putting all its eggs in one basket. Weetabix is number two in the United Kingdom's top 10 selling breakfast cereals, with a promotional spend of £15 million focused on a product once described as 'a dour, sugarless flaked wheat block that looks like it was designed by the Soviet Cereal Secretariat in 1951'. In fact, Weetabix is the SAS of the breakfast cereal market compared to Kellogg's Red Army.

The SAS of the cereal market

The right choice must depend on the circumstances, the market dynamics and the capabilities of the competing suppliers. If there is a strong demand for low-cost suppliers in the market then Strategy 1 may be the preferred option. The greater the potential for differentiation, the more attractive Strategy 2 or 3 will become.

The 'wonder watch'

Suppose you had just invented the 'wonder watch', a wristwatch that performed well against the whole of the following range of requirements:

- to tell the time;
- jewellery;
- an investment;

- a badge of status;
- fun;
- a fashion accessory;
- a stopwatch;
- a calendar;
- deep-sea diving;
- a gift;
- a calculator;
- and plenty more…

What strategy would you follow? If it really does manage to do all these things (unlikely, I know, but just play along with me) then isn't Strategy 1 the right choice, with all its economies of scale?

The problem will be price. You might be able to sell this watch as an item of jewellery for £100 and as a badge of status for £500, but simply as a means of telling the time, perhaps only for £30. (That is to say, if that is what someone is looking for, that is what he or she would be prepared to pay.) In an open market with no segmentation strategy, the lowest common denominator will win through: £30 for the most incredible watch ever invented.

Strategy 2 looks better, positioning the watch in different segments, but it would be necessary to do a lot of redesign for this to work; it can't be exactly the same watch, and before long you don't have one 'wonder watch' any more but six different products to suit six different sets of needs.

Strategy 3 will force you to focus, perhaps on the segment with the greatest potential for revenue, share, profit – it's up to you – but again it is no longer a 'wonder watch', just a great piece of jewellery, or sports watch, or…

The moral of the story? Perhaps the 'wonder watch' is not such a great idea. The 'one size fits all' approach will lead you down a path of missed opportunity unless the one most important driving force for you and the market is reducing costs through uniformity. Even here, this is segmentation, by omission. You produce a low-cost uniform product, but only certain groups of customers will buy it; the rest will look elsewhere. Perhaps then the real moral of the story is that you can't avoid segmentation, even if you want to!

And then what…? The marketing mix

The marketing mix will be discussed in more detail at the end of this chapter, in the section on positioning. For the moment, suffice it to say that each segment must be serviced by and managed through its own unique *marketing mix* made up of the four P's: product, price, place and promotion.

BENEFITS OF SEGMENTATION

There are many benefits to be had from good segmentation:

- an enhanced understanding of the market dynamics, particularly the notion of the market chain running right through to the end consumer;
- an enhanced understanding of competitor strengths (the competition will differ by segment), and so the opportunities for competitive advantage;
- greater understanding of the needs, attitudes and behaviours of customers;
- a better chance that you will see how to develop the capabilities of your business in order to match those needs;
- a basis for organizing and structuring your business – focusing the whole supply chain on the customer;
- improving your ability to manage the marketing mix in a customer-focused way;
- enhancing your opportunity to add value, gain competitive advantage, and build barriers to entry for competitors or substitutes;
- enhancing your opportunity to create, maintain and defend price premiums.

Always remember you are doing this in order to focus your limited resources on those areas of the market where you will have the best match between your capabilities and the customers' needs – the best opportunities for competitive advantage. It doesn't mean that you will necessarily turn business away if it appears outside these areas, simply that you will be able to determine your priorities more clearly when faced with any choices.

'Wool is only wool if you let it'

The recent story of the Australian wool market is a nice example of how segmentation can be used in a mature and challenging market, in pursuit of a price premium. Synthetic materials have been slowly replacing wool for many years, and prices have been in what looked like terminal decline. The search began for segments that would offer price premiums, and the answer has been high fashion.

The demands in this segment are for lighter-weight fabrics with close-to-the-skin comfort, perfect for fine and superfine grades of wool. Interestingly, before this segmentation began to be pursued in practice, the prices of both 'broad' and 'fine' wool were falling together, dropping by 1998 to 35 per cent below the base of 1995. Since that time, and the implementation of segmentation strategies, the two grades have seen prices diverge – broad wool falling further, to 40 per cent below the 1995 base, with fine wool recovering to +15 per cent on 1995 prices. At October 1998, superfine wool stood at A $7 per kilogram; by Q1 2000 it was A $20, showing a 140 per cent premium over broad wool.

The Australian wool industry is still in difficulty – supply outstrips demand, and prices for broad wool are still in decline – but segmentation has at least allowed suppliers to find some prospect of better prices, and suppliers are starting to shift their emphasis towards more fine and superfine production.

There have even been cases of farmers keeping their fleeces locked in bank vaults, so high is the possible price for the absolute finest grades.

THE SEGMENTATION PROCESS

Discipline is required in an area with so much choice, to ensure that good options are not missed and, more importantly, to ensure that we do better than accepting what already exists...

There are three principal steps:

1. **Identifying the criteria for segmentation**:
    – market mapping;
    – opportunity analysis;
    – leverage points;
    – who buys, what, how, when, and where?
    – some common (and not so common) criteria...
2. **Targeting – the selection of segments**:
    – the Directional Policy Matrix:
        – attractiveness;
        – resources and capability.
3. **Positioning**:
    – the marketing mix;
    – perceptual mapping.

STEP 1: IDENTIFYING THE CRITERIA FOR SEGMENTATION

Market mapping

A good start will be to draw up a *market map*. This is a diagram illustrating all the routes to market for your product or service – what the marketer calls the *market channels*. The example shown in Figure 15.2 shows the main routes (much simplified) for a manufacturer of adhesives: specialist, industrial and consumer.

The map presents in the broadest sense some options and choices for segmentation. If it is to be useful in this process, you must be careful to include *all* channels, and not just those used by your own business. Start with the full picture and you reduce the risk of lulling yourself into a false sense of security.

The next stage is to focus in on the best possible means of segmentation.

Opportunity analysis

● Note the size of the market and the percentage of sales at each 'junction' along the different channels. This will normally be done as percentages of sales volume, although using sales value or profit may be more illuminating.

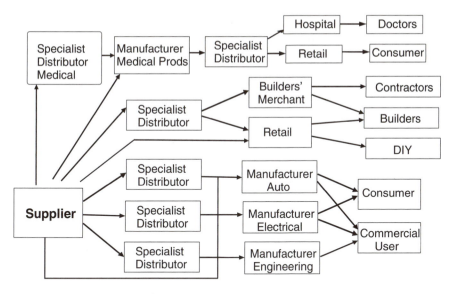

Figure 15.2 _The market map_

- Note the size of your own business, and the percentage share, at the same points.
- Note your competitors' size and shares at the same points.

Doing this will help you to compare your historical performance to the total opportunity, and who you are up against in each area. To repeat, the segmentation process must start with the whole market, not just your own sales, otherwise, not only might you miss opportunities, but you will ignore potential threats.

Leverage points

Where to segment? There are many choices, each with its pros and cons. At this point, statistics will get us only so far; we must now engage our brains.

Examine the market map for what we will call _leverage points_. These are points in the chain where critical purchasing decisions are made. Decisions are made at every point, but where are the big ones: the _fors_ and the _againsts_, to buy or not to buy?

- Are decisions made globally, regionally or locally?
- Do distributors make the choice to present your products to the market, or do they simply service demand?
- Is it the players along the channel that make the important choices, or the end user?
- When looking at distributors as leverage points, are you in competition simply with direct alternatives to your offer, or must you also persuade

distributors to give time and attention to you in preference to unrelated products that might have more attractive margins, or might be easier to sell?

Push or pull?

If your product has a strong reputation, a good brand name and a decent market share then you might expect to be in 'pull' marketing. Your efforts in the marketplace create a demand that pulls customers into the channel of supply. Without such reputation and market position, you will be more used to 'push' marketing: persuading the channels of supply to take your products and sell them on to the next step using their own efforts.

With a pull strategy, segmenting by end user may work for you, while the push strategy may find more success segmenting somewhere in the distribution channel. The choice must depend on who has the most influence on the sale being made.

Who buys, what, how, when and where?

A market never bought anything – it always turns out to be people! We must aim to understand the buying habits of people at each junction, and of each potential grouping of customers, particularly if we aim to segment by end user or consumer.

Returning to the adhesive supplier's market map, we can identify three distinct market segments, and we can also identify the most significant leverage point along the channel to market in each case, by understanding the balance of push and pull in each case, and by looking closely at purchasing behaviours along the chain. This is shown in Figure 15.3.

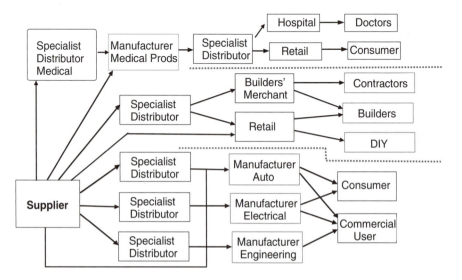

Figure 15.3 *Leverage points in the market map*

1. The _medical market_ – where the adhesive is used in the construction of syringes. It is unlikely that end users, whether regarded as hospital, doctors or patients, can be made to care much about the nature of the adhesive used. If the adhesive allowed a certain construction of syringe that benefited a certain use, then maybe a pull strategy could be employed, but it is a very long shot, and in reality we must recognize that it is the manufacturer of the syringes that has most influence over the choice of materials. Buyers here have some very precise specifications for the product, and expect a good deal of help from suppliers in delivering bespoke solutions. They buy in large quantities, with long-term contracts. They are _'technical spec'_ buyers, to whom price is of less significance than quality and security of supply.

Different channels, different buyers

2. The _building and DIY market_ – where there is far more to be achieved by trying to influence the choice at the end of the channel. It should not be assumed, of course, that professional builders and DIY users share the same needs, attitudes or behaviours; they represent at least two distinct segments. DIY users have little or no expertise, want something 'dependable' and are heavily influenced in this respect by branding and advertising. They buy in small quantities, irregularly, and want to find the product in DIY superstores. They are no-hassle _'convenience buyers'_. Professional users are very different in almost every respect – though don't suppose the badge 'professional' means they are not influenced by brands and advertising. Such users develop strong loyalties over time. They may be termed _'tradition and heritage buyers'_.

3. The _industrial and specialist use market_ – is this push or pull? Is it the distributor or the user who decides, or can be made to decide? We need to explore the nature of the purchase further, and we find that the specialist distributors have built up reputations for service and advice, acting as consultants for the varied projects and uses of their customers. Distributors need a range of products to meet the spectrum of demand, and want buying terms that give them a large enough margin to justify the technical support they offer to customers. They are _'commercial buyers'_.

Three very distinct segments, at three very different points along the channels to market, each requiring a very distinct offer (see 'Segmentation and the marketing mix', page 148).

Some common criteria, business to business (B2B)

Table 15.1 summarizes 10 typical criteria for segmentation in a B2B environment, grouped into three main types or characteristics.

Table 15.1   *Criteria for B2B segmentation*

Organizational Characteristics	Industry type Size of firm Geographic location
Product Characteristics	End-use benefits Frequency and scale of purchase Specification
Buying Characteristics	Distribution channel Purchasing function and policy Buyer characteristics Lead influence on purchase

The paints example

ICI Dulux used a range of criteria like these to assess the trade market for Dulux paint. Its marketers had identified, among others, two potential segments deserving of more attention: the small firm of decorators and the major contractor firm. They compared the two segments against the criteria summarized in Table 15.2.

Table 15.2   *Segmentation: trade paint*

Base	Major Contractor	Small Decorator Firm
Size of firm	200+	1–5
Size of purchase	Industrial scale, larger pack size	Domestic scale, smaller pack size
Specification	Professional	From client, usually a homeowner
Distribution channel	Direct from supplier	Builders' or decorators' merchant
Purchasing function	Professional buyer direct to supplier	Owner/manager through merchant
Lead influence on purchase decision	Price and cost analysis	Client specification and brand loyalty

Segments and brands

Finding the two segments to be so very different, they concluded that not only were two distinct marketing mixes called for, but two separate brands must be used. A new brand was launched to target the major contractor segment, Glidden Paint, with Dulux Trade targeting the smaller decorator firms.

When they looked at buying behaviour in particular, they found that the brand loyalty of self-employed professional decorators and the influence of their client (a brand-aware homeowner) made the use of the Dulux brand a must. The buyer for the major contractor demanded cost reductions that would have compromised the main brand had it attempted to work in both segments. A new brand was the perfect solution, and one already existed in the world group (Glidden was the main ICI paint brand in the United States).

The nesting concept

Developed by Benson P Shapiro and Thomas V Bonoma, the nesting concept aims to help work through the complexity and range of criteria by suggesting a hierarchy, as shown in Figure 15.4.

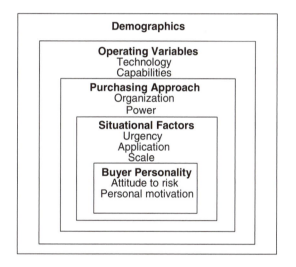

Figure 15.4 *The nesting concept*
Source: Benson P Shapiro and Thomas V Bonoma, How to segment industrial markets, *Harvard Business Review* (May–June 1984)

The model suggests that demographics provides the starting point, and the most basic criteria on which to segment, but that within that basis are four further levels of increasing specificity. First come the operating variables, such as the client's technology, its capabilities, its use of products and brands. The nest within that nest looks at purchasing approaches – the way that clients buy. Next come situational factors: the product application, the urgency, the scale. Finally come the buyer's personality, attitude to risk, motivation, etc.

A general observation can be made that the closer to the central nest you get in your attempts to segment the market, the harder the task becomes in practice, but should you succeed, the more likely you are to find a unique basis that will give you competitive advantage.

No pain, no gain

Novel segmentation

There is a problem with using the most obvious way to segment a market: your competitors are probably seeing things just the same, and where's the competitive advantage in that? The pursuit of novel ways to segment (provided they pass the 'viability' test – see page 127) will often unearth new understanding of the dynamics of the marketplace and gain you significant competitive advantage. It is well worth the time, and the trial and error, to find such methods. Here are two such examples.

'When you finally realize that it's not East Anglia that buys your product, but farmers; then you're on to something'

A fertilizer manufacturer found its product to be in slow decline in a mature market. It decided to segment as a means to finding new offers, testing first the more obvious 'cuts': crop type, geography, seasonality, etc. Finally it hit on the simple truth noted earlier in this chapter: wheat didn't buy fertilizer, and nor did East Anglia; it was farmers every time!

Farmers came from different backgrounds and had widely differing attitudes, aspirations and buying behaviours. Once the manufacturer started to explore these factors, it began to understand (almost for the first time) what *really* made people buy its product, or not. The final segmentation was done on the basis of attitudes and needs, the traditional family farmer for instance having a rather different outlook as compared with the graduate of an agricultural college managing a large estate.

Division of the market into seven segments allowed the business to prioritize its attentions on those that would respond best to its own strengths. The resultant marketing mixes helped the manufacturer target its product better, add more relevant value, structure its own operations to suit customers' needs, and gain a significant increase in revenues and profits. The resultant 'types' are illustrated in Figure 15.5.

Figure 15.5 *Farmer 'types', used in segmentation of the market for fertilizer*

A supplier of compounds to the pharmaceutical industry had segmented for some time by therapeutic area: there was an asthma segment, a heart segment, a cancer segment, etc. This really did very little for the supplier, as not only did every one of its competitors do the same, but it found the behaviour and attitudes of separate customers to be quite different even in the same segment. What it found (with hard-won experience) was that it was not so much the therapeutic area that determined behaviour as the phase of development that the drug was at.

A drug must pass through a series of checkpoints on its way from research to market, including efficacy tests, trials, and regulatory approvals, and these fall into four distinct phases. A pharmaceutical company will have rather different concerns and needs moving from one phase to the next, but they are quite precise and uniform within a single phase, providing an excellent opportunity for segmentation for the observant supplier.

At the earliest stage, the pharmaceutical companies want speed and flexibility from suppliers, with price and quality some way down the list. As the development proceeds, the requirement changes to a greater need for quality and reliability, and then an absolute ability to gain regulatory approval, and finally to issues of scale, capacity, and the reduction of production costs. The supplier was able to identify these stages, or phases, as quite discrete segments, based on specification requirement, and develop offers that met the needs, attitudes and behaviours almost regardless of drug type.

Not what, but when…

It hardly needs saying that Monsanto has had a rough ride over GM foods. In part we can see some reasons why, from its choice and management of its target segments. Monsanto segmented by farmers – the benefits of GM were largely for farmers – and so the communication of the benefits of GM foods was put to farmers. Of course, there was a market chain that ran down to the consumer, through food producers and retailers, and the consumer was far from convinced. Consumers buy products, not technologies, and with large doses of hindsight we can see how Monsanto compounded its problem by promoting the technology as a means of communicating the benefits to farmers.

Compare this scenario to the success enjoyed by Zeneca with a GM tomato used in the manufacture of tomato paste. The GM tomato had significant consumer benefits: a superior taste as it clung to the taste buds, and a superior coating ability for things such as pasta.

It is an increasingly recognized truth that most value in the chain is usually added closest to the consumer, and if GM suppliers are to break through the barrier of GM resistance, they will need to develop and communicate genuine consumer benefits. Some are just on that line, seeking for instance to 'find a food that prevents osteoporosis' – a headline from a Du Pont advertisement in its 'To do list for the planet' range.

There is such a temptation in B2B environments to segment by your own products that I will close this section with a reminder to avoid that particular sin. Let's consider four choices for the basis of segmentation:

At all costs, try to avoid the cardinal sin: segmenting by _your_ products

- your own products;
- your own technologies;
- the customers' applications;
- the customers themselves.

The first two are to be avoided: they are inward focused and unlikely to find you a group of customers sharing similar needs, attitudes and behaviours.

The customers' applications are a much better basis on which to segment, though you should ask yourself, do all customers who need a product for application X share the same needs, attitudes and behaviours?

The customers themselves come top of the list, from a textbook view, but now I must remember that this is not intended to be a textbook, but rather, a practical guide. Perhaps it is the case that, in most B2B cases, segmentation by the customers' applications is the most practical approach, but if so, I would urge you to take great efforts when considering issues such as key customer management (see Chapter 19) to distinguish sub-segments of customers, distinguished by needs, attitudes and behaviours, within those larger groupings segmented by application.

Some common criteria: consumer/fmcg

Table 15.3 summarizes 10 typical criteria for segmentation in the fmcg environment, grouped into three main types or characteristics.

Table 15.3 *Criteria for consumer segmentation*

Macro Characteristics	Socio-economic
	Demographics
	Age and sex
	Income
Circumstantial Characteristics	Regionality
	Family or household size
	House size/location
Lifestyle Characteristics	Psychographics
	Aspirations
	Rate of adoption

Some of these deserve a little more attention.

Socio-economic classification

Probably the most common method of consumer segmentation in the United Kingdom, and much used by the advertising industry, is the socio-economic classification of A, B, C1, C2, etc. This is an attempt, increasingly crude but nonetheless popular, to classify people on the basis of their social class, status and occupation. It makes certain assumptions about disposable income (that those in class A have higher income than those in class B, and so on), and about discretion and taste (that those in class A are more selective than those in B, etc). Table 15.4 lists the main classifications.

Table 15.4   *Socio-economic classifications*

	Class	**Status**
A	Upper middle	Higher managerial, professional
B	Middle	Middle management, administrative
C1	Lower middle	Supervisory, junior management
C2	Skilled worker	Skilled manual
D	Working	Semi- and unskilled manual
E	Low subsistence	Pensioners, casual, unemployed

The distinctions work as a crude shorthand, but if used on their own could lead to some strange results. For instance, we might find the Pope and David Beckham occupying the same segment... Pensioners, low subsistence? What about those on two-thirds of final salary who have paid off their mortgage and whose kids have flown the nest? Are all semi-skilled and unskilled manual workers the same, and assumed to have low disposable incomes? What about the 18–22 age group, in such jobs but still living at home with few commitments beyond next Friday night? This group has one of the highest disposable incomes in the country!

An out of date and out of touch methodology?

Perhaps better suited to the targeting of communications (hence the advertising industry's continued use of them), the classifications are increasingly suspect as providing any coherent set of needs, attitudes and behaviours – vital for good segmentation.

Demographics

Simple demographics are fast losing their appeal as a basis for segmentation: people aged 25 to 35 are not exactly a coherent group with similar needs, attitudes or behaviours. Marks & Spencer long relied on the 'middle-class' and 'middle-aged' consumer as the yardstick for its positioning. A 54 per cent dip in profits in 1999 forced it into a rethink, including the launch of the Autograph range of clothes targeted not at an age group, but at an 'attitude' or 'lifestyle' group.

Lifestyle characteristics

The past 20 years has seen much attention given to lifestyles in preference to socio-economic classifications. A huge range of terms have arisen, including the Yuppie–Dinky terminology. One such range of terms, even giving a breakdown as percentages of the UK population, is summarized in Table 15.5.

Table 15.5 *Lifestyle segmentation*

Lifestyle	Description	% of pop
Self-explorers	Self-expression and self-realization; reject doctrine in favour of individual awareness; 'spiritual'	15
Social resisters	Caring and altruistic, concerned for society and the environment; can be intolerant	14
Experimentalists	Highly individual, fast-paced enjoyment, materialistic, pro-technology, anti-authority	11
Conspicuous consumers	Acquisitive and competitive, concerned with position and show. Pro-authority and pro-hierarchy	19
Belongers	Conventional, traditional, seeking to fit in. Family orientated and resistant to change	18
Survivors	Class conscious and community spirited. Aiming to 'get by'. Hardworking and apparently happy with their lot.	17
Aimless	a) Young unemployed seeking 'kicks', anti-authority. b) Old, focused on day-to-day existence in trying circumstances	5

Source: Martin Christopher and Malcolm McDonald, *Marketing: An introductory text*, Macmillan, London, 1995

Better, but still too blunt

It is easy to criticize any such listing, particularly out of context, although it does seem that any basis of segmentation that puts a 17-year-old unemployed seeker of 'fun' in the same segment as an elderly couple living on a meagre pension has something to explain. Is a possible explanation (though not an attractive one) that this 5 per cent of the population is what we have come to call an 'underclass', not to be considered a prime target for the marketer?

Using generic lifestyle definitions is always going to lead to problems when faced with the specific circumstance. Much better, if you have the time and the resource, to construct your own distinctions that work in your own market. Such distinctions tend to evolve over time as experience and research hone the analysis. At this point, lifestyle segmentation merges with psychographics: an attempt to map out consumer attitudes, defined by emotions and perceptions.

Psychographics

Having discussed ICI Paints in the B2B environment, we might look at how ICI dealt with the consumer side of its market.

Dulux is an excellent example of a brand that has evolved through changing market circumstances, always keeping in touch with its consumers through a deep understanding of their needs, attitudes and behaviours, and updating its basis of segmentation accordingly.

In the 1960s the boom in DIY was based to a great extent on a raft of new products that were easy to use; Formica led the way, but also Fablon, hardboard, and paints such as Dulux Non Drip Gloss. Segmentation based on product types and product usage was quite appropriate in such a climate, and so it stayed for many years.

Into the 1970s and attitudes were changing. DIY was an established norm and consumers were seeking more: they wanted to transform their homes. Dulux became an aspirational brand, and new segmentation was required. Terms such as _planners_ and _appliers_ evolved, and soon became segments, each needing its own marketing mix, not least because planners had to be targeted early in the decision process, through magazines and TV, while appliers could be targeted in-store, with advice and information.

The more demanding 1980s and 90s saw consumers seeking increasing personalization of their homes. The 'nesting' culture (an updated form of the Englishman's home being his castle, where a desire for personal and private spaces strongly influences attitudes and behaviours) called for another look at segmentation. Planners were not just planners any more. Figure 15.6 gives a diagrammatic description of the new segmentation using psychographic terminology.

FMCG brands must continually remake themselves to survive – segmentation provides a key

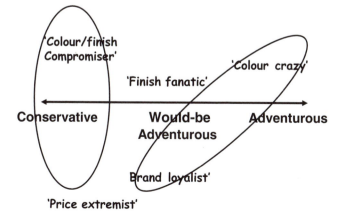

Figure 15.6 _Segmentation for paint consumers_

Consumers are identified as either conservative, would-be adventurous or adventurous in their attitudes to decorating, and their use of paint in particular. Around that spectrum of attitude there are other emotions going on. With regard to the end effect, there are those who want to use colour, those who focus on the finish and those who compromise between the two. Looking at their purchasing behaviour, we can identify those who are brand loyal (usually to Dulux as the brand leader) and those who buy on price (most often the own-label consumer).

Different slices of this spectrum can be seen to be more attractive than others, both in terms of premium pricing and also as allowing a match with Dulux's main capabilities. The brand-loyal colour crazy are prime targets, whereas conservative price buyers are less attractive.

Rate of adoption: the 'adopters curve'

This model is equally applicable to B2B, but we discuss it here, under criteria for fmcg, largely because it is here that it has seen most use.

When a new product is launched, there is usually a vanguard of ardent enthusiasts who jump on board almost regardless of the product's merits. Sometimes it goes no further and the product dies, remembered only as a fad supported by a clique of fanatics; there were certainly a *few* enthusiasts for the Sinclair C5!

If a product is to succeed, it has to go beyond that narrow following and find a wider audience. It has to progress beyond the *innovators* to find the *early adopters*. Everett Rogers captured this concept in his much-quoted 'adopters curve' shown in Figure 15.7. The curve shows how most new products or ideas go through stages of adoption, first by the innovators, a small but enthusiastic group, then by the early adopters, who help make the

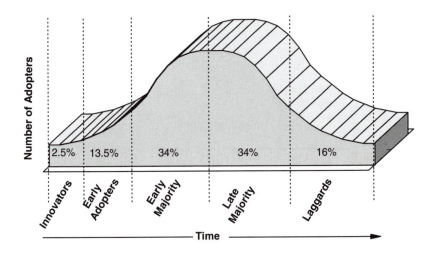

Figure 15.7 *The adopters curve*
Source: Everett Rogers, *Diffusion of Innovations*, 4th edn, Free Press, New York (1995)

product something of wider appeal. The early majority provide the volume sales that drive down costs and turn the product into a mass-market one such that the late majority come sweeping in to buy. Laggards are those who resist till the very end, or perhaps never succumb.

A classic example of such a development is the electronic pocket calculator. At its invention it was bought as an advanced scientific instrument, predominantly by businesses and institutions, doubtless requiring approval by the capital acquisitions committee. It was not long, however, before a new segment of the market opened up, spurred on by government legislation (note PESTLE – see Chapter 9). Once the use of calculators in GCSE maths exams was approved, every little Johnny and every little Jane rushed home to demand that their parents buy them one. They were cumbersome instruments, often with a mind-boggling array of functions from cosines to reciprocals, but this new demand from the _early adopters_ brought prices tumbling down. Before long, the pocket calculator was an established item for businesspeople, and this _early majority_ helped drive prices even lower, until calculators were being given away free as promotional items; the _late majority_ were engaged.

An interesting feature of the model is the role of the innovator – sometimes a positive force, but not infrequently a drag on the market's uptake. The Internet is a case in point. Early users of the Internet were portrayed as 'nerds': sad characters with no social life who sat up late at night surfing the Net in search of other such lost souls. Whether valid or not, this image of the early users served to hold back wider acceptance of the Internet perhaps for as long as two years.

As a model for potential segmentation, the adopters curve holds much promise. A marketer can plan the development of a product through these stages, changing the marketing mix as each new group is targeted. The proposition must be quite different for each group. For innovators, the talk might be of novelty, experimentation, leading edge and trial. Such a proposition would frighten the late majority, just as the innovators would be bored by talk of 'tried and tested' and lengthy evidence of success, such as would appeal to the late majority.

Looking ahead to Step 3: Positioning – the adopters curve spans the process

STEP 2: TARGETING – THE SELECTION OF SEGMENTS

Once you have found the criteria, or basis, for segmentation that best suits your business, the next step in the process is to select those segments that merit targeting. Here we must go back to the Marketing Model described in Chapter 2. The aim of this model is to achieve a match between your capabilities and the needs of the market. It is in part by considering this matching process and finding where it can be done best that we will select our target segments.

The tool we will use is the *Directional Policy Matrix* (DPM), a tool that we will meet again in Chapter 22 when considering the management of a portfolio of products. Here we use it to consider and manage a portfolio of segments.

Figure 15.8 shows a DPM, plotting segments based on two sets of factors:

- Their attractiveness.
- Our likely capability in matching the needs, attitudes and behaviours of those segments. (The classic DPM places *'our relative strengths'* along this axis, meaning, are we better or worse than the competitors, as perceived by our customers? For this purpose, I have substituted that with *'our capability'*.)

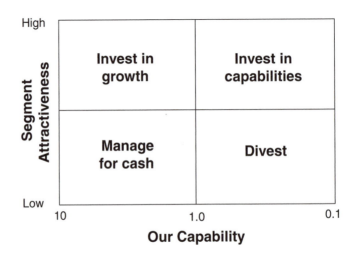

Figure 15.8 *The Directional Policy Matrix: selecting segments*

The DPM is one of the classic matrices, growing out of the famous Boston Box (also see Chapter 22). It can be put to use whenever there is a need to prioritize resources or select targets for investment. Assuming all resources to be finite, and your investment strategy to be based on likely returns, the four boxes suggest different approaches, also indicated in Figure 15.8.

Segment attractiveness

A range of factors should be identified that will determine the attractiveness of the segment to your business. These might include any of the following, or any additional factors that are relevant to your own circumstances:

- size: volume, value, profit opportunity;
- growth potential: volume, value, profit opportunity;

- ease of access;
- opportunity for a match;
- whether they are 'early adopters': do they pick up on new ideas and products, or do they wait until the market has tested them?
- whether they will value your offer;
- level of competition (low being attractive).

Our capability

Again, a range of factors should be identified that will determine your level of capability. These might include any of the following, or any additional factors that are relevant to your own circumstances:

- resources: production capacity, etc;
- ability to differentiate;
- cost levels;
- budget for promotion;
- sales force;
- access to distribution channels;
- image and reputation;
- product quality;
- service levels;
- speed of response.

Using the DPM in practice

Chapter 22 will describe a process for scoring the items under consideration (in this case segments; in Chapter 22 it is products) against these two sets of factors – attractiveness and capabilities – and so placing them on the matrix. The DPM is a tool to aid decision making; it doesn't make the decisions for you, and the labels on the matrix – invest, divest, manage for cash – are only suggestive of your chosen strategy.

Trial the DPM on this book's CD ROM

(The CD ROM attached to this book contains a simple DPM tool that can be used to plot your segment options.)

STEP 3: POSITIONING

Having chosen, we must now 'make our case' to the members of those segments – why us? We do this by deploying the _marketing mix_ (the four P's), so aiming to develop a unique offer against each segment – our _proposition_. If different segments are managed through the same mix then we should be asking the question: are these actually different segments or are we positioning ourselves (in one, or perhaps both) with the wrong proposition?

The Proposition

Segmentation and the marketing mix

The *marketing mix* is that range of tools, or levers, used by marketers to influence demand and gain competitive advantage. There are four levers: *product, place, promotion* and *price*, traditionally known as the 'four P's' and shown in Figure 15.9.

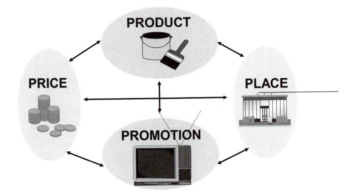

Figure 15.9   *The marketing mix*

Demand is influenced by the total mix, each of the four P's working in relation to one another:

● product: the range, quality, packaging, after-sales service, etc;
● price: premium, discounted, purchasing terms, etc;
● promotion: communication of the offer to the customer – advertising, PR, sales force, etc;
● place: the route to market – distribution channels (direct, retail, wholesale, etc).

Not only do the four P's interact with each other, they must balance with each other for a successful mix. New product launches are particularly prone to *misfits* in the mix.

From misfit to sixties icon...   When Babycham was first launched, the product, promotion and place were well thought out, but the price was too low. This was a drink ('fake' champagne) that men bought for their girlfriends to impress them (remember, this was back in the 1950s!). But at such a low price, who was going to be impressed? The product was relaunched at a suitably ego-enhancing price and remains one of the icons of a different world.

... and nineties icon   When Land Rover launched the Range Rover, it was *place* that was out of step. Customers had to go to traditional Land Rover dealers for this new, upmarket, premium-priced product. Having responded well to the adverts, they sometimes found themselves trudging down a muddy track to a showroom that exuded all the imagery of agricultural machinery…

The 'proposition'

Each segment will require its own particular mix. Indeed, if it didn't, that segment would probably not be a 'viable' one as defined by our test questions above. The sum total of this mix is what many would call the *proposition*: the reason a customer should buy your product or use your service.

The proposition may well emphasize one element of the mix more than the others: the lowest price, the most widely available, the best known, the most reliable – what marketers call a 'single-minded proposition'. This doesn't mean the other elements don't count; the most reliable product should be sold at a premium through channels that are also reliable (it wouldn't do much for the credibility of such a product to be sold through 'Crazy Mikey's Discount Heaven'). The lowest-price offer may need heavy promotion to generate the volume required to keep cost down, and the channels of supply will need to be mass market – and so it goes on.

By preparing a different and specific marketing mix for each segment, the business ensures that it will meet the needs of each grouping of customers in a more focused way. At the same time, it enhances its opportunity for maximizing profits through premium pricing, or differentiation, or the offer of a lowest-cost option – whatever the dynamics of the particular segment demands.

The airline industry provides an excellent example, and Table 15.6 shows a much-simplified summary of its 'outline' segmentation. Customers are divided into classes: First, Business, Economy and Standby, each with its own needs, attitudes and behaviours. They are similar enough *within* the class for aggregation, and different enough from the next for discrete

Table 15.6 *Outline segmentation in the airline industry*

	Product	Price	Promotion	Place
First	Luxury / ego	€6,000	Direct to 'club' members	Direct
Business	Priority / flexibility	€2,800	Business journals	Company on-site travel agents
Economy	Standard	€850	Press, magazines	Travel agents
Standby	'Risk'	€250	Ceefax, Internet, 'small ads'	Internet, airport desk

treatment through four different marketing mixes. The result? On a flight from London to New York, passengers will be paying anything from 200 to 6,000 euros for the same seven-hour flight!

Of course, it isn't the same *flight* at all, even though the passengers might take off and land together. The four classes have paid different rates because they sought different things. Standby passengers have a different attitude to risk from that of business travellers: they are happy to purchase a degree of risk (they might not go!) for a discount. First-class travellers may behave differently in their purchase of the ticket as compared with economy travellers: they may have a regular journey that the airline 'manages' for them, while economy travellers prefer to shop around.

Beyond this outline there are segments within segments (sub-segments) and endless potential for variants and micro-segmentation (in theory, micro-segmentation could consider each passenger as an individual segment), but this outline makes the point well enough about the opportunity for different pricing and rewards based on different offers and cost structures.

Times change, and so must propositions

Positioning must reflect the dynamics in the market, and as those dynamics change, so must the proposition.

Chemist, pamper parlour, or unofficial adjunct to the NHS? Boots marches on...

Boots the chemist has been more than just a chemist for some time, and after many years of moving towards a kind of variety store, Boots is repositioning itself into the service sector, with in-store opticians, dentists and chiropodists. In part this is a continuation of the shift from chemist to 'pamper parlour', but it also sees Boots taking on (from the beleaguered National Health Service) a new role in auxiliary health care. This new positioning is one that its existing brand strengths, based on responsibility, trust and confidence, make particularly attractive.

Perception is all: perceptual mapping

Segments are made up of people with similar needs, attitudes and behaviours. Those attitudes, in particular, can take us away from the world of facts (and logic), and into the world of perceptions.

Customers' perceptions often have a way of differing from the suppliers' views – and you can guess which are the ones to care about! Clive Sinclair (now Sir Clive) had a clear view of his Sinclair C5: an energy-efficient, environmentally friendly, low-cost means of transport. His potential customers saw it as a death trap. Predictor, the self-use pregnancy testing kit, has tried hard through its promotional messages to stress the positive, not to say joyous, results of its use, but there are still large numbers of people (particularly students!) who regard it as something that you use to discover the worst.

As with all communications, the message _received_ is of more significance than the message _sent_, and this is a vital truth to remember when seeking to position your product or service in the chosen segment. The four P's will help you to determine the elements of your proposition, but we need to turn to the idea of perceptual mapping to help ensure that we actually occupy the space in people's minds that we intend.

Figure 15.10 shows one of a variety of possible perceptual maps for the motorcar market. This particular one looks at two factors, price and performance, comparing a sample of makes and models based on consumer opinion in a particular segment. It is very important to remember that this map does not show _actual_ positions as based on any comparisons of list price and technical specifications; it represents the perceptions of a particular group of customers. Facts may argue another case entirely, but it is perceptions that lead to people spending their money as they do.

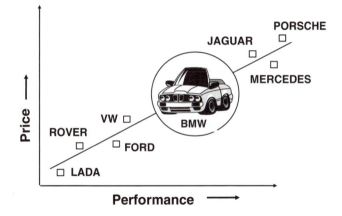

Figure 15.10 _Perceptual mapping_

The perceptual map can be used in a number of ways. As here, it is used to assess where target customers place your proposition and to compare that with your intended proposition. Another use would be to plot the competition and to look for any 'gaps' in the map. Such gaps may be opportunities for you to offer a unique proposition. BMW was arguably the first manufacturer to position a middle-price, mid-sized, high-performance car (perceived), exploiting a gap that had stood open between the likes of Ford and Vauxhall on the one hand and Porsche and Ferrari on the other. Exploring the 'white space' of such maps can be fruitful ground for identifying segments, as well as positioning the offer.

Trial and error (again!) of various permutations of factors (for there is more to choosing a car than price and performance) will help to identify a range of options for segments, and to assess the current positioning of competitors, and so the opportunity for a unique positioning.

SEGMENTATION AND MARKET RESEARCH

The last thing to say about segmentation is something that must by now be abundantly clear: the more you know about your market, the more powerful will be your method of segmentation and the more effective your positioning. Market research is vital unless you are to rely on gut feel and inspiration. Quantitative data will be required for the market mapping exercise, and after that, qualitative data will be required as you delve further into customers' attitudes, behaviours and perceptions. The search for the right basis for segmentation will in fact help to highlight the sorts of questions that you should be asking. As the search progresses, you will uncover more and more that you just don't know.

Don't despair, this is good (!), provided that you have both the motivation and the budget to seek better understanding as a result. Time and money are issues here, and we are of course back to the basics of the marketing model: company capabilities. How many segments you can operate in will, in the final analysis, depend as much as anything else on how many you have the ability to understand.

16

Branding

To brand or not to brand? We are talking here not of logos and slogans, but of genuine exercises in branding. This chapter will consider three strategic issues surrounding branding:

1. brand architecture;
2. brand positioning;
3. valuing the brand.

Chapter 20 will look at the details of brand management on a tactical level.

But first, why does branding matter? The answers to that could fill an entire book, and many thousands have been written on this very theme. I will mention just three reasons:

- Branding improves profitability.
- Branding builds loyalty.
- Branding reduces risk.

Branding and profitability

Research by PIMS (Profit Impact of Market Strategies) shows that in the UK food market the number one food brand in any particular sector has an average profit margin of 18 per cent while the number two brand has an average of only 4 per cent. Remember that these are averages: many number two brands run at a loss. Not surprisingly, a good number of these number two brands have withdrawn from the game.

These figures suggest that in the food business at least, it is not branding *per se* that is profitable, but *successful* branding, and in this market that means being the brand leader. In other markets there is still room for a multiplicity of brands, but being the biggest often helps.

Table 16.1 shows the average return on investment (ROI) assessed across 3,000 diverse UK businesses, looking at how they stood in terms of market share (brand strength) and quality.

Table 16.1 *PIMS research on brands and return on investment*

	Low Quality	Medium Quality	High Quality
High market share	21.00	25.00	38.00
Medium market share	14.00	20.00	27.00
Low market share	7.00	13.00	20.00

These figures alone are by no means conclusive, but they suggest some truths that other pieces of evidence would give backing to: investing in brands to gain market share is as rewarding as investing in the product to improve quality, and if a good-quality product also has a good brand standing, it will be even more likely to return good profits. Strong brands tend to return good profits for a variety of reasons:

- Top brands command premium prices.
- Winning new customers is easier and so less costly.
- Good brands win customer loyalty, and loyal customers will cost less to retain and service.
- A strong brand gives negotiating power to the supplier.
- High market share gives you presence in the market, and that brings knowledge, and that allows vision, and that facilitates an ability to change (but only if you choose to learn).
- A good brand evidences a unique match between company capabilities and market needs. A good brand is therefore an expression of competitive advantage.

Branding and loyalty

Consider three alternatives to branding, in the attempt to win customer loyalty:

- *Monopoly*. Loyalty does not result from monopoly; watch how customers will jump ship, almost regardless of the relative merits of the new offer, when a new player enters the field previously held by a monopoly: British Gas and its industrial customers, British Telecom and the new wave of providers, IBM and the PC story.

- *Bribery*. Loyalty does not result from bribery: retailer loyalty cards, credit card membership reward schemes, air miles. This is bribery, and when the bribe is withdrawn or the novelty wears off, the customer looks elsewhere.
- *Discounting*. Loyalty does not result from discounting. Many studies have shown that when consumers buy a 'cheaper' product on a price basis, they still yearn to buy the higher-priced, big-brand-name alternative, but money won out this time – but just wait until they win the lottery…

True loyalty results from the relationship between the supplier and the customer, and the brand is a vital vehicle for defining and managing that relationship. Sure, branding is an expensive thing, but just consider for a moment the costs of winning loyalty through the kind of alternatives considered above.

Branding and risk management: the brand 'halo'

Chapter 12 showed how risk increases as a business moves from a growth strategy based on penetration into one based on market extension, or the yet more risky territory of new product development, or beyond that, diversification. The moral of the Ansoff matrix was not that you should avoid growth strategies based on anything but penetration, but that you should aim to reduce the risks of other strategies by whatever means appropriate. Branding is one of the most successful strategies in such a pursuit.

Virgin's halo (that's around the brand; it's not yet Saint Richard)

Virgin has diversified its business activities more often, and at a faster pace, than almost any other company in business history, and yet it handsomely beat Ansoff's forecasted 15 per cent success rate. The answer lies in the way it does its market research (thoroughly), the way it works with experts (particularly suppliers) and the way it uses its brand. Each new Virgin activity benefits from the success of the ones that went before. People wanted to buy Virgin's PEPs (personal equity plans) because they had been impressed by the way Virgin ran its airline, or they liked Virgin cola, or they liked Richard Branson. Virgin has enjoyed the effects and benefits of the *brand halo*.

The brand halo works as it sounds: providing a prefabricated protective surround to the new venture, so easing its way, even when the new venture might be as unconnected from the previous ones as cola is from airlines or mobile phones are from trains. The halo effect allows the marketer to infuse the new venture with the brand values (hopefully saintly ones!) of the existing ventures.

So, after that short validation of the art and science of branding, back to the three strategic issues: brand architecture, brand positioning and valuing the brand.

BRAND ARCHITECTURE: PUTTING IT ALL TOGETHER

Almost anything can be branded: products, services, people, places, even ideas. If that is so – and most companies have more than one product or service, plenty of people and lots of ideas – then how are we to avoid an overwhelming and ultimately damaging cacophony of brands, each shouting over the other? There is a need for some order and method, and this is what we mean by the term *brand architecture*.

Brands are used in an amazing variety of configurations. Kit-Kat is a brand, but so too is Nestlé, its owner, and so we have Nestlé Kit-Kat. Does that combination of brand names strengthen or diminish Kit-Kat as a brand? Sarsons is a brand (remember 'Don't say vinegar, say Sarsons'?), and so is Crosse & Blackwell, under whose umbrella Sarsons is marketed, and so is Nestlé, which owns Crosse & Blackwell. So do we have Nestlé Crosse & Blackwell Sarsons, and if so, what does that do for us?

Unilever has over 1,500 different brands in use around the world, most of which we would not identify with the parent company, whereas almost everything that Microsoft does (and we can include alongside Microsoft the likes of Virgin, Mitsubishi, Yamaha or Shell) goes under the same *corporate* name.

The need for a variety of architectures

Brand architecture is the study of these different configurations, but before we describe some of the principal 'designs', we should ask why there is a need for these different approaches. Such an understanding will help us to avoid the jerry-built results of poor architectural design. Brands can be strengthened or weakened as a result of their place in the grand design.

Let's take as our starting point a company with a number of existing brands and some potential new ones in the pipeline. It faces the question, should these brands be developed as independent entities, or might they benefit from being built into a more uniform architecture?

The matrix shown in Figure 16.1 (developed from a concept introduced by Professor Peter Doyle to consider the desirability of building corporate brands) will help us to answer this question.

The vertical axis asks whether the target markets are broadly similar to each other or display significant differences. The key to sameness or difference is usually to be found in the behaviours and attitudes of the target customers.

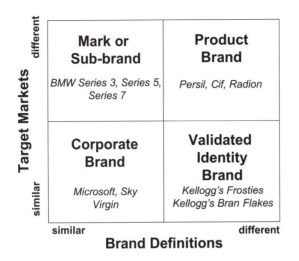

Figure 16.1 *Brand architecture (after Peter Doyle)*

The horizontal axis asks whether the values expressed by each brand definition (see 'positioning', page 147) are broadly similar to each other or whether they display significant differences.

Where markets are alike, and brand definitions share the same values, that is where the greatest scope for corporate branding lies, with all its benefits of efficiency and economies of scale. Where there is no similarity between markets, and the brand values are quite distinct for each proposition, then there will be a greater need for unique *product brands*.

There are two other options shown in this matrix, to be discussed in the following pages: what we will call the *validated identity brand* and the *sub-brand* or *mark*.

Why does this matter?

Think of the brand as a personality (an idea to be developed in Chapter 20). Would you expect one individual to be equally convincing in front of audiences with widely differing expectations? Can the same comedian, with the same act, get the same laughs from a working man's club in Wigan and a vicarage garden party in Esher? You wouldn't think of booking the same turn for both occasions, so why do we sometimes expect as much from our brands? How would you feel about receiving as a gift a nice box of Boeing chocolates? Not *too* bad? So how about flying to Australia on a Cadbury 747?

Sometimes, imposing a corporate brand or a validated identity brand could seriously limit the potential of a product brand or a new product launch.

Ford struggled for years to move into the higher-priced luxury end of the car market and ultimately found it easier to buy Jaguar in order to achieve its aims. Rebadging the

Who'd buy a Jaguar...

... if it was called a Ford?

Jaguar as a Ford would have been a disaster. The high *emotional charge* (see Chapter 20) of car brands makes them a particularly interesting case in this debate. Toyota chose to launch its new quality car under the Lexus brand; Honda chose to create the Acura brand, because the target markets were sufficiently different from its current ones, and its planned brand definitions were also very different.

Product brands

Persil, Cif and Radion – three of Unilever's brands, all three positioned in the same market, and each standing independent of each other and of any Unilever mantle. Some might think this inefficient, but each brand targets a unique customer group – a segment – and so each brand has a unique definition. This is so fundamental to the strength of a brand, its evidencing of a unique match between capabilities and customer needs, that any pursuers of business efficiency through brand consolidation should be very cautious before they act to destroy such value, often built over many years.

A few years back, I could eat out at Whitbread, or Whitbread, or Whitbread...

Walking round my home town one summer evening a few years ago, I counted eight different restaurant brands all owned by the same parent: Whitbread. There was a Pizza Hut, a Pizzaland, Dome, TGI Friday's, Costa Coffee, Jim Thompson's Spice Island Trading, a Beefeater and a Brewers Fayre. Most of their clientele would not know the link, and why should they? What advantage would Whitbread have gained from that? The people in each restaurant were quite different, a credit to Whitbread's ability to link segmentation with branding. There would have been room for only one Whitbread-branded restaurant in the town, and then anyone of my age would probably mistake it for a pub!

Sub-brands and marks

Where a supplier has different products placed in different and distinct markets but wishes to share some common values across them, or to transfer the values from an existing product to a new one, then the use of a sub-brand architecture can work well. This is quite typical in the car market, where the essential values that define the brand are appreciated by all its customers, but some of them want a small car, others a medium car and yet others a luxury model. Hence the BMW Series 3, 5 and 7 – different *marks* of the same brand.

Validated identity brands

Some product brands choose to make more of their parent company's name: Kellogg's Frosties, Kellogg's Bran Flakes, Kellogg's Rice Krispies, etc. Different from pure product brands, these are sometimes called *family* brands, *umbrella* brands or *validated identity* brands, and this last name suggests the purpose. Individual product brands can be given greater authority by making it clear whose stable they come from. Kellogg's provides a protective umbrella to product brands that might not stand up so well on their own – would Pop Tarts have been launched as successfully without such a validated identity? And how about corn flakes? Such a common name or simple descriptor of a product is hard to register as a brand in the legal sense, but putting it under a validated identity 'umbrella' means that Kellogg's Corn Flakes becomes a brand that stands out from its paler imitators.

An important point here is that the validated identity approach can work well when all the products under the umbrella are in the same or similar markets – in this case, breakfast cereals. But what if we go beyond that? How would we feel about Kellogg's bathroom scourer? It can be done, of course, but we are moving into a different kind of brand architecture here, to be discussed later: *corporate* branding.

When does a product brand become a validated identity brand? The dividing line is not clear, but it might be said that if the company name is bigger or better known, or carries more value, than the product brand name, then that's a validated identity brand. Persil is not such a brand. Lever's name may appear on the box, but it is not Lever's Persil; it's just Persil. The question for the brand manager is, will attaching the company name enhance or diminish the brand?

Validated identity, or sub-branding?

When Nestlé purchased Rowntree and so acquired the Kit-Kat brand, it quickly put its own name in place of Rowntree's. Many accused Nestlé of throwing away value built over decades, but it simply believed that Kit-Kat had sufficient value that was separate from its old parent, and that Nestlé provided just as good a validation as Rowntree, as well as offering savings through uniformity and efficiency. Many might still beg to differ.

And how about this one: sub-brands or validated identity brands? Paint is not just paint: there is paint for inside, for outside, for wood, for metal, and so the list goes on. The end uses (markets) are very different, but the one paint manufacturer may want to establish a commonality between all its products across its markets – hence Dulux Weathershield, for outside masonry, and Dulux Satinwood, for interior woodwork…

Corporate brands

One of the most contentious issues in branding over recent years has been the value, or otherwise, of the corporate brand. There are four broad arguments:

- that this is simply an exercise in corporate egotism that has little value for the brand or for the customer;
- that huge cost savings can be had through corporate branding (but beware of handing the management of your brands over to the accountants);

- that this is a matter of culture, and some believe that culture can be changed;
- that some very positive synergies are to be had when uniform corporate values can be applied across a range of different products, businesses and markets.

It's just a Japanese thing...

Turning to culture, we can see that the Japanese have long accepted the benefits of corporate brands. You can buy a Yamaha-branded motorbike, hi-fi, piano, yacht or electronic organ without, it seems, being unduly confused. This is not just a Japanese phenomenon; in India the Tata brand encompasses almost every business activity from banking to motorcars, and from fmcg to industrial chemicals. Such brands often break the architectural 'rules' shown in Figure 16.1, but they succeed for reasons well understood in Asia, and slowly being realized elsewhere.

Back in Japan, Mitsubishi uses as one of its corporate slogans, 'from noodles to atomic power', a statement that calls on a very Japanese perception of the role and status of business in society. Would the British be as happy trusting atomic power to Heinz, makers of spaghetti hoops?

A much-quoted study carried out by the Henley Centre in the 1990s showed that in the United Kingdom, many consumer brands are trusted more than the police or the royal family, and indeed, more than those brands' corporate owners. Among brands winning high levels of trust were Pepsi, Mars and St Michael (product brands), while among the less trusted were Shell, Microsoft and Sky (corporate brands).

It would seem that, in the United Kingdom at least, a product brand, particularly one with a clear personality and compelling emotional charge, can be loved and cherished, while we remain wary of big business. Or is that just what the media and certain pressure groups want us to feel? Do Shell's tussles with Greenpeace have an impact on how we see Shell at the pump? Do we worry about Microsoft's products because the government worries that Microsoft is growing too dominant and powerful? The answer is, of course, yes – for some. It all depends, of course, on the reputation of the corporation in question.

The attribute brand (not to be confused with a tribute band...)

Sir Richard Branson calls Virgin an 'attribute brand', arguing that it has a value of its own quite independent from the specific product to which it might be attached. The brand is a reputation, and in this regard Virgin follows the Japanese practice. Branson has indeed attacked what he calls the 'stilted Anglo-Saxon view of consumers' that insists that a brand must relate directly to a product. Much of Virgin's success as a corporate brand has been to do with its ability to portray the Virgin business as a role model of good and modern business practice, championing the customer, breaking with convention and sounding a challenge to existing norms and authorities.

The brand's values are of course personified in Sir Richard Branson: entrepreneur, adventurer, and friend of the consumer. There is always a new twist to any Virgin venture, a twist that makes use of those corporate values. Virgin didn't just sell PEPs (personal equity plans); it took out the middleman. It doesn't just fly aircraft; it gets you to the airport on a Harley Davidson limo-bike (and there's no reason why brands shouldn't borrow from others to help build their own definition). Hotels with 'standby' tariffs, mobile phones with attitude, and bridal shops for brides (not just the bride's mother) – these are all applications of the corporate brand values: championing the customer in style. The success of the Virgin corporate brand depends on the continuing relevance of those values.

Branson has made it clear that he wishes Virgin to be the most respected brand, not necessarily the biggest, and in corporate branding, reputation is all.

The lesson taught by those who succeed in the pursuit of a corporate brand is that such a brand can sometimes play on a higher level of awareness and impact than the product brand. A product brand must identify and match the needs, attitudes and aspirations of a targeted market segment; it is necessarily concerned with the 'micro'. The corporate brands definition requires a big-picture approach, building values that match the political, social and economic mood of the time. So long as big business is venerated in Japan, corporate brands such as Mitsubishi and Yamaha will thrive, but economic failure, the end of the 'job for life' culture and a few too many corporate scandals could lead to a rethink.

Downsides of the corporate brand

'If it don't fit, don't force it' is good advice in this matter. There are other risks. Does putting all your eggs in one basket overstretch the credibility of that basket? Sir Richard Branson doesn't think so: 'Each time Virgin entered a new business all the conventional pundits whined that we were stretching our brand too far. Rather than worrying too much about brands being stretched too far, people will have to stretch their imaginations further.'

Of course, the imagination is a powerful thing, and how might it work if you are sat stranded somewhere between London and Manchester, *on a Virgin train*, and your mind turns to that flight you have booked to Johannesburg next week, *on a Virgin plane*...

If a company like Nestlé *were* to have all its products under the one name, what would be the impact on the supermarket shelf? It could end up looking rather like one of those 'despised' private labels... Or if it were hit by a food scare on one of its products, how might that impact on all its other products?

Global or local?

Theodore Levitt set the scene for the global brand back in 1983 when he asserted that 'The world's needs and desires have been irrevocably homogenized.' It was doubtful whether they had, except in a very few markets, but this became the mantra of brand managers seeking a global pitch.

The 18th 'immutable law' of branding, according to Al Ries, is that all brands should be global brands, and he cites Heineken as an example of a brand that knows no borders. Good example, and *if you can do it*, then the benefits are enormous, but where does that leave segmentation and positioning? In very few markets do we find that 'the world' is a useful segment. Would you sell vodka in France in the same way you would sell it in Poland? In truth, Heineken does not make that attempt: the brand name may be global, but the brand definition has some very local treatments.

'Some brands are born global, some have globality thrust upon them'

In 1999, ICI Paints sold its Autocolor brand to long-time rival PPG. Autocolor was the paint brand for the car refinish market, the 'you bend 'em, we mend 'em' business, as insiders called it. Some observers were surprised: the business was a success and a technical jewel in the ICI crown, but as a global brand it was a non-starter. John McAdam, Executive VP for Coatings at ICI, was clear about the sale: 'Technical markets are global... if you are not in the top three – forget it.'

Things are different in the decorative paint market. Back in the 1980s, when ICI bought in quick succession a number of leading brand names around the world – including Valentine in France and Glidden in the United States – the plan was set for a process of 'Duluxization': the creation of a truly global brand. No more, as John McAdam points out: 'Decorative markets are different from technical ones because you can be no 1 in the UK and be nowhere in Italy.' Instead, the policy is to use local brands where they have strengths and resonances and to build a global portfolio of strong brands that includes Dulux, Glidden, Valentine, Cuprinol, Hammerite, Polyfilla and Polycell. John McAdam concedes, 'We thought we could apply a UK solution to the US, without doing regional research.'

Or 'glocal'?

We have come through many manifestations of how to deal with the apparently shrinking world. First came the rather brutal 'one size fits all' approach, particularly from the United States, with all the concomitant charges of US imperialism. Then we had the softening 'think global, act local' approach. *Glocal*, with its underlying desire to demonstrate that 'we're all the same really…', brought some uncomfortable stereotyping, and then came the rather ephemeral idea that we are one 'global village' – less a statement of the brotherhood of man and more a clumsy attempt to find workable global segments.

Not so daft…

Now it would seem that we are back to 'think local, act local' – at least, that is the view of Douglas Daft, CEO of Coca-Cola, the world's most truly global brand. Daft quite rightly dismisses the idea of there being a market segment called 'the world': 'We were looking at similarities, not differences, and we didn't stand for anything in particular for the individual.' It will be interesting to see just how far Coca-Cola allows the development of local brand definitions to go, and how keen local managements will be to take up their new freedoms.

BRAND POSITIONING: A PLACE IN MIND

Brand positioning is more than just stating your case; all brands do that, whether they are successes or failures. The real test for a successful brand is, does it find, or create, a relevant space in the target customer's mind, and does it cement its brand definition and values there? This chapter deals with finding and creating the space; Chapter 20 will look at the methods used for cementing the resultant brand definition into that space.

Positioning isn't easy; there are all sorts of wrong positionings awaiting you:

- *Underpositioning*: where you stand for nothing in particular, occupying no space in the customers' mind, and giving them no reason to buy, or even to care.
- *Overpositioning*: where you are so narrowly specific that once the handful of target customers have bought, you're done.
- *Confused positioning*: where you're just trying to be too many things at once, and contradictions and conflicts abound.
- *Irrelevant positioning*: 'So your brand will help remove the stains inside my radiators without my having to close them down.' Who cares?
- *Doubtful positioning*: making claims that nobody believes, and only the most gullible will become your customers – not a good recipe for building sales by word of mouth…

Get it wrong, and you face the costs of repositioning, though just sometimes there is a happy ending…

Marlboro, one of the earliest filter-tip cigarettes, was originally positioned to appeal to women. Failing to make great headway there, it tried to target men, who considered its filter tip positively 'sissy'. Marlboro adopted a cowboy as an image and repositioned the brand as 'the he-man's smoke'. The rest we know.

Second time lucky for Marlboro

Boldly going…

Usually, a brand must try to avoid a 'middle-of-the-road' positioning, but taking any kind of extreme stance inevitably means that some will disapprove. The Benetton campaign of the 1990s is an example of such positioning, but many have 'learnt' from the success of that brand. A sense of disapproval has now become an important facet of some brands, creating as it does an 'in-crowd' feel for those who *do* approve. Nowhere is this more important than when a new brand tries to break into a mature market. Häagen-Dazs was launched in an environment that said 'ice cream is for kids', and in order to create a new space in people's minds, it had to escape those associations. The brand was shown with adult interactions, sometimes with provocative images that could bring only disapproval from some, but helped establish a loyalty from those specifically targeted. (Getting the market segmentation right is essential for such a strategy.)

Some brands even manage to play cleverly on their realization that not everyone likes them. Marmite sought to position its unique taste by recognizing that some folk just can't stand the stuff: 'I hate Marmite' posters ran alongside the 'My mate' posters in its advertising campaign.

'I hate Marmite'

The positioning process

There are three steps:

1. Establish the *broad positioning*. This may be at market level, or even company level (see 'Brand architecture', page 156).
2. For each target market or segment, develop the *specific positioning* – this will include the *value context* of the brand.
3. Cement the brand definition on the customers' mind, making a positive impact on their *total business experience* (see Chapters 17 and 20).

The process is illustrated in Figure 16.2.

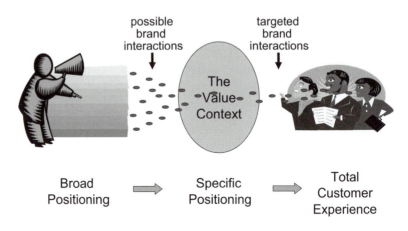

Figure 16.2 *Brand positioning the process*

Broad positioning addresses the way in which your brand will help the business to grow (Chapter 12 – does it reduce the risks?), how it will help you to compete (Chapter 13 – differentiation or lowest cost?), how it will work alongside your chosen drivers (Chapter 14) and how it will help you to secure that unique match between capabilities and needs (Chapter 2), segment by segment (Chapter 15). You will see by this proliferation of chapter references that a good brand will provide much of the glue that holds a business and its marketing plans together.

Brand glue

Specific positioning results from segmentation. Good segmentation (see Chapter 15) will give you a deep understanding of your customers' needs, attitudes and behaviours. Matching these with your own capabilities (see Chapter 2) will help you select the specific _benefits_ that make up your offer. This will be your specific positioning: the value given to the customer, the representation of your leading capabilities, and your basis for competitive advantage. We might also call this your _brand definition_.

Brand definition

Specific positioning: sourcing the brand definition

There are many sources for the brand definition:

- the _emotional charge_ of the brand (see Chapter 20): does your brand claim simple authenticity, or a particular level of performance, or satisfaction in use, or is it even a badge of social expression?
- the _personality_ of the brand (see Chapter 20) – whether it is male or female, young or old, cool or dynamic, hip or hop…;
- specific benefits;
- the _value context_.

We will now consider the last two of these.

Specific benefits

As every sales professional knows, a benefit is what the product or service does for the customer. It is quite distinct from a feature – which is simply a fact.

In the world of branding, what a product does for a customer can sometimes be quite complex. Volvo has for many years defined its brand through the benefit of safety – that's easy enough. 'No FT, no comment' makes clear the benefit that that newspaper seeks to bring its customers. Berri, an Australian fruit juice, has defined itself through the benefit of patriotism – it is '100% Australian owned'. Many a malt whisky brand has taken heritage and traditional values as its source benefit – which starts to get a little more complex. The Hovis brand reassures us with 'It's as good for you today as it's always been.' Some brands even find their source benefit through comparison to the competition: Avis 'tries harder'; Duracell 'lasts longer'.

There is always a danger of claiming too much, and so confusing customers with too many benefits. In general, the greater the number of benefits argued, the more diffused the brand definition becomes. While this might allow the brand to work across many segments, it will also tend to leave it open to competition that might take a more single-minded approach.

Some brands focus on just one benefit, so maximizing their impact and their credibility. Others manage a range of benefits. The Aquafresh brand of toothpaste selects three: protection, whiteness and fresh breath. The red, white and blue bands in the toothpaste

The Aquafresh three-in-one

help it to communicate these benefits even at the point of use – a valuable customer interaction.

The value context

An important part of the brand definition is a statement, in the customer's mind, of value received. Figure 16.2 showed how the range of possible interactions inherent in a brand must be funnelled through a *value context*; in other words, the selected interactions must all work together to express the nature of the value received. There are several choices of value context, and all can work; the trick is to make sure you remain consistent:

- *Getting more for more*: the 'reassuringly expensive' Stella Artois, or premium-priced Häagen-Dazs or Starbucks.
- *Getting more for the same* — the Lexus. 'Perhaps the first time in history that trading a \$72,000 car for a \$36,000 car could be considered trading up,' runs one of the ads.
- *Getting more for less* – the so-called *category killer* retail brands such as Toys 'R' Us and Wal-Mart, whose scale and buying power promise bigger ranges, greater choice and lower prices.
- *Getting the same for less*: Tesco, with its high-profile 'rip-off Britain' campaign to sell Levi's jeans at non-rip-off prices.
- *Getting less for much less* – 'stripped down' brands such as easyJet, the Formule 1 hotel chain or the Lidl supermarket chain. These examples show that the 'giving' part of the equation is not always money; it might be the sacrifice of amenities, an acceptance of risk, or a 'managed level of discomfort'.

The options that do not appear here, 'getting the same for more' and especially 'getting less for more', are two value contexts taken up by fast-declining brands!

In a B2B environment, the value context may be expressed in a slightly different way, referring back to a model already encountered: Wiersema's value drivers (see Chapter 14). Now, rather than considering our own value driver, we must identify with the target customers'. If the customers are driven by *operational excellence* then brand values such as consistency, reliability and cost reduction will need to come to the fore. If they are driven by *product leadership* then innovation and creativity will be more likely sources for the brand definition. And if they are driven by customer intimacy, it may be values such as flexibility, or the ability to understand, that will need to come shining through.

Repositioning: brands die (if you let them)

The 1950s was a boom period for concentrated fruit squash drinks and Treetops was a leading brand with an eye-catching bottle design. The brand definition was about economy and thrift, and very appropriate for the time. Today, most of us will happily pay more for a 250ml bottle of flavoured mineral water than for a litre of squash that might make 20 pints. We will even pay a huge premium to have that same squash (though not Treetops) in a small cardboard box, ready diluted. The value of convenience has overtaken the value of thrift in this market, but Treetops failed to move with the times, and the values.

It is perhaps to be expected that those brands with the clearest positioning and the strongest definition will have the hardest task of changing as times change. It is a feature of anachronisms that they were once absolutely spot on…

Some brands become liabilities and should be killed or sold. Others may still provide a nice income stream as they are progressively run to grass. And then there are those brands with enough long-term value to make it worth the risk and the cost of repositioning. The risk is twofold: if you fail, not only is the investment lost, but now try going back to where you came from.

Repositioning is usually harder than the initial positioning: there is the question of existing perceptions and beliefs. Rather than providing a good foundation on which to build, the existing brand heritage is often an obstacle to change.

Leaving home

It's the same with people. Imagine that someone wants to change her personality. She might change her clothes, her hairstyle, her accent, her behaviour, but the problem is that her family and friends still remember who she was before all this confusing messing about. If a person really wants to change his or her personality then the answer is usually to leave home. Repositioning a brand often involves much the same process.

In sickness, and in health…

Time was when Lucozade was what your mother bought for you when you were ill. Generations have grown up identifying the brand with illness and recuperation. It was a clear positioning, but once it was well established, the potential for growth was rather limited. SmithKline Beecham, the brand's owner, conducted a brilliant campaign over a number of years to reposition the product as a high-energy 'sports drink'. SmithKline Beecham had identified the potential in this segment and it had a product with many of the necessary attributes. High-profile product endorsements from the likes of Daley Thompson were used to great effect alongside new packaging designs and new target retail outlets. Lucozade is still a favourite choice for those overcoming illness, but it now also occupies a position well away from the invalid's bedside table. Its 'new-life' success results from having selected the appropriate parts of its existing definition and personality, and using these to act as a protective halo on the brand's journey to its new home.

Changing the mood

Not all repositioning has to be this dramatic. Leaving home is an extreme step with extreme risks. Sometimes repositioning can be effected through changes of mood.

Finding a new emotion

Predictor, a self-use pregnancy testing kit, found that its personality was not entirely suited to its growth aspirations. The product was well thought of, reliable and responsible, but it suffered from some negative associated images: unpleasant surprises, let-downs, unwanted pregnancies. It was too often a product that you bought when trouble was looming. While that might have been a base on which to position the brand – a promise of performance in use – it wasn't where Predictor wanted to be. Its marketers wanted the brand to have a more upbeat emotional charge, and so a more prominent place in the customers' mind: personal fulfilment. A combination of a packaging redesign and an advertising campaign demonstrating the joy, private and public, of discovering your dreams come true helped to put the brand on to this new level.

You're either in, or you're out

Irn Bru, a brand of fizzy drink with an almost fanatical following in Scotland, had for many years made much of its rather minimal iron content: 'made in Scotland from girders', appealing to an increasingly ageing audience. Figure 16.3 illustrates the extraordinary change of mood developed, with great success, in order to build sales among the new generation of 'fizzy drinkers'.

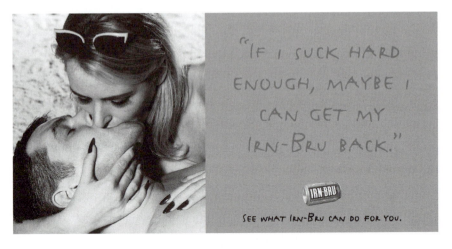

Figure 16.3 *Changing the mood*

The Irn Bru case again illustrates the high-risk tendency of some brands to appeal to the 'in crowd' and in so doing risk the disapproval of those beyond the target audience. Good segmentation is vital for such a strategy.

Changing with the times

Repositioning along with the changing times is the lowest-risk strategy, but calls for a surprising flexibility of mind. Its main obstacle is all those who cry out, 'If it ain't broke, don't fix it' – the death knell of many a brand.

Having once been one of the toys of the century, Lego spent much of the closing years of the 20th century slowly slipping out of style (and into a loss in 1998), until repositioning in pursuit of a new ambition: to be leading brand for families with kids – not just bricks, not even toys, but families with kids. Mindstorms, Technic, Mybot, lifestyle kids' clothing and watches, the Legoland theme parks, and licensing deals with Star Wars and Winnie the Pooh, are all part of that strategy. Business results are up, and this old timer is making a brand new impression.

Lego, no longer just a pile of bricks

Repositioning from behind

When a company is aware of a poor image for its product, it will need to do more than just tell people how great it is. Humour is a favourite tack, and there have been many adverts that appear to knock the advertiser as a means of changing people's perceptions. A recent UK television ad for a Skoda car has a car park attendant apologizing to a worried car owner (a Skoda owner) for the vandalism done to his car – some little devil has stuck a Skoda badge on the front. Humour, recognition of the current perceptions, and a clever point about how things have changed, yet there are some (not you, of course) who are still behind the times.

VALUING THE BRAND

It is clear that brands are hugely valuable properties that will have received significant investment over time. Not so very long ago, brand managers may have been inclined to talk of the 'inestimable value' of their brand. Of course, they meant this in praise of its undeniable, but immeasurable value, but no longer should they take such a trusting and accepting view.

In 1985, Reckitt & Colman bought Airwick from Ciba-Geigy, with a good chunk of the payment being for 'goodwill', the accountants' term for the value of such apparently indefinable things as Airwick's customers and the Airwick brand. In fact, 'goodwill' makes these items quite definable, placing an actual market value on them. The normal accounting practice would have been for Reckitt & Colman to pay the money but see no increase in the net assets shown on the balance sheet – not a new problem, but Reckitt & Colman had a new solution: they decided to capitalize the value of the brand.

In 1987, Grand Met bought Heublein, owners of the Smirnoff brand. Grand Met announced that it would include £588 million on its balance sheet for acquired brands.

These two moves were unusual but not revolutionary: Reckitt & Colman and Grand Met were only valuing acquired brands as part of the complexity of acquisitions and valuations. The real revolution came in 1988, when Philip Morris paid $12.9 billion for the Kraft food company, a sum that was four times the book value of the tangible assets in the business. What Philip Morris was really paying for was the intangible assets of the brands.

In the same year, RHM decided to value all its brands, not just newly acquired ones, and after much debate in learned journals, many more have followed their example. Brand managers now have an additional responsibility: as well as building the value of the brand in the customers' eyes, they now must also please the accountants. The problem has become how to value the brand, and as yet there is no one agreed method.

Methods of valuation

The task was relatively easy when a company was buying a brand as part of an acquisition: what it paid was what it thought it was worth; the market decided. But what if you already owned the brand? Three methods stand out from the crowd:

- *The existing use method*. This attempts to value the brand on the basis of the price premium it receives over its generic competition, plus a calculation for the level of recognition the brand has in the market and the esteem in which customers hold it.
- *The earnings multiple system*. This calculates something called *brand earnings*, largely based on the cash flow provided by the brand, and multiplies that by a figure based on *brand strength*. Brand strength is a combination of factors, including market share, global presence, investment, and any brand protection measures taken.
- *The Interbrand system* (as developed by the firm of that name). Recent profitability is multiplied by a number between 1 and 20 that represents a balance of seven important aspects of the brand:
  - its leadership position;
  - its likely longevity;
  - the stability of the market in which it operates;
  - its globality;
  - its future trend;
  - the level of marketing support;
  - its legal protection.

Each of these allows a good deal of room for subjective analysis, but as the practice becomes more common, so do the standards used for this kind of analysis.

Implications for brand management

The 'how to' of brand valuation need not detain us longer, but what about the impact of brand valuations on the role of the brand manager? Brand valuation is a discipline that forces the brand manager to focus on some rather important issues:

- What actually represents strength and value in our business – is it the brands?

- What is the relative importance of our brands when compared to, let's say, our physical assets?
- If a brand has a value then it can be sold. What will be best for the business: selling a brand or continuing to invest in it?
- Valuing brands helps puts a price on licensing and royalties.
- The value of a brand is not based solely on today's receipts; as with any investment, it is also based on tomorrow's potential. The practice of valuing brands forces the business to regard those brands as investments over time, making quite clear the brand manager's responsibility to build and sustain that investment, consistently. (Remember this argument the next time the boss asks for a cut in the advertising budget!)

Part IV

Delivering the value

17

The segment audit

From here on, we focus on individual segments. All the tools and processes discussed in the rest of this book must be applied to each segment, separately, so building up unique offers and propositions designed to meet the precise needs, attitudes and behaviours of the customers in those segments.

DELIVERING THE VALUE

Chapter 9 introduced the notion of the market map and the market, or value, chain. At that point in the *marketing process* – the *strategic audit* – we used the notion of understanding the big picture, the opportunities and the threats. Here, now that we are working at segment level, the *segment audit* takes it one step further: looking for opportunities to develop a value-based offer, and to deliver that value to the customer, for the appropriate reward.

You may be working in a business that is highly commoditized. You may have chosen, as your route to competitive advantage, the lowest-cost supplier option (see Chapter 13). But don't think that means that this discussion of value is not relevant to you. Value is in the eye of the beholder, and may be interpreted in many ways as a result. By a value-based offer, I mean no more than an offer that presents the appropriate value, as perceived, and as required by that beholder: the customer.

DEFINING VALUE

Value is in the eye of the beholder. I will say that many times in this book, and yet still some folk insist on seeing it otherwise!

Consider the following circumstance. You want to sell an X-ray machine to a hospital. It already has a favoured supplier, and plenty of experience with that supplier's products, but you want to break into this hospital. You realize you have to provide a reason for it to change, and you consider what value you bring to the party. There is no doubt – and the whole industry praises you for this – no doubt at all that you provide the finest training in the business to users of your machinery. You decide to make this your lead point in the presentation: the folk in the radiology department will be fully trained, and never better, and for free, to use your new machine. You will even train them on aspects of radiology outside the bounds of your own equipment – and how's that for a value proposition? But you don't get the business, and can't understand why...

You thought you were making a value proposition, but what did the customer see? It saw the need for training, a need that would never appear if it just stayed with its existing supplier. It didn't see any value; it just saw costs – the cost of change.

Sometimes the customer sees value in your offer that you never imagined – like the lady who always buys the same brand of yoghurt, whatever the price, or promotion, or claims from rival products. She is a schoolteacher and has found the containers to be ideal for use as paint-pots and glue-pots, and who knows what else. One day the manufacturer redesigns the packaging, and the lady stops buying the yoghurts, never to return as a customer...

The challenge for the marketer is to discover – from the customer's perspective – what the customer values, or might value, or could be persuaded to value, and then develop propositions that deliver that value. This is also the starting purpose of the *segment audit*.

SEGMENT AUDIT TOOLS

We will consider three tools (each to be revisited in later chapters):

- value chain analysis (see also Chapter 18);
- the total business experience (TBE) (see also Chapter 18);
- shared future analysis (see also Chapter 19).

Just as with the strategic audit, the tools used here, and the questions they ask, are designed to help us make some critical decisions: what value, delivered to whom, and how.

VALUE CHAIN ANALYSIS

A value chain is a series of activities, in chronological order, carried out when producing your offer, whether it be a product or a service. It starts with an idea, moves on through investigatory stages, proceeds to the sourcing of materials, then on to 'manufacturing', and then to the selling of the product or service. The chain does not end there: as we saw in the idea of the market chain (Chapter 9), we should follow the offer right through to the end user.

Why 'value' chain? Because it is to be hoped that at each step, value is added. Each step will undoubtedly result in additional cost – running trials, purchasing materials, converting those materials, storage costs, sales costs, and so on – but also, if the business is to prosper, it should result in additional value. Provided the amount of value added exceeds the amount of costs, we are on our way to a profitable concern.

There are plenty of people employed to examine the supplier's own chain – supply chain managers – looking for steps that are superfluous, or that add too much cost, and seeking greater efficiencies, etc. The marketer's task is to examine the value chain of the market segment and, hence, the customers within that segment – looking for opportunities to add value.

Adding value to the market chain

The process

Chapter 18 will go into detail on how to use this tool (found there in the guise of an 'activity cycle') in order to generate ideas for adding value, and to select from those ideas the components of the value proposition. At the audit stage we commence that process. The whole process comes in four stages:

1. Define the nature of the _total business experience_ (TBE) sought by the members of the segment. (In consumer markets it may be better to call this the _total customer experience_, but we will carry on using TBE for the discussion that follows.)
2. Draw out the chain, identifying the gaps in your knowledge and taking steps to fill those gaps.
3. Assess the 'importance' of each step to the customer. Importance can be assessed in many ways: the level of risk involved, the existence of a problem, the potential for value to be added, etc.
4. Brainstorm activities that will make a positive impact on the steps in the chain, and select those that will form the value proposition, to be offered for the appropriate reward.

An academic approach to marketing might seek to define at what point this tool and process is part of the audit stage, and at what point it becomes part of the decision-making and planning process. This is not an academic textbook (if it were, you would probably not have stayed with me so far!), and such debates are for the birds! In this chapter we have introduced the tool and process, but for sake of clarity it will be best to leave to Chapter 18 the more detailed description of its use.

THE TOTAL BUSINESS EXPERIENCE

Marketers talk a great deal about adding value, and there usually follows a frantic pursuit of new ideas to help gain competitive advantage, but so often a vital ingredient of the equation is left out. Adding value to what? The answer is, adding value to the customers' desired experience, and that experience may extend well beyond what the suppliers have been used to regarding as their products' 'arena'.

Ask any salesperson and he or she will tell you that customers don't buy features; they buy benefits. Customers are less interested in the facts about a product than in what it will do for them. But are today's customers even more demanding than that, seeking solutions, perhaps even *experiences*?

Traditional sales practice (much simplified) has sought to identify a set of benefits behind a product or service and present them to customers as efficiently as possible. Traditional marketing practice (even more simplified!) has sought to segment markets so that those benefits can be presented to groups of customers in a consistent and focused way.

The notion of the *total business experience* takes us one step further down the marketing path: seeking solutions that impact on the customer in a more holistic way. It is the fourth stage of 'marketing sophistication' as described in Table 17.1.

Let's take as an example a company that sells fertilizer to farmers, and at the first stage that means all farmers.

Stage 1: 'Take it, because that's what I'm offering, and I know you want it…'

You regard your customers as essentially the same, and you deliver a standard product or service – you probably talk 'features'.

Oomph!

Your product is fertilizer, in three bag sizes, and it contains the magic ingredient 'Oomph'.

Stage 2: 'It's all in the presentation…'

You uncover customer needs that allow you to present those features as relevant 'benefits'. The product or service may remain much the same, perhaps with some minor cosmetic changes, but you are starting to recognize your customers as being different from each other, often expressed through some kind of customer segmentation.

Oomph plus!

You have segmented your market, perhaps by crop types, and so now you have to address yourself to wheat farmers. The magic ingredient 'Oomph' is still there, but a reformulation has made it particularly beneficial to wheat growers: 'Oomph Plus'.

Table 17.1 *The stages of marketing sophistication*

	Stage 1	Stage 2	Stage 3	Stage 4
The Offer	Features	Benefits	Solutions	Total business experience
Customers	All	Segmentation	Key accounts by type	Individual key accounts
Marketing Approach	Sales-led marketing	Traditional four P's marketing	Traditional marketing in transition	Relationship marketing
Sales Approach	Traditional 1:1	Enhanced 1:1	Key account management	Partnership key account management
Competitive Advantage	First, largest, best known, or perhaps none!	Ability to communicate benefits	Quality of solutions	Quality of relationships
Supplier Organization and Focus	Sales focus	Marketing focus	Customer focus	Value chain focus

Stage 3: 'Tailored just for you…'

You uncover a deeper set of needs that forces you to make more substantial changes to your product or service, recognizing the increasing individuality of the customer. This allows you to present your offer as a tailored solution. This is usually done only for a small group of customers: your key accounts, perhaps even types of key account.

You have identified a trend towards minimal use of chemicals, and have developed some low-application formulations of your product, still containing 'Oomph', but the real trick now is the application rate. On the basis of this trend, and your ability to meet the need, you have identified a key account 'type': large farm, keen to minimize chemical use, wheat production for human consumption, likes high-tech solutions, 'early adopter'.

Less Oomph!

Stage 4: 'Managing the customers' total business experience…'

You uncover a breadth of needs that allows you to understand the customers' values and aspirations in full. This is not just with regard to your offer; you understand their 'total business experience'. Your tailored solutions are now designed to have a positive impact at all levels of this business experience – before, during and after the use of your particular product or service. Indeed, your customers regard you as more than a simple supplier of a product or service; you now add value at many (why not all?) points of their business experience. You have achieved the status of key supplier.

Oomph? What's that, and who cares?

Many of your farmers, you discover, regard fertilizer application as a very low-grade task in the great scheme of things. It takes a lot of time, time that they could use for doing other things, only all these new high-tech fertilizers make it difficult to pass the job on to a jobbing contractor. Your offer has now been transformed. You no longer talk about 'Oomph' or 'Oomph Plus'; indeed, you rarely mention the product at all, for your business now is in providing a managed fertilizer application service for key farmers. You charge by results (a percentage of farm profits), not by volume of material, and you are continually developing formulations to reduce the volumes required. Indeed, your joint aspiration is to move to a stage where you can use more environmentally friendly alternatives and be rid of 'Oomph' for good.

The key to success here, in moving from stage to stage, is the ever-improving understanding of what your customer wants. Features tend to be supplier focused; benefits begin to consider the customer; solutions are about meeting requirements; but addressing the total business experience requires you to go beyond this, beyond expectations, to anticipating the customers' needs.

At its best, you understand their aspirations, not just with regard to your products as a supplier, but with regard to their total business, and so you have an opportunity to enhance their total business experience. For the farmers in our example, the TBE is being able to forget about the fertilizer issue altogether and spend their time on more profitable, or more challenging, or perhaps just more interesting activities; it all depends on the farmer.

TBE in the oil supply industry

Another example of a supplier going beyond benefits, and enhancing the customer's TBE, is found in the oil supply industry. BP, among others, has identified that it has a certain expertise in managing fluid supplies on a customer's site. For key accounts, it will offer to manage the customer's total 'fluid requirements'. This will almost certainly involve taking responsibility for the supply of products outside BP's own portfolio, perhaps in some cases even working with a competitor's products. As with the fertilizer example, the focus moves to reducing the volumes of product required, and improving efficiencies of use. The focus is squarely on providing value rather than lowest prices. Indeed, the price of the product becomes almost irrelevant, as the services are charged for in more creative, more *holistic* ways.

Identifying the customers' TBE

In the bad old days, sometimes we would tell our customers what they needed, and sometimes we were lucky and we got it right. Then, *sometimes* wasn't enough, and we realized that we had to learn to ask, and some of us are still learning…

But now we hit on some problems:

- What if our customers don't know what they need?
- What if things are changing around them so fast, they can't see a clear way forward?
- What if the things they keep telling us they want are just, well, what they think they _should_ be saying? Everyone wants a lower price, a better product and slicker service.

Remember the tale about Alexander Graham Bell, from Chapter 3? When he invented the telephone, he toured the United States, showing it off to what he hoped would be interested businessmen. After one such session, he was approached by an apparent enthusiast: 'Mr Bell, I really like your new toy. It's my daughter's birthday party tomorrow, and I would be very grateful if you would come along to show it.'

Well, the great man was incensed: 'It is not a toy!' he exploded. 'Don't you realize that this will revolutionize communications, and your business? Just think, with one of these you can talk to a customer three hundred miles away.'

The businessman thought for a moment, and then answered, 'But Mr Bell, I don't have any customers three hundred miles away...'

Unfortunately, telling them isn't enough.

But sometimes, even _asking_ your customer is not enough. Who knew that they needed Post-it notes before they were invented, or the Internet, or a telephone? The job of the marketer is to identify and understand what their customers _might_ want, based on their _latent_ needs, aim to provide it, and to sell them the vision. And how do you gain this new _insight_?

Benchmarking?

Useful, but why should we think that everyone else has seen the light? And anyway, we want competitive advantage, not a 'me too' solution.

Market research?

Of course, but asking traditional questions will get traditional answers. Yes, of course they want a lower price, a better product and slicker service – hardly an _insight_.

My own company once commissioned a piece of research to see why training managers chose particular training suppliers. The answers seemed very worthy – value for money, value for time, leading edge, and all the rest – only we knew that wasn't the truth; at least, not the truth that went to the root of their desired experience. The truth of the matter was that many training managers chose the supplier least likely to make them look foolish. See it from their standpoint: they arrange an event, they commit people's time – it is their reputation that is on the line if the trainer turns out to be an embarrassment.

How did we know that? Because we focused on what the training managers wanted from the *total experience* of doing business with us: their TBE.

So, don't do market research? None of this is arguing against market research. Research is vital if we are to understand our customers and their needs. What this argues for is the *kind* of research required: research into the customers' motivations, aspirations and values. And beyond that, you need to uncover the things that they didn't even know themselves.

Thinking for the customer

Remember, customers are lazy. This is not a prejudiced remark; it is just that if they ask for anything, they ask for what seems to them the simplest solution. When buyers ask you to provide consignment stock (stock held on the buyer's premises but remaining your property until the buyer calls it off), are they really wanting consignment stock? Perhaps they want to reduce their working capital, and consignment stock seems a much easier option than installing electronic data interchange (EDI) and efficient response ordering. Easier for them, but not for the supplier, and, in the end, not the optimal solution for either.

Customers may find it difficult to articulate their desired *total business experience*; they may even lie to save themselves time, money or effort. It is the supplier's responsibility to understand its customers well enough to be able to articulate that experience for them and to argue for the appropriate activities to meet it, not just the simplest.

The following case study looks at one company that has been remarkably successful in identifying its customers' requirements by understanding first the customers' customers: the end consumers. And on the basis of that understanding it has been able to add value for its customers well beyond simple product benefits, and secure a handsome reward in return.

The NutraSweet® **case study**	NutraSweet brand sweetener, generally known as aspartame, is a high-intensity sweetener used in a wide range of food and drinks around the world. The fact that it has a brand name is perhaps the most important point, as NutraSweet aims to create consumer demand for the 'invisible' raw material used in well-known brands such as Coca-Cola or CareFree (chewing gum). Its aim is to create value for the end consumer and, most importantly, also for the 'carrier' product.

In a market where consumers had all sorts of doubts about artificial sweeteners, from taste to health concerns, NutraSweet created strong consumer demand that resulted in a pull for its product even through massive 'carrier' brands such as Coke. How did its marketers do it?

The strategy was clear from the start: NutraSweet had to have a strong consumer franchise. Just being a superior product would not be enough. That way, not only would the carrier product gain all the credit and reward, but without consumer awareness of the product the reward to be gained would be slight and short-lived. One tactic in this campaign was the 'gumball' promotion. Millions of these sweets were made with

NutraSweet's product and mailed direct to US households. This was an unashamed assault on the taste buds of the end consumer. At the same time, the marketers made use of a clear brand logo: the NutraSweet 'swirl' stamped on the packaging of a range of low-calorie products.

Consumer awareness was only the start, of course. To be sustainable, such a strategy must also mean something to the 'carrier', NutraSweet's immediate customers. Here a range of activities was in place. First, a clear patent for aspartame allowed it to negotiate long-term deals with market leaders in the food and drinks industry. The patent expired in December 1992, and many in the industry had expected this to signal a move towards commodity status for aspartame. Instead, both Coca-Cola (1991) and Pepsico (1992) signed long-term partnership deals with NutraSweet – actions far from the expected hunt for the lowest-priced alternative. Both Coca-Cola and PepsiCo seemed to feel that it would be a competitive disadvantage to be without the NutraSweet brand, a validation of NutraSweet's consumer-focused strategy.

Second, NutraSweet sought to collaborate with its direct customers in promoting the 'carrier' products, gaining in return the application of its logo to the packaging.

Third, experience in the food as well as the drinks market allowed NutraSweet to improve its product, in particular extending its shelf life, something that had been an early limitation. Such improvements allowed broader applications and experience that led to further improvements, and so the virtuous circle continued.

Fourth, as well as attending to its customers' requirements regarding end consumers, NutraSweet also attended to its customers' own business requirements. As volumes increased, so economies of scale became apparent, and these were shared with customers through steadily falling prices. This was important, as some customers might have become uncomfortable that NutraSweet had some kind of hold on them through its consumer franchise that might tempt it to exploit its position. Steadily reducing the prices put paid to any such thoughts.

Perhaps the greatest value that NutraSweet brought to its customers and to the end consumers was in recognizing that the full potential in the low-calorie market had not yet been realized. NutraSweet was able to identify with the end users' desired total business experience: they wanted low-calorie food and drink that didn't taste strange and that was safe (saccharin had been the cause of a number of consumer 'scares'). NutraSweet tasted like sugar, felt like sugar in the mouth, and had no consumer health scares. As for the food and drink manufacturers, where their desired total business experience was double-digit growth, then NutraSweet contributed significantly. Diet drinks grew dramatically while others saw more sluggish performances.

So, the secrets of NutraSweet's success? First of all, a good product with unique competitive advantage. Second, a strong consumer franchise, important for a supplier a few steps down the chain from the end consumer. Third, working in partnership with their customers, both focused on the end consumer. Fourth, and most important of all perhaps, identifying what both consumers and manufacturers really wanted – their desired total business experience – and delivering it.

Chapter 18 will continue this process into the identification of value propositions, but for now, we will turn to the third tool to be used in the segment audit: _shared future analysis_.

SHARED FUTURE ANALYSIS

Shared future analysis is ideally suited for use against an individual customer. As such, it is an excellent tool to be used in the practice of key account management. We use it here to assess the nature of the segment's needs, and our capabilities against those needs. A good match promises a good shared future. Of course, if we have segmented well, these two uses should come to the same thing, because isn't a segment meant to be a group of customers with similar needs, attitudes and behaviours? Shouldn't one customer be able to represent them all in a segment? Well, let's hope so!

The shared future analysis is a form of SWOT analysis, but used with more analytical rigour, forcing us to make the link between opportunities and strengths, threats and weaknesses.

The process

We need to fill in a form, shown in Figure 17.1.

		What future issues *excite* the customer?				What future issues *worry* the customer?			
+ sign(s) *we make a positive impact on their ambitions or reduce their worries*	**- sign(s)** *we detract from their ambitions, or compound their worries*	1.	2.	3.	4.	1.	2.	3.	4.
What are we perceived as being good at?	1.		+++		+			+++	
	2.	*'Attack' these*				*Help resist*			
	3.	+++	*issues*		++	*these issues*			
	4.							++	+
What are we perceived as being poor at?	1.	*Ensure these*				- - -		- -	
	2.	*things don't*				*Resolve, or*			
	3.	- -	*cancel out the*			*withdraw?*			
	4.		*'attack' issues*					-	

Figure 17.1 *Shared future analysis*

Start by putting your own business out of your mind and putting yourself entirely in the customers' shoes. This is vital. Now try to identify the things that excite the customers about their future, and the things that give them cause for worry.

The example shown in Figure 17.1 is that of a consumer-branded food manufacturer whose marketers are excited by such things as the growing trend towards health and fitness, and the consequent expectations from food.

They are worried by the prospect of food scares, and by the ever-increasing power of retailers who threaten to displace their brands with their own. Try to identify some kind of priority, so ranking the issues from left to right in the top two boxes of the matrix.

Of course, in doing this there is no substitute for speaking with the customers. Aim to speak with as many people as possible, and well beyond the buying office. If this is difficult, then at least speak with your own people who have contacts with the customer. Ask them what the customers talk about all the time – not a bad guide to what excites them and what worries them.

Now turn to your own organization, but keep yourself in the customers' shoes. What do they see in you that will help them achieve their dreams, and what do they see in you that turns their worries into nightmares? Do you help or hinder their progress? Do you reduce or exacerbate their concerns? In other words, what are your strengths and weaknesses as they apply to the customers' ambitions and fears?

Again, there is no substitute for talking with the customers, but this takes some subtlety. The aim is not to get them focused on a long list of complaints and insecurities!

List these good and bad capabilities in the two side boxes, again with some attempt at ranking from top to bottom.

Before moving to the next step, stop for a bout of honest reflection. Are these really the things that excite and worry them, or just what _you_ would like them to be excited and worried about? Are the listings of your good and bad capabilities as seen through their eyes and not through yours? If they don't know about your particular brilliance, whatever it might be, then you can hardly list it here as a good capability.

Why this pause for reflection? Because we are about to use this analysis to determine our direction for the foreseeable future; it will be as well to have it right!

Now consider each vertical column (excitements and worries) in turn, working down through your capabilities, good and bad. Against each of these, indicate with a plus where there is a positive contribution (use a scale of one to three pluses to represent the size of the contribution) and with a minus sign if your lack of capability either detracts from an ambition or makes worse something that worries them.

Using the analysis

What we now have is a snapshot of your likely future together – pluses indicating the things to talk up, minuses the things to resolve. Hopefully there are plenty of pluses in the top left quadrant; these are areas to be bullish about. Pluses in the top right indicate that you are well placed to ease their worries; let them know this!

Too many minuses in the bottom left may outweigh the pluses in the box above. Aim to reduce or remove these weaknesses if you believe they cancel out your strengths.

Finally, too many minuses in the bottom right suggest that you make their worries even more hair-raising. You must either resolve these problems or conclude that you and this segment don't have much of a future together.

18

The value proposition

The segment audit has helped us to understand the dynamics of the segment, and in particular the nature of the value added and sought by the players in that segment. This chapter takes us on to the creation of propositions designed to deliver the appropriate value.

Let us just remind ourselves of the process:

1. Define the nature of the total business experience (TBE) sought by the members of the segment. (In consumer markets it may be better to call this the total customer experience, but we will carry on using TBE for the discussion that follows.)
2. Draw out the chain, identifying the gaps in your knowledge and taking steps to fill those gaps.
3. Assess the 'importance' of each step to the customer. Importance can be assessed in many ways: the level of risk involved, the existence of a problem, the potential for value to be added, etc.
4. Brainstorm activities that will make a *positive impact* on the steps in the chain, and select those that will form the value proposition, to be offered for the appropriate reward.

Now let us consider an example from the airline industry: flying transatlantic, business class, to visit a customer and make a sale. We might consider this a fairly precise, discrete and viable segment.

Chapter 17 discussed the meaning of total business experience (TBE). In this example we will define it as 'to do the deal'. In other words, it is something more than the experience of the flight; it includes what goes on before and, more especially, what goes on afterwards. What the airline seeking a value proposition needs to do is to identify what, within the realm of its product and service, will help this customer do the deal? And it should go even further and ask itself, how might we extend our product and service to secure this aim?

The next step is to list all the activities that your customers currently have to go through to achieve their TBE – this is their own personal value chain. Table 18.1 charts such a list from initial route enquiry through to the return trip.

Table 18.1   *The customer's value chain*

Customer activity
Route enquiry
Ticket purchase
Receive tickets
Drive to airport
Park in long-stay
Shuttle bus to terminal
Check-in and luggage
Security
Passport
Waiting
Boarding
Safety procedures
Take off
Watch a movie, play games
Read, talk, work
Meals and drinks
Sleep
Meals and drinks
Landing
Disembark
Passport and Immigration
Luggage
Customs
Into the terminal
Find taxi
Check into hotel
Business meetings
Reconfirm flights
Recommence the process…

So far so good: we know what our customer is up against.

The next stage is to try to assess the importance of each step to the customer. There are many ways to do this. In this example I have chosen to identify the potential problems at each point: the list of things that could go wrong, and might stop the customer 'doing the deal'. Table 18.2 suggests such a list of potential problems, and then moves on to the next stage, that of identifying some possible actions that would have a positive impact on the customer's total business experience.

Table 18.2   *Value chain analysis: problems and potential solutions*

Customer Activity	Problems	Positive Impact
Route enquiry	Confusing alternatives No personal incentive	Corporate client service 'Air Miles' packages
Ticket purchase	Frustrating admin	Electronic commerce
Receive tickets	Worry of not receiving	No ticket – electronic ticketing
Drive to airport	Time, getting lost...	Limo door to door
Park in long-stay	Time and hassle	No need given the above
Shuttle bus to terminal	Time and more hassle	No need given the above
Check-in and luggage	Queue, debates over cabin baggage...	Completed in limo
Security	Time	Fast track
Passport	Time	Fast track
Waiting	Time	
	Lack of business facilities	Deliver direct to business lounge, with IT and secretarial services
Boarding	A rush for locker space	Larger lockers, wardrobes
Safety procedures	Fine, but you didn't listen – heard it all before…	Cartoon video, personalized briefings?
Take off	Long waits on the tarmac	Fast-track arrangement with air traffic control?
Watch a movie, play games	Great, but caught a cold from the guy next to you	New air-conditioning
Read, talk, work	Couldn't because of noisy neighbours	Design seating so that it can be 'closed' off from neighbours
Meals and drinks	OK, but the choice and timing is so limiting	Offer a buffet rather than a served meal

Table 18.2 *continued*

Customer Activity	Problems	Positive Impact
Sleep	Couldn't because the seat was too small	Put beds in business class
Meals and drinks	You usually have an earlier breakfast	Have a buffet option
Landing	Never-ending circling and circling…	Fast-track arrangement with air traffic control?
Disembark	A tedious wait – so close and yet so far…	Psychology…
Passport & Immigration	Big delays	Fast-track arrangement Schedule to arrive at less busy times
Luggage	Worry of non-arrival	On-arrival limo service handles collection
Customs	Time	Check on departure, not arrival?
Into the terminal	Tired, can't send your e-mails…	Arrival lounges with showers, business services
Find taxi	Huge hassle	On-arrival limo
Check into hotel	Tired and emotional….	Check-in handled by limo
Business meetings	Lots of admin, no support	Airlines associate hotels to provide support – book venues?
Reconfirm flights Start over…	Plain nuisance etc	Not required …

Of course, not all the ideas for positive impact will work, nor should you seek to attempt them all. We will come to a screening and selection process later in the chapter. For now, remember that this stage of the process is a brainstorming one, expanding your horizons before narrowing in on your choice of activities.

Perfect flight or perfect holiday?

The Virgin Atlantic flight from London to Orlando, Florida, serves another segment: holidaymakers. The TBE in this segment may be something like 'the perfect holiday' – so how does the airline extend its service into ensuring that is achieved? How about allowing customers to check in, on the last day of their holiday, not at the airport but at Disney World? This gives them a whole extra day's holiday – and that is value!

What we see here is a different segment and a different value proposition, but it is the same tool that gets us there.

Chain or circle?

The marketer should always try to map out the value chain from as early in the customer's process as possible, to as late as possible. In many cases it will be both convenient and illuminating to divide the value chain into three sections: the before, the during and the after, as shown in Figure 17.1. This also shows the chain as a circle, recognizing the fact that in most cases we are wanting to repeat the customer's experience with us again and again and again! At this point, we may refer to the process as the customer's *activity cycle*.

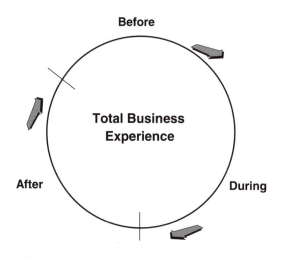

Before

Total Business Experience

After

During

Figure 18.1 *The customer's activity cycle*

'Before' relates to all the activities that occur before customers become directly involved with purchasing and using your product or service. This will include their generation of ideas, their identification of needs, their selection process, vendor ratings, trials, supplier negotiations and purchase. 'During' includes all the activities from purchase through to use, whether that be final consumption or an intermediate use. The 'after' section of the value chain includes all those activities for customers in their own market: the customers' customers.

Having made this division, you may now discover that you have bias towards one portion of the chain. Not only do you know the steps better, but you already provide a lot of value against those steps. And maybe, just maybe, so do your competitors.

Now you need to start to use the tool to look for ideas beyond your current points of contact with the customer, and away from the competitors' offer, so helping you in your search for that unique match between capabilities and needs described by the Marketing Model (Chapter 3).

Products or solutions?

Where suppliers have a poor understanding of the steps around the customer's activity cycle, or perhaps only know about a small portion of the cycle, then the chances are that they are selling products, and only that. This situation is shown in Figure 18.2.

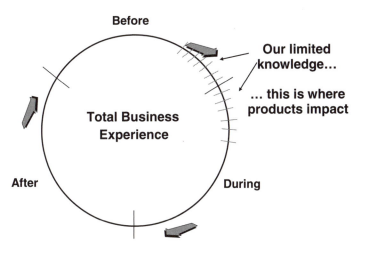

Figure 18.2 _Limited impact on the activity cycle_

If, however, a supplier has a much wider understanding, and has found the means to make an impact on that cycle at multiple points, then the chances are that this supplier is selling solutions, as indicated in Figure 18.3.

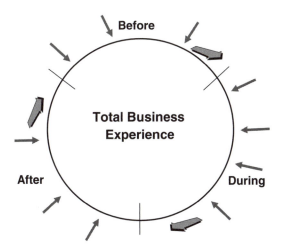

Figure 18.3 _Multiple impact on the activity cycle_

Selling solutions takes joined-up thinking...

Or at least they should be selling solutions if they realized the breadth of their impact. Often the 'left hand' of a complex supplier will not know what its 'right hand' is doing, and there are in fact already many pieces of added value, but nobody is joining them up in one coherent proposition. Chapter 20 will return to this idea, placing the responsibility for 'joining it all up' in the hands of the brand manager, for brand management is about coordinating the range of interactions the product or service has with the customer, so representing the customer's total experience of that brand.

MAKING A POSITIVE IMPACT

We now have a range of *possible* activities that *might* make a positive impact on the customers' TBE. Of course, no supplier could work on all these at once, and in any case, no customer is likely to want them all at once. The next step is to screen these possibles, selecting the priority actions. The following is a suggested checklist – the *positive impact analysis* – to be applied to each possible action:

- Does it add value to the total business experience sought?
- Does it remove a problem?
- Does it reduce a problem?
- What value does the customer put on this?
- Does it impact on the customers' core values (Wiersema's value drivers, for instance)?
- What does it cost them – time, money, other?
- Would they pay for it as part of a service?
- What will it cost you to provide?
- Can you charge enough to cover cost, or make a premium?
- Can you secure your fair share of the value added to the market?
- Do you have the capability?
- Can you work with a partner to bring the capability?
- Does it give you sustainable competitive advantage?
- Does it enhance your service to other customer groups, segments, markets?
- Does it help you avoid competitive disadvantage (see page 195)?
- Does it give you 'lock-in' – in other words, is this something that will tie your customers to you, and is difficult for your competitors to replicate?

Using a selection matrix for screening activities and projects

If the number of potential activities is large or complex, you may want to go one step further than asking the screening questions as a means of identifying the runners. You could use a modified version of a Directional Policy Matrix (DPM – see Chapters 9 and 22).

The vertical axis would now be the attractiveness *to you* of the project or activity, and the horizontal axis will measure the attractiveness of the activity or the project to the customer. Each axis is made up of a number of factors, which might include the checklist questions used in the screening process, and any additional factors that may apply in your own circumstances.

A typical list for attractiveness to us might include:

- Will revenue earned (or protected) outweigh the costs to us?
- Do we have the capability?
- Can we develop the capability – is there a partner to bring the capability?
- Does it give us competitive advantage?
- Does it enhance our service to other customers or markets?
- Does it give us lock-in?

A typical list for attractiveness to the customer might include:

- Does it reduce or remove a known problem?
- Does it impact on our (the customer's) core value drivers?
- Does it reduce risk?
- Is it of high value (using the customer's definition of value received)?
- Is it of low cost to us?

Use a similar weighting and rating system as described in Chapter 22 to complete the matrix. Projects that fall into the top right-hand box are the most likely to be progressed and those that fall into the bottom left those most likely to be dropped.

When a project falls into the top left box then the next question to ask is: could this be made more attractive to the customer? It is very important not to invent attractions that are not there; it is very easy to justify any action if you lie hard enough. The point of the question is simply a double check.

Similarly, question those projects that fall into the bottom right – are they really so unattractive to you? If they benefit the customer so highly then cannot this be turned to your advantage? Not another excuse to lie to yourself, simply a double check.

'Lock-in'

Lock-in is a matter of huge importance. Any supplier can do things that are of value to the customer, but whether they bring sustainable competitive advantage is another matter. Extended credit is certainly of value to a customer, but it is very easy for a competitor to match or even to offer more. Such added value is short-lived: the competitive advantage is not sustainable, and, worst of all, it can start a process that will spiral out of control as competing suppliers vie to improve the last offer.

Sustainable competitive advantage comes from activities that encourage loyalty, and that competitors are not able to match without costly effort.

Sustainable Competitive Advantage: the Holy Grail

Buying loyalty rarely works. Frequent flyer miles are said to be about loyalty – but they are very often false loyalty; the customer goes elsewhere as soon as the scheme is stopped. Worse, everyone can do them.

Telemetry and lock-in

The secret of 'lock-in' is finding an activity or service that the customers value, that the customers would rather not perform themselves, that the competitor doesn't offer, and that doesn't involve handing the supplier too much power. The e-revolution has facilitated a number of new opportunities in this regard, by suppliers doing business *inside* the customer's own organization and supply chain. An example is the use of telemetry, where the supplier monitors product usage by the customer and handles the reordering process automatically. The bar code that is swiped through the supermarket checkout is an example of telemetry, or sensors placed two-thirds of the way down a silo of liquid that trigger an automatic order when the level reaches that point. A degree of lock-in is achieved, because for the customer to go elsewhere, the system has to be manually overridden, an action only to be considered if there is a real and dramatic competitor advantage.

It is a delicate balance: 'lock-in' implies supplier power, and suppliers should tread carefully. The airline that offers to manage its corporate clients' full business travel arrangements must take great care not to abuse its position: London to Moscow via New York (the airline has no direct flight to Moscow) is not value; it is an outrage!

The lock-in that got them locked out!

Perhaps the most famous example of a misplaced attempt at lock-in was that of Apple. Apple had a truly splendid operating system, but wanted to hang on to it and to use its strength to sell its own machines; you could only have it if you bought an Apple computer. This effectively restricted the value that consumers could receive, and when Microsoft allowed MS-DOS to be put on any machine you liked, Microsoft won the day.

Lock-in can be unpopular if used for too obviously selfish ends. Much of the complaint against the development of genetically modified seeds is that they are designed to resist the effects of the supplier's own pesticides, a clear attempt to lock the customer in to the purchase of those pesticides. Somewhere along the line, the intention to help farmers improve their yield becomes confused with other, more selfish intentions. The notorious 'terminator gene' that would prevent the crop from producing new seed was a step too far, particularly when considering sale to Third World countries, and that particular attempt at lock-in was withdrawn.

Gaining a share of the value

You do a thorough positive impact analysis (PIA), select an activity and come up with an innovation. Will you be able to get your fair share of the added value in the market? Of course, one of the PIA questions was just this, but how to judge? If you supply to the 'owners' of the market, then it is certainly true that your definition of _fair_ will have to be modified. 'Owners' tend to get the lion's share. That doesn't make it a bad move, however; perhaps it secures your position with that 'owner', and you might consider that very good value.

Your best chance to gain a fair share is in doing the analysis ahead of customers' demands. By waiting for them to ask, the potential reward of your activity diminishes immediately. By being proactive – by offering solutions to problems they are only just becoming aware of – you increase your chances of _fair_ reward.

Sometimes suppliers will choose to allow the chain a greater share of the value, because they stand to gain something in return – not a bad definition of 'fair share'.

When Toyota launched the Lexus car in the United States, it wanted dealers to offer levels of customer service that would leave competitors standing. It knew this would mean dealers having to invest in new systems, people, training, etc. Its solution was to allow dealers a substantially higher margin on selling the Lexus than was the industry norm, with the proviso that this margin went towards customer service improvements – a fair share of the value created by the whole Lexus package.

Fair shares for all

Gaining advantage or avoiding disadvantage?

The PIA process will help to identify those activities that will add most value to your customers' business. Some of these things may be unique to you; we might call them _differentiators_, and they provide a real source of competitive advantage.

Don't fall into the trap, however, of thinking that added value ideas have to be big and bold, and that small, nitty-gritty activities are too mundane to be worth anything. While the big ideas may well gain you advantage, it is equally important to avoid suffering disadvantage by failing to attend to the smaller things, the everyday things. Here we might identify another class of activities: the _givens_. These are the things that must be in place for business to be carried on.

Avoiding disadvantage is as important as gaining advantage, and may well involve attention to a more mundane list of activities – just the sort that might be discounted as administrative, clerical or even (if we were honest) dull. Making sure, for instance, that invoices are raised in a way that corresponds to the customers' requirements will rarely win you the business, but it may well help secure your position – and failing to do it will certainly lead to your disadvantage against those who can.

Customers will be unlikely to see the value in your grand proposition if they feel that you are letting them down on the everyday front. Had to ring a call centre recently? What did the experience make you feel about the bank, or the insurance company, or the car hire firm behind that call centre? Enough said.

By understanding the customers' *total business experience*, and by looking at the options for making *positive impact* on that experience, you will also be able to distinguish those activities that will gain you advantage and those that will help you avoid disadvantage: the 'differentiators' and the 'givens'. It may be useful to list them separately, and perhaps give particular attention to the 'givens' – that is, if you thought they might be ignored in all the excitement!

Adding value by *removing* features

It is easy to get into a mindset that says that to add value you must always do more. Sometimes, *less* really is more.

Understanding the customers' value chain allows us to ask the vital question: what elements of their experience with us are valued most (some perhaps hugely so) and what parts are valued least (perhaps not at all)? If elements of the experience are not valued at all then they can only represent unnecessary costs in the customers' eyes, so why not remove them? The result is a stripped-down offer that truly meets the customers' value perceptions, and one with lower costs to boot. If those lower costs are then passed on to the customers through a lower price then their perception of value received will be even greater; folk might even to talk of 'bargains'!

SOME HINTS ON USING THE PROCESS

- Involve a cross-functional team; each member will see a different aspect of the value chain, and so the different opportunities.
- Use PIA as a means of uncovering gaps in your knowledge and so as a spur to further research.
- If possible, involve real customers (but take care not to build unrealistic expectations).
- Examine the *value chain* from the customers' perspective, from before they are involved with you as a supplier, during their involvement, and beyond that involvement. Very often the most value can be added at the 'before' and 'after' stages. The 'during' is perhaps already fine; real competitive advantage often lies in stretching the boundaries of your relationship with customers.
- Don't stop at considering the customers' value chain; include the customers' customers, and beyond, all the way to the consumers. Go beyond your customers.
- Identify activities that are 'givens' as distinct from 'differentiators'.
- Ensure the 'givens' are in place.
- Seek out options for competitive advantage through the 'differentiators'.

- Be open-minded about the need to work with partners.
- For each screening question, set parameters for good, OK, bad.
- Use it to establish priorities: A, B, C activities.
- Use it to determine project teams.
- Repeat the exercise regularly, backed up by market research, customer surveys, customer involvement.

19

Relationship management

That relationships – whether between B2B suppliers and customers, or between consumer brands and their end users – have become a vital source of competitive advantage is one of the most significant realizations of the late 20th century. I say 'realizations' – relationships had always mattered, but it is only in recent times that they have been seized upon as a positive part of the marketer's toolkit for delivering value.

Chapter 24 will remind, and warn, us that marketing is something that must be done *with* customers, and not *to* them. The purpose of this chapter is to show how that can be done through managed customer relationships.

Straight away, another warning: managing customer relationships might sound as if we are telling them how to behave, how to react, how to relate to us. It shouldn't. We are far more concerned with developing relationships that will make customers feel they are working in partnership, with an equal ability to manage their relationship with us.

We will look at five aspects of relationship management:

- the market-focused structure;
- key account management;
- customer classification and distinction;
- customer service;
- customer relationship management (CRM).

THE MARKET-FOCUSED STRUCTURE

Relationship management sees customer contacts as opportunities for collaboration, not simply as a selling or promotional activity. In some cases it will go beyond that, aiming to integrate the outcome of those collaborative relationships into the operation of the business. This is a three-stage process:

1. Build relationships with customers designed to improve understanding of the real needs, opportunities and value required.
2. Ensure that this understanding is shared by all those within the supplier's organization who will be active in delivering the resultant value.
3. Align the business to deliver the value.

None of this will be possible if the business is organized along what we will call 'silo' lines, as shown in Figure 19.1.

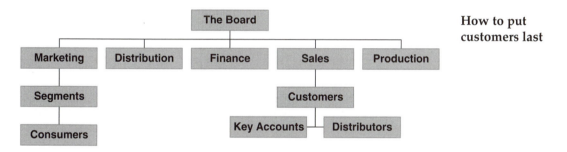

How to put customers last

Figure 19.1 *Silo business structures*

Such structures encourage an inward focus, not to say an introspection, often based on power politics – hardly conducive to the sort of thing we are seeking.

What then is the right structure? This must of course depend on circumstances. No precise blueprint will help you, and in any case, one thing is for sure: it will never be perfect! Let's say you want to be a customer-focused business, and you have only two customers; sounds easy? But what if one of those customers has a strongly centralized organization dominated by purchasing and supply chain management, and the other customer is a loose federation of regional sites each focused on a particular technology? Unless you divide into two businesses, however you structure yourself you are likely to be wrong at least half the time!

Figure 19.2 shows not so much a structure as an intention, with service functions providing the core, operating in support of those parts of the business with direct customer contact.

Getting yourself to the centre of the customers concerns

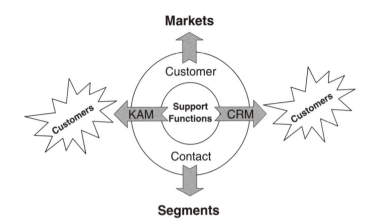

Figure 19.2 *The market-focused 'intention'*

There are many points of contact with the customer: through markets, segments, key accounts, CRM systems, Customer Service, Internet portals, and many more besides.

KEY ACCOUNT MANAGEMENT (KAM)

The following is necessarily a very quick summary of what is a large topic, and one of increasing importance to the marketer. For a fuller treatment, please refer to *Key Account Management*, 3rd edition, by Peter Cheverton, published by Kogan Page, 2004.

The KAM process

Figure 19.3 suggests a logical process for working through the KAM challenge. It is not a strict chronological flow: most businesses are plunged into the fray of managing customers, so in reality all this must happen at once. The discrete steps are important, however. KAM is demanding on your organization's resources, and it is vital to ensure that they are being applied to the right targets, and for the right reasons.

Why KAM?

Here are perhaps the eight most typical reasons that companies choose to practise KAM:

- customer consolidation;
- global customers demanding a uniform approach and service;
- new purchasing practices;

Understand the Opportunity

↓

Select the Targets

↓

Prioritize the Resource

↓

Plan the Entry Strategy

↓

Build Diamond Team Relationships

↓

Develop the Value Proposition

while all the time…
avoiding the sins and the pitfalls, and
developing the skills, processes and disciplines

Figure 19.3 *The KAM process*

- the supplier's own complexity – multiple business units…;
- a growth opportunity requiring prioritization of resources;
- the fact that your products alone no longer provide a source of competitive advantage: *relationships matter*;
- the desire to sell solutions, not products;
- the pursuit of *abnormal* returns for abnormal efforts…

There is a difference between the first four and the second four. The first four are what we might call 'defensive' reasons: because we have to – new purchasing practices being a particular stimulus. The second four are 'aggressive' reasons: because we believe practising KAM will give us an advantage. It may seem that the latter reasons are the better, but in truth, it is often the former that make companies do it!

Figure 19.4 indicates the way in which KAM has been used to redress the balance between supplier and customer; a balance weighted in the customer's favour as the result of what we might call the 'purchasing revolution'.

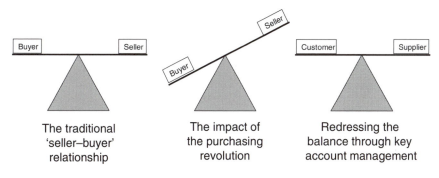

Buyer
Seller
The traditional 'seller–buyer' relationship
Seller
Buyer
The impact of the purchasing revolution
Customer
Supplier
Redressing the balance through key account management

Figure 19.4 *Redressing the balance*

Pursuing key supplier status

Buyers have become more professional: they have greater access to information on suppliers than ever before, and they are using it. A typical use is to identify key suppliers, or preferred suppliers, or perhaps even strategic suppliers – necessarily a very small number of the competing crowd. KAM is to some large extent the pursuit of key supplier status.

What is a key account?

A key account is an investment of the company's time, people, assets, energies and capabilities. The investment anticipates a future return, superior to that to be expected from a traditional sales approach. The key words here are 'investment' and 'future'; key accounts may not be your largest customers today. Indeed, your largest customers today may already be, to some extent, the past.

What is KAM?

If a key account is an investment, then KAM is the management of your investments, or, put another way, managing the future. Figure 19.5 reminds us what is involved in that: balancing objectives with resources and the true opportunity; with KAM providing the ability to identify the real opportunity, and so position the appropriate resource.

Figure 19.5 *Managing the future*

We have seen in Chapters 17 and 18 one important way to identify the real opportunity: to understand the market chain *beyond* your customer. At the same time, the key account team must be building relationships within the customer's organization to ensure a full and proper understanding of the customer's needs, and expectations for value. Their task is to penetrate the customer's decision-making process.

Penetrating the customer's decision-making process: the snail

Let's consider the example of a food flavours supplier selling to an fmcg food manufacturer. The supplier has a particular capability for developing novel flavours, and what it wants more than anything else is early access to new product developments, so that it can get its ingredients listed. If we consider how new ideas for such products emerge from a typical fmcg company, the result might look something like Figure 19.6.

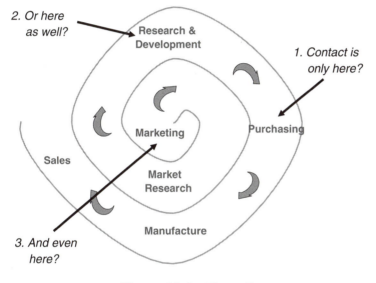

Figure 19.6 _The snail_

Typically, a new idea sees the light of day in the marketing department and develops by working its way through a series of other departments: first to market research for an earlier evaluation of interest, then on to R&D to be certain it can be made, then manufacturing to prepare for scale-up, purchasing to source the materials on a large scale and finally the sales force to sell it into the market. The development may not be entirely linear, with plenty of overlaps and backward loops, but it is a reasonably accurate picture of many such new-product developments.

Now let's consider the supplier and its contacts. If its relationship is primarily with the purchasing people – not untypical – there are some pros and cons for the supplier:

Out on a limb...

Pros

● If an idea has reached this point in the snail then it is probably a genuine requirement, not a speculative one; an order could be on its way soon.
● You will be discussing real details, not 'wild blue yonder' forecasts.

Cons

- The conversation is going to be about price – perhaps not the supplier's strongest suit.
- It may be too late; another supplier may already be preferred, and talking with you is just a ruse to get the price down.
- You may not have enough time to develop whatever is required.
- You probably only get to hear about existing product opportunities, not those all-important new ones.

Getting closer...

Perhaps the supplier has managed to penetrate further into the customer's 'snail' and has a relationship with the R&D people; now there is a different list of pros and cons:

Pros

- The conversations are about technical ability – your strong suit.
- You have time to develop your proposition.
- If you get specified by the R&D folk, it will be hard for purchasing to pressure you on price.

Cons

- This new product still may not see the light of day; this could be a risky investment of your time and effort.

Getting to the heart

And what if they penetrate even further, to the marketing people?

Pros

- Being in at the start gives you plenty of time to get your act together.
- You can head off the competition before they even hear of the opportunity.
- The conversations are about the future and collaboration.
- The customer is taking you into their confidence.
- This will not be about price.

Cons

- Marketing have a hundred great ideas and only three or four turn into real successes; this could eat up your resources in speculative trials.
- Perhaps the customer's R&D folk don't have much time for their own marketing people, you could be seen by your prime contact as collaborating with the internal enemy!

The downsides are not to be ignored, but if they can be managed, the upsides are overwhelming. Consider the customer's ambitions. The snail is necessarily a slow process, and most fmcg companies seek to increase their speed to market. In pursuit of this aim, they will attempt to modify the snail, to break down its linear nature, perhaps talking of _process re-engineering_ or _supply chain management_ or _matrix management_ as they do so. Whatever the terminology used, they require suppliers who will help them, suppliers with the ability to manage complex relationships across functions, businesses and perhaps even continents. Such suppliers will be regarded as key suppliers, and this is the true significance of the key account relationship: the achievement of key supplier status.

So far so good, but don't expect a lone sales professional to achieve all this on their own – not even the ones who seem to wear their underpants on the outside! This is a task for a key account _diamond team_.

Not a job for Super-rep... but a team

The KAM relationship model: building diamond teams

Figure 19.7 illustrates the way in which a key account relationship might grow, through distinct phases. It will grow for a combination of two reasons:

- the supplier's strategic intent – _it believes this to be a good investment_;
- the customer's strategic intent – _it believes this supplier to be a good partner_.

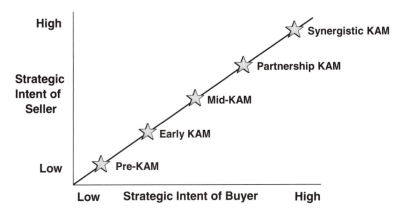

Figure 19.7 _The KAM relationship development model_
Adapted from a model developed by A F Millman and K J Wilson, From key account selling to key account management, _Journal of Marketing Practice: Applied Marketing_, 1 (1). pp 9--21 (1994)

Early KAM: the bow tie

The early KAM relationship may resemble that shown in Figure 19.8.
  Some possible characteristics of this stage might include:

- Principal contact is between two people: salesperson and buyer.
- The relationship may be competitive, each seeking to gain advantage.
- At worst, the relationship may be confrontational.

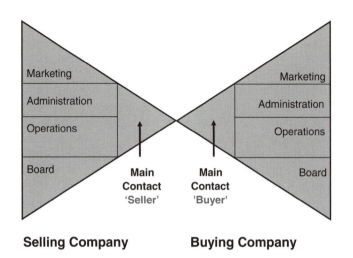

Figure 19.8 *Early KAM: the bow tie relationship*
Adapted from Key *Account Management: Learning from supplier and customer relationships,*
Cranfield University School of Management (1996)

- The buyer may see any attempt to gain access to other contacts as a threat to their own position and power.
- Price discussions dominate: the buyer focuses on costs.
- The supplier focuses on increased volume.
- Suppliers are judged on unspecified performance criteria.
- The customer is still assessing alternative suppliers.
- Disputes can lead to long-term breaks in supply.

This is probably the most typical sales relationship, the classic 'bow tie', and it is a dangerous stage. It is all too easy, and apparently attractive, just to stay here. The salesperson is in full control of the relationship, with no distractions from badly informed colleagues – and they get all the praise for success! This is the stage that promises a place in the limelight at the next sales conference.

Moreover, the buyer may also be quite happy with this state of affairs: they are secure, know all that goes on with the supplier, and can keep all their carefully guarded secrets.

The buyer as gatekeeper matched with the salesperson as superstar makes for a relationship with a built-in resistance to change, but the downsides of staying here are many:

- Expertise on both sides is seriously under-utilized.
- Seller and buyer are expected to be all-round experts – an unlikely state of affairs.
- Information flow is restricted as buyer and seller jockey for negotiating position.

- When information does flow, it is littered with 'Chinese whispers' as it is translated along the chain: expert to non-expert, to non-expert, to expert... and back.
- Projects and activities are held up by the sales/purchasing bottleneck.
- There is over-reliance on one relationship, and if it breaks (buyers retire, salespeople get promoted) then the whole thing must start again; the future is permanently at risk.
- Salespeople become 'kingpins' who cannot be moved on for fear of losing the business. (Rewrite that last point's comment: salespeople retire, buyers get promoted...)

A major limitation of this kind of relationship is the way that it denies the supplier full access to the customer's internal processes, and to the customer's market. A salesperson might have very little knowledge of what happens to their product once it is bought, still less how the customer operates in its own market. These are serious gaps if the supplier is to understand how it may best help the customer.

Sometimes the denial of access will be deliberate. In the retail industry it is not unusual for buyers to limit a supplier's access to contacts, and so to valuable information. It is a matter of power, and ownership of the market. In the past, major brands often dominated relationships as a result of their consumer knowledge and huge advertising budgets. Increasingly, the retailer's enhanced knowledge of consumer behaviour – through, for instance, electronic point of sale and loyalty cards – is shifting the balance. Knowledge is undeniably power, and why should it be shared with suppliers? Many purchasing organizations are becoming increasingly concerned about the leakage of valuable information to suppliers, with no tangible return.

That said, there are advantages to this kind of relationship: it is simple, it is relatively low cost, it is controllable – and if it gets you where you want to go, there may be no need to go beyond it. But take care with such certainty; be sure it is not just complacency.

Partnership KAM: the diamond team

It is likely that if the target customer is important enough to your future (ie a key account) then you will wish to develop a relationship that looks more like the one in Figure 19.9. This leaps a step in the model shown in Figure 19.7, but we will return to that mid stage in a while.

Some possible characteristics of this stage might include the following:

- Key supplier status is awarded.
- Relationships are based on trust.
- Information is shared.
- Access to people is facilitated.
- Pricing is stable.

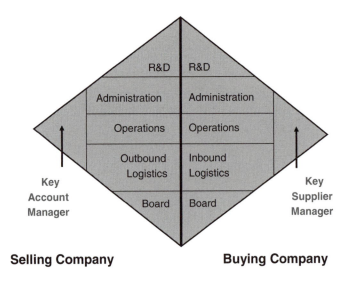

	R&D	R&D	
Key Account Manager	Administration	Administration	Key Supplier Manager
	Operations	Operations	
	Outbound Logistics	Inbound Logistics	
	Board	Board	

Selling Company   **Buying Company**

Figure 19.9 *Partnership KAM: the diamond relationship*
Adapted from *Key Account Management: Learning from supplier and customer relationships*,
Cranfield University School of Management (1996)

- The customer gets new ideas first.
- Continuous improvement is expected.
- There are clear 'vendor ratings' and 'performance measures'.
- There are possible contractual arrangements.
- Value is sought through integrated business processes.
- Value is sought through focus on the customer's markets.
- 'Step-outs' are permitted.
- The key account manager's role is one of coordination and orchestration.
- The supplier's main contact, while perhaps still the commercial buyer, is now focused on developing the supplier's capabilities rather than challenging them.
- The supplier's total organization is focused on customer satisfaction through 'supply chain management'.

This is where the benefits should start to flow. With the proper deployment of expertise on both sides, with the more open and honest transfer of information, and with the resultant improvement in customer understanding, the supplier has the potential to move towards significant competitive advantage. By taking the right actions it may even secure key supplier status, with its attendant increase in long-term security.

If a major downside to the 'bow tie' of early KAM was the denial of access to the customer's internal processes and to its market, the main advantage of the 'diamond' relationship is in seeing those conduits of understanding opening up. At this point of the KAM journey, the path to providing genuine solutions to the customer's problems changes from a rutted track to a metalled road.

Moving from bow tie to diamond

But watch out. As contacts proliferate, so does the speed of activity and the risk of saying and doing the wrong things. People without experience of 'sales' will be put in front of customers, and some of them might just panic at the prospect. The biggest danger is rushing things: confusing the customer, confusing your own team – a recipe for chaos and disaster. So, some things to help us navigate the path: 1) the mid-KAM stage; and 2) the contact matrix and GROWs. I will deal with these in turn.

Mid-KAM

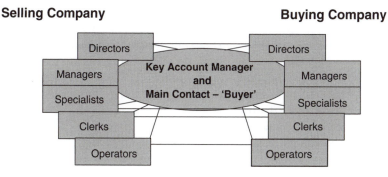

Figure 19.10 _Mid-KAM_

Adapted from _Key Account Management: Learning from supplier and customer relationships,_
Cranfield University School of Management (1996)

Some possible characteristics of this stage (Figure 19.10) might include the following:

- Principal contacts start to facilitate other contacts, through mutual desire to increase understanding of the customer's processes and markets.
- There is an increase in the time spent in meetings.
- There is a focus on reporting those meetings, actioning minutes, etc.
- Increased trust and openness are developing.
- Links are informal, and are still facilitated through the salesperson and buyer.
- It is perhaps at this stage that the greatest chance for 'mishaps' occurs; expect setbacks.
- This is a lot of work for both seller and buyer!

This is the transition stage between the classic 'bow tie' and the 'diamond' of the partnership KAM stage. It is a stage full of sensitivity, and, if the supplier is wise, involves slow, measured steps forward.

Noting that the buyer is quite likely to feel threatened by any increase in contacts 'beyond their control', the key account manager must ensure that all these new contacts are cleared with the buyer and arranged *through* the buyer. The key account manager will almost certainly have to be involved in putting the contacts together, attending the first meetings, and perhaps further. Ideally, the buyer will also be involved in these meetings, but if not, their outcomes will certainly have to be reported to the buyer in full.

How many key accounts can be managed?

Add to this activity a briefing and coaching role, and we can see the biggest problem of this stage: the potential overload of activities for the key account manager. The question raised when looking at this stage is, how many key accounts can an individual key account manager have responsibility for, if the supplier is passing through this stage? Add to this the fact that the mid-KAM stage can go on for many months, perhaps even years, and we must think seriously about how many customers can be classified as key accounts.

One possible result of this period of hard labour is that it can be all too easy to throw in the towel. It can be seen as just too much effort, not worth the candle – and, after all, the resultant benefits of moving towards partnership KAM are unlikely to flow for some time. The temptation to go back to the relative comforts of the 'bow tie' will be strong. Resist!

Proceeding through the transition mid-KAM stage can be very hard work indeed. At times it will seem more effort than it is worth, to both sides. This will call for all the patience, understanding and resolve you can muster. It will call on every skill and tool within your grasp, and some that are beyond your reach. At this point, you will need friends and allies. This, let it be understood very clearly, is not a task for loners.

Tips on moving from bow tie to diamond

- Don't expect your journey to be one way; there will be U-turns and side alleys.
- Remember that the strategic intent must be mutual, and even then, don't expect the customer to make it easy for you. You will have to lead a lot of the way, and while stamina and persistence will be two valuable assets, so will subtlety and finesse. You will know when you are getting there: when the customer starts to pull.
- Remember, the buyer has a lot of power when they are the only point of contact. Your efforts to develop broader contacts might be for the good of the buyer's company, but the buyer might not see it as good for them! You are about to threaten their control.
- To sell or not to sell? If the customer sees your 'selling' activity as a pushy concern for satisfying your own needs, then don't be surprised if you come up against obstacles. If the customer perceives it as seeking solutions to its problems, then the doors will start to open.

- Some customers will demand that the key account manager should not be a 'salesperson' at all, but a business manager and a relationship manager.
- Some customers might not like being called 'accounts' – so this is a word for internal use, not your business card (in the end, you can call them whatever makes them feel good!).
- Don't let your organization loose on theirs with no direction and no control; chaos can be the only outcome, quickly followed by a rapid raising of the customer's drawbridge.
- Don't allow the commercially 'innocent' members of your team to be taken for a ride by the customer. Brief them first, and, above all, train them. This goes for everyone, including the boss (actually, especially the boss…).
- Don't describe this journey, internally, as an initiative. Many companies have had 'initiative overload', and your own team will steer clear of this latest 'nine-day wonder'.
- One sure 'killer' of progress from bow tie to diamond is the unrealistic tightening of travel budgets; strong relationships require personal contacts.
- Be careful how you present your intentions to the customer; being told that you wish to be more 'intimate' may concern the buyer, confuse him or her, or worse!
- Take care if you are the first to use the word 'partnership'. Try to hear it on the customer's lips first.
- Perhaps your customer will use 'partnership' as a trap. 'Let's work in partnership,' they say, meaning 'You tell us your cost breakdowns, then we'll take you to the cleaners.'
- Recognize the need to move from hunting to farming (see below).
- Use two simple tools: the contact matrix and GROWs (see below).

From hunters to farmers

Key account management and relationship marketing are vital activities in mature markets where competition is tough and the customer's decision processes are complex. But what about times of rapid growth; might all this just slow you down?

There is a time to hunt and a time to farm; the marketer's task is to know when to make the transition.

With the opening up of the telecommunications market in the 1990s, the appearance of new players such as MCI, WorldCom and Mercury saw a frenzy of hunting, and quite rightly so, as the opportunities were there to be seized by the most energetic. Within just a few years, however, the easy targets were gone, and the original players such as BT were starting to win back their lost customers. The time for farming had arrived, with a new focus on customer retention and growth rather than just new customer acquisition.

When the market is a jungle, hunt…
… but for how long will that work?

The contact matrix and GROWs

The contact matrix and GROWs are two simple tools designed to ensure that control is maintained as relationships become more complex. Figure 19.11 shows a contact matrix, a simple grid that shows who in the KA team is responsible for seeing whom, in the customer.

	Key Account Manager	Your team member	Your team member	Your team member	Your team member	Your team member
Buying Director	XXX					
Their team member	XX	Ken Reilly - John Smith G - Secure order for xxxx R - Present solution yyyy O - Brief team on progress W - 3rd July, London				XX
Their team member					X	
Their team member	X			XXX		X
Their team member		John Harris, Site Manager Specifier Problem holder Laggard	XXX			
Their team member						XXX

Figure 19.11 *The contact matrix*

For each point of contact, a GROW should be drawn up. GROW is an acronym standing for:

- **G**oal – what is the big purpose of this relationship?
- **R**ole – what activities will this person carry out?
- **O**bligation – to the team; what are their responsibilities, limits to authority, etc?
- **W**ork plan – the nitty-gritty of dates and schedules.

Key account plans and marketing plans

Where is the marketer in all this? Key account managers are clearly going to be important people, and it is increasingly the case that they are not promoted sales reps, but senior managers with the authority required to get things done. So, is this a sales takeover? KAM is not a sales initiative; it is a business initiative, and calls on the participation of all functions if partnership KAM relationships are to be formed and if the outcome of those relationships is to be used to drive the business. As such, it must involve marketing, and marketing should take a keen interest – indeed, more than a keen interest: key accounts are part of their market and segment plans.

Figure 19.12 shows how key account plans are in fact subsets of segment plans. In identifying key accounts (see page 214) it is necessary to have done the market segmentation first. The figure shows two key accounts in two segments, and none in a third. This is quite normal; there is no rule that says there must be key accounts in every segment. Indeed, some would argue that if KAM is about developing understanding, and if a segment is truly a group of customers with similar needs, attitudes and behaviours, then there is only need for one key account in any segment!

Key Account Management is very much part of the marketer's responsibility

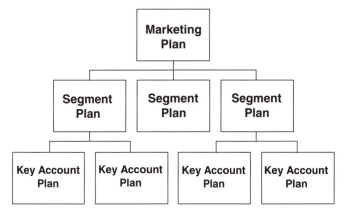

Figure 19.12 *The planning hierarchy*

Without segmentation, the selection of key accounts will tend to suffer from 'sizeism'. Comparing customers against attractiveness factors (see page 214) becomes difficult if you are dealing with a range of segments: what seems attractive in one may not be so important in another, and so the scale of business becomes the only truly comparable factor – hence 'sizeism'.

Avoid 'sizeism'

CUSTOMER CLASSIFICATION AND DISTINCTION

How many diamond teams can you form? Not many, given the requirements and given your resources – and, as important as either of these considerations, given the number of customers deserving them. Selecting only a small number of key accounts makes it possible for the appropriate resources to be applied to develop the relationships, and the organization can cope with the resultant rise in activity levels. Having too many key accounts will result either in no effect at all or, worse, in splintering your capabilities into little, ineffective pieces.

Identifying the key accounts – and the non-key accounts

Using a modified version of the Directional Policy Matrix already described in Chapters 9 and 15 (and to be described again in Chapter 22), you can identify your key accounts as being those customers that are attractive to you and that regard you in a similar light. This mutuality is important, as we will see when looking at the development of the relationship itself. Figure 19.13 shows such a matrix. (You will note that the flow of the horizontal axis is reversed, with *HIGH* on the right. There is no particular reason for this; it is just the way two matrices have developed, and conventions formed. Such are the minor frustrations of marketing!)

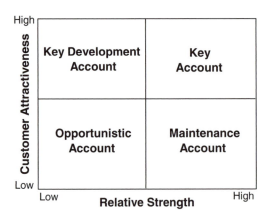

Figure 19.13   *Customer classification: identifying key accounts*

The elements that determine how attractive the customer is to you will depend on your own priorities, but should be focused as much on the future as possible. Your relative strength is based on the customer's perspective, and hence whatever criteria it uses to measure and select suppliers. These *vendor ratings* will be unique to each customer.

Making it happen: customer distinction

Once the key accounts are identified, you will also have identified three other categories of customer:

- key development accounts;
- maintenance accounts;
- opportunistic accounts.

Each of these will require its own sales and service strategy. Indeed, without such it is highly unlikely that any progress will be made with the key accounts.

Figure 19.14 shows how 'energy' must be freed up from maintenance and opportunistic accounts, to be invested in key and key development accounts.

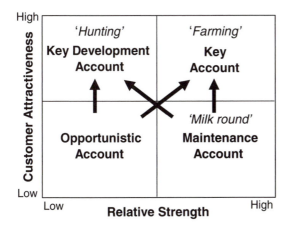

Figure 19.14 _Freeing up the energy_

The labels suggest some generic sales approaches: the _hunter_ for the key development accounts, seeking to penetrate and make quick wins; the _farmer_ for the key account, nurturing and building for the future; and the _milk round_ for the maintenance account, finding means of servicing these customers regularly, without any risk of loss, but without the expenditure of time from people who will be more valuable targeting key and key development accounts. This may mean the more active involvement of customer service in 'selling', or the use of tools such as Internet portals or customer relationship management systems (see page 219).

The design of specific sales and service packages for each classification of customers might include distinctions based on the following:

- profitability and the time horizon;
- level and depth of contacts;
- nature of commitment to the customer;
- contracts – long or short, or none at all;
- allocation of resources;
- nature and number of projects;
- provision of services;
- charging for services;
- terms and pricing;
- use of distributors.

CUSTOMER SERVICE

Good customer service wins every time, and is a vital part of any relationship management strategy. It is a source of differentiation in an increasingly uniform world. It builds loyalty, so aiding customer retention. It plays a key roll in supporting key account management – and so the list goes on.

Bad customer service is another thing altogether; just consider the following. Good news about your service can travel fast, but not nearly so fast as bad news. Here is an example of an increasingly common style of complaint about bad service, made to a major corporation:

> I would be grateful if you will settle my problem as a priority and keep me informed of your actions either by fax or e-mail (not by post as this is too slow). If I don't hear from you within two days I will contact your HQ in the US. I will also inform dedicated mailing lists on the Internet and the consumer watchdogs here and in the States. I will ensure that the maximum number of people get to hear about the way your company treats its customers. I run my own company and would never dream of treating my customers like this.

The interesting aspect is not the complaint itself but the intention to do something about poor service, to 'get even'.

The keyboard is mightier than the sword

A recent news story concerned a young man whose wedding had been ruined by a bout of food poisoning among the guests at the reception. He had received no help from the hotel concerned, whether by trying to explain the outbreak, deal with the problem, or take any interest whatever. He was not looking for an admission of guilt, simply a dialogue, but the hotel chose to wash its hands of the whole affair. The man discovered that the hotel chain had not yet registered an Internet site using its own name, so he registered one with its name and posted a series of articles on his plight for anyone who might be thinking of using the chain to read. Vindictive, or simply another case of the pen (or in this case the keyboard) being mightier than the sword?

Customer service and differentiation

Some people buy Heinz baked beans in Fortnum & Masons, knowing full well that they are paying a premium. The premium is for the environment, the experience, the prestige, and the impeccable service. Some of these people are one-off tourists, but plenty go back week after week.

Some professional buyers will pay a premium to a supplier that manages its stock for it, or provides quality assurance checks, or contributes to forecasts, or will break bulk, or help out with emergency deliveries, or provide expert technicians to work problems through on the customer's premises. With such service, who would want to bother about changing supplier?

Some hard-nosed businesspeople will pay a premium for a photocopier that comes with a 'no questions asked' guarantee to have the copier replaced. Xerox gained nearly five market share percentage points when it introduced such a guarantee.

Customer service and customer retention

Bad service loses customers. Consider the following statistics showing reasons for a B2B customer to change its supplier:

- Few than 10% change because of changes in their own personnel (often the outgoing suppliers excuse, but rarely the sole truth);
- Fewer than 10% change because of a competitor's offer (the costs involved in changing often outweigh the benefits of an apparently 'better' offer);
- Fewer than 15% change because of dissatisfaction with the product (getting suppliers to improve their product is often easier than changing supplier);
- More than 65% change because of poor customer service, often expressed as 'indifference' shown by the supplier or a member of staff at the supplier.

It is interesting to note the use of the word 'indifference' in relation to service. Few customers expect 100 per cent perfection; to err is human ('but to really foul things up requires a computer' – *Farmer's Almanac*, 1978), it is said. What really gets to customers is the supplier's failure to act in response to a problem, or even to recognize that anything has occurred. Too many suppliers are afraid that any recognition of a problem will imply an admission of guilt, so let's keep quiet and hope it goes away (and, as we see, the customer often does).

When customers 'snap'

Of course, when there are no competitors, or demand far exceeds supply, bad service doesn't matter, or so many businesses have thought. All seems well as the sales graph points skywards, and then the market starts to level out, or a new player arrives on the scene. Now come the frantic pursuit of customer loyalty schemes and the price-cutting exercises that turn customer retention into an expensive activity. Worse follows as customers that seemed entirely happy suddenly 'snap' and go elsewhere. Of course, the truth is that they were probably far from happy, but had no alternative but to stay with their existing supplier. They were on the *low competition curve* shown in Figure 19.15.

When customers have few alternatives, their level of satisfaction must be very low indeed to warrant the effort involved in changing supplier. When choice is wide and easy to take up, the competition curve can 'snap' like a

Figure 19.15 *When customers 'snap'*

piece of high-tension wire, and the smallest dissatisfaction can see them on their way.

The splendid value of good customer service

On average, winning a new customer costs five times more than the annual cost of retaining and maintaining an existing one. The importance, and value, of customer service in keeping customers is huge.

Developing a customer service offer

Strategy, people, processes

First, what do you wish customer service to achieve for your business, and how? Is it principally about retaining and maintaining existing business through high levels of customer satisfaction, or is it about winning new business, perhaps through a sales-orientated 'and will there be anything else, madam?' kind of approach?

Then comes a debate: which is the more important, the people or the processes? The 'right' mix must depend on the market needs and the supplier's capabilities; strictly applied 'formulas' for customer service delivered through tightly managed call centres will suit some strategies, while others will demand the personal attention of empowered staff.

The debate is sometimes blurred by internal drivers: call centres, and especially those sited in low-salary countries, have been attractive to suppliers because they help bring down the costs of customer service, but are they attractive to customers? A recent survey from Contact Babel, using ICM research, showed that one in seven Britons who knowingly came into contact with a call centre based overseas reacted by removing their business.

The Marriott hotel group realizes that its own staff are at the heart of any customer service strategy, and if staff turnover gets too high then they start to have customer service problems. Marriott found a correlation between reducing staff turnover and increasing customer retention. A 10 per cent reduction in staff turnover at a particular hotel would lead to a 1 to 3 per cent decrease in lost customers, and that translates to an increase in revenue across the chain of between $50 and $100 million. Marriott consider its investment in customer service through staff retention a sound one.

Good people = good service

Perhaps you have been lucky enough to receive the perfect customer service, and if you did, I'm prepared to bet it was down to the people involved. Probably a small business where the people you were working with had the authority to do what you needed. The challenge for larger suppliers is to replicate that kind of service across a wide range of customer contact points, perhaps even across different countries and cultures. How do you develop a process that will do that, without killing the human element that made it so good in the first place?

A 'good' process is one designed for the benefit of the customer, one that can be changed as customers' needs change, one that delivers value to the customer, and one that enhances the supplier's ability to improve that value over time. In a small business that might mean no more than regular meetings of the staff concerned, to discuss failures and successes, in pursuit of improved ways of handling their customers.

In my own business, we meet after every major event, such as our one-day master classes, to discuss what we could do better next time; and we add ideas to an action checklist. Last time around it was to put a needle and thread in the materials box, as one of our delegates had developed an embarrassing hole in his trousers…

Good processes = good service

In a large business this will call for rules, agreed service levels by categories of customers, and almost certainly the use of customer relationship management (CRM) tools.

CUSTOMER RELATIONSHIP MANAGEMENT

'We installed CRM last month, and now we have the world's best, and most expensive, address book.' So said one cynic, perhaps missing the point, or perhaps simply echoing the experience of many.

The potential offered by CRM is huge, but it seems that too few get to see it materialize. Perhaps the mistake is seeing this as another 'let's do something to the market' process, whereas it should be opening the doors to a new ability to work *with* the market.

CRM doesn't have to involve complex software, or even software at all; it is a process for collecting data on how customers behave, determining their needs from that data, and presenting the business in a way that will meet those needs. It might be as simple as a tone of voice or a style of service, or as complex as a solution to a business problem. Sales professionals have been doing this for years, in their heads. What has not been so easy in the past has been the transfer of what is in those sales reps' heads to the business as a whole.

CRM, in its software mode, seeks to harvest and share data from every customer interaction. A supermarket gets data from the point-of-sale scanner and your use of a loyalty card; the B2B supplier gets it from a variety of manual and electronic ordering processes. Each interaction with customers has the potential to provide information about their needs, their buying behaviour, their perceptions, their concerns and their frustrations.

New techniques come along so quickly as to make examples seem positively antediluvian, but here are just three from the Web site arena:

1. Analysis of the customer's *clickstreams* as they work their way around your Web site and into your system can reveal how they go about making their choices – do they look for information first, do they check for alternatives?
2. The *virtual sales assistant* allows customers to ask questions, and in so doing reveal much about their interests, their certainties, their doubts and their priorities.
3. Some sites allow customers to interrogate *virtual customers*, to seek 'opinions' of the product or service, and through this interaction the customers will display a whole range of concerns, attitudes and perceptions.

Such information is kept in a *data warehouse*, and at this point the amount of information can be mind-boggling. Without sophisticated *data mining* techniques we would soon be pining for 'old-fashioned' market researchers with clipboards! Data mining seeks patterns in the data; patterns of behaviour that indicate concerns, interests or needs. We are back to the world of the sales professional but in a modern guise – with systems instead of people looking for *buying signals*. Customer behaviours can be tracked to see if they indicate such things as a willingness to pay more for speed, or a desire to set a specification, and so it goes on.

Of course, concerns abound as to how such relationship management techniques can or will be used. How many of us would want our bank to analyse our behaviour in this way, even if it did do so in order to provide us with a better service?

Boots is a big user of various CRM techniques, but it makes clear that it would never seek to use them for individual customer selling; health care is too sensitive an issue to be seen to be prying. Boots aims to aggregate the information to identify trends and to customize its offer, but not to individualize it.

Customization and individualization

Perhaps the most exciting application of CRM technology is its use in the design of the offer itself. CRM data provides the basis, should you wish it, for a much more detailed segmentation study, creating sub-segments or micro-segments based on the real behaviours of your customers. Some argue that we will be able to segment right down to individual customer level – already a feature of the B2B and service environment through key account management, though perhaps not really required in fmcg circumstances? Tesco used to manage its customers through six segments, but the use of CRM systems has allowed it to build that into the hundreds, so ensuring a higher degree of relevance, and hence success, in its promotional messages.

Does such individualization necessarily bring competitive advantage? Suppliers of products with a standard core but a variety of possible add-ons have much to gain in this way – witness Dell and its online 'configurator', allowing customers to design their very own Dell. This allows the customer into the supplier's own systems, rather as if we were able to go and knock on the factory door and submit our own request.

I loathe the whole business of buying a car; for some it is a joy, but for me it is just one long series of compromises and frustrations. I make my choice, only to find that the model I want can't have the type of seat I want, and the one that has the seat I want won't take off the boy racer spoilers... The car manufacturer that is able to regard me as an individual segment and allows me to talk directly to its factory in order to design my own car spec will have my undying loyalty.

The problems with making such a notion reality are of course many and complex, but the challenge is on. First, current manufacturing systems will stand in the way of such 'interference' from customers. Second, the supply chain logistics could easily be frozen solid by such 'infinite variety'. Third, and for now perhaps the biggest issue, in many markets there will just not be enough takers to make such a proposition economical. Of course, once customers wake up to what they can get from a supplier, and once the demand starts to build, then manufacturing and supply chain systems that cannot oblige will leave their owners looking like dinosaurs. Competitors that _can_ oblige will start to siphon off the customers prepared to pay for such a service, most likely the high-margin end of the business, and the dinosaurs will find themselves in a potentially vicious circle of decline.

Looked at from the other perspective, the supplier that offers such choice will be the supplier that builds the most detailed knowledge of customer requirements and motivations. This knowledge is then used to drive better value propositions, and so we see the start of a virtuous circle of growth.

CRM: marketing's baby, or IT's toy?

Simply installing a CRM system will do nothing for the supplier or for the customer. In too many cases this is what happens, because the CRM strategy is not properly set or owned by the marketing department. This happens particularly when the marketing folk are daunted by the technical complexities and hand the whole thing over to the IT specialists…

20

Brand management

Two or three hundred years ago, branding was something you did to a cow. A brand declared rights of property and ownership, and meant, particularly in remote Scottish glens, 'keep your hands off!'. It is a nice irony that one of the key social and economic phenomena of the past hundred or so years should turn the words' meaning on their head: the 21st-century brand most determinedly declares 'get your hands on!'.

Chapter 16 laid out the strategic issues behind branding: its purpose, how to manage the brand architecture, and how to position the brand. This chapter turns to the ways in which brands must be managed in order for them to take their part in delivering the value. We will examine five key areas:

1.   the history of delivering value;
2.   the brand relationship;
3   building positive associations – *moments of truth*;
4.   brand extensions;
5.   the learning brand.

THE HISTORY OF DELIVERING VALUE

Trade marks

The history tour starts in 1876 with the United Kingdom's first registered trade mark; the red triangle still used today by Bass, the brewers. Brands had existed before that, but this marked their official recognition. So why now?

The explosive rise of urban populations during the industrial revolution meant that by the close of the 19th century only a tiny fraction of people still bought direct from the original producer. The age of mass production and mass distribution had arrived. Where their parents would have made bargains with artisans to 'make to order', or shopped at local stores for goods that were finished on the spot, late 19th-century consumers were having to put their trust in a middleman, or indeed a string of middlemen. The late Victorian tippler never met the man who brewed his ale, but the red triangle told him that he was as safe with it as if the brewer had been his neighbour. The brand as we know it today began its life as a simple mark of authenticity.

There's only one ENO

ENO's 'Fruit Salt' carried the following caution in 1903: 'Examine the bottle and capsule and see that they are marked "**ENO's** 'Fruit Salt", otherwise you have been imposed upon by a **WORTHLESS** imitation.'

Brands were trade marks, and trade marks were brands. The honour role of 19th-century consumer brands that are still with us is remarkable when we consider the huge changes in all other walks of life. Anchor butter, Avon cosmetics, Bassett's Liquorice Allsorts, Baxter's soup, Beecham's pills, Bird's custard, Bovril, Brooke Bond tea, Cadbury's, Clark's shoes, Coca-Cola, Colman's mustard, Fyffe's bananas, Heinz (even the '57 varieties' goes back that far), Horlicks, Hovis, Jacob's biscuits, Johnson's baby powder, Kellogg's, Kodak, McVities, Omega watches, Parker pens, Pears soap, Robertson's Golden Shred marmalade, Rowntree's Fruit Pastilles, Schweppes (strictly speaking, late *18th* century), Slazenger tennis rackets, Tate & Lyle sugar, Wrigley's chewing gum, Yale locks – they all started life over a hundred years ago.

Promises, promises

By 1911, Kellogg's was already spending $1 million in the United States on advertising the familiar red signature, one of the world's most consistent claims to authenticity. But imitators abounded, and brand managers had to look beyond simple statements of authenticity; they began turning their brands into promises.

The promise might be for a better taste, purer ingredients, a longer life, a better physique, and to begin with these promises could sometimes get out of hand.

Dr J. Collis Browne's 'Chlorodyne' was advertised in 1902 as follows:

The most wonderful and valuable remedy ever discovered. Chlorodyne is the best remedy known for **coughs**, **colds**, **consumption**, **bronchitis**, **asthma**.

Chlorodyne effectually checks and arrests those too often fatal diseases – **diphtheria**, **fever**, **croup**, **ague**. Chlorodyne acts like a charm in **diarrhoea** and is the only specific in **cholera** and **dysentery**. Chlorodyne effectually cuts short all attacks of **epilepsy**, **hysteria**, **palpitation** and **spasms**. Chlorodyne is the only palliative in **neuralgia**, **rheumatism**, **gout**, **cancer**, **toothache**, **meningitis**, and etc. Caution – Beware of **Piracy** and **Imitation**.

(Collis Browne is still available today and is said to be good for treating diarrhoea.)

This period is rich with examples of products and advertisements that tried to 'hit' on every front at once. Carter's Extra Concentrated Lemonade offered 'Lemonade in a moment' – but not only that, it was also a 'prophylactic against cholera'. And to top it all, in case anybody thinks the notion of 'cost in use' (see Chapter 28) is a new one, the tag line was 'goes farthest – therefore cheapest'.

The unique selling proposition

As consumers grew more 'brand literate', so the promises had to moderate, and advertisers began to latch on to rather more single-minded claims as a means to give direction to the brands in their charge. In the 1940s Rosser Reeves led the way with unique selling propositions (USPs) and brands became very single-minded. USPs gave brands competitive advantage, and some USPs remain to this day. Volvo still 'owns' safety as a proposition in the car market, so much so that it has to try that much harder whenever it wants any message other than safety to be heard.

Campaigns such as 'Birds Eye – the modern way to cook', or 'Chew Wrigley's, Freshen your Taste!' might seem rather tame and innocent today, but at the time they were seen by many as aggressive and intrusive. The USP gave critics and competitors alike something to shoot at, and this was its drawback. If all your eggs were put in that one basket, what happened if someone came along with a better product? You might claim best performance, but new technology could outflank you.

The brand image

By the 1950s, admen like David Ogilvy were working to go beyond simple promises; they wanted to build 'brand image'. If a brand could acquire an image, a personality even, then that would enhance its protection against competitors. This was not simply the trick of a clever copywriter (though many of today's famous novelists had their writing apprenticeships in the post-war advertising agencies), this was marketing as defined by the Marketing Model in Chapter 2. A brand needed credibility to build its image (company capability) and it needed customers that would value that image (market needs). Only then would big advertising budgets bear fruit.

Making a house into a home	ICI, as one of the world's largest chemical companies, had credibility as a paint manufacturer, but it recognized that the new DIY paint buyers wanted more than technology in a tin. People wanted to turn their houses into homes, and that meant the warmth of family life. The Old English sheepdog (or Dulux dog, as most people have come to call it) was added to ICI's paint brand to give it that warm family feeling, and a brand *personality* was born.

Brands were becoming more complex, multi-faceted, eliciting emotional responses, and, as a result, they were able to command premiums for longer. The brand was a route not only to competitive advantage, but also to long-term security.

The 'T Plan'

In the 1960s, the J Walter Thompson agency was working with its 'T Plan', an intellectual concept that a brand was a synthesis of *knowledge, beliefs* and *emotional projections*. In other words, a brand was something that you knew about, that you might be able to state 'facts' about, facts that you believed to be true and that engendered feelings and emotions that went well beyond the product or its USP. It was these emotional projections that were most important. Volvo might 'own' safety as its USP, but the emotional projections were even more important: this was safety with a purpose, protecting your family. In the end it is this emotional projection or what we might call 'emotional charge' that gives Volvo its brand value, not the statistics about safety records or crash tests.

THE BRAND RELATIONSHIP

Take a quick look at the three pictures on the next page. Don't take too long over any of them, just a few seconds, and then move on.

The emotional charge

If you took the time, you could probably now fill a whole side of A4 with the various facts, pieces of knowledge, ideas, thoughts, beliefs, promises, expectations and emotions that just a few seconds exposed to three well-known 'brand images' have communicated to you. You can say so much because these brands carry clear 'emotional charges', the result of the way in which they interact with the customer, or even the way in which they build relationships with the customer.

Figure 20.4 repeats the model introduced in Chapter 16, dealing with how brands are positioned. We are now moving to the right of the model, and the way in which brands interact.

Figure 20.1 _Coca-Cola logo_

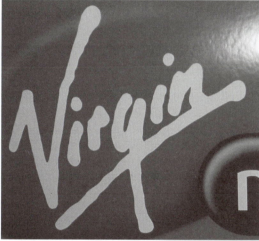

Figure 20.2 _Virgin logo_

Figure 20.3 _Mercedes logo_

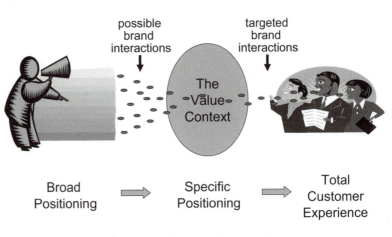

Figure 20.4 *Brand interactions*

Brand interactions and emotional charges

Brands are the sum of our interactions with the things that we buy. Those interactions represent a relationship, and, like human relationships, they can work at different levels of emotional charge.

Some brands call on consumers' emotional responses more than others. The reasons are numerous and complex, and depend most importantly on the individual consumer's perceptions. The following are some of the factors involved:

- the price paid;
- the frequency of purchase;
- the risk involved in the purchase;
- the risk involved in use;
- the conspicuity of the purchase;
- the importance of consistency;
- the utility of the product or service;
- the tangibility of performance;
- the number of brands competing for attention.

The factors do not work in isolation, nor do they always work in the same direction: just because an item is low priced, regularly purchased and has a utilitarian purpose, that doesn't mean that it can't have an emotional charge. Toilet paper is a case in point: the Andrex brand spends a lot, and does so consistently, to build emotional responses that go beyond these factors. The Andrex puppies used in UK television advertising exude messages of softness, warmth, care and responsibility (at the same time as helping communicate messages about the length of the roll!) – a subtle blend with a strong appeal.

Interactions – one or many?

A brand aiming at longevity needs to develop its definition on the basis of a range of customer interactions. Solo interaction brands risk replacement, either by changing times, or by lower-cost/price imitators.

Kodak is one of the world's most instantly recognizable brands, and it must be hoping that it is identified less with its product – film – than with the nature of its interaction. If Kodak is a film, then it's in trouble: digital is here to stay. If Kodak is about the interaction – photography and, more importantly, memories and the sharing of memories – then it might just survive.

Kodak: film or photography?

The retail brand has grown over recent years to become one of the strongest examples of branding. Why? It's not just about money; it's about the number of interactions that the customer has when shopping, and so the number of opportunities that the retailer has to develop a positive relationship. Figure 20.5 lists just some of those interactions.

- Location, Location, Location
- Free bus
- Free car park
- Spaces for mothers with kids
- Architecture and design
- Greeter and trolley host
- Deliver your laundry
- The crèche
- Kids' trolleys
- Smells of the in-store bakery….
- Salad bar
- Samples
- Demonstrations… *retail theatre…*
- The broccoli saw and grape scissors…
- The bunny bag…

- Related merchandise…
- Lunch
- The toilet stop… and a retail brand soap…
- Book a weekend away treat
- Thursday night is singles night….
- Queue at a sweet-free checkout
- Self-checkout
- Bag for life
- Bag packing
- Loyalty points
- Collect laundry
- Umbrella…
- Cheap petrol
- Home delivery

Figure 20.5 *Some retail brand interactions*

Interactions and loyalty

It is the job of a brand to create and maintain loyalty, and the more complex the relationship the consumer has with the brand, the greater the chance of success. Loyalty to a make of car is an excellent example. You are considering buying a new Mercedes. It is a high-price item, purchased rarely.

Buying the wrong car is a big mistake, driving the wrong car is a big mistake, plenty of people will draw conclusions about you from the car you drive, your father had one and it was great, you will use it every day for important business calls, you can feel its performance beneath your foot and, after all, there is only one Mercedes.

Perhaps, but for someone else the price is outrageous, they don't care what people think, it's only for a runaround, they never go above 30 mph and for them, a car is just a car. People and their different priorities: it's what brands are made for.

A brand can develop a high level of loyalty and emotional charge in the group of people at whom it is targeted. In so doing it may even antagonize those for whom it is not intended. Ever seen a TV ad that just makes you want to scream? Chances are, you weren't in the target audience.

Times change, and so must the interactions

DHL works hard to create its brand value around reliability and speed. The emotional charge for DHL comes from the business community's need to do things fast, globally. A brand that facilitates that is a hero brand. And then, along comes e-mail. Suddenly there is less need for such heroics: huge documents can be sent in seconds with no need for a fleet of planes, boats and trains. The brand must change into something other than a specialist emergency service.

The types of emotional charge

Table 20.1 defines four types of emotional charge, looks at the role of the brand against each, and shows some examples.

This table is not intended to pigeonhole particular brands, only to help express a concept. Of course, there are crossovers between the levels, and

Table 20.1 *Brands and 'emotional charge'*

'Emotional Charge'	The Role of the Brand	Examples
A social expression	Facilitate a feeling of belonging	Rolex watches; Hofmeister
Satisfaction or fulfilment	Win a premium price	Janet Reger; Cadbury's
A promise of performance in use	Influence choice	Crest toothpaste; Fairy Liquid
A guarantee of authenticity	Make choice easy	Kellogg's; Citizens' Advice Bureax

brands that work on more than one; that is their strength. There are many consumers who would fail to tell Kellogg's Cornflakes from a retailer's own label in a blind test, yet would gain genuine satisfaction from pouring their favourite breakfast cereal from a reassuringly genuine Kellogg's box.

Let's consider each of these levels of emotional charge, starting at the lowest level and rising in intensity, illustrated by examples from an fmcg, a business to business company and a service industry.

The brand as a guarantee of authenticity

In the days of the USSR, Borjomi sparkling mineral water from the Caucasus in Georgia was said to be the third best-known brand in the Union; the Volga car and Aeroflot took the top spots. By 1996, after nearly a decade of the kind of free enterprise that encouraged the rise of piracy and gangsterism, as much as 90 per cent of what went under the Borjomi label was said to be counterfeit! Then came the advertising campaign reminding consumers of the distinctive packaging of the real Borjomi ('beware imitations'), and the not insignificant financial crisis of 1998 that killed off many of the poorly financed counterfeiters. By 2000 the claim was that 90 per cent of Borjomi sold was genuine.

Keeping ahead (when all around are losing theirs)

The value of a strong trade mark or logo is clear when there are many players in the market and customers simply want an easy choice that they can trust. This is the home of the USP.

- *Fast-moving consumer goods*: Kellogg's and the famous 'if it doesn't say Kellogg's on the pack, it isn't Kellogg's inside the pack'.
- *B2B*: Hewlett-Packard replacement ink cartridges – this will work, and it won't wreck those expensive printers you've just had installed.
- *Service*: Citizens' Advice Bureaux – the advice will be genuine.

Of course, the Rolex logo or the Lacoste label is proof of authenticity just as much as the Kellogg's signature, but here we see one of the ironies of branding: if authenticity were all it is about, who would ever *knowingly* buy an imitation Rolex watch or a fake Lacoste shirt? That people do (though few would admit to it) only shows that some brands work on much higher levels of emotional charge and that some people are prepared to lie, even to themselves, to reach those levels.

The brand as a promise of performance in use

If a brand makes a promise of performance then it must be able to prove it. Often the proof is in the longevity of the brand, but this can be a problem, as Coca-Cola found when it tried to launch a new formulation. New Coke was a flop for a host of reasons, but one was undoubtedly the fact that many consumers felt a promise had been broken.

231

The higher the price tag or the risk involved in the purchase, the more important is the promise. Some products give long lists of their features as proof – computer hardware comes to mind – but good brands can achieve the same end more effectively. While a motor car will quote fuel consumption figures and torque ratios, the evidence of performance is promoted by more intangible imagery, references and associations. Condoms may print statistical evidence of their testing procedures on the packet, but for most people it is a matter of trusting in a particular brand name. When Durex started to market its more exotic range (the pursuit of satisfaction in use, not just performance), some consumers questioned for a moment whether the brand still retained its absolute trustworthiness and reliability.

- *Fast-moving consumer goods*: Fairy Liquid's famous comparison tests, or the Duracell battery in the Christmas toy that goes on, and on, and on…
- *B2B*: A brand such as Lycra promises performance on two levels – as a high-performance raw material for clothing manufacture, and as an aid to sales of that clothing through its strong consumer franchise.
- *Service*: KPMG and Simon-Kucher have brands that are able to promise performance through the 'honour role' of their client list.

The brand as satisfaction: pleasure or fulfilment

One of the best examples of a brand acting as an aid to satisfaction is the label on a bottle of wine. Simply seeing the bottle, if we recognize the name and think well of it, can convince us that the taste will be, and is, good. Try it for yourself in an open and then a blind test and just see if that isn't true, and if you disagree with me then at least you will have enjoyed the inquiry.

There is plenty of hard evidence that headache sufferers will feel better treated or soothed by taking a brand of analgesic that they have heard of rather than an unknown generic. Placebos masquerading as well-known brands have been shown to be more effective than placebos in plain white boxes.

Can a washing powder be elevated to the level of satisfaction or fulfilment? The marketers of Persil believe so, and have for many years advertised the product as something more than just a guarantee of clean clothes. The inference of the message is a clean family, putting the washer into the role of protector and carer. If this doesn't quite put washing on a par with eating chocolate or watching movies, by injecting that element of pride into using the brand it certainly raises it above that of plain drudgery.

- *Fast-moving consumer goods*: Dulux paint: not just colour for your walls, but a means of 'transforming your home'. Or Dunlop golf balls: just hitting them makes you feel better about your golf. Or Cadbury's Flake, a simple product that has achieved levels of sensuality rarely seen in confectionery.

- *B2B*: 'Nobody ever got fired for buying IBM.' This famous phrase makes plain that commercial buyers buy on more than product performance: there is also the question of job security.
- *Service*: Consider a training organization such as INSIGHT Marketing and People. It is not unusual in the training business to have someone ring you and say that they want their team to go through one of your courses because 10 years ago *they* went on it and they still remember the good time they had, and the amount they learnt, and the great trainers, and the use it has been...

The brand as a social expression: ego, conformity/nonconformity

Sometimes this is just plain conspicuous consumption; driving a Jaguar, wearing a Barbour jacket and carrying those green plastic bags from Harrods even when shopping in Waitrose.

Sometimes it is about confidence, and the need to have your decisions justified. Seeing other people wearing the designer jeans you just bought can upset some people, but for most it says, 'whew, you did the right thing'. Social expression can be about conformity or nonconformity, and brands can fit either of these positions. Drinking Pimm's on ice in an East End pub can set you apart from the crowd, while Hofmeister lager will make you one of the lads (for the reverse scenario, think Henley Regatta).

Hofmeister was launched successfully in the United Kingdom, targeted at young, working-class males, a closed shop where beer is concerned, and group conformity is the key. Hofmeister used George the bear, a 'dude', to gain itself street credibility, and of course those who don't see the appeal of George just aren't in the target segment.

Are you a 'dude'?

The subtext of many car advertisements is more about reassuring you that you have in fact *already* made the right decision *and* it will be respected by your peers than it is about trying to influence you in the first place.

- *Fast-moving consumer goods*: Rolex, Hofmeister, Remy Martin.
- *B2B*: Gore-Tex allows manufacturers to position their product on the right level, passing on the boast of superiority to their own consumers, and allowing the consumer to be in with 'those in the know'.
- *Service*: American Express is said to say something about the user, and saying that is saying it all.

It might seem from looking at these examples that a brand would always want to appeal at the highest level of emotional charge, but this is not always the wisest ambition. For one thing, sustaining a brand image at the level of social expression is an expensive activity and requires a continuity of credibility over a long period of time.

The B2B emotional charge

The examples already given have shown how the B2B and service circumstances can be accommodated within this model, but perhaps the word 'accommodated' confesses to a weakness; it has to be squeezed to fit. Figure 20.6 considers the nature of customers' expectations with regard to the performance of a B2B or service brand, placing them in an ascending order of importance, so allowing the brand manager to position his or her own brand at the most appropriate level of emotional charge.

Figure 20.6 *The 'emotional charge' of the B2B and service brand*

The list in Figure 20.6 is based on the increasing significance of a supplier, and so a likely increasing level of loyalty to a brand that manages to make the appropriate positive impact.

There are, of course, some significant 'ifs' and 'buts':

1. It is only indicative of typical expectations, not a complete list.
2. Rarely do customers expect all of this, and still less often do they get it, but nor are they mutually exclusive requirements. A brand may form its definition around an almost endless variety of mixes and matches.
3. If there are different requirements in your market, then add them in!
4. Expectations change as markets change.

Price busters and cost reducers

New entrants to a market have often donned the price-buster mantle, or its more sophisticated elder sibling, the cost reducer. It is also an approach taken by brands trying to shake up a long-established market with incumbent brands dozing quietly.

Companies offering business training through the Internet have tended to lead with claims of cost reduction, a brand definition that they can substantiate with some ease. Moving up to the level of performance enhancer or business improver (brand platforms occupied by many of their more traditional competitors) will present a much harder challenge if it is to be substantiated with any conviction.

Easy to do business with

American Express takes all the effort out of corporate business travel – that is its claim. The Amex 'in-plant' is a common feature of many a large business, taking on all the tasks short of making the trips themselves. This 'easy to do business with' brand now has to take on the challenge of those managers who think the Internet makes it easier for them to do it themselves. The fact that Amex might be better tuned in to the business environment may just give it the edge.

Steady as a rock

The TetraPak is a good example of a brand that is 'steady as a rock'. Its numerous users, often creating new markets made possible by the packaging technology, depend on the absolute reliability of the brand. And if things *do* go wrong then they depend on the ability of the brand to put them right. TetraPak has much at stake if its product fails the customer, and the customer knows that, and so a strong bond of common interest is forged between supplier, customer and consumer.

Lifesavers

DHL works hard to define its brand around reliability and speed. Driven by the business world's need to do things fast, and globally, DHL represents a 'lifesaver' brand. Just hearing the letters DHL brings a sigh of relief – not a bad emotional response to associate with your brand. And then, as already mentioned, along comes e-mail. Now, huge documents can be sent in seconds, with no need for planes, boats and trains. The DHL brand must change into something more than a specialist emergency service – perhaps a provider of wider business solutions that recognize the changing demands of truly global businesses?

Tuned-in performance enhancers, solution providers, business improvers and market builders

If a consumer brand must tune into social and life values, so a B2B brand must tune into the commercial environment of the time.

The Intel brand captured the loyalty of PC manufacturers for a variety of reasons, not least because the brand was both a performance enhancer, through the ever-increasing speed of its ever-diminishing chips, and a market builder, through its consumer franchise. Times change, and PC builders are becoming more interested in cost reduction in a maturing, not to say saturated, market. Should Intel take its brand down a price-buster road, perhaps with its high-volume Celeron microprocessor line, or does it stick to its market-builder definition by encouraging the development of software applications that will demand its high-speed capabilities? The launch of the Pentium III Xeon microprocessor, specifically designed to improve the performance of large Web sites and e-business applications, fits the latter direction. Which would you choose?

Brand personalities

To refer to brand personalities is another way of talking about the emotional charge. Figure 20.7 shows a rising level of possible relationships that a brand may aspire to.

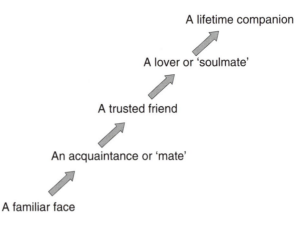

Figure 20.7 *The brand as a personal relationship*

How do you see the brands you use?

As an exercise, see if you can identify a brand that fits at each level shown (there are no right answers here; this is pure subjectivity), and then try to assess what it is that has put it there. Is it the product, the advertising or the nature of the interactions? I am prepared to bet that as you rise up the levels, so the answers to that question shift towards the interactions.

Defining the personality: identifying the personality gap

Another exercise: consider your own brand. Who would your brand be if it was:

- a movie star?
- a comedian?
- a newsreader?
- a politician?
- a sportsperson?
- a writer?
- a TV 'personality'?
- a game show host?
- etc.

You might even ask:

- Is it male or female?
- How old is this person?
- What are the person's politics?
- What religion does the person follow?
- Is he or she married with kids, or single?
- How's the person's health?
- How does he or she respond to stress and crisis?
- etc.

This is a great exercise to do with a group of colleagues – especially a cross-functional group. There might be some surprises...

Even better, do it with groups of customers (but do it with the help of a professional market researcher, and one experienced in brand positioning). This will tell you how your brand is currently perceived. Again, there may be some surprises in store.

Now some questions:

- Did they define your personality as you wish it to be?
- If not entirely, is it at least close, and if so, what tweaks are necessary to be seen as you wish?
- If not at all, how will you reposition to be seen as you wish?

There is of course one last question, and always worth asking: if that is how they see us, can we live with that? It may not be the personality you wished for, but if it works then you should at least consider hanging on to it.

BUILDING POSITIVE ASSOCIATIONS: MOMENTS OF TRUTH

It is the brand manager's responsibility to ensure that every interaction with the customer builds and enhances the brand's definition. This includes the choice of the name, the logo, the packaging design, the sales approach, the management of customer relationships, the advertising, the appearance at the point of sale, the characteristics of the product or service in use, after-sales support and, not to be forgotten, the handling of complaints. Each one of these 'steps along the way' is an opportunity for a positive customer inter-action, and each one is what we might call a *moment of truth* for the brand.

What's in a name?

A new brand can have a name specially designed to suit its definition; an old brand is stuck with what it has inherited. How much does this matter, and should a brand ever consider changing its name?

Plenty of product brands carry their founder's or inventor's name, though we have long since stopped making associations with any real person and are often surprised to learn that there was indeed a Mr Firestone or a Mr Goodyear.

Almost any name can grow to represent the brand definition, *provided it has time*. Of course, a good word with positive associations can also become associated with a poor brand definition: Lada is Russian for 'beloved'.

> 'What's in a name? That which we call a rose
> By any other name would smell as sweet.'

Al Ries argues that Shakespeare, at least when it comes to brand names, was wrong, 'which is why the single most important decision in the marketing of perfume is the name'.

Sounds like...

Choosing a word or name that sounds like or might even be confused with another attention-grabbing word is another approach – FCUK being perhaps the most controversial of recent times. It's just abbreviation, they say, for French Connection UK.

Abbreviations

Abbreviations can of course become brand names, and it is often a surprise when we learn their original meaning. 3M says innovation and invention, hardly words that the Minnesota Mining and Manufacturing Company would bring to mind. Who would be enthused by the products of the Bayerische Motoren Werke? BMW to you and me.

Magic letters...

Certain letters appear more commonly in brand names than in normal everyday use, the letters X, K and O being the most notable. Dulux, Kodak, Knorr, IKEA, Exxon, Xerox and Oxo are just some of many that attract our attention through their unusual appearance.

A formula

Kodak was coined by George Eastman in 1888, being 'short, vigorous, incapable of being misspelled... and in order to satisfy trademark laws it must mean nothing.' Not a bad formula. We might extend Eastman's formula a little, to say that a brand name should meet at least the majority of the following criteria:

- It should be short and vigorous. They don't come much shorter or more vigorous than Oxo, or the new football boot brand from Umbro: Xai.

- It should be incapable of being misspelled or mispronounced – though Knorr and Nestlé have successfully ignored this criterion for decades.
- It should be unique to the brand. The search for a unique name can be long and frustrating; it's amazing what has already been dreamt up…
- It should be consistent with the desired brand definition. Old names will have already grown into this position; new ones must be chosen with care: Häagen-Dazs is a pure invention, but has all the right Scandinavian connotations to be intriguing and suggest some expertise in things icy…
- It must sit within the existing brand architecture. 'Sane' might be a great name for a new hotel chain that specializes in stress-reducing therapeutic stays, but perhaps not so good if it is included as a sub-brand under the Holiday Inn umbrella…
- It should be capable of international usage without causing embarrassment or cultural offence.
  This was ignored successfully by the likes of FCUK, and ignored to its cost by Chrysler when launching the Nova motor car in Mexico ('no va' means 'doesn't go').
- It should be capable of grabbing attention. FCUK certainly keeps this rule, at least.
- It should be capable of being protected – not a common word or simple descriptor. A word that means nothing will fit the bill nicely, but might end up meaning just that – nothing.
- It should be liked by the target audience. This needs research and more research – and don't rely on one drunken session of the marketing team!

Here is some provocative advice from Lexicon, a brand development company:

1. 'Are we comfortable with the name – then it's OK but not great.' A great brand name should provoke.
2. 'Does the name break any rules? If not, try again.' A great brand name needs to do better than just fit in.
3. 'Can we use the name to make a promise or tell a story?' This is a 'must have'.

Is 'owning the word' good for a brand?

Some regard it as a strength of a brand name that it becomes the generic for a product or service – to *Hoover* the carpet, to *Sellotape* a package, and then to *FedEx* it to Sydney. But how often have you hoovered the carpet with a Dyson, sellotaped with Scotch Tape, or FedEx-ed that package by DHL? How often have you ordered a Coke in a café and been served an anonymous cola without comment?

Awareness through use of your brand name as the generic is a great thing, but we have seen that branding is about more than simple awareness; it is about associations. If customers will happily associate other people's products with your brand name then where does this leave your own brand definition?

Becoming the generic is good provided that you really *do* own the word, and continue to retain that ownership. That takes massive and continuous investment, continued vigilance, continuing evolution and a refusal to rest on your laurels. A great and glorious heritage is not enough.

Changing the name

Great outrage, letters to *The Times* and much free publicity attends the change of a well-known brand name. Remember when Marathon became Snickers and Opal Fruits became Starbursts? It was as though a part of your childhood were being stolen.

The cost can be huge: when Andersen Consulting was forced to change to its name to Accenture, the total bill was reputed to be well over £100 million – so why do it if not forced? The pursuit of global consistency is the reason behind Snickers and Starbursts, and, managed well, the change can cause less disruption to sales or loyalty than the letters of outrage might have suggested.

Timing can be everything in such matters. Unilever resisted for years switching the name Jif, used in the United Kingdom, to Cif, the name used across the whole of continental Europe. Cif was thought to sound too much like the slang for a particular type of venereal disease. The rise of AIDS has taken the attention off such 'second-grade ailments', and Cif is now thought thoroughly safe and respectable.

Other reasons can involve needing to change a name that has just grown out of date, or is too restrictive in its scope. When the United Kingdom's Post Office changed its name to Consignia, it argued that it would give it international standing. It can certainly be seen that 'The Post Office' is not the most helpful of names overseas, but 'Consignia' just plain didn't work at home, and was abandoned with little regret by anyone.

Perhaps in the end it is just a way to give a flagging brand a new lease of life through all the attention the change brings; 'the artist formerly known as Prince' comes to mind.

Logos and slogans

Logos

Figure 20.8 is perhaps all that needs to be said about the importance of a good and consistently used logo.

The logo is the fast means to recognition, eliciting subconscious responses that can often tip the balance of the sale. B2B brands should never underestimate the power of a logo in this regard. For many years, the best-selling fertilizer in the agricultural market was ICI's 'blue bag'. The ICI

Figure 20.8 *The importance of the logo*

roundel and the familiar blue bag were all that farmers needed to see to convince them of the product's quality. The logo represented the firm's reputation and became one of the most familiar sights in barns across the United Kingdom. And, of course, once the logo becomes recognized, resist the temptation to change it every year.

Slogans

Slogans can be dangerous things: they have a habit of backfiring when times change. British Rail's 'This is the age of the train' was coined on a wave of enthusiasm for public transport that soon dissolved, and the slogan looked less and less convincing with every passing year. 'Let's make things better', a slogan from Philips, the Dutch electronics firm, was a sitting duck for any headline-writer each time the company had a product flop or a serious customer complaint.

In trying to expand customer perceptions beyond the obvious, the United Kingdom's Post Office adopted the slogan 'delivering value', but too many found it an easy pot-shot, saying that they would prefer it if the Post Office just managed to deliver letters.

Sometimes slogans can be too clever. 'Guinnless isn't good for you' back in 1984 perhaps called for too many second-takes.

Think of slogans as short-term tactics, not fundamentals of the brand definition.

Packaging: the Cinderella of branding

The packaging industry has been under much pressure in recent years, with buyers more interested in reducing costs than in adding value. The tragedy of this is that packaging, used well, provides huge scope for building brand definition through customer interaction.

Even Kit-Kat has succumbed to the cost and efficiency argument in preference to enhancing the brand's interactions with its customers. The new flow-wrap packaging will certainly reduce costs, but dropping the tin-foil wrapper means the loss of a significant part of the consumer experience. A small but important interaction with the consumer has been removed, and what is still a therapeutic break-time treat has edged just a little closer to being a chocolate wafer biscuit.

Packaging exists for many reasons: to ship, to protect, to preserve, to identify, to help in use, to store and to dispose. We should also add to this list, to help build the brand.

Packaging the interactions

- Consider a paint brand with a brand definition of 'colour and transformation'. Wouldn't it be great if the paint cans were transparent so that customers could see the real colour and not just a tiny colour chip?
- Limmits, the range of slimming biscuits, come in slim shapes with silky black wrappers – 'just as I would like to be,' say many of its consumers, 'slim and sexy'.
- Consider a fine malt whisky that has built a brand definition through images of peat bogs and faithful retainers. It has worked hard to distinguish itself from those ordinary blended whiskies, and yet there it sits on the off-licence shelf, just another bottle of brown spirit. Enter the cardboard tube: a small step for packaging but a giant leap for the sales of high-quality whisky, particularly if purchased as a gift...
- Consider a brand of photographic film that centres its brand definition on perfect colour representation. How will it look if the boxes lined up on the shelf vary in hue from dark to light?
- The Angostura bitters bottle positively screams its unique individuality: the label is way too large, the text on it far too small, but it is instantly recognizable and it works.
- The toilet duck was a brilliant example of a brand capturing a unique identity – visually, through the distinctive shape of the bottle, but also emotionally, through our belief that now we really can reach those germs that have been stubbornly evading us.
- If your business is in the supply of bulk materials to industrial customers, how could new packaging help identify your brand as the easiest to handle, to store, to maintain or to renew?
- Even in disposing of the product, the packaging can give the brand one last customer interaction. The Evian brand has made good use of plastic bottles that can be crushed down to a quarter of their original size after use. A brand that stresses the purity and ecological soundness of its product has successfully added another positive association to its image: the reduction of landfill on disposal.

Customer relationships

Every human point of contact must also aim to build positive associations.

Jan Carlzon, when CEO of SAS, described these human points of contact as the brand's 'moments of truth', and he went on to quantify them. SAS looked after 5 million passengers a year, and each passenger would probably meet five members of SAS staff. That meant that there would be 25 million SAS-brand moments of truth, 25 million opportunities to build and enhance the brand, but also 25 million opportunities to let the brand down. Sales and customer service training became high priorities to support the SAS brand definition.

Moments of truth

Not long ago, I picked up an Avis car at Copenhagen airport – at least, I tried to, but unfortunately the person behind the desk was 'the abominable no-man'. 'Nothing but diesels,' he said, 'nothing but estates', he said, 'nothing with air-conditioning', he said – 'and you didn't specify any of that when you ordered,' he said. I had, because I always do, and so I suggested I might try the Hertz desk. 'You do that', he said. 'We try harder' had never sounded so hollow…

Inventing new interactions and associations

Borders and Barnes & Noble, two US booksellers, pioneered the invention of several new interactions with their customers: armchairs, in-store coffee shops, meeting spaces for societies, barber-shop choirs… Who could name a bookstore brand before all that?

A good source of positive associations is to be found in other people's brands. Little Chef features Bird's custard on its menu, McDonald's builds its brand through the use of the likes of Cadbury's and Nestlé in its product lines, and of course the arrangement is mutual. Heineken has often associated itself with other brands' imagery, including a healed-up cut in a piece of silk and, famously, the Dulux dog seen painting a wall – all part of the 'reaches the parts that other beers cannot reach' campaign.

A brand can benefit by building on the stories that sometimes attach themselves. Ford has not suffered from the 'any colour so long as it's black' tale, Ben & Jerry are the subject of countless urban myths (in the United States at least) of what they do with their profits and what causes they support, and the Body Shop benefited hugely from the high profile the media gave to its founder and campaigner for all sorts, Anita Roddick. A charismatic boss can be a great asset to a brand or a business. Even the ICI 'brand' became 'exciting' under the leadership of John Harvey-Jones.

Cadbury World is one of the few tourist attraction 'theme parks' run by a brand that is not primarily in the entertainment business. Many say it has no business to be doing this, not least some within the company, who could point out that it has lost money more years than it has turned a profit. Of course, it is there for reasons other than profit; its financial target is in fact to break even. Cadbury World helps cement the brand's definition: quality and fun. It doesn't exploit the brand, it helps to build the brand, and

Much more than just chocolate (as if that wasn't enough already!)

the vast majority of its millions of visitors will have had their perception of the brand enhanced by this wonderfully creative and wholly positive interaction.

B2B brands can perhaps benefit the most from extending their customer interactions beyond the confines of their product. Selling services and solutions rather than products is a common strategy, but it is not always easy to get the due reward. Using a brand to identify the package of services and solutions as a distinct entity, separate from the competitors' 'product', can help enormously.

Finally, a brand can always use a little help from associations with liked and respected personalities, provided of course that they are the *right* people for the brand. You own a brand of jeans aimed at 'cool' teenagers; how pleased would you be if the prime minister took to wearing them? (What goes for 'cool' is endlessly surprising, and the oddest folk can become icons of teenage cool, so who knows…?)

The Internet interaction

Of course, the Internet has provided a whole new medium for interaction, with many consumer brands operating Web sites that offer product information, deals and, very often, advice that helps position the brand on a much wider footing. The Pampers Web site has become a popular source of advice on all aspects of mothering, so taking the brand definition far beyond a simple supplier of nappies.

The interaction is two way, providing information to the brand owners on how to steer their brand positioning in the future. Consumers are given a new channel of enquiry in this exchange, and with equal access to competitors' sites, there is an increase in the transparency of the brand for the consumer. Choice is made easier, comparisons are made easier, and in some cases genuine enquiry into value received can be made. In this way, the Internet promises to keep brands on their toes as much as it gives them a new medium of interaction.

There is a dilemma here for the typical fmcg branded product. Consumers tend to buy baskets of groceries, not individual products, so won't the brand's Web site inevitably lose out to the retailers? The offer of advice through the Web site is one response, but perhaps there are more cunning ones in store. Where would you expect to find information on Jaffa cakes? In the McVities site or on a kids' site? Put yourself in the shoes of the consumer…

Owning time itself? — Swatch is keen to make a radically new, but hugely relevant, association between its brand and the notion of time. Universal or Internet Time, 'launched' in 1998, divides the day into 1,000 beats, and time zones are gone. Should it catch on, who knows what we might be saying in years to come? Perhaps 'Swatch Time' in place of 'Greenwich Mean Time' – even 'log in with me at 800 "Swatch Time"' – a powerful association indeed.

BRAND EXTENSION

As many as two out of three new product launches are examples of brand extension. This is where an existing brand is used to support the launch of a new product. The reasons are clear: new product launches are very risky, most fail, and using the 'halo' of an existing brand (see Chapter 16) can help to reduce that risk. If the market is also new, then the risk is even greater and the halo effect yet more important.

Brand extension comes in different forms. The simplest is the launch of the existing product in a new format. Soap powder takes on a liquid form under the same brand name, or Mars bars are shrunk into bite-sized pieces and launched as Mars Little Ones. Some would argue that this was really still brand augmentation, with the brand chasing much the same market with much the same product – or does the Mars Little Ones proposition target a new buyer in a new circumstance? This is more than playing with words: augmentation is relatively safe territory, dealing with what you know already; genuine extension enters the higher-risk zone.

Next up the ladder of extension is the launch of what we might call companion products under the same name. Gillette razor blades will add Gillette razors and then Gillette shaving foam. Once each brand extension is successfully established, the process of brand augmentation will recommence, adding Gillette shaving gel to the shaving foam range, and so on.

The highest-risk brand extension is when the brand leaves its own territory. Virgin, as we have seen, is adept at this, reducing the risk through use of the brand halo effect and ensuring that it translates the existing brand values to the new market. Caterpillar has had success with its rugged outdoor clothing line, as has JCB, which has also moved into children's toys – with mini yellow diggers in abundance. These are extensions that 'make sense', which is to say that the target customer can see the relevance and accept the translated brand values. For JCB, durability, functionality and a rugged outdoor quality were all values and images that could be transferred to a range of clothing.

Some extensions make less sense.

Cosmopolitan took its brand into yoghurts and flavoured mineral waters, Philip Morris considers taking the Marlboro brand into hotels. Some brand extensions come naturally; some are forced for reasons of growth targets – dangerous ground for the brand manager.

'If it don't fit, don't force it'

The problem with too much extension…

Some branding consultants like to discuss the brand definition as its DNA, its unique signature. Brand extension, or 'brand stretching' as it is sometimes called, stretches the DNA. Do we reach a point where one stretch too many weakens the genes and we start breeding halfwits and chinless wonders? And if it does fail, the backlash will be felt by the original brand…

THE LEARNING BRAND

Brands evolve; at least, the best ones do. And as they evolve, they learn – or at least… Figure 20.9 illustrates the process of evolution.

Figure 20.9   *Brand definition and brand evolution*

Brands evolve in response to changing customer expectations (if they are listening brands), and those expectations are in turn prompted and managed by the very process of evolution. Out of this process comes the *brand definition*.

In a circular process, the brand manager can jump in wherever they choose, acting or reacting. 'Acting' can bring successes like the Post-it note or Amazon.com, but it is a risky business. Brands said to be 'before their time' are generally brands that acted rather than reacted, forcing their brand definition on to the market rather than allowing it to evolve with that market.

Forcing it…

In the 1970s, Levi Strauss attempted to move into the formal menswear market, with the Levi name sown into off-the-peg suits: Levi Tailored Classics. The market research warned against it – 'people are not ready for such a big step – why not try separates first?' – but it went ahead and paid the price of forcing a brand into territory that was not yet ready. People had expectations of the brand, and this move didn't fit.

Reacting reduces the risk of failure, but also increases the risk of being overtaken by competitors – a delicate balance.

Listening and learning

Shortly after the First World War, Kimberley Clark launched a brand in the United States called Kleenex. It had a surplus of cellucotton (used as the filter in gas masks) and believed it had found an outlet. The war was over, people were after a little gaiety, and sales of make-up boomed. Kleenex was launched as the ideal make-up remover, and very good it was, but the brand hardly set the world alight. There was a good deal of brand activity but to no avail: this was a small market and there were plenty of alternatives.

Then the folk at Kleenex started to listen to their customers, and they discovered a whole new set of interactions going on that not only were unexpected, but in truth filled some of them with dismay. People were using Kleenex to blow their noses. Fine, there's a market out there, but how do you promote such a product? The answer was to let the brand evolve.

Existing customers had certain 'polite' expectations of Kleenex, and nose-blowing messages might cause some disturbance, so the first step was to target a different audience, and who better than children – they of the runny noses?

Parents were encouraged to buy Kleenex for their kids to stop them being antisocial and unhygienic – a tall order, but Kleenex, it seemed, had the answer. In the 1930s, Kleenex hit on the slogan 'Don't put a cold in your pocket', and the adult market was hooked. The brand's positioning was changed from a niche market to a mass market, and it did it through a process of learning and evolving – a vital quality of any successful brand.

Figure 20.10 shows how a brand should learn while acting. Brands help customers to make choices, and, when they have done so, they are helped to feel good about their choice. The key for the learning brand is to understand precisely what it is that makes customers feel good about their choice. This is far more important than having got them to make the choice in the first place: what if they chose you because, in truth, there was no choice? Once the brand manager knows what made the customers feel good, they are well on the way to understanding what _could_ make the customers feel good, and so the brand evolves.

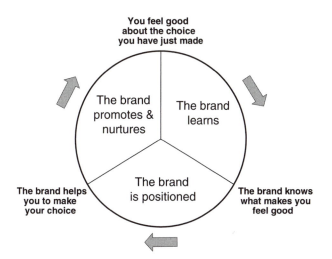

Figure 20.10 _The virtuous circle of a learning brand_

The complaint is a gift...

Brands can learn by taking note of the complaints that arise, and can improve their standing by managing them professionally.

TV watchdog programmes will go to great lengths to chastise a famous brand that has let the customer down. The brand manager who vacillates with weasel words is on a hiding to nothing. The brand manager who responds with bucketloads of apologies and enough free product to last the customer a lifetime gets away with it, but is the customer satisfied, and what of the millions of others watching at home, with no free products?

In too many cases the brand manager takes the easy route of a voucher or a free sample. I know of several big brands that, if you simply send them a letter saying that you bought the product *in one of the big retailers* and you are not happy, will send you a bundle of vouchers by return.

Brand managers should ensure that they move into overdrive to investigate a problem. And when they discover the causes – report them to the customer, put right the problem, and give evidence of a better level of reliability in the future. That way, not only will they have learnt something about the customer's real concerns, and not only will they have plugged a gap in their operational excellence, but they will have built another link of loyalty in the chain between themselves and the market.

21

Functional alignment

No man is an island, and that is for sure when discussing the task of marketing. The best plans, at least in terms of what you hope to do, will come to grief if they don't win the support of those who have to make them happen. That last sentence betrays the truth of many a supposedly good plan: it has concentrated on what we want to do, and gives little attention to whether we are able to do it. We are right back to the leftsider–rightsider debate from Chapter 2. A good plan must attend to both sides.

THE SUPPLY CHAIN

Figure 21.1 shows a model of a supply chain. It covers all the steps involved, and hence the people and functions involved in doing what you do: sourcing materials, converting them into your product, and selling them to your customers.

These are the hearts and minds that you have to win if your marketing plan is to succeed, if you are to hope to deliver the value you have identified, and if you are to reap the reward you deserve. This issue is touched on in several places throughout this book, in particular the chapters on place (Chapter 26), when dealing with supply chain and the sales team; price (Chapter 28), when working alongside the sales team to audit price effectiveness and to implement pricing decisions; and, in particular, relationship management (Chapter 19).

Support Activities Infrastructure	– Legal, Accounting, Financial Management	
Human Resource Management	– Personnel, Pay, Recruitment, Training, Manpower Planning, etc	
Product & Technology Development	– Product and Process Design, Production Engineering, Market Testing, R&D, etc	
Procurement	– Supplier Management, Funding, Subcontracting, Specification	Value Added – Cost = Profit

INBOUND LOGISTICS	OPERATIONS	OUTBOUND LOGISTICS	SALES & MARKETING	SERVICING
eg Quality Control Receiving Raw Material Control etc	eg Manufacturing Packaging Production Control Quality Control Maintenance etc	eg Finishing Goods Order Handling Dispatch Delivery Invoicing etc	eg Customer mgmt Order Taking Promotion Sales Analysis Market Research etc	eg Warranty Maintenance Education / Training Upgrade etc

Primary Activities

Figure 21.1 *The supply chain*

Aligning behind key accounts

The task of key account management, described in Chapter 19, has many obstacles, not the least of which is an organization built on traditional functional silos, as shown in Figure 21.2.

The task requires a cross-functional approach represented by the matrix-style organization illustrated in Figure 21.3.

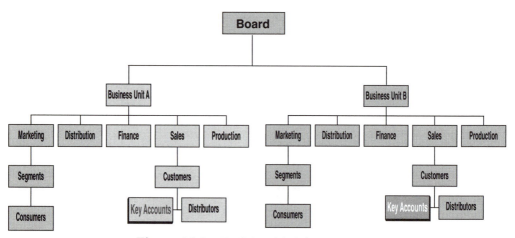

Figure 21.2 *Traditional 'silo' organization*

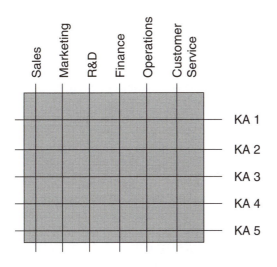

Figure 21.3 *The inevitable matrix of KAM*

Whose responsibility is it to make this happen – sales' or marketing's? The key account manager may well be a salesperson, working in that traditional silo, but the practice of KAM is part of relationship management, which is most certainly part of the marketer's concern. Of course, both sales *and* marketing should be working hard, and together, to break down the traditional functional barriers; it is they that have the most to gain by doing so, and the most to lose by shirking the responsibility.

Business partners

This supply chain may of course involve people outside your own business, perhaps even outside your own company. In high-tech industries or those requiring significant R&D investment, such as pharmaceuticals, it is increasingly common to find business partnerships, whether formally established joint ventures or simple contractual arrangements (not that the contracts involved are ever simple!). This adds another level of challenge to the marketer's task: seeking alignment between two sets of people who may well be based in different countries, or even continents, probably come from different business cultures, and may not always fully understand the ambitions and objectives that were discussed at senior level between their two companies. Even more reason, then, for taking the time and the care to complete a capability audit of who can do what, and where.

THE CAPABILITY AUDIT

Throughout the planning process we must be continually asking, 'Can we do this, are we up to it?' And if not, can we be made better? This is the job, in part, of the supply chain manager, but it is also the job of the marketer. There is a danger at this point that the marketer becomes the auditor of their colleagues, and the marketing department the police force of the company. This is not likely to win hearts and minds.

The solution is to get everyone to audit themselves, but for that to be effective, they must start by all singing from the same hymn sheet. Ultimately, of course, this is something that can only be fully done at the most senior level. The marketing plan must be part of the board's thinking. In recent years, different functions have elevated their status to boardroom level: what used to be the distribution department has become supply chain and sits on the board; what used to be the staff department has become human resources and sits on the board; and now we see issues such as safety and risk management jostling for boardroom space and attention. It is to be hoped that marketing already has its place, but too often, as we discussed in the first chapters of this book, marketing is seen as the people who make the brochures. It is by applying the professional skills described in this book, by adopting the disciplined processes and by preparing a detailed and evidenced marketing plan that looks into the future as well as detailing this year's tactics that marketing will gain the necessary respect and time at senior levels.

Persuasion skills?

Must the marketer become a skilled persuader? The answer is yes, inasmuch as one of the key skills of persuasion is to 'persuade by involvement'. That is to say, don't preach, don't even present; get them to present to you, get them telling you how they want to help.

Writing the plan and then presenting to those who will make it happen is doomed to failure: it starts with a debate, moves on to argument, turns to naked opposition and ends in recriminations. Much better to involve them from the start, and not just because that is good persuasion technique, but because it is good marketing technique.

My own experience, working as a trainer of marketing skills in companies, is that most people outside the marketing department, once they discover that marketing is not a black art but has a process, demonstrate an enormous desire to be part of the marketing activity. More than that, they demonstrate skills and capabilities essential to the task. The wise marketer will get such people on board from the very start. Often, a good way to achieve this is in fact a mixed-function training course – and the marketing folk present are often surprised at just how much their so-called non-marketing colleagues know.

Assets versus customers?

In any manufacturing company there is a need to decide which is more important: the customers' needs, or the occupacity of the plant (occupacity is the measure of how close to full capacity a plant is run). This may seem an odd question after all that has been said about the need to focus on customers, but the marketing model requires us to look also at our capabilities. If the only way to produce a competitive product is to reduce costs through full-capacity manufacture, then cherry-picking niche customer needs may not work for you.

We are in chicken and egg territory, of course. It can be argued that if you are sitting on a massive plant that needs filling with large-scale product lines, while the true opportunity is for niche products, then someone in marketing went wrong years back when the factory was built; it was clearly the wrong capability. If only life were so simple! The reality is that you need to fill the plant, at least for now, and so in the short term you must focus on a particular set of customer needs: those that relate to large orders.

In order to avoid such binds, both marketers and manufacturers must be talking together, ensuring that their respective functional plans are in line with each other. And that trick must be repeated with the operations people, the sales team, the customer service folk, the R&D department – and so it goes on.

Making it happen through drivers and performance measures

Chapter 14 looked at Wiersema's value drivers: operational excellence, product leadership and customer intimacy. It is easy to see how different functions within the same company might choose different drivers. Operational excellence? That's the manufacturing crowd. Product leadership? That's R&D. Customer intimacy? Well, that's the sales force. And so we have a recipe for disaster. The answer, as discussed in Chapter 14, is to choose the driver for the business, and then, rather than denying the importance of the other drivers, ensure that their performance targets and measures are appropriate. A business driven by customer intimacy can't afford an operationally poor manufacturing capability, but nor does it want one driven by occupacity to the exclusion of all other questions. Measuring the flexibility of the plant in switching between lines may bear more fruit.

22

Portfolio management

You can have a portfolio of many things: of companies, of markets, of segments, of customers, and of products. The principles of portfolio management and the two tools deployed – the *Boston Box* and the *Directional Policy Matrix* – are broadly the same in each case. As we are discussing, at this stage of the book, the choices taken within a particular segment, I have chosen to discuss portfolio management in relation to a portfolio of products. Chapter 19 covered similar ground in relation to a portfolio of customers.

THE CHALLENGE

The CONNECT case study (Chapter 10) looked at a company with a tight range of products that was attempting to launch a rather different range in a rather different market. Undoubtedly the existing market was at a late stage of maturity, with a number of external circumstances accelerating it towards decline. The new products had plenty of potential but also plenty of challenges. Which range deserved the lion's share of the company's attention?

Most businesses manage a range of products, and the questions of priorities and resource allocation are continually pressing ones. Very often, the answers boil down to the powers of persuasion of individual product managers or the personal preferences of the boss. Sometimes this gets the right result, but who would want to depend on it?

Managing a portfolio of products is undoubtedly harder than managing a single product company, but, if done well, can lead to a far more secure and successful future.

THE BOSTON BOX

An excellent tool is at hand, the _Boston Box_, complete with its exotic language of _stars_, _cows_, _dogs_ and _problem children_. Developed by the Boston Consulting Group, the matrix (see Figure 22.1) seeks to guide the marketer in a number of decisions:

- how to allocate resources;
- how to manage each product;
- what to expect, in financial terms, from each product.

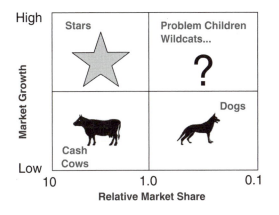

Figure 22.1 _The Boston Box_

The vertical axis measures the future growth rate of products in the portfolio – a judgement of each one's position on its product life cycle (PLC). The horizontal axis measures the product's market share, with high share to the left and low share to the right.

Why these two measures? I will comment on their limitations a little later, but for now, growth is used as an indicator of attractiveness, and share is used as an indicator of strength in the market.

A product in the top left box, a _star_, is clearly a good thing: there is future growth potential and you have a commanding position in the market with this product.

A product in the top right has a question mark against it: can this _problem child_ be nurtured into a star, can this _wildcat_ be tamed? It occupies an attractive market or segment, but perhaps you are a relative newcomer, or there is very strong competition. Will effort here be worth it, and, with limited resources, which of the products in this box should get the investment?

A product in the bottom left, a _cash cow_, is there to be milked. Your high share indicates a strong position, but the growth has gone. It is a place to be looking to reduce high-cost resources and effort.

The bottom left box contain the *dogs*, products to be divested or strictly managed at low cost of effort or resource.

It might appear from this rather simplistic summary that you should want all your products to be stars. But stop to consider what sort of business this would give you. Indeed, what sort of business would you have if all your products occupied just one box?

- All *stars* – apart from requiring huge investment to keep pace with success, this is perhaps a business with a cloud over its future. Products reach maturity; what then?
- All *problem children* – a business with a promising future if only it had income to invest today!
- All *cash cows* – a business with plenty of cash, but to what long-term purpose?
- All *dogs* – a business soon to be out of business.

The ideal business will have products in at least the star, problem child and cash cow boxes – a balanced portfolio, just like a balanced investment portfolio. The sense of this becomes clearer if we consider the cash flow implications of products in each box as shown in Figure 22.2.

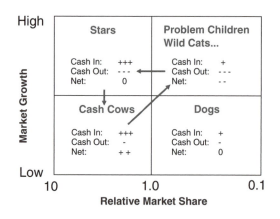

Figure 22.2 *The Boston Box and cash flow*

The positions are of course rather stereotyped. Some stars will have large positive cash flows, but it is not uncommon for stars to cost almost as much as they reap. Similarly, some dogs will be positive or negative, but the point to consider is the need for a balanced portfolio. A business without cash cows will need to borrow heavily from outside. Cash cows provide the means to invest in the problem children to turn them into stars, and, as sure as eggs are eggs, today's stars will become tomorrow's cash cows.

This analysis is valuable in so many ways: allocation of resources, emphasis on the marketing mix (problem children are heavy on promotional effort, cash cows need careful price management), even determining the ideal product manager for each product. A cash cow might need an accountant's approach to cost control, an approach that might stifle a problem child to death, while a star calls for more careful management than might seem to be the case: big products can steal resource and profits like nothing else in a business (except perhaps big customers...). Table 22.1 indicates some generic strategies and activities for products in each of the four boxes.

Table 22.1   _The Boston Box: generic strategies and activities_

Activity	Star	Problem Child	Cash Cow	Dog
Strategy	Maintain growth	Select priorities for investment	Maximize earnings	Divest or manage for cash
Share	Maintain or grow	Invest to increase	Maintain	Focus on profit rather than share
Product	Augmentation and extension	New product development	Rationalize	Rationalize
Price	Price leader	Penetration	Stabilize or raise	Raise
Promotion	High level	Aggressive for share	Reduce, for maintenance	Minimize
Place	Broaden	Focused	Maintain	Rationalize
Costs	Focus on economies of scale	Controlled budgets	Focus on supply chain costs	Aggressive reduction
Working capital	Tighten controls	Increase	Reduce debtors	Aggressively reduce
Production	Expand	Expand and invest	Maximize 'occupacity' and efficiency	Free up utilization
R&D	Broaden application	Expand, trials and pilots	Managed projects	None?
Personnel	Upgrade in key areas	Increase, training and development	Maintain and reward for efficiency	Reduce
Investment	Fund maintained growth	Fund growth	Limit fixed investment	None?

Limitations of the Boston Box

The simplicity of the Boston Box is both its main attraction and its main failing. On the plus side, most businesses can make the measurements and comparisons required – growth and share – but on the minus side, is growth the only determinant of an attractive product or market? Must you have a big market share to have a strong position? Of course not, but here we see one of the strengths of the analysis rather than a weakness: the way in which it raises these very questions and encourages us towards a more sophisticated model: the DPM.

THE DIRECTIONAL POLICY MATRIX

A development of the Boston Box is the Directional Policy Matrix (DPM – see Figure 22.3), already discussed in Chapters 9, 15 and 18 – clearly an important and versatile tool.

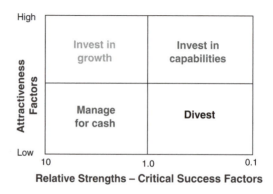

Figure 22.3 *The Directional Policy Matrix*

The essential difference as compared with the Boston Box is the way the DPM allows for a number of factors to represent the two axes, under two general headings. The vertical axis is a combination of factors that measure attractiveness. The horizontal combines factors to measure your relative strength in the market. This avoids the limitations of the Boston Box, and also forces you as a marketer to a more wide-ranging assessment of what works for you, and what works for customers.

Market attractiveness factors

What makes a product attractive to us? Some factors to consider might include the following:

- Volume of sales.
- Value of sales.
- Profitability of sales.

- Future growth potential (volume, value or profitability).
- Stage in product life cycle.
- Portfolio fit – does the product fit with others in a range?
- Is it valued by customers?
- Is there an opportunity for competitive advantage?
- What is the level of competition (low being attractive)?
- Investment required (again, low being attractive).
- Specific customer demand.

Your own business circumstances must determine your selection, and the weighting you might give to individual factors.

Whatever your final choice, you must be able to apply these factors to each of the products in the portfolio, measuring them against each other. In identifying these factors you will go a long way to identifying the sort of business you want to build in this segment, a useful exercise in itself.

Relative strength factors

These factors will measure how the customers in the segment perceive your capabilities. Remember, when doing this exercise, that it is their perceptions that matter, not yours. Your R&D department may be telling you that your product is superior to a competitor's, you may even be able to evidence this by blind testing, but if the customers vote with their feet and purchase someone else's in preference to yours, then it is their perception that makes them do so.

Identifying these factors may well be harder than identifying the market attractiveness factors, and not surprisingly. Proper identification may call for market research, particularly into issues such as customer satisfaction ratings, and if it does that, then the exercise will have been useful even if taken no further.

While for market attractiveness factors the purpose is to compare each product against a common list, with these relative strength factors you will need to measure each product against its competitors. Some examples of the criteria used might include:

- brand name;
- brand awareness;
- innovation;
- price;
- costs in use;
- service levels;
- quality;
- supplier's investment in the market;
- value in use;
- long-term sustainability;
- supplier's experience.

Completing the matrix

The following tables are designed to help you compile your analysis. Software packages are available to help with the process (indeed, you will find a simple version of a DPM in the CD ROM attached to this book), but it is no bad idea to commence with a paper exercise, however rough, for several reasons: it quickly identifies the black holes in your knowledge of the market; it makes a team-wide analysis easier to carry out; and, most importantly, it engages the brain rather than your typing fingers.

Attractiveness

Table 22.2   *Attractiveness factors*

	Products								
Attractiveness Factor									
1									
2									
3									
4									
5									
6									
Total									

Average score: (Total of all scores divided by number of products rated)

- Enter your products across the top of the grid shown in Table 22.2.
- It is advisable to select a list of about six factors. Of course, more will exist, but this will help to focus the analysis.
- Enter a score from 1 to 10 for each product against each attractiveness factor. The higher the score, the better the fit of the product.
- Calculate the average score. This will be used to place each product on the matrix, higher or lower than the average.

Relative strength

Table 22.3   *Relative strength vis-à-vis the competition*

Product:		Competitors			
Relative strength factor	**You**				
1					
2					
3					
4					
5					
6					
Total					

- For each product under consideration, identify six relative strength factors that represent the customer's criteria for choosing a product. These are the factors that determine your success or failure against the competition.
- Complete one table (Table 22.3) for each product rated in Table 22.2.
- Place you and your competitors across the top of the table and enter a score from 1 to 10 for each, against each factor. Remember to ensure that this scoring reflects the market's perception, not your opinion!

Placing the products

Using the information from these two tables, you can place each product on the matrix.

From Table 22.2, if a product scores higher than the average score, then it will be in one of the two upper boxes; if lower than average, it will be in one of the two lower boxes. To identify which of the two, use the results from Table 22.3. Where your product scores better than your _best_ competitor's, you will occupy the right-hand box. If you score worse, you will occupy the left hand.

Generic product strategies

This section comes with a health warning. Each box carries a generic piece of advice: how to manage products in that box. Please note: it is generic advice. Your own circumstances may cause you to ignore that advice, but if you do, make sure you understand why you are ignoring it, and can justify your actions.

- Top left: invest in sustaining your winning position.
- Top right: invest in developing a competitive advantage.
- Bottom left: manage for cash.
- Bottom right: divest.

In a business that allocates products to product managers (a typical fmcg scenario), you might even go so far as to allocate those products on the basis of the skills and abilities of the product managers. Bottom left products call for managers who will keep an eye on costs and will go to great lengths to find small savings, while a top right manager will need expertise in market research and the development of value propositions. Being given a bottom right product may be a sign of something else…

Part V

The tactical mix

23

The tactical audit

By this stage of the marketing process, your own specific needs for information will be just that: very specific. Remember, the purpose of this audit is just the same as that of the strategic audit and the segment audit: to help you make the decisions required, and at this stage in the process those are the decisions concerning the marketing mix:

1. Is our promotion working?
2. Does our price properly reflect the value received?
3. Are we pursuing the right channels to market?
4. How is our product received?

In addition, we will want to monitor performance against plan, which includes the above questions and also some broader ones, such as:

1. What market share do we have?
2. What are competitors up to?
3. How satisfied are customers?

The channel audit is a significant undertaking, and is considered in the chapter on place, Chapter 26. Here, I have chosen two additional examples to illustrate the sort of thing that might be going on at this point: 1) customer satisfaction surveys; and 2) tracking of promotional effectiveness.

Note: the fact that they come under the heading of 'tactical audit' does not mean that they are one-off activities; both should be part of a longer-term campaign of research. It does mean that the information they provide is to be used in helping with the tactical implementation stage of the marketing process.

CUSTOMER SATISFACTION SURVEYS

Perhaps you are losing customers at a rate, and in a way, that is beyond the normal trends. You might want to understand why, and commission research into customer attitudes, perhaps a customer satisfaction survey. But is this the best time to do so, when something in the market (a competitor? your recent price rise?) is possibly prejudicing customers against you? Customer satisfaction surveys are not best used as one-off crisis management tools (nor are they intended to bring warm glows to the supplier!); they should be used to provide guidance to future activity. This is a case for long-term investment; indeed, jumping in and out of such activity can be more damaging to customer perceptions than not engaging in it at all.

Aiming to understand

Asking customers what they think of you is not as easy as it might seem. The question 'are we expensive?' is unlikely to prompt a constructive response from a busy customer. A better approach might be to ask customers to consider first of all what is important to them in dealing with a supplier. By keeping this general, you will help avoid sending the customers down an avenue prompted more by a recent failure on your part than by a genuine assessment of their own requirements. Of course, using an 'independent' research agency will help take some of the heat out of such a situation, but increasingly customers will not respond to such general approaches. They want to know who is behind the questions, and why (and what they're going to do about it!).

If you establish a list of expectations from the customer and ask them to rank them on a scale of 1 to 6 (1 being least important and 6 most important), you will be able to plot the horizontal scale on the chart shown in Figure 23.1.

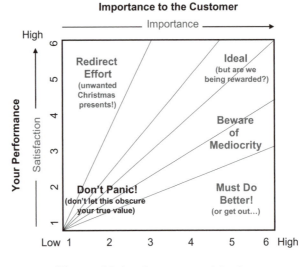

Figure 23.1 *Customer satisfaction*

(Incidentally, using a scale of 1 to 6 is much better than 1 to 5 for any of these sorts of ratings. A scale of 1 to 5 allows sitting on the fence – everything gets 3 for average – while 1 to 6 forces the respondent above the mid point or below.)

Now ask the customer to evaluate how well you perform against each of these factors. This really does call for expert help. Questionnaires or interviews can be framed to get any answer you might want, but presumably you want the truth. This rating, 1 for poor through to 6 for excellent, will position the factors from the horizontal scale on to the vertical scale.

The results of such a simple analysis are often most illuminating:

- Those factors that appear in the top right are fine. They are important and you perform well, but you might like to ask, are we being properly rewarded for this excellent performance?
- In the top left we see excellent performance, but against things that don't matter all that much. This is the realm of the unwanted Christmas present, and we all know what we think of the people who give us those! You need to redirect effort from here, possibly even stop certain activities.
- The bottom right is of course where alarm bells should be ringing, and if you really cannot improve, you should be thinking of getting out.
- Finally, bottom left, and don't panic! Buyers may love to pick on these things as part of the negotiation exercise, but if you are certain that they really are of minor importance, don't let them obscure your true value. That is not to say that you should be happy with poor performance – they may be small issues, but psychologically they may get blown up out of all proportion.

Such an analysis can be used for many different purposes: improving performance on the bottom right factors, reducing effort and resource (perhaps) from top left factors, and getting a better reward for the value delivered through the top right factors.

When you have plotted your own performance, another step might be to do the same for the competition. The value of this is more than the obvious benchmarking exercise. What it helps you to see is where you beat your competitors _when it matters_, not just where you beat them, and also where you underperform _when it matters_. Such an analysis is a good example of research that will illuminate your understanding and direct your efforts rather than supporting your current prejudices (remembering David Ogilvy's complaint from Chapter 7, that too many people use market research as a drunk uses a lamp-post: for support instead of illumination).

One you have started out on this track, the possibilities begin to get exciting. How about using such studies with particular customers, as a means of sharing strategies, developing ideas for partnership, and generally planning a successful shared future? Why not indeed – but take care, there are bear traps around this corner. It is very easy to raise customer expectations

… but take care to manage expectations

through such activities and then see them come crashing down again when what materializes is less than they hoped for. Take care to manage expectations, and seek the help of the experts in conducting such studies; the returns will almost always justify the costs.

TRACKING OF PROMOTIONAL SPEND EFFECTIVENESS

Knowing which half worked!

If you spend millions on TV advertising, surely you should also spend the tens of thousands required to be sure of its efficacy? Henry Ford once said that half of the money spent on advertising was wasted; unfortunately, you could never be sure which half. 'Tracking' is one way of being more certain.

Many big spenders in the area of fmcg advertising have started to look more carefully at the efficacy of that spend. In the old days they might have commissioned studies to measure 'top of mind' recollection (how many people polled would mention a brand unprompted) and slept more soundly when the results were 75 per cent plus. Then they started to wonder why a 75 per cent unprompted recollection turned into a 20 per cent brand share. Clearly, such a simple measure of advertising effectiveness was not enough.

A typical tracking study might ask three main sets of questions of its audience, and it would ask them before the campaign, during the campaign and after it, in order to identify the impact and the 'stamina' of the campaign:

- *Cut-through*. What awareness is generated by the campaign – who has it reached and how well do they recall it?
- *Beliefs and perceptions*. What values and promises did the campaign raise, and what level of belief do you have in them? Has it enhanced your perception of the product/brand/company?
- *Disposition scale*. What action will you take as a result of this campaign? Will you buy the product now or in the future? Will you recommend it?

A typical study of this kind might cost about £80,000 using a sample size of 300 a month, tracking a campaign over three to six months. Expenditure of this kind would relate to an advertising spend of over £5 million, a small proportion of the total spend.

24

The four P's... or the four C's?

For years, when it comes to the tactical mix, people have spoken of the four P's – product, place, promotion and price. Indeed, I am about to do the same thing, but before I do, we might pause to consider a word of warning from no less than Philip Kotler.

We all accept the purpose of these four P's – the marketing mix – namely, to define our proposition in each market segment, uniquely. The mix represents the levers of demand; levers that can be pulled by the marketer through an amazing range of subtle gradations, resulting in propositions as distinct and as 'refined' as the greasy-spoon café and dinner at the Ritz. They all use that same mix. The art of using the mix is in the balance achieved, not a focus on any one element in isolation.

What came before the marketing mix? The elements were all still there, of course, but they were not drawn together in a coherent strategy. This was in the days of the 'make and sell' philosophy, when perhaps life was easier, and choice was certainly more limited. I recall my induction training on joining ICI back in 1981: 'The sixties and early seventies', we were told, 'were the Midas years – whatever we made and sold turned to gold. As we enter the eighties, there is a distinct danger that we enter the My God! years – competition has arrived.' The result was an urgent need for marketing training throughout the company, which turned the 1980s into a decade of success and record profits.

The mix was born as an attempt to escape the limitations of that 'make and sell' philosophy, and it worked. It introduced the idea that customers were influenced by more than the hard facts of a product, and so encouraged a greater spirit of inquiry into the dynamics of the marketplace, its segments and its customers. The language used was not particularly revolutionary and suited the predominantly manufacturing-based economy of the time.

The problem – and here we turn to Kotler's warning – is that the mix can easily become a set of things that we do *to* the market. But marketing, we are reminded, is something that we must do *with* the market. So, Philip Kotler, in his book *Kotler on Marketing* (1999), suggests an alternative to the four P's: the four C's, encouraging us to look at the market through our customers' eyes. Not that the four P's don't do this, if understood and used properly, but perhaps the choice of words used in the four C's makes it easier to express the outward-looking intention of the marketing mix.

For practical purposes of defining the marketing mix, most people still prefer to stick with the P's, as I have in fact done in the following chapters, but the alternatives are as follows, with some slight modification (and, I hope, improvement):

- *Product* becomes **customer value**, reminding us not only that everything is in the eye of the beholder, but also that successful products must provide genuine value to the customer.
- *Price* becomes **cost to the customer**, reminding us that price is simply a marker and that the full costs in use are of much greater significance in most purchases.
- *Place* becomes **convenience**, which is certainly a much better term than 'place' (which has always been suspect, but starts with the letter P!), encouraging us to remember why we consider routes to market in the first place: to make it easy for our customers to get hold of our offer.
- *Promotion* becomes **communication**. This is perhaps the most important change of emphasis, recognizing that good promotion should aim to develop into a dialogue with the customer.

Cynics might say that this is mere semantics, but the true marketer will recognize the important differences in tone, a tone that will be used in the following chapters even though I have still adhered to the 'P' words.

25

Product

Marketing, as we know it today, had its roots in the mass-production industries of the 19th century, and so it is no surprise that the definition of 'a product' for many years referred to something that was entirely tangible: a product was something that was made. Sure, it could be anything from a pin to an ocean-going liner, but it was very much a 'real thing'.

In more recent years the application of the word 'product' has broadened considerably, not only in marketing circles but also in common usage. Now it is quite normal to hear a holiday described as a product. A pension plan, a theatrical performance, a premier-league football match – all are products. Even a country can be seen as a product: the Seychelles tourist board recently employed an executive from Coca-Cola to help market these particular holiday islands. Sporting superstars from Tiger Woods to David Beckham are often described as marketable commodities, though the word 'commodity', as we will see, is hardly a suitable choice. Even bishops in the Church of England call for new thinking in marketing their product, though whether they mean their church, their creed or their Lord is not always clear.

A product is in fact much more than a tangible item, a 'thing'. For the marketer, a product is something experienced by the customer, in a wide range of senses. Dinner at the Ritz is far more than the food consumed; it is very clearly an experience. So for that matter is a Big Mac: the customer is experiencing more than the food itself, whether that be speed, convenience, mobility or the security of certainty. There is a risk of getting into the territory of Chapter 28, price, but it is clear that what we pay for a product such as a Big Mac cannot be calculated by itemized costings of bun, patty and lettuce leaf; the experience itself has a value.

So, product managers are responsible for more than an item: they are responsible for the image, the associations, the reputation and the ultimate value of that item. The ubiquitous can of baked beans (Heinz, of course) has more in common with a performance of *Fidelio* at the National Opera House than at first appears.

THE COMMODITY

A commodity is – a failure

Economists speak of commodities as shorthand for things that are bought and sold, but marketers have a more precise definition. For them, a commodity is a failure. If a product really has no value above its component parts then the marketer has failed in his or her task. Any profit made by the seller of such a thing comes only from the service of getting it to the customer, not from the product itself, and at such a point, of course, it ceases to be a commodity!

If value has been added, then the product is no longer a commodity. Now, if the marketer allows that service of delivering the product to become valueless, then he or she may as well be giving up…

By this definition it is hard to think of any real commodities. Water has long since ceased to be one; sugar is more subtle in its variations than ever before; even such 'known-value items' (KVIs) as flour and tea have escaped the clutches of commoditization. The ease of self-raising and the healthiness of wholemeal, the convenience of tea bags and the taste sensations of camomile, burdock and agrimony – such have been their salvation.

ADDED VALUE

Added value is not an artifice of marketers and advertisers, despite what the cynics might think. A product ceases to be a commodity and takes on value not when the marketer says it has, but when the customer perceives it to have done so. Value is entirely in the eye of the beholder.

Value is in the eye of the beholder; and there are beholders, and there are beholders… (we might call them segments)

A sales rep for a pharmaceutical company told me how she once spent a thankless 15 minutes with a doctor, trying to extol the value of a new drug. The doctor would have none of it, and so the rep left a sample and prepared to leave. Opening the packet, the doctor called her back, saying, 'You didn't tell me they were blue.' The drug was intended for those likely to be already on a variety of pills, and for this doctor the ability to distinguish this pill as 'the blue one' was a definite plus. Fine, but going into the next surgery on the journey plan and opening with 'Let me tell you about this new drug; it's blue…' was hardly going to work!

Value has nothing to do with the costs of manufacture of the said product. If a cardboard disk illustrating a cartoon character that comes free with a bag of potato crisps happens to be the one that completes your collection, then who is to deny its value, even though its cost of manufacture may have been tiny? The value of a lifebelt to a drowning man is beyond calculation...

Nor is the complexity of the manufacturing or distribution process a guarantee of value added, though it should be the purpose of the manufacturer to ensure that these processes do just that.

Consider the 'widget', that 'thing' at the bottom of some beer cans that makes the beer froth. Starting life as a bunch of component parts, this 'nascent widget' has very little value at this stage. When it has been formed together and put in the bottom of a can, it has added a good deal of value by virtue of the effect it has on the beer when poured. But this is only part of the story. For the rest, and the lion's share of the value, we must turn to the consumer. Beer drinkers had long criticized canned beer as a poor substitute for the real thing from the tap. The 'widget' (as coined by Guinness) performs the miracle of translation, delivering draught taste with all the convenience of the can – true added value, if you're a beer drinker.

The added value widget

The core and the surround

Of course perceptions can be influenced: we will pay four times more for a bottle of wine in a restaurant than we would have paid in the supermarket, and yet we may sit there and discuss the good value of our choice. We will pay perhaps 20 times as much for the convenience of a diluted box of Ribena as for the equivalent amount made from the bottle of undiluted Ribena plus glass and tap water. What is happening here is that we are influenced by more than the thing itself: we are influenced also by what marketers call its *surround*.

PepsiCo famously conducted a huge consumer research project in the United Kingdom, asking people to blind-test Pepsi against its main competitors. The results delighted its executives: 55 per cent of people preferred their product. The tests led directly to a long advertising campaign showing the amazement on consumers' faces when they were asked to blind-test colas and found that their favourite was indeed Pepsi. The campaign did not bring the hoped-for ejection of Coca-Cola from the number one spot, however: there was a problem. It seemed that when people knew what they were drinking, as opposed to in blind tests, 65 per cent preferred Coca-Cola!

When telling us we like it isn't enough

Thus, we are influenced not just by the tangible taste, but also by the product's surround. This idea is illustrated in Figure 25.1.

A product has a core: what it is. Value is added by a number of tangible things, things that can be touched and measured – the quality, the packaging, the availability, a warranty, etc. Further value is added by a range of intangible issues such as trustworthiness, heritage or reputation. These

Figure 25.1 *The core and the surround*

issues are in the realm of perception, and can be brought together under the banner of the 'brand'. It is very often the case that the greater value is added in this intangible surround, and it is also here that the longer-term competitive advantage is gained.

At their core, both Pepsi and Coke are 'black, sweetened drinks' (BSDs). How much would you pay for a 'BSD'? Not much value added so far. The value is added in layers. First the tangible elements: the secret ingredients, the taste, the design of the bottle, the look of the logo, the availability of the product. These tangible things add value, but most value is added by the brand and its associated images: everything from youth to tradition, energy to relaxation, heritage to 'cool', the American dream to the global family.

Malt whisky drinkers will tell you that they can distinguish the taste of one malt from that of another with some precision – hence their preference. This may be so, but nonetheless, the distillers of those whiskies will go to much trouble to build broader associations around the core of their product. There is the name, the bottle shape, the romance of its place of origin, and the image of ancient retainers practising time-honoured traditions with equipment that might just raise the eyebrow of a local food inspector. Would we value an identical taste so much if we knew it to come from a stainless steel vat in a chemical plant?

The battle of the petrol pump shows how in the pursuit of competitive advantage a product can take on a range of associations, tangible and intangible, well beyond its original essence. At its core, petrol is petrol; it is not an unknown occurrence to see one company's tanker filling the underground tanks of a competitor's station. Even when a company develops a unique formulation, a genuine tangible difference, how much is this a factor in determining our purchasing behaviour? Each of us has his or her own reasons for choosing a particular make of petrol, some tangible, some less so.

The following lists a range of those reasons, in no particular order of preference, culled from a consumer research study:

- The station is on my way to work.
- The station is on my side of the road, so I avoid having to turn across a stream of busy traffic.
- The station has a shop.
- The station has a cash machine.
- The station has clean toilets.
- There is good protection against the rain and the wind.
- They've got a car wash.
- I collect the loyalty points.
- I'm collecting the free gifts.
- They stock my favourite brand of cigarettes.
- The pumps are fast.
- The pumps don't dribble.
- They always have a copy of my morning paper.
- It's a great place to buy a quick breakfast.
- I believe that their petrol is best for my engine.
- I don't like the environmental record of the company across the road.
- I broke down once and they helped me out.
- The queues are short.
- I like the people behind the counter.
- I trust them not to put funny stuff in the petrol.
- It always seems to be the cheapest.
- It seems to give me the most miles per gallon.
- I trust the name.

Some of these are tangible reasons, some intangible, but whichever they are, fewer than half have anything to do with the petrol itself. The purchase seems to be more down to the mix of services and related products than to the core product. And even when we do have reasons that relate to the petrol itself, they are about beliefs and perceptions as much as about known facts. Each of us would rate those reasons differently, each of us fitting into some segment of the petrol market: the business traveller, the convenience shopper, the seeker for bargains, or the points collector, to name just a few possibilities. Value is added in different ways depending on the segment, and the product is perceived differently depending on the segment. This can get complicated: as a business traveller, I resent standing in queues behind people doing their grocery shopping, yet at the weekend I am the first to give thanks for late-night milk and bread!

The surround for service and B2B suppliers

Is this notion of the core and the surround just for fmcg suppliers? Absolutely not: for a service provider, the surround is of even greater importance.

A 'good' service takes more than the service

Service providers must add at least three ingredients to the core service provided: the people, the systems and the evidence of capability. Take the example of a training provider. The question of who will deliver the training is often of much greater significance to the customer than is the nature of the content. The quality of training is more than the quality of the course: a good product is one that links the training to the delegates' work, before, during and after the event. The customer takes on a degree of risk when selecting the training provider: what if they waste our time, what if they don't understand our needs, what if they send us down the wrong tracks? The training company must be able to evidence its capability, perhaps through references, an impressive client list, the opportunity to sample the wares, or perhaps a book on the subject that demonstrates its credibility and status in the big wide world.

B2B suppliers must also take note of the surround. They may think that their product is chosen solely on performance and price, but the truth is usually more complex, and more beneficial to the supplier that does attend to the surround. What about availability, what about the mode of supply, what about customer service, what about the breadth of the portfolio? Then, further out; what about flexibility in providing variants, or speed of response? And, further out still, what about questions of reputation, customer confidence and trustworthiness?

Figure 25.2 suggests an alternative model to that shown in Figure 25.1, where the surround is made up first by specific benefits, then by services and finally by solutions. This language may better suit the B2B environment.

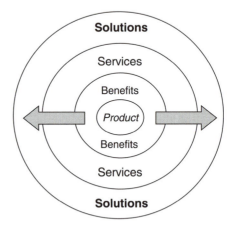

Figure 25.2 *The B2B surround*

A fertilizer manufacturer initially tried to differentiate its product through specific benefits: it was good for application in areas of high rainfall. This worked, until the competition matched those benefits. It turned next to services: providing advice to farmers on application, which worked fine, until the competition matched its offer. Then it turned to solutions. Realizing that what the farmer really wanted was a better crop, and didn't want to be bothered by the niceties of how, it offered to apply the fertilizer itself, being paid by a share of the improved yield and profitability of the crop. Of course, competitors may still copy that, but the closeness of the relationship with the customers' business provides a higher level of security (or 'lock-in') than the earlier offers of benefits or services.

Solutions and 'lock-in'

Givens and differentiators

While it is very often in the outer circles of the 'surround' that the most value is added, this shouldn't lead us to suppose that the core is unimportant. Products that promise the moon in their surround but are rotten at their core are products that fail in the long run. Products have to work: drinks must refresh, and they must be good for us if that is what they claim. The higher the profile established by the surround, the greater the crash when something at the core fails. The withdrawal of Perrier water after it was found to have traces of benzene in it made front-page news.

There were more headlines in 1999 when Coca-Cola had to withdraw millions of litres of product in the Benelux countries after traces of dioxins were found. Food safety issues have become headline news not just because we care about health, but also because food manufacturers make such public claims for the purity, freshness and general well-being to be had from their products. Coca-Cola was criticized by many not only for the product's problem, but also for the way it handled the problem. The management in Atlanta were slow to comment, and when they did, it was to say very little. When that caused a problem, they snapped to high-profile response mode with a dramatic product call-back. The watchers were not impressed: 'givens' (see below) are *very* sensitive things if they go astray.

'Givens' may be taken for granted, but not by the supplier!

We might regard the core, and those things closest to the core, as 'givens': things that just *have* to be right, or you are not in business. Away from the core we are looking at what we might call 'differentiators', the source of competitive advantage. When choosing our petrol, we assume that all brands will work – that is a given – but it is some mix of the factors discussed earlier, the differentiators, that will determine our preference. Let's consider two example sources of product differentiation: packaging and customer service.

Packaging

Packaging might be, at any one time; a practical means of supply, the product's persona, its advertisement, and sometimes even its source of competitive advantage. Kodak film comes in yellow boxes, but not just any yellow. The colour consistency of that packaging is vital to a product that is claiming perfect colour representation. The package is a part of the product's credibility.

As was pointed out in an earlier chapter, Limmits, the range of slimming biscuits, come in slim shapes with silky black wrappers, 'just as I would like to be,' say many of its consumers; 'slim and sexy'. The traditional Coca-Cola bottle shouts heritage, the Angostura bitters bottle positively screams its unique individuality. Packaging can even communicate complex messages such as trustworthiness, provided it is given time. For many years, ICI delivered its fertilizer products in distinctive blue bags, and farmers would order 'blue bag' from their local wholesalers and heave sighs of relief when they saw it stacked in their own warehouse – a sign of a safe decision taken.

Novel packaging can allow new uses for existing products. The TetraPak has allowed a variety of drinks from milk to orange juice to be offered in ready-to-drink, long-life or other convenience modes. In the convenience drinks sector it is arguable that the package is in fact the core of the product, not the contents. For many a food shopper with a busy lifestyle, the sight of a microwavable container is almost more important than what comes inside. I have often put back on the shelf the doubtless tastier but oven-cooked option and chosen instead the convenience version – convenient and with value added, thanks to the packaging.

New materials have allowed suppliers of bulk materials to industrial users to supply in quantities that suit the customer's production schedules, not the limitations of the supplier's packaging. The value of this is clear: deliveries of product direct to the point of use reduce lead times, remove the need for storage and allow the customer to concentrate on manufacturing rather than the management of inventory.

One of the dilemmas for the marketer is that novel packaging can often take longer to develop than the product itself. With an ever-increasing emphasis on speed to market as a means of commercial success, this must inevitably leave some good packaging ideas on the drawing board. The solution lies in seeing packaging not as a last-minute add-on, but as an integral part of the product, whether core or surround.

Packaging is not an afterthought; it takes planning

One of my favourite examples of this attitude is that of Dulux Paints, which developed a square can for a new product, Once Gloss, a one-coat paint. The novelty of the design suggested the novelty of the product, but this is not the story I wish to tell. The marketing manager knew that this novel design would be perfect to emphasize the originality of another product, only he didn't yet know what that product was; it lay in the future. He ordered a large production run in the confident assurance that it would suit 'some' future new product launch, and that waiting for the product would mean missing the boat on the packaging. A year later, Dulux launched 'Kids Zone', complete with novel square can, and it was a great success. Brave, open to criticism of poor focus, but eminently practical and ultimately wise.

Customer service

Customer service should be regarded as part of the product surround, and a part that will often reap rewards much beyond the apparent costs. The key to success is finding the appropriate kind of customer service, which means 'appropriate to the product it surrounds'.

During most of the 1990s, customer service managers were obsessed with getting their staff to answer the phone before the fourth ring. This was a noble endeavour, in some cases... A hotel with its telephone number on the information board at a busy airport that answers its telephones on the fifth ring, or worse, is a hotel going out of business. The supplier of a unique and complex high-tech product (perhaps a piece of software for use by engineers) should worry more about what gets said when the telephone is picked up than about how quickly it is done.

PRODUCT LIFE CYCLES

Products must be managed (hence the need for product managers) for a host of reasons, but perhaps mostly because they are like living things. Products are born, nurtured, encouraged to learn and grow; they mature, grow old, and perhaps at some future date they die. The idea of a product life cycle (see Figure 25.3) is hugely valuable to those wishing to manage this process, as it provides them with the same guidelines that a good parent would want for bringing up baby and sending it out into the big, wide world.

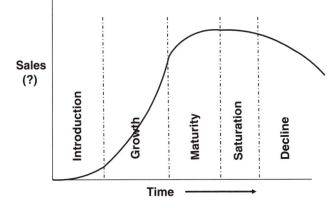

Figure 25.3 _The product life cycle_

The following are the stages of a typical product life cycle (PLC):

- _Introduction_ – typically a time of high investment and slow uptake.
- _Growth_ – if it takes on, it can take off, with resultant volumes bringing costs down, so fuelling more growth.

- *Maturity* – the product's success brings in competitors to share the spoils, and life starts to get a little harder.
- *Saturation* – too many players are crowding around the honey pot, spoiling the game for everyone.
- *Decline* – with the fun gone out of the game, the suppliers lose interest and the product declines towards death.

The timeline is hugely variable, depending on the nature of the product. The life of a successful pharmaceutical might be measured in decades; a successful confectionery bar may come and go within two years; while a PC seems to have a life cycle that extinguishes on purchase!

This cycle isn't inevitable. Many products die at their introduction; many products get a new lease of life at maturity, just as with people. But perhaps the analogy between product and person is ultimately flawed. People are born, they grow, they mature and they die, but products don't have to; that is up to the market, and the product manager.

Using the product life cycle

The PLC analysis allows for three distinct uses by the marketer:

- the 'comparative' use;
- the 'advisory' use;
- the 'dynamic' use.

The comparative use

The comparative use is like taking your baby to the clinic to make sure that it's putting on the right weight for its age. Parents who are proud of their children might get strange ideas about their progress if they didn't stop occasionally to compare notes with others. Baby might be growing fast (babies do), but what if everyone else's is growing twice as fast? Your mother might tell you that little Sally is quite tall enough, that's how big you were at her age, but what if today's environment promotes much faster growth? The PLC can be used to plot your product against a range of benchmarks: other products in your own range, the competition, and the market cycle. This last is particularly valuable, as it encourages an understanding of that cycle and shows your performance in the only arena that matters. Knowing that you are down when the market is up allows you the choice of taking action. Without that kind of knowledge, most of us would blunder on regardless.

The advisory use

The PLC can be used like one of those manuals on child care, and with the same warnings: each child and each product is unique, and the environment is infinitely variable, but guidelines are nonetheless helpful, and some are given in Figure 25.4.

The PLC

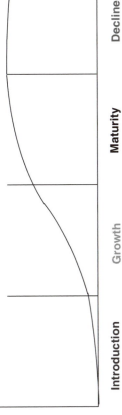

POSSIBLE CHARACTERISTICS

	Introduction	Growth	Maturity	Decline
Sales	Low	Rapidly rising	Peak sales	Declining
Costs	High per unit	Falling	Low per unit	Rising?
Profits	Negative	Rising	Maximum	Declining
Customers	Innovators	Early adopters	Majority	Laggards?
Competitors	Few	Growing	Over-capacity?	Possible shake-out?

POSSIBLE OBJECTIVES

	Introduction	Growth	Maturity	Decline
	Create Awareness	Maximize share	Maximize profit	Reduce costs

POSSIBLE STRATEGIES/TACTICS

	Introduction	Growth	Maturity	Decline
PRODUCT	Basic	Develop	Extend lines	Rationalize lines
PRICE	Premium	Penetration	Matching others	Cut or raise?
PROMOTION	Awareness	Build brand	Stress benefits	Reduce or niche?
PLACE	Selective	Many outlets	All outlets	Rationalize
SALES EFFORT	Targeted	Heavy	Reducing	Alternatives?

Figure 25.4 *The product life cycle: advisory use*

Take great care to note the use of the word 'possible' in Figure 25.4. These are not prescriptions for success, but generic advice. One of the loudest debates is whether prices should be cut or raised when a product enters the decline phase. The argument for raising price is the one of milking a product that will die anyway; the argument for cutting is that fewer and fewer people want to buy it and you still have a factory to fill. The real answer must depend on four things:

- What are your competitors doing?
- What will the market stand?
- How much volume is required to keep your production efficient?
- What do you plan to do about this decline?

The last point takes us to the third and most important of the uses for the PLC analysis: the dynamic use.

The dynamic use

The dynamic use is the PLC use that least suits the analogy with a human life. Marketers have an advantage over the parent: they can postpone nature, or bring it on. They can behave as no good parent would, yet still be doing the right thing. They can force their child to change its character; they can favour another child in preference to this one; they can raise new children that will chase this one to a premature grave; they can even choose to kill their offspring outright.

Marketing is about choices, and nowhere more so than in the choices facing the product manager with regard to the PLC. The tragedy is that so few product managers see the choices in time. In theory at least, no product need ever decline, and maturity can be put off indefinitely. Continual growth is possible, provided that the marketer is on hand to do the right things. Even if maturity and decline become inevitable, there is always the option of a new product to replace the old, but the big question is usually, when?

Consider a car manufacturer whose leading model has seen a few years of spectacular growth but is now showing signs of reaching maturity. Other manufacturers have caught up with what was once a revolutionary new design, and market share is beginning to slip. There are choices:

1. Do nothing.
2. Take action to revive the existing model: *augmentation, range extension, relaunch.*
3. Find a new market for the product: *repositioning.*
4. Launch a new model to replace the one in trouble: *new product development.*

The first is acceptable only if analysis of the market suggests that this is a temporary blip or that the market is no longer attractive. Incidentally, such an analysis is all too tempting for a company that resists change, and is so often a fool's paradise, or a sanctuary for post-rationalization.

The second choice seems immediately the most attractive, appearing to call for a level of effort within the current capabilities and comfort zone. But is it enough, or is it even warranted?

The third is tempting, but perhaps more challenging than imagined.

The fourth is a dramatic step, but one that may already be too late…

Augmentation

As products move through the growth stage, wise product managers will be on the lookout for opportunities to 'augment' their product. This may mean a range of activities including additional features and benefits, new design or styling, new packaging, or range extension. These are actions intended to give the product a 'kick', to set it on a new growth path away from the threat of maturity (see Figure 25.5).

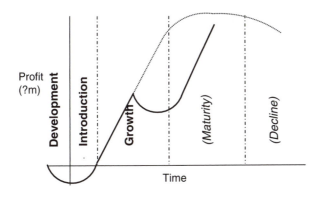

Figure 25.5 _Breathing new life…_

The classic case is of the 'new, improved' product, whether it be a soap powder or a motor car.

Cars are managed through this process to an increasingly preordained plan. The launch model is quite basic – its novelty being enough to ensure success. As time goes by, a stream of extras are applied; things once optional become standard. A sure sign of a car approaching the end of its life cycle is when it carries every conceivable extra as the standard offer.

If we remember the 'adopters curve' from Chapter 15 (Figure 15.7), we will see the sense in such a strategy. The innovator's requirements are different from those of the early adopters, and those are different again from those of the early majority. If product managers can identify the needs of these groups of customers then they can plan the development of their product to meet them. The Japanese have long been regarded as experts in this practice of planning by use of the adopters curve, a concept that has often been resisted by Western firms driven by a spirit of invention and technological expertise. Philips has been the source of more innovations in the electronics and hi-fi market than perhaps even it chooses to recall – the reluctance being because of its failure to market so many of these new ideas well enough. If we look for a cause of its relatively poor track record, we can see it in its apparent reluctance to manage the product life cycle. Too often it has launched a new product with a range of features and benefits more suited to an early majority audience, not the innovator, and too often an Asian Pacific competitor has captured the market with a more appropriate PLC strategy.

The concept of the core and the surround (see Figures 25.1 and 25.2) gives another insight into the strategy of augmentation. The first activities outside the core will be seen as differentiators by the market, but over time they become givens. The successful supplier must continually seek new differentiators, often searching further and further from the core, and in time these activities too will become givens. Doubtless the first petrol company to offer free plastic daffodils with its petrol stole a march on the competition, but soon it was the norm for customers to pick up free gifts at the petrol station. Already the attachment of a grocery shop is almost a given; now the search is on for yet more differentiators: cash machines, takeaway meals, free newspapers and who yet knows what.

In the grand scheme of things, product augmentation is a relatively low-cost activity with attractive returns if done at the right time. Getting the timing right, however, calls for a high degree of forward planning.

Range extension

Once there was white paint, but white paint was approaching maturity, so over the past 20 years it has branched out. First there was brilliant white, then natural whites with just a hint of colour; ultra-white was fast on their tails, followed by one-coat white, classic white, romantic white, and ever onwards. Where once there was a single product, now there are a dozen. Such range extension is a common strategy in the fight against product maturity. Our beleaguered motor car might choose to revive its fortunes through the launch of new variations on the theme: an open top, a sports model, a diesel option.

The strategy can be played too far, of course, and the plethora of white paints leads to confusion not only for the consumer, but also for the retailer taxed with ordering and displaying the many variants. Shelf space, a real-world issue, might force a halt to such endless extension.

The product relaunch

Revitalizing a classic

The strategy of relaunching a product is best illustrated with a set of case studies.

Coca-Cola relaunched its main product as Classic Coke back in 1985 after the failure of a new-formulation Coke. New Coke was a mistake, and a costly one, and the subsequent relaunch of the old product was a rearguard action, but the result was spectacular as new life was breathed into an old product. After the disaster of New Coke, the relaunch was greeted as a triumph, and, with much hindsight, an act of genius!

Getting lucky...

In January 2000, Subbuteo announced that its world-famous football game was to be withdrawn from the market. There was much talk of the attractions of video games and the like, and a good deal of news coverage of the announcement, and then a cry of protest from fans. By February 2000 the product was 'reprieved' amidst even more publicity. Famous footballers were called on to endorse the product – a vital ingredient for the predominantly young male audience – and sales of an old and mature product are set to see a revitalization.

Getting clever...?

Kellogg's spent heavily on relaunching Corn Flakes with a series of adverts that showed grown-ups 're-experiencing' the taste of the cereal as they took breakfast with their children. The messages were a clever combination of nostalgia and retro styling with simplicity and wholesomeness, all in a world of complexity and sophistication (which, if we limit ourselves to breakfast cereals, is of course largely the doing of Kellogg's!). An old and mature product was given a well-deserved boost based on values and qualities that were there all the time; they just needed restating.

Getting it right!

Repositioning

If analysis tells you that your own product's slowdown is the result of a similar slowdown in the total market, the costs of augmentation or relaunch may be hard to justify. Time to look for pastures new. An example of this is discussed in Chapter 16: the Lucozade story (page 167).

New product development

As a means of avoiding maturity, new product development (NPD) may at first seem an odd choice. If the new product takes sales from your existing one, doesn't that just make life worse? Are you not just becoming your own competition? And there of course is the answer: who would you rather took sales from your existing product – you or the competition? This raises the question, when is the right time to launch a new product that will cannibalize the sales of your existing one? Figure 25.6 considers the options.

By redrawing the PLC to measure profit rather than sales, we begin to see the answer.

The 'sensible' answer seems to be to wait until maturity. Why kill your own product before it has had the chance to grow to its full extent? This is where we need to throw away the child-rearing manual... A new product

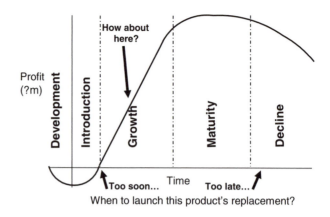

Figure 25.6 *The product life cycle, profit and new product development*

will require investment, a potential net loss, just at the time when profits are levelling out or even declining for the existing product. More than this, NPD will require sanction from senior management or the board. Will they sanction such expenditure when they look at your current business performance – maturity to saturation? We might add a third problem: NPD requires a great deal of corporate energy to succeed, energy that might just be starting to ebb away as the existing product enters maturity or saturation. And a final problem: NPD takes time – time to develop, time to launch, time to get established – and time is something you are fast running out of at the maturity stage. By waiting this late you are effectively raising the stakes on the success of your new product: if it fails, all is lost.

Very often the right time to launch a new product is while the existing one is still growing. Even though the launch will hasten the decline of a perfectly healthy product, consider the advantages. Profits are good, so investment can be accommodated. The business is still attractive, so the board will be happy to sanction your investment. Energy levels are still high, so the prospect for success is good. The only problem is that awful cliché that should be banished from any business looking at its future, 'If it ain't broke, why fix it?' This cannot be the thinking of the product manager. Sure, your NPD may shorten the life of your current product, but isn't it better that you should be in control of that, rather than your competitors? The challenge for marketers is taking the rest of the organization with them. This is really a question of inertia. If a business has been in the habit of NPD as prescribed here, then the challenge will not be so great. If NPD is a rare thing, then watch out for the cries of 'If it ain't broke…'

New product development and 'stage-gate'

Watching out for the cries is, of course, not enough; much better to have a means of handling them in advance. The stage-gate process is much used by

compan ng ideas and easing
their dev ess will be designed
to be ap; s a generic path that
will be d

Stage- ideas that come out
of a mar, et the business, the
greater th re that only the best
ideas get

Stage-g t of those functions
that must 'If it ain't broke…'
then they gate aims to ensure
that all are

One wa rocess such that it
speeds yo ones back to the
drawing b quicken the pace of
NPD, not gs down through
committee process.

The gener

Starting wi ure 25.7, must be
worked thr again.

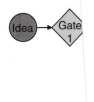

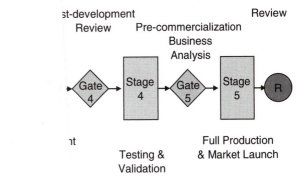

Figure 25.7 *The new product development stage-gate process*

At any point the project can be sent back on a loop to an earlier stage, but
heed the warning about slowing things down. Of course you need a process
to weed out ideas that would be failures or would drain resources for poor
return, and to ensure the successful launch of the good ideas, but above all
else the process should be designed to speed your product to market. It is
quite possible that over the next decade it will be 'speed to market' of new
products that becomes the main beacon of competitive advantage. Make
sure stage-gate helps you to this goal rather than hindering you.

The rate of new product development

Figure 25.8 shows a 'perfect' scenario for the staging of NPD and PLC.

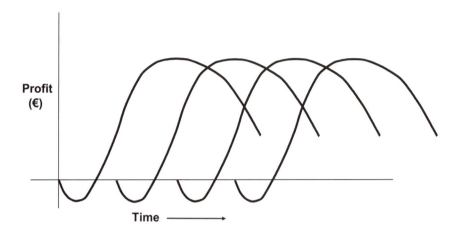

Figure 25.8 *New product development and product life cycle 'staging'*

It is 'perfect' because the cost of investment of each new product launch is balanced by the profits of an existing product or range. It is 'perfect' too because the company has a balanced portfolio at any one time of launch products: those in growth, and those in maturity. This might be considered a marketer's holy grail, but beware: there is only any point launching these new products if there is a market demand! We are right back to our discussion of the right- and left-sider from Chapter 2: this 'perfect' scenario is very much a left-sider's world.

Product development and the customer's product life cycle

Product improvement means different things at different moments in its life cycle. At the growth stage, improvement might mean better quality; by maturity we might be looking more towards cost reduction as a means of product improvement. This shift in the target for product developers can be a serious problem if R&D departments operate remotely from marketing departments, particularly as the lead times for some product improvement projects leave suppliers working on changes that were required years before and are now of little relevance. Translate this problem into a B2B environment, where it is the customer's product life cycle that needs understanding as much as your own, and the challenges become clear.

For many years, Intel has improved its chips by making them faster, as have its competitors. Companies will develop a culture based on such experience: continuous improvement, with improvement defined as speed.

While this is of huge benefit in the present, they must take great care not to allow this culture to blind them to the shifting targets brought by the customers' advancing product life cycle. As the PC market heads into maturity, will the target still be speed, or might cost or service become more significant? Deciding such questions is one of the many tasks of the marketer.

Watching the customer's market chain

As the market matures, Intel has to develop expertise well beyond its own manufacturing capabilities if it is to win the 'speed is best' battle. In order to persuade PC manufacturers that speed matters, it must now influence the end-user applications. Intel invests in companies that are developing applications for which speed is of paramount importance – an example of influencing the chain beyond the immediate customer in order to support your own product development. So far so good, but a logjam has been reached. The Internet is now one of the key drivers of any PC manufacturer's strategy, and here speed becomes an issue: the Internet is slow. It is the bandwidth available rather than the microprocessor that determines the kind of applications that can be used. Now Intel must look even further afield, for it depends on the development of more broadband access for the success of its 'speed is best' strategy.

The launch of the Pentium III Xeon microprocessor, Intel's most sophisticated to date, marks Intel's attention to customers' needs and their PLC: the Pentium III Xeon is specifically designed to improve the performance of large Web sites and e-business applications. The benefit of such attention is clear: this is a high-margin area for Intel, as opposed to the lower margins it receives from its high-volume Celeron microprocessor line.

Product development cannot be carried out in a vacuum; the supplier must look well beyond its own R&D lab to understand the forces and dynamics in the market that will shape the nature and appropriateness of its product. Success for Intel is dependent on more than a slugging match over who has the fastest chip. First, the debate must be made a relevant one.

26

Place

Place is without question the most poorly named of the four P's found in the traditional marketing mix. In order to have something starting with the letter 'P' we end up with a term that severely misrepresents and underestimates this significant part of the marketer's concern. There is a suggestion in 'place' that we are dealing only with where the product is sold to the final customer: the buyer's office, the showroom, the retailer. On that basis, too many marketers abandon this part of the mix to the sales force, for surely *they* are responsible for managing this end of things?

'Place' is not the final destination: it's the whole journey

Place is not just about *where* the product or service is sold; its real concern is with the whole enterprise of getting it to market – order reception, logistics, the *channels of supply* – and with supporting the product or service throughout its journey – before the sale, during the sale and after the sale. Of all the elements of the marketing mix, place probably requires the involvement and coordination of the widest range of functions within a business: distribution, supply chain, sales and customer service, and these are all the proper concern of the marketer, as was discussed in Chapter 21.

Rather than 'P' for place, we might prefer 'C' for *channels of supply*, or even 'C' for *convenience*, as suggested by Philip Kotler (see Chapter 24).

Note: relationship management (including key account management and customer service) is often considered to be a part of 'place', but I consider it to be too important on a strategic level to include here as part of the tactical mix. It has received its own discussion in Chapter 19 in Part IV, 'Delivering the value'.

The channel manager

'Channel manager' is a job title much on the increase as the importance of this aspect of the marketing mix comes ever more to the fore. Why the increase in importance? Place always mattered; it is simply that as products and prices and promotions grow more uniform among competitors, so it is that companies start to see the route to market as a genuine source of competitive advantage. There are opportunities for cost reduction by reassessing the use of channel partners, and through greater efficiencies within the supply chain. There are also opportunities to add value through knowledge and expertise, all dependent on the right choice of channel partners. And a final reason for the new-found interest: it is within channel management that the impact of the e-revolution has perhaps been most dramatic, providing new capabilities in logistics, supply chain management and customer management.

Is the channel manager a marketer, or part of the operations group, or even part of the sales team? Where they sit tells us a lot about the business's priorities, its source of competitive advantage and its chosen value drivers (see Chapter 14). Within operations: this is a business driven by operational excellence. Within sales: this is a customer-focused business that sees service management as a key source of competitive advantage. Within marketing? Perhaps we will return to this question at the close of the chapter.

CHANNELS OF SUPPLY

The routes to market

Your business is faced with a variety of routes to market, or channels of supply, and an early task within the management of place is to make your choices and determine your priorities. Figure 26.1 shows just some of those options.

Should we supply direct to the end user? Should we work through wholesalers, or distributors, or agents? Only once that is clear can the channel manager get down to the task of managing the channel.

New channels to solve old problems?

There has been a lot of controversy recently in the United Kingdom over banks closing rural branches. The banks argue that new channels such as the Internet not only force them into this decision, but also provide the consumer with adequate alternatives. They are also looking at other alternatives. Lloyds TSB has an arrangement that allows Post Office branches to carry out some simple banking tasks on its behalf. The Post Office, particularly in rural sub-post offices, suffered a significant loss of business as over-the-counter payments of social security benefits came to an end, but now perhaps there is a potential win–win outcome for banks, the Post Office and consumers alike?

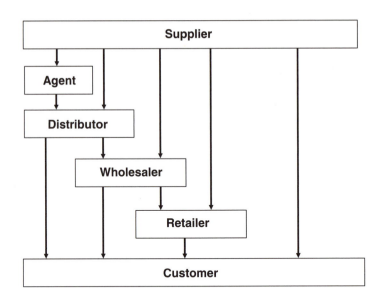

Figure 26.1 *The possible routes to market*

The channel audit

We will ask a series of questions to help us with this choice:

- What are the channels available?
- Who are the current players in those channels?
- What are the dynamics and market shares of those channels?
- What is the nature of our own activity in the channel – push or pull?
- Do we wish to alter the balance of our own activity?
- How do we regard the players in the channels – as customers or as channel partners?
- What is the value added by each player in the channel?
- What is the utility of each player in the channel?
- How manageable (by us) is each player in the channel?
- How dependent are we on the existing channel players, and should we be aiming to alter that dependency?
- Could we/should we create a new channel?

The channel map

We begin to answer these questions by returning to the idea of the market map, introduced in Chapter 9. Figure 26.2 shows such a map (the example is a provider of travel insurance), annotated with the share of business flowing through each channel.

This map lays out the various routes to market, or the channels of supply. At this point the map should aim to trace all the possible routes, current *and*

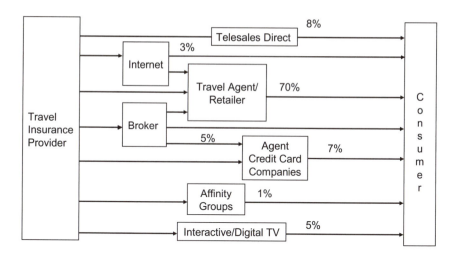

Figure 26.2 *The channel map*

potential, so that we don't get trapped in a 'well, we've always done it that way' syndrome – all too easy in this particular neck of the marketing woods. Of vital importance, then, is ensuring that the percentage shares of business by channel are for the market as a whole, not just for your own business. If we start out with the picture as we experience it today, and only that picture, then we are unlikely to be able to change it; it would be like seeing the world in only two dimensions, when we all know that there is a third. (The advice of V K Chakravati comes readily to mind (see Chapter 8).)

The map should also aim to assess the relative shares of our own and our competitors' business along these channels.

It is not always easy to get to grips with the dynamics of these channels, partly because you start out with the blinkers of your current choice and experience, and partly because they are too often the carefully protected 'territory' of the sales force. Their complexity is often embellished with anecdotal stories, usually designed to terrify the uninitiated, and the power of channel players can sometimes be magnified to a point that not even the players themselves would recognize.

Getting to grips with the dynamics is one thing; seeking to change them is quite another. You have what you inherit: agents with contracts written 30 years ago, distributors who know more about the market than you do (and want to keep it that way), wholesalers who extract margins for doing, well, not very much from what you can see, and salespeople who might have done your product justice a decade ago, but no more. Try taking that on and see the vested interests rise against you. This is precisely why it is so important to start with the data, to be able to distinguish the truth from the war stories.

The audit follows much the same path as we examined in the segmentation process, looking for 'hot spots' or points of leverage. These are the points in the market map where the real decisions that affect your success in the market are made: to buy or not to buy. Is the hot spot at the final consumer, or is it somewhere in the channel? In other words, are you engaged in *push* or *pull* marketing?

Push or pull?

Nike spends millions on persuading us to buy its shoes, and we respond in droves, going eagerly to the retailer, expecting to find them on prominent display. If we don't see them, we probably go somewhere else; we might even complain to the store. This is pull marketing. The supplier is targeting customers right at the end of the chain and pulling them into the channel of supply, the retailer. The retailer doesn't need much persuading to stock the products, nor does the wholesaler or the distributor; the shoes will sell themselves. And in a remote country or territory where Nike has no physical presence, finding an agent will be child's play; everyone will be fighting for the nomination.

The supplier of an unbranded adhesive used in the manufacture of a wide range of things from silicon chips to packaging materials sells its products through specialist distributors, each focused on a particular market. The users of those silicon chips, whether Dell or the user of Dell's PC, are not too concerned whose adhesive was used, provided it works, and the further they are from the adhesives supplier, the less they care. When this adhesives supplier calls on the specialist distributor, it has a problem: why should it be *the supplier's* adhesive? The distributor shows the supplier a competitor's product, saying that it carries a lower price, or comes in a more convenient pack size, or the competitor is doing a better job in helping the distributor sell the product to the silicon chip manufacturer. This is push marketing. The supplier has to persuade the channel to accept its product, and it has to push it down the line with incentives and rewards.

Some people play the game at both ends: a car manufacturer has large-scale advertising campaigns to pull us into the showroom, and dealerships incentivized to get us walking out with one of Ford's products. In reality, most businesses will combine both push and pull. The differences are in the balance: branded fmcg is more pull than push and a lot of B2B is predominantly push.

Can that unbranded adhesive supplier redress the balance and develop more 'pull'? The task of developing a brand and promoting it to end users is a significant one, a long haul, but this is not the only thing that determines a pull strategy. The supplier could develop relationships with the silicon chip manufacturers to find more about their needs, and use that knowledge to help the distributor make the sale, perhaps even working on the distributor's behalf. It could go further down the chain to the PC manufacturer and see if there were any positive implications from the choice of the bonding technology used for the chips, so helping the silicon chip manufacturer make its sale, so helping the distributor with its sale. And even the consumer – if the bonding technology were part of the balance between size and speed, understanding the consumer's preferences might just give the supplier something to take back through the channel. 'Pull' is not just about big-budget promotional spend; it can be about relationships, and about the kind of knowledge that comes from those relationships.

Finding the right balance between push and pull is of great importance, because it will impact on your strength in the market, it will influence the cost structure of your business, and it will determine your reward. It will also determine how you view your customers and how you manage them. Table 26.1 indicates some of the differences, admittedly in a rather black-and-white fashion, but designed to help you find your own particular shade of grey.

Table 26.1   *Push or pull strategies*

	Strength	**Cost Structure**	**Reward**	**Customers/Partner**
Pull	Suppliers own the market Able to 'select' channel partners	Investment in promotion	Higher margins Security through the brand	Channel partners
Push	Dominant channel players own the market Fight for customers	Investment in sales Discounts and rebates	Lower margins Margin is 'shared' with distributors	Customers

Rewards

I should say more about the issue of reward. Think of it from the distributor's point of view. You present the distributor with an unbranded, non-supported product, with no knowledge of the market to give direction, and ask the distributor to sell it for you. Who will need to make the investment? Who will be taking the risk? Who will expect a good reward? Distributors and wholesalers need good margins for such propositions, and the supplier will need to 'share' the total margin in the channel with the channel players.

Or perhaps you present the distributor with a gold-plated certainty – a big brand name, a promotional campaign about to break, a high level of demand, a knowledge of the market that allows you to direct the distributor's effort – and you ask it to take the orders and deliver the product. You are making the investment and taking the risk; *you* will expect the reward. Indeed, you may even be in a position to select your distributors, a position of strength indeed.

Customers or channel partners?

What all this starts to make clear is just how you should regard the players in the channel: are they customers, or are they part of your distribution network – channel partners? We are still talking in very black-and-white terms here, whereas the real world is tinted in every imaginable shade of grey, but let's continue with the two situations discussed above under 'rewards'. For the unbranded unsupported case, the distributor is a customer – to be won, to be persuaded, to be cajoled, and to be rewarded for taking on the next step in the chain. In the second case, the gold-plated one, the distributor is a means to an end, an extension of the supplier's own distribution network, an extension of the supplier's own sales team – a *channel partner*, to be managed and rewarded for its service.

Costs and capabilities

It may seem that so far I have painted a rather glowing picture of the pull strategy and a life of toil and frustration for the push strategy. Perhaps we should redress the balance a little. Sure, pull is great, if you can do it. We are back with company capabilities: do you have brands with strong customer franchises, the money for major promotional activity, the knowledge of the market to know what hot buttons to press, the capacity to handle demand, the resources to talk with the players downstream? The cost structures of a company pursuing a pull strategy can be frightening; the upfront investment is huge – and in a new market with a new product, we know the risks involved.

A pull strategy might suggest to you that you don't need distributors; if there is such a great demand then let's cut out the middleman. Capabilities again. Do you have the systems to cope with the flood of orders from big and small, do you have the physical capability – the warehouses, the fleets of vehicles – and will these costs be justified by the extra margin you get from cutting out that middleman? Specialists can often work more efficiently and effectively than generalists, and a good specialist distributor should be able to operate at lower costs than you, *and* earn a living. If you can work with your distributors as if they are true extensions of your own distribution network, if they really are channel partners, then why not enjoy the benefits of a sales and logistics operation working at a lower cost than you could achieve, and providing a more appropriate capability? The answer may well depend on how manageable these 'partners' really are, of which more later.

The push strategy requires its own set of capabilities – the ability to find good distributors, just for one. As Russia emerged from the Soviet Union and began opening its doors for business, suppliers from the rest of the world found that they had a problem. In the old days, the government handled the buying and the distributing. Once you understood the rules, life was relatively simple: one contact, one order, and you were supplying the USSR! With the fall of the Soviet Union, these buying committees started to disappear, and in their place was – nothing. Finding a good distributor was hard work, particularly as so many of the crop that did appear were financially unstable, or worse.

Direct supply, or taking the long route?

The simplest route to market is direct supply. Build a Web site, install an order reception system, get to know the mailing options, and you have an instant channel to market. Such is the dream of many, and in too many cases such is the underestimation of the task. Building beautiful Web sites is easy; it is the infrastructure behind them that determines your success or failure. easyJet and Dell are two famous examples of direct supply through the Internet, and they have both invested heavily in the systems needed to make this happen. Many have tried to establish retail operations through the Net, the 'clicks without the mortar', but it is arguable that only two have truly succeeded in building a sustainable business: Amazon and Netflix (the latter is a video and DVD sales and rental operator in the United States).

At the other extreme, we might choose to manage a series of players in a long channel to market, such as that shown in Figure 26.3.

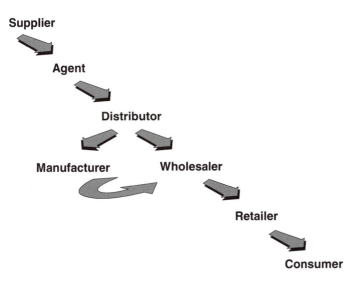

Figure 26.3 _The 'long' channel to market_

Each plays its part in adding value – or if it doesn't, such that it only adds costs, then it should be removed from the channel, if that is possible.

The agent will have specialist knowledge, an understanding of the 'rules' of the territory or market, will have local contacts, and will charge for that value added, usually through some form of commission. The distributor will handle large volumes delivered from the supplier and 'break bulk'. It may also do something to the product: repackaging, dosing with additives, or testing its application. In a B2B market the product may now pass to a manufacture as a 'raw material' or component, coming back into the wholesale–retail channel in its new form.

Wholesalers take the product to the local level, providing a sales force, credit terms, delivery, customer service, etc. The retailer handles the consumer, the enquiries, the complaints, the after-sales service.

Value in the channel

Having mapped out the existing and potential channels, taking into account the options discussed above, you must now look at their relative merits. A good start will be to assess which channels add most value – or, to look from the negative position, which channels add most costs. The precise definition of value, and to whom it is added, will of course depend on your own marketing objectives, but might include things such as speed to market, ability and willingness to invest, expertise, and capability.

For each channel under consideration, work through the route from supplier to the end consumer, noting against each point in the chain the function performed, a definition of the value added, and, if possible, a quantitative estimate of that value. Table 26.2 shows this analysis for a consumer product exported from the United Kingdom to Eastern Europe. As the product itself is not changed at each stage, it is possible to note the price at which each point in the chain sells, and the margin that each point makes. The price achieved at each point represents only a very crude assessment of the value added, assuming as it does that the customer in each case is happy to pay that price and by so doing recognizes that value has been added. Doing the same thing for a product that is modified, or changed entirely, *en route* to the final consumer is a much harder task, but one that repays the effort. Remember, the purpose of the exercise is to discover where value is being added, and by whom, in order to assess whether the rewards of channel players are justified, and to be able to answer the bold question, should we be doing this differently?

Having done this analysis, we can use it to answer some simple questions:

- Does each channel player add value to its immediate customer?
- Does each channel player add value to the final consumer?
- Do any channel players add more cost than value?
- Is the channel player's reward justified for the value added?

Table 26.2 *Value in the channel*

	Function	Value Added	Price	Margin
Supplier	The product	The great idea…	£10.00	10%
Agent	Expert knowledge	The ability to trade	(commission)	5%
Distributor	Breaks bulk	?	£12.5	20%
Wholesaler	Sales effort	Service to local independents	£14.4	13%
Retailer	Customer service	Promotion, advice and after-sales service	£21.6	33%

- Does each channel player add value to your business?
- Are there alternative channels? – e-commerce, licensing, franchise, etc?
- Are any of the channel players dispensable?
- Could you take on any of the functions?
- Do you have the appropriate capabilities?
- Could you take on any of the functions at a lower cost than the existing channel player?
- What impact can you have on the activities of the channel player?
- What impact can you have on the reward received by the channel player?

In the analysis from Table 26.2, it is not clear what value the distributor adds. How significant is the break-bulk activity? This would be deserving of further inquiry, as it may be possible to re-engineer the supply channel straight to the wholesaler, freeing up to £2.50 per item, either to pay for the costs of this direct supply, or to invest in market development, or to take as additional profit.

There are more specific questions to ask depending on the circumstances. Let's suppose that you are supporting a major promotional campaign in the market, a significant attempt at a pull strategy. Does the share of reward in the channel represent a just return for your and others' efforts? Perhaps the retailer's margin represents a reward from an earlier period where a greater 'push' was required in the market; should that margin now be reduced?

Utility and manageability in the channel

We must now assess the channel players on two broad bases: their utility and their manageability:

- Their _utility_ – do they perform a valuable role for you and the customer, and will they continue to do so in the future? (As always with marketing, the future role is more significant than the current, raising another of the problems between sales and marketing in this area: their different planning horizons.)
- Their _manageability_ – are you able to influence their activities and their rewards? Will they work to your agenda?

Note: some care should be taken with how we think about the second of these two issues: the manageability of distribution channels. There must be a very clear world of difference between influencing channels and behaving anti-competitively. The UK car market has been under close inspection because it is believed that car manufacturers 'manage' the channels unfairly, particularly with regard to the prices at which distributors can or may sell – leading to an estimated £1,100 excess charge per car sold to the consumer.

Let's work through an example of the assessment of these two factors, as they are seen in the market for decorative paint sold to professional users in the United Kingdom. There are five main options, shown in Table 26.3, along with their share of the current market, a comment on their future share, and an assessment of their utility and manageability.

Table 26.3 *Channel options and priorities in the professional decorator market*

Channel Option	% Share of Current Market	Future Trends	Utility	Manageability
Supplier-owned chain of decorator merchants (our own chain)	12%	Stable	Very high, but unlikely to see a significant increase in market presence	High – although issues abound over allowing the chain to operate as a genuine merchant, not a supplier's 'puppet'
Competitor-owned chains of decorators' merchants	40%	Stable	Almost zero!	Almost zero!
Traditional independent decorators' merchants	26%	In slow decline – under threat of faster decline if new entrants come in from the retail sector	Declining utility as customers begin to regard them increasingly as behind the times, particularly with regard to price and service	Moderate – good relationships as a result of a long trading history
Builders' merchants	11%	Fast growth	Aggressive price and service propositions are increasing their significance in the customers' eyes	Low – trying to forge a new style of operation in the market
Retail outlets	11%	Prospect of major growth should a big player make a serious entrance	Significant if they succeed in establishing a presence in this highly traditional market	Very low – new entrants likely to want to create their own position, independently of suppliers

We could now plot these different channels on a four-box matrix, Figure 26.4, based on their relative utility and manageability. The matrix can be used as a first view on which channels will offer the greatest prospects for development to our own agenda (top right), those that will require the most effort to 'manage' towards our agenda, but will probably be worth the effort (top left), and those that we may choose to manage with a lower order of priority (the bottom right) or perhaps not at all (the bottom left). (This is of course the classic Directional Policy Matrix used in yet another guise, and no harm done there for being so versatile!)

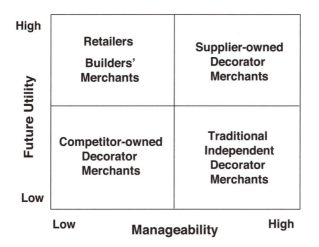

Figure 26.4 _Channel options and priorities_

The _wildcat_ or _problem child_ channels (see Chapter 22) are the newly emergent retailers and to a lesser extent the newly aggressive builders' merchants. Should the paint supplier actively pursue the retail wildcat?

Here are some typical _fors_ and _againsts_ – and you might like to consider what else you would want to know before making your decision. First the reasons _for_:

● There are some very strong and significant players here.
● Their trading practices _may_ be the way of the future.
● Should one of them make a serious entrance, it will gain share quickly.
● We need to be in partnership with them before this happens, not attempting to forge partnership after they have made their move.
● We must certainly not be seen as impeding their progress.

And against:

● Our existing customers will be very displeased.
● Our own decorator merchant chain will be impacted – we are supporting our own competitors.

- The sales force will not support the move.
- The risk of failure by the retail sector in entering this conservative market is high, with the consequent waste of our resource in supporting retailers and the unnecessary bad PR with existing customers.

Having made your decision – and let's suppose it is to chase the retailer channel actively – how would you go about it? We must turn at this point to the question of channel management.

CHANNEL MANAGEMENT

Back to a question posed earlier in this chapter: direct, or take the long route? There are very different management tasks involved in these two extremes, and every shade of grey along the spectrum of choices in between.

Here are four examples, each illustrating a novel choice when looking at routes to market, each seeking to create to some extent a new route, and each calling on a very different set of channel management tools and skills.

Seasonal opportunism

Fantastic Fireworks, based in Luton, has a turnover of around £1.5 million, with about £800,000 from managed firework displays and £500,000 from what it lightly calls 'mail order'. The remaining £200,000 comes from sales through temporary sales sites based on farms. This arrangement suites both parties fine: the farmers get a 20 per cent commission on a sale or return product at a time of year when other sources of income are slim, and Fantastic Fireworks gets a safe and instant sales network for the short pre-5 November season.

Sweating an asset

Somerfield, the supermarket group, had recently started a delivery service to some of its competitors: small independent grocery shops, particularly in rural areas. It will deliver its total range of products at wholesale prices, *including* its own-label lines. The service helps utilize an asset that was not being 'sweated' as much as the operational people would have liked, and helps extend the Somerfield brand presence into new areas.

Seeking a better reward

Farmers' markets are growing in popularity with farmers and consumers alike. Consumers get to talk directly to the supplier and can enjoy the experience of sorting their potatoes from the earth in which they were grown, or of carrying away their Brussels sprouts still attached to the stalk. Farmers get to sell at prices hitherto undreamt of, learn a lot about what consumers really want (as opposed to what wholesalers and retailers tell them they want) and by all accounts enjoy themselves into the bargain!

Video Island, a small United Kingdom-based firm, is trying to establish a rent-by-post service for DVDs. It is not a new idea, and the owners readily admit to using an existing business model pioneered by Netflix in the United States. Customers express a series of preferences for DVDs and receive three by post, returning them as they choose and receiving replacements as they do. The range available to them is staggering, more than any 'bricks and mortar' outlet could support, and it is this, alongside the armchair convenience, that holds the greatest attraction for potential customers.

The biggest challenge is in finding the customers, and finding them fast, and it is here where perhaps the most novelty (from a channel management perspective) is to be seen. Video Island is not going it alone, but is partnering with such respectable and highly trusted names as Tesco, MSN, Comet and Toys 'R' Us, providing them with what is in effect an 'own-label' DVD subscription service.

What is particularly clever about this plan is the way that it creates so many potential winners along the channel: the retail partner adds a service, Video Island gains instant access, and even the film companies and DVD suppliers are happy, as this service promises to open up the back catalogues for business (the high street rental outfits tend to stock only the latest releases and a very small backlist of evergreens).

**'Win–Win–Win'
Ensuring benefits
to every link in the
chain**

And two further channel management options, each demanding a very different management approach: licensing and franchising.

Licensing

For a fee or a royalty, you pass your technology, expertise, intellectual property or brand name to another business, allowing it to manage the channel of supply in its own territory or market. This is an attractive option for markets or territories where you have no ability to reach the customers, or perhaps where you have very little interest in reaching them but are pleased with the income. But beware: licensing has a nasty way of coming back to bite you. Today's lack of ability or interest may all change tomorrow, and then what of your 10-year contract that allows someone else to reap the reward in return for your easy life? And is licensing the easy life in any case? Licences need to be supported and managed. Your product or your name is in the licensee's hands, and so is your reputation. Take care not to regard licensing as the easy way to handle non-core markets.

Franchising

Franchising is another option for channel management: setting other people up in business with your formula but, as compared with licensing, perhaps retaining a greater control over essential elements of the mix. Many McDonald's outlets are franchised, but they are obliged to buy their materials through tightly regulated channels, and they are obliged to maintain very strict operational and management standards. The speed with which a new idea can penetrate the market is phenomenal with the use of franchising, and if cash flow would otherwise be likely to impede your progress then this can be a very attractive option.

Channel management rules?

With such a range of options, it is clearly not going to be possible to identify one set of rules for managing channels, and rather than giving a vague and generic list of guidelines, I have chosen to illustrate in more detail one specific channel management task, as an example: managing distributors.

Managing distributors

Imagine you left the management of place entirely in the hands of your own sales force, to do as they wished. Can you imagine anything worse? I certainly can. Imagine leaving the management of place in the hands of *someone else's* sale force.

When you make significant use of distributors, you are handing chunks of responsibility over to a third party, and you should want to know what is going on, and to be in control. If you are operating principally in push mode, with the distributor seen as a valued customer, then 'managing' that distributor takes on a different connotation, though one of no less importance, from that of managing a *channel partner* in a pull scenario. The tone of voice will need to be more subtle, your expectations will be modified, the balance of power in any negotiation will be rather different, but the motivation remains the same: to learn as much about your customers as possible and to retain control over the sale of your product or service. Remembering these points of difference, let's look at some of the ways of managing distributors.

Selection

The best way is to start by selecting your distributors carefully – easier said than done if you have inherited your predecessor's selection, or you are in a market with precious little choice. Whether you have a real choice or not, there will be value in trying to identify a list of qualities that would define the perfect distributor. These can be used in any selection process, but they can also be used in assessing existing distributor performance, forming the basis for improvement plans – the core of any management process.

The list might include any of the following:

- the distributor's market knowledge and experience;
- its market coverage;
- its track record and reputation;
- its commitment to, and enthusiasm for, your product;
- low (or no) competitor involvement;
- the size, quality and reputation of the distributor's sales force;

- the frequency of sales calls;
- the distributor's product knowledge, application knowledge, etc;
- the quality of its customer service;
- its costs of operation;
- its willingness to discuss costs of operation;
- inventory control – whether it will hold stock; whether it will manage that stock effectively;
- its manageability – whether it will work to your agenda;
- whether it will share information on its customers;
- whether it is open to suggestions for improvement;
- whether you can you develop shared business plans;
- the quality of relationships;
- the distributor's expectations for reward.

The real world operates over and above all these points, and the balance of power between the two parties is a constant theme, whether witnessed in regular negotiations or experienced through working relationships. Nowhere will it be more felt than in the area of monitoring and improving performance.

Performance improvement plans

Unless you have the world's perfect distributor there will always be areas for improvement, and unless you are the perfect supplier the same will apply to your own operations. An indication of a good relationship will be your ability to discuss things openly and constructively, and the existence of a performance improvement process. The way in which you go about this process will have much to do with the success of the relationship; as with sales teams, the marketer tends to get the distributors it deserves.

The ideal scenario is a two-way process set as a regular feature of the relationship, not an occasional response to emergency and crisis (rarely the best environment for collaboration and improvement!). Both sides should list their aspirations against a number of issues and then compare notes. Where are the likely points of conflict, what actions are required to reduce or avoid that conflict? There are probably two parts to the table: issues between your two businesses, and issues in the marketplace. You may end up with a table that looks something like that in Table 26.4 (an example only, not an attempt at a full list).

If we look at just one of these issues, we can see the kinds of differences that may appear between 'managing' a distributor in a strongly _push_ or a strongly _pull_ scenario.

Range and stockholding

In a _push_ scenario the supplier's aspirations are usually for greater stock commitments from the distributor – looking for breadth and depth, while the distributor's aspirations may be just the reverse! The actions to resolve these

Table 26.4 *Performance improvement planning*

Our Relationship	Supplier's Aspirations	Distributor's Aspiration	Potential Conflict?	Actions to Reduce/Avoid Conflict
Range and stock holding				
Prices and discounting				
Margins and shared costs				
Terms and conditions				
Training programmes				
Complaint procedures				

Market issues	Supplier's Aspirations	Distributor's Aspiration	Potential Conflict?	Actions to Reduce/Avoid Conflict
Customer selection				
Sales effort and targets				
Prices and discounting				
Promotion				
Customer service package				
Supplier's support package				
Complaint procedures				

differences may lie in the area of incentives or 'deals', or perhaps some form of vendor-owned and -managed stock. Consignment stock (where stock is held on the distributor's premises but remains the property of the supplier until it is drawn to be sold) is one of the means of persuading reluctant distributors to take on new ranges, but there are significant drawbacks.

First, it is almost always enormously costly to the supplier – ask any accountant. Second, it is notoriously hard to manage and control; staunch opponents of consignment stock will sometimes refer to it as 'lost' stock! The third drawback is the impact that such arrangements can have on the distributor's 'energies' behind your products. The supplier wants its products pushed, but filling the distributor's warehouse with supplier-owned stock is not perhaps the best way to give the distributor an incentive to work hard.

In a *pull* scenario the supplier will be much more able to influence the distributor's range and stockholding through market information and sales forecasts. Details of a specific promotional campaign for instance can be used to 'instruct' the distributor to build stock. The *pull* scenario might look much the more attractive for managing the distributor, but don't forget that the supplier must be involved in a whole range of activities and investments to initiate this pull – activities and investments that the *push* strategy supplier is not required to undertake.

Training

A key ingredient of any supplier's support package will be the provision of training. At the very least, this will be product training for distributor staff, but there is scope to go much further. Distributors will often look to their best suppliers for help in providing training for their own staff; what better way to cement relationships between the two teams than joint training?

Sales training provided to both supplier and distributor sales teams, together, in the same room, can be used to explore relevant issues within the market, and can be as useful as a joint planning session as it is valuable as training. Some care is required, however, to ensure that the supplier is not seen to take too dominant a role, with accusations for instance of 'brainwashing'. The use of an independent trainer rather than the supplier delivering the training itself will often help to avoid these problems.

One of the best examples that I have seen of using training to cement relationships and develop channel partner capabilities involves PPG, a supplier of refinish paint to the car repair market. Many of its customers are independent spray shops – small businesses with huge training needs, but precious few resources to hand. PPG delivers a programme of training on a range of 'running a small business' issues, and customers pay to participate in the programme (at a subsidized rate, but one high enough for them to appreciate the 'value'), including how to raise their own prices in the marketplace – an issue of some interest to the supplying company!

Training customers to increase their prices!

Joint business planning

If a distributor is a true channel partner then this will be evidenced by the desire on both sides to develop a joint business plan. Many suppliers see distributor business plans simply as a range of sales targets to be imposed and then achieved, and are surprised when distributors fail to get excited by such treatment! A genuine channel partnership plan may look something like the following (loosely based on a real example from the UK agrochemicals market):

- a joint statement of intent (what do both parties seek from the relationship; what are their expectations?);
- the values and aspirations of the supplier and the distributor;
- a SWOT analysis of the target market, with strengths and weaknesses of both parties identified;
- an identification of customers and target customers – also key accounts where appropriate;
- a statement on the needs and aspirations of the target customers;
- the value chain analysis (see Chapters 17 and 18);
- the sales proposition;
- the support package: supplier responsibilities, distributor responsibilities – budgets – the customer service package – training programmes;
- specific sales targets;
- the *service level agreement* (SLA);
- action lists (who, what, when?);
- key performance indicators and review criteria.

Such plans not only take time to develop, but require high levels of trust and collaboration. Don't expect them to come easily, and certainly not of their own accord. The marketer's role in making such plans happen will bring them into very close collaboration with their sales colleagues, a collaboration that can only be of benefit to all concerned.

LOGISTICS AND SUPPLY CHAIN MANAGEMENT

Being able to deliver, on time and in full, is just one of the things a business has to be able to do these days merely to be on the page. But it isn't so very long ago that measures such as OTIF (on time in full) were used to express the competitive advantage of one supplier over another. This is the story of logistics in the marketing mix: a continuous effort to improve, a few blissful months every now and then of genuine competitive advantage, and then everyone else catches up and it's back to being just one of life's givens. Of course, get logistics wrong and everyone knows about it.

Logistics has long been one of the less glamorous areas of marketing, but one where the greatest damage can be done very quickly through disregard, carelessness or lack of discipline. The logistics experts are the unsung heroes of the supplier's offer, yet there is increasing evidence that in most markets, from fmcg through business to business and service, being 'easy to do business' with is seen to be of vital importance – often even the number one issue on the customer's list of vendor ratings. How many times would you go back to a mail order firm that sent you the wrong things? How long would you stay with a bank or credit card company that put other people's charges on your monthly statement?

As markets mature, as they become more and more competitive, and as the need for competitive advantage increases (just when it is becoming hardest to achieve), so issues of supplier reliability are raised to new levels of importance. In such markets it is becoming the supplier's ability to forecast accurately and to 'deliver' with speed that is increasingly dividing the winners from the losers. If in the past we saw so often the battle of the brands, with market share the key indicator of who was winning, then perhaps the future will become the battle of the supply chains, with a whole new range of victor's metrics.

In some markets it is not so much the battle between products or brands, but the battle between supply chains

Efficient consumer response

An example of such a metric is *effective consumer response* (ECR). This is the idea that in, let's say, a retail environment, each time a consumer purchases a product, an automatic reordering process is set in motion. Wal-Mart not only has raised ECR to the level of a science, but has established it as a key to its success. The point-of-sale scanner starts the process, and a complex series of algorithms convert this 'fact' into a specific order, running right back up the supply chain to the original manufacturer of the item. The algorithms must take note of such things as seasonality, promotional schedules, manufacturing and delivery lead times, shelf life and perishability, and more.

Supply chain management

The rise of *supply chain management* as an activity within most large businesses is witness to this, and an excellent example of how internal operations are being focused on to the customer and the marketplace. Figure 26.5 illustrates how this external focus is taken back into the operational functions of the business and beyond, to purchasing, and beyond that, into the supplier's suppliers.

The dialogue between marketers and operations can only be a productive one in this respect. The objectives of the manufacturing plant or the purchasing department can be defined by reference to measures of customer satisfaction as well as internal measures of operational efficiency. The plant can still aim to maximize its occupacity (a measure of its efficient use of its total capacity) – not because greater occupacity is simply a 'good thing', but because of the understanding of the benefits that can accrue to customers through reduced costs, and the potential for competitive advantage. Such an approach will help to remove those conflicts of interest between operations

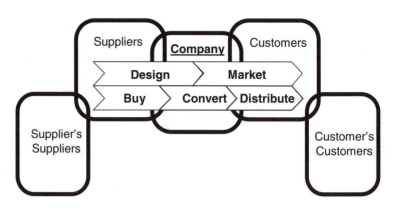

Figure 26.5   *The supply chain*

and marketing, as both focus on the same ends. Terms such as 'appropriate occupacity' will help determine the path that operations must take between the huge efficiencies of uniformity (an old-fashioned plant manager's Holy Grail) and the market's needs for variation and flexibility (an old-fashioned marketer's Holy Grail).

By understanding the supply chain, marketers can set themselves two targets: to improve the efficiency of the chain in order to drive out costs, and to improve the effectiveness of the chain in supplying the customer. Within logistics and the supply chain lie both routes to competitive advantage: lower costs and greater differentiation.

Mapping the supply chain

Any business that is seeking to reduce costs through supply chain efficiency, or improve service to customers through supply chain effectiveness, will benefit from regular reviews of that supply chain. A hugely valuable exercise is to map out the chain from start to finish, and a very low-tech but highly effective way to do it is to plaster a blank wall with Post-it notes. For every step that is carried out, write a separate note – and find yourself a *large* wall, because things can get surprisingly complicated. Start with the customer's order, in all its varieties – whether received through the sales rep, or a telephone call, the faxed order, the electronic order, the standing order – and follow it back into the organization and out again to the final delivery to the customer, and then beyond to the invoice and final receipt of payment.

Aim to follow the chain back into production and then beyond that into your own purchasing activity. Involve the experts in this exercise: customer service, internal sales, distribution, supply chain, master schedulers, purchasing, salespeople, credit controllers – each will add their own Post-its to the chain.

By keeping it visual in this way, you will begin to appreciate the complexity of what might have seemed to you just a straightforward order

Arm yourself with Post-it notes, and a very large wall...

and dispatch system, and the need for close inter-functional relations to ensure its smooth operation. You might also be pleasantly surprised by the evidence of the capability within your organization to achieve what now looks like something of a minor miracle every time you deliver an order!

Once you have plastered the wall with yellow squares, place large black crosses on those points that cause problems: the credit check that takes three days, the bottleneck in the packaging department, the high level of errors in the invoicing office. Place large red crosses on those points in the chain that are absolutely vital handover points from one function to another: sales pass the order to the factory, the warehouse hands responsibility to the transport company, etc.

Stand back and note where you need to look for improvements (black crosses) and where you need to ensure the absolute reliability of the process (red crosses). Think of it as a relay race, each runner passing a baton to the next, and look out for the places where the baton might just get dropped.

This may all sound rather archaic in an age of high tech and software packages, but there is still no better way to *really* understand the dynamics of the supply chain. Of course, it is not just the problem spots that you are seeking out. Chase down those unnecessary links and those backwaters of inactivity and delay, and hound them into extinction. The aim should be to seek means to shorten the chain, speed the process, debug the system, and allow the customer as close access as possible to your own systems.

How would it be if you allowed the customer to place its order direct on your factory: chaos, or a route to competitive advantage? The marketer's interest in the supply chain should be around making this possible: providing customers with such close access to your supply chain that they are effectively locked into the relationship simply because it is so easy for them to do business with you.

MARKETING AND SALES

Throughout this chapter, references and allusions have been made repeatedly to the thorny issue of sales and marketing collaboration. It should be clear by now how important an issue this is, and what the kinds of obstacles are that stand in its way. Conflicts between sales and marketing, as with conflicts between nations, flare up precisely because they are such close neighbours. Sometimes the sales force are made to feel the poor cousin to marketing, sometimes they feel that they are there to pick up the pieces of marketing's mistakes, and sometimes (and it has to be admitted) they are just dyed-in-the-wool cynics. The truth of the matter is that marketing gets the sales force it deserves. How the product is sold into the market is marketing's responsibility, and if they choose to shirk it then they must learn to put up with the result.

Key account management, discussed separately in Chapter 19, has done much to bring sales and marketing together. In a sense, a key account is like a market segment, often in a very real sense. The management of that segment has perhaps fallen more to sales than marketing, but sales have been called on to take a broader view than their traditional sales approach has required (farming rather than hunting), and certainly a longer-term view (a key account is defined as an investment, and key account management is defined as managing those investments). In short, they have been called on to behave and think like marketers.

Which brings us to the unanswered question from earlier in the chapter – who should be responsible for channel management, sales or marketing? That it is a joint responsibility is clear, and if that sounds too much like sitting on the fence, then let me jump down very clearly on the side of marketing: channels to market (place) are but one part of the mix, and it is the marketing manager who controls and manages that total mix. Allow sales to hive off this part of the marketing edifice, and the whole architecture will start to wobble.

27

Promotion

Club biscuits once 'owned' the UK market for the break-time chocolate biscuit until it chose one year to pull back on advertising and regard the money saved as extra profit. Club was, after all, the brand leader; what harm could one year do? It was its bad luck (or marketing myopia?) that this decision corresponded with a massive campaign behind the Penguin biscuit with Derek Nimmo's famous stuttering tag line. Penguin never looked back, and Club never regained its position.

'P-p-p-pick up a Penguin

Promoting a major brand has to be a long-term activity; consistency of spend is vital – hard as this might be for financial directors to understand. But this isn't the only story for promotion, and it is a subject that extends well beyond the realm of seven-figure TV advertising campaigns.

The key for any promotional strategy is its objective: know what you intend to achieve, and you will avoid most of the pitfalls of wasted activities and the kind of overspent budgets that make new government offices look like well-forecast bargains.

THE PURPOSE OF PROMOTION

You might engage in a promotional activity in order to:

- grow the total size of the market;
- grow your own sales volume;

- increase market share;
- support a sales drive;
- improve distribution;
- attack a competitor's offer;
- develop awareness of your product, or brand, or company;
- influence the customers' needs and desires;
- effect the customers' perceptions of your proposition;
- overcome prejudices;
- gain trial for your product or service;
- increase frequency of usage;
- reinforce existing behaviour;
- establish a unique link between your proposition and the customers' needs;
- establish or build credibility;
- dispel rumours of your imminent decline;
- demonstrate social or political awareness;
- affect customers' disposition to buy your product;
- inform customers of a change to your proposition;
- inform customers of a change in the market environment.

This is a far from exhaustive list, but it illustrates how easy it would be for a promotional campaign to become a cacophony of competing voices. You might want several of these things, but take care not to be too greedy: a promotional activity that tries too much will end up achieving very little. Each one of the ambitions listed above is unique, and will very likely require a unique promotional treatment.

THE CAMPAIGN AND THE COMMUNICATION

The promotional campaign is bigger than the individual communications within that campaign, and will have broader objectives than any individual communication or activity within that campaign. The campaign might include a variety of media, each used for its character and merit in effecting a particular response – TV for awareness and developing desire, the press for disseminating information, a sales offer for stimulating purchase, etc. Each individual communication will need to have a very specific and focused objective.

The promotional objectives

Be pedantic about your promotional objectives: write them down for the whole campaign, and for each specific communication and activity, using the following construction:

- This promotional activity… *(define the medium and method)*
- will, or is intended to… *(state the intended 'effect', the planned response from the customer or the market, to include a verb – gain, build, achieve, win, convert, dispel, etc)*
- with the target audience… *(specified)*
- to the following timings… *(specified)*
- with the following results… *(specified – impact on sales, share, profits, etc.).*

An example for a new brand of lager might read as follows:

This £3 million TV campaign of 30-second commercials placed at prime time will gain trial for Hogshead lager among men aged 18 to 25 living in the Granada TV area between 1 May and 30 June resulting in a 160 per cent increase in sales (to £1,200,000) over the period and a prompted brand recognition rate of 90 per cent among the target audience. It will also support the trade-based promotional campaign intended to gain initial distribution.

The importance of this apparent pedantry cannot be overemphasized, for the following reasons:

- When you are briefing external agencies, it must be crystal-clear what you are asking them to do for you.
- When asking your own business for the necessary budget, you must be able to quantify the target return on investment.
- The effectiveness of promotion must be measured, just as with any other activity, which requires a clarity on what it was you set out to achieve.
- The realm of promotion, more than any other part of the marketing mix, can suffer from what we might call the *feel-good* syndrome; liking the execution can often blind the marketer to whether it achieves their original intention. Being able to refer back to objectives is vital in such an environment.
- Lazy objectives lead to lazy activities, with confused messages and confused customers…

Clarity of purpose

Let's suppose that you want to increase awareness for British beef; the past 10 years of scandal and tragedy will have worked a treat for such an objective! Perrier never received as much attention as when it was discovered to contain benzene. Building awareness is not enough; it must be awareness to a purpose.

The first golden rule of promotion

The most important thing to remember about any form of communication, whether it be a one-to-one conversation or a £5 million TV campaign, is that the message received is more important than the message sent. Customers have existing perceptions of you and your products, and those perceptions will affect what they see and hear. Placing adverts on French TV that extol the delights of British beef, no matter how expensive or well produced those ads, would almost certainly backfire while there is still any climate of suspicion or mistrust around the product. Worse than failing to achieve their intended response, they would risk setting off a greater wave of cynicism and disbelief.

When a company is aware of a poor image for its product, it will need to do more than just tell people how great it is. Humour is a favourite tack, and there have been many adverts that appear to knock the advertiser as a means of changing people's perceptions. The Skoda advert featured in the case study on page 169 is a good example.

The single-minded proposition

The human brain is a remarkable thing, but when faced with a barrage of promotional messages it reaches overload surprisingly quickly. Any single customer communication should not attempt to say too much. How long do you expect to keep the customer's attention – perhaps only a few seconds, perhaps 30 in the case of the average TV advert, maybe more for a piece of magazine 'advertorial', and substantially less for an Internet Web site passing under the surfer's temporary gaze. With this in mind, saying one thing but saying it clearly and memorably, and saying it so as to elicit the intended response, is a very good idea indeed. Perhaps there is much that can be said about your offer, but if you try to say it all, you will almost certainly lose the customer's attention – and perhaps worse, you risk losing your own credibility.

Over the course of a promotional campaign it may be possible to build up a series of single-minded propositions, but each specific activity within the campaign should aim to tackle just one at a time.

Saving the earth efficiently

Kyocera, the office equipment manufacturer, recently ran a series of press adverts for its Ecosys printer range with a strong central theme and a series of individual messages, one per advert. The campaign was designed to establish a clear link between Kyocera's unique capabilities (based on its technology) and a single-minded identification of the customers' needs: business efficiency and environmental concern. Each advert identified a different aspect of the technology, but a consistent tag line was used throughout: 'because business demands efficiency and the earth needs attention'.

How many things might there be to communicate about a grocery retailer such as Asda? Plenty, so why for so many years have its adverts concentrated on the one single image: a hand patting a back pocket, indicating the money saved by shopping at Asda? Because it works.

THE EFFECTIVE COMMUNICATION

The proposition is only the start. An effective communication must achieve the following:

- It must reach the target audience.
- It must penetrate the audience's attention through a combination of timeliness, relevance and simplicity.
- It must communicate the _intended_ message.
- It must _bond_ the message to the brand name.

Many high-cost adverts fail this test, sometimes on all four points; the production costs of an advert do not guarantee its effectiveness.

Reaching? The brilliant Web site with every latest interactive technique is entirely wasted if nobody can find it.

Penetrating? The TV remote control has threatened to consign TV ads to the 'mute dustbin', and so advertisers have had to raise the production quality of their work to ensure that it stands out from the programming surrounding it! The commercial breaks during the US Superbowl are the most expensive spots of the year, attract the most ambitious (and expensive) advertisements, and also attract a huge audience tuned in to see the ads just as much as the game...

Intended? I once saw an advert for cigars that showed a dinner jacket-clad man sitting opposite an admiring companion, the source of her admiration clearly being the cigar on which he puffed. The tag line insinuated that as well as the more obvious things, your choice of cigar was one of the ways that you demonstrated your concern for your loved ones. Unfortunately, this particular advert had the government health warning pointing out that passive smoking can cause cancer – so much for love and attention.

Bonding? One of the perils of _not_ being the brand leader is that your advertising often gets mistaken for that of the number one in the market. For many years when I was working on the Dulux paint brand, I would receive congratulations (or sometimes criticism) from friends and relatives on our latest advert, only to discover that they had just seen one of Crown's, the long-time number two player.

The second golden rule of promotion

Telling people stuff is not enough; you have to elicit a response. You will want to know what they think about what you have told them, so feedback is important, and you will want them to do something positive about what they have heard. Good promotional activities engage the customer in a 'conversation' – the communication 'C' of Kotler's four C's (see Chapter 24).

THE CHOICE OF MEDIA: PROS AND CONS

Each medium has its own strengths and disadvantages, depending of course on your intended outcome. The following lists compare the pros and cons of the main media choices, taking into consideration such issues as cost, the precision of targeting, the nature of the impact, and the all-important generation of a positive response.

Television

The strengths of television are the following:

- You control the message.
- Close targeting is possible through slot bookings.
- The promotion will have huge impact with good recall.
- It builds high awareness quickly.
- It has a good impact on perceptions and latent needs.
- There is a strong branding opportunity.
- It builds credibility.
- It provides the opportunity to build over time, whether by reinforcement through repeats or by the development of a theme.
- It enables regional targeting and flexibility.

The disadvantages are as follows:

- The cost is high – not only of that of buying space, but also that of production.
- There can be occasional problems with placement associations.
- Television is increasingly impersonal, given the development of other, more direct media.
- It is still a largely national medium. Few TV adverts travel well – witness the popularity of TV programmes that find 'Johnny foreigner's' ads so hysterical!

The ability to book specific slot times for TV adverts provides a high degree of targeting and minimizes the old problem of unplanned and embarrassing placement associations. There are still occasional problems, as with the advert for slimming products that ran adjacent to a breaking news story on a dreadful famine in East Africa.

The cost of TV still makes it the medium for big players, and production costs are such that small campaigns are rarely cost-efficient. Cutting production costs leaves you with an ad that, unless it captures some kind of cult following, will be first victim to the remote control zapper.

TV ads have to be better made than the programmes they sit next to; they have to be funnier, stranger, more arresting, or just find some means to engage our attention. The 'what on earth is this an advert for' technique is one angle; the running story is another – witness the Gold Blend saga of next-door neighbours, or the 'Nicole? Papa?' soap.

Radio

The strengths of radio are the following:

- It offers the opportunity for local tailoring.
- It provides the ability to 'talk' to people in their home.
- The low cost allows for high frequency.
- It is an 'immediate' medium, good for prompting action, and is therefore a favoured medium for retailers.

Its disadvantages are as follows:

- Sometimes the audience size will be quite low.
- Lack of visuals is a problem for many propositions, though a creative agency should be able to 'paint pictures' with words and sounds.
- There are problems with national campaigns.

National press

The strengths of advertising in the national press are as follows:

- It gives the ability to react quickly to events and developments in the market.
- Messages can build over a run of days – 'tease' campaigns of the 'what's coming tomorrow?' variety abound.
- The medium is good for making offers, particularly time-related ones.
- Promotional offers can be made for the advertiser by the newspaper itself – holidays, flights, train tickets, etc.

The disadvantages are the following:

- The cost is high.
- There can be problems of placement associations.

easyJet makes very effective use of 'buy now' ads for its low-cost European air fares. The placement in a daily paper gives the ad an immediacy and sense of urgency, and, at least in easyJet's early days, the 'association' with the big-name papers was important in helping to build credibility for a new business taking on the big boys.

Special-interest press

The strengths of the special-interest press as an advertising medium are the following:

- The advertising is highly targeted.
- It is possible to enter into more complex messages – particularly with inserts, rather than ads in the magazine itself.
- You are among 'friends' and can be more informal with your approach.

There are some disadvantages too:

- Everyone else is there; overload can be a problem.
- Production costs are high relative to the audience reached when compared to the costs for more mass media.

Being smart, with an audience that knows you...

Kodak once ran a one-page ad in a leading photography magazine that consisted simply of a plain yellow page with the text 'our real advert is on pages 5, 12, 28 and 37'. On each of these pages would be a beautiful photograph as part of an article, with a reference to the film used – Kodak, of course. This was a clever way to maximize impact on a slim budget with almost no production costs – usually a high part of the spend for a company such as Kodak.

The use of the 'advertorial' is common in many magazines – adverts dressed up to look like articles, or articles that are thinly disguised adverts. The credibility of the magazine can suffer if it makes too much use of this technique, and so opportunities are not always easy to come by.

Trade press

The strengths of the trade press as a medium for advertising are the following:

- It provides good targeting.
- It is possible to build a market presence through regular use.
- The medium is good for reinforcing the single-minded proposition: 'leave it to Lonza', etc.

- It is also good for more complex messages: readers will accept more text in the trade press than in other magazines.
- It is good for new entrants.

The disadvantages are as follows:

- Impact is low.
- The effect is of a slow burn; it takes time to generate awareness.
- There is a danger of overload: your immediate competitors will probably use the same media.
- Advertising claims can sometimes cause problems for salespeople confronted by 'local' issues for which the advertising is not wholly relevant.
- Small target audiences = small production budgets = dull, 'home-made cut and paste' ads.

Posters

The strengths of advertising by means of posters are the following:

- It is good for visual messages.
- It is good for tease campaigns (remember Sid?), 'surprises' or shock tactics: Benetton, FCUK, etc.
- It offers local targeting – even down to specific streets.
- A continuous presence is possible.

The disadvantages are as follows:

- Production costs are high in relation to the audience reached.
- Great care is needed to manage placement.
- Bonding the brand to the message is not always easy.
- There are problems with defacement!

A DIY brand with a small budget for a new product launch was able to use posters very effectively. The product was a fairly complex wood treatment product – not an impulse buy, and one where reputation and dependability would be important. Posters were placed on the main routes to major DIY stores such that consumers would see them just before arriving at the store. In-store, consumers were faced with a bewildering choice of options, but the last thing sown in their mind _outside_ the store was an image of this manufacturer's product, and the association helped build a sense of credibility and trust.

The problem with bonding the message to the brand finds posters, ironi-cally, a popular medium for non-supplier-specific campaigns. Trade and manufacturer associations will often use posters to promote the market rather than any particular supplier. British beef, pure wool, milk – these have all had the poster treatment. The UK bed manufacturers often use posters to tell us to replace our beds more frequently, for health reasons of course, using posters almost as a public service medium.

The Internet

The strengths of advertising via the Internet are the following:

- There is huge potential for an interactive exchange: promotion becomes communication, and becomes a trading exchange.
- It is possible to build huge demand – but be careful that you can respond.
- It is perhaps essential for a modern image.
- It is great for updating messages or materials.
- It enables small players to look as good as the big guys, and thereby provides opportunities for the Davids to take on the Goliaths.
- It offers the opportunity to provide large amounts of information to those who want to search.
- Customers' 'use' can be monitored.
- Getting established is easy, but it is also easy to be incredibly dull!

But there are disadvantages:

- It isn't 'free': people still have to know where to find you, which involves expenditure on more traditional media. Posters in particular have enjoyed a boom from the dotcom brigade.
- Many sites are clearly amateur, uninspiring and ultimately frustrating.
- Internet advertising requires a substantial back-up of people and logistics to deal with the responses; yes, Victoria Secret's Web site in the United States *did* get 250,000 hits *an hour* just before Christmas 1999 (Victoria Secret is a lingerie retailer), but when it crashed for three days owing to the overload, lost sales were estimated in the millions of dollars.

Here's a 'great' idea for a domain name for a United States-based home cleaning service: www.SpruceSpringclean.com (maids in America…?) – but without a great deal of traditional promotion, who's going to hear of it? One of the ironies of the boom in the electronic medium for promotion is that traditional advertising media have enjoyed a parallel boom. When the search provider AskJeeves.com was launched, it was promoted by a campaign using TV press and posters that was no less costly than a traditional pre-Internet era campaign. You still need money to get yourself heard.

A Web site can of course be much more than a promotional vehicle, but when it is used on that level, the following tips may be helpful:

- The Web site design must hook people within four seconds or most visitors will leave. Get an expert to help with the design; this is not a job for the youngest member of the marketing team just because they happen to be 'Internet literate'.

- For those customers searching for something specific, the 'two clicks and you're there' rule is a good one.
- Content and design must be changed regularly if you want people to keep returning; old Web sites can get 'tired' very quickly.
- The use of banners on other people's sites can be very wearing if transfer is not fast and if it doesn't take you to precisely where you want to get.
- Aim to generate a response – and then handle that response immediately.
- Use the medium to develop an understanding of what people are looking for.
- Monitor usage and conversion rates.

Frighteningly, only about 40 per cent of enquiries through company Web sites are answered at present. Remember that this is communication: that's like putting the phone down on a customer halfway through the conversation, 6 times out of 10!

Direct mail

The strengths of a direct mail campaign are as follows:

- If you have good databases, the advertising is highly targetable, even personalized.
- The message is very controllable and there is the ability to go well beyond the single-minded proposition.
- It provides an opportunity to establish dialogue with customers.
- It is relatively easy to measure effectiveness.
- The cost of start-up is relatively low.

The disadvantages are the following:

- There is an identification with junk mail.
- Hit rates are low – usually well below 1.5%.
- The effectiveness is dependent on the quality of your mailing lists.

Most people hate junk mail, so we are pleasantly surprised if something of genuine interest lands on our doormat. The secret to direct mail is being relevant, and for that to happen, the quality of the database is everything.

Telemarketing

The strengths of telemarketing are as follows:

- The cost of start-up is relatively low.
- It gives the opportunity to engage in a conversation with the customer.

- It gives the opportunity to do research on real customer needs and perceptions.
- It is easy to start up without competitors knowing, and easy to close down without the market knowing you have 'withdrawn'.

The disadvantages are the following:

- The telephone is probably regarded as the most intrusive of all media.
- There is a danger of creating strong antipathy (and a place on the next TV exposé of 'cowboy' sales techniques).
- The hit rate is low.

Some of the potential benefits of telemarketing – the extended conversation and the opportunity for research – are only achievable if the staff engaged on the job are sufficiently briefed and trained, and, most importantly, allowed the time to engage in such pursuits. The strictly time-bound and results-based regimes of many telemarketing operations may work actively against this aim. If this is a purpose of your exercise then careful selection and briefing of the agency or staff providing the service will be required.

Exhibitions

The strengths of promotion through exhibitions are as follows:

- Exhibitions provide direct contact with customers and potential customers.
- Exhibiting is good for trade relations.
- Exhibitions are a good platform for new-product launches.
- They provide a shop window.
- Exhibiting establishes presence and credibility.
- It gives opportunities for customer entertaining.
- It generates sales leads.

The disadvantages are the following:

- The cost is high (if you try to keep costs down too much, you run the risk of looking tacky).
- Exhibiting makes high demands on staff time.
- Your competitors will usually be present (and might outshine you or out-entertain you).
- Once you have started, it is difficult to pull out without incurring negative comment: 'I see so-and-so can't afford to be here this year…'

Sponsorship and celebrity endorsement

The strengths of sponsorship and celebrity endorsement are as follows:

- It gives you a high profile.
- It offers an opportunity to link strong values and perceptions to your own proposition, so enhancing your own product's perception.
- With the right vehicle, it provides an opportunity to substantiate your proposition.
- There are entertainment opportunities.
- Success builds success.
- It offers the opportunity for a unique position or statement.

The disadvantages are the following:

- Failure breeds contempt!
- The wrong associations can be embarrassing, and not all eventualities can be planned for (eg Pepsi and Michael Jackson).
- There are complex targeting issues.
- It can build opponents as well as supporters – particularly where sports teams are sponsored: it might be supposed that not many Manchester City supporters own Sharp appliances and few will now sign up for Vodafone contracts (see below).
- It needs a long-term commitment; withdrawal can be difficult, with negative PR.

Aprilia, the Italian motor scooter manufacturer, was outraged when, having secured the Spice Girls to endorse its product, Gerri Halliwell promptly left the group, leaving Aprilia with a highly embarrassing set of non-usable images and materials.

And then there were four...

In February 2000, Manchester United signed a £30 million, four-year sponsorship deal with Vodafone. This came after 18 years with Sharp, and there was a good deal of talk from observers about how Vodafone will aim to extract a whole lot more value in its 4 years than Sharp did in its 18. Vodafone will certainly plan to 'leverage' the deal well beyond the use of hospitality boxes. The deal illustrates how sponsorship can be used beyond simple promotion, taking it into the realm of the other P's in the marketing mix. Manchester United is the product and Vodafone the distributor, quite literally. The Manchester United Web site gets 75 million hits a month, and access will soon be available through mobile phones.

Making sponsorship relevant

Product placement

Product placement includes such things as DIY products used on TV home improvement programmes, or retailers providing items for fashion magazines. Its strengths are as follows:

● Costs are low.
● It enables you to build credibility over time.
● It offers a high profile.
● It can turn on sales very fast.

Its disadvantages are the following:

● There is low control of the message – with occasional surprises if your product is slated!
● There is a proneness to short-term bursts of enthusiasm.

Delia, the supermarkets' darling

UK supermarkets now try to find out in advance what products Delia Smith will be using in her TV cookery programmes, as she only has to mention a new type of cream or some little-known vegetable for the shelves to be emptied of these things the following day. Delia once famously exhausted the UK supply of sun-dried tomatoes as that humble vegetable was rocketed to superstar status through her programme.

'Product placement' is an art. Philips once scored a coup by having a number of its highest-tech products 'placed' in the latest Bond movie. Endorsements by fictional (or long-dead) characters sometimes seem to be more powerful (and more believable?) than those by the real and the living.

Product placement comes in various forms, including having your product associated with another that is in turn promoting itself. Soap powders might feature particular washing machine manufacturers in their advertising, Little Chef might place Bird's custard on its menu, the Dulux dog might be used by Heineken to demonstrate how its beer really does reach the parts other beers cannot reach (the dog was shown doing the painting for its owner while the owner relaxed with beer in hand).

Nor is this just for consumer brands. Rockwell Automation has promoted its name to investors and customers alike as a supplier to Nestlé, associating itself with Nestlé's success in the ice-cream market. 'Rockwell Automation is helping Nestlé scoop the market in ice cream with perfect flavour and consistency' runs the ad, placed in the share price section of the *Financial Times*.

PR

The strengths of PR are the following:

● It is a subtle approach – not being seen to promote.
● It is good for managing the big issues and the top-level messages.

Its disadvantages are as follows:

- It needs very professional management; amateur attempts can lead to big problems.
- It is hard to measure its impact or effectiveness; it is often a matter of 'faith' (it's much easier to measure its failings!).

Sales promotion

The strengths of sales promotions are the following:

- They can be highly targeted.
- Their impact is measurable.
- Increased sales during the activity can reduce the sort of cash flow problems associated with most other promotional activities.
- Sales promotions build distributor commitment.

The disadvantages are as follows:

- There are forecasting problems, as in Hoover's famous debacle with the airline tickets (see Chapter 7).
- The effect is a short-term one: when the promotion stops, so can the sales.
- The promotion can become established as the norm.
- Promotions can devalue the brand, particularly if price is always the vehicle.

When Brake Bros, a leading food supplier to the catering industry, introduced a 'buy one, get one free' offer, this was a relatively unusual form of promotion in the catering trade. It was pleasantly surprised by winning 2,000 new accounts. It didn't allow the success to go to its marketers' heads, however: 'Our challenge now is to make those regular customers', was its wise reaction.

BOGOF (not to be confused with 'sell one, deliver one free')

The role of the sales force in promotion

In many B2B environments the face-to-face contact provided by the sales force can be the single most important part of the promotional effort, allowing genuine dialogue and feedback. Unfortunately, the costs are high, and as sales forces reduce in size, the time given to genuine promotion, rather than straight selling, can shrink to disappearing point. The trend towards smaller sales teams has seriously reduced the ability of many B2B suppliers to promote themselves in the market. Is this a case of misplaced cost-cutting zeal?

The instant sales force – just add Innovex

Nowhere has the impact of a sales force been more important in recent years than in the pharmaceutical market, evidenced by the great care taken with selection and training, but nowhere does the cost of such sales teams hit harder on the bottom line.

The launch of a new drug is a phenomenally expensive exercise: perhaps $1 billion goes on promotion costs in the first two years, and a significant slug of that is taken by the cost of the sales force. The drug companies have looked for ways to reduce this cost, and a popular option has been the idea of the contract sales force. Companies such as Innovex will provide a bespoke sales team to the drug company, making it possible to create the ideal team for the promotional period, and then will disband the team at the end of the campaign.

SELECTING AND BRIEFING AN AGENCY

The huge number of agencies available to help with every conceivable form of promotion can be rather overwhelming, particularly when faced with the need to select just one. And there are sharks out there... Too many large agencies behave as if they are from a superior species, while too many one-man bands feel that their own business experiences are sufficient to warrant charging you for their help – yet it is precisely with some of these smaller agencies that the real gold dust can be found. So, how to make the right choice – is it reputation, size, personal chemistry, experience?

Selecting the right agency starts well before reaching for the telephone directory. It starts with an absolute clarity about your own promotional objectives. You will need to brief the agency, so start by preparing that brief. Once the brief is completed, the sort of agency best placed to help will already be that much clearer.

The briefing

The agency will need to know all of the following (and if it says it doesn't, then perhaps it is not the agency for you):

- the key characteristics of your company, brand and product;
- the market performance;
- the market dynamics;
- the main competitors;
- the main trends in the market;
- market segmentation;
- any previous promotional activity and its impact;
- any restrictions on your ability to promote – financial, legal, moral, etc;
- the target market, segment, customers;
- the purpose of the promotional activity – the desired outcome, the target audience, the timings, the specific results required;
- your single-minded proposition – unless you are engaging their help to determine one for you;

- supporting evidence for this proposition;
- the desired brand positioning;
- the preferred media;
- timings and budgets.

Agencies that show too much concern with the last of these points before understanding your purpose and objectives may be helping you with your selection process.

Once the brief is complete, select the agencies you wish to have a response from. Don't go for too many. First, the briefing process is time-consuming. Second, receiving the agency proposals will be even more time-consuming. Third, it is unfair on an agency to ask it to put in a significant amount of work if it is one of a large number under consideration. In the past, it was the norm for agencies to charge 'concept fees', but this practice has all but disappeared as competition has become fiercer. As a result, some agencies are beginning to feel taken advantage of by clients who brief, listen and then steal their product: their ideas. Don't even think of doing this!

Getting to the shortlist of agencies to brief will be a combination of references from colleagues, perhaps ruling out those used by the competition, and an assessment of their track record of success in similar areas. This last is not a question of 'advertising awards' and the like; rather, it is an assessment of how successful the clients of the agency have been.

Some 'rules' on briefing the agency

1. Take the time to give a full briefing.
2. Give the agency a written copy of the brief.
3. Be very clear on objectives, timings and budgets.
4. Agencies should welcome your creative thoughts, but try to leave the final creative process to the experts.
5. Ask for the agency's questions.
6. Encourage a critical assessment from the agency.
7. Give the agency as much information as possible on your selection process: timing, criteria, competitors, etc. Help it to do a good job; you are not setting it an obstacle course to test its initiative.
8. Give the agency a date by when you want its response, and specify in what format.
9. Be very clear on how you wish the agency to respond: is it just ideas, or do you want a full campaign proposal?

Some 'rules' on receiving the agency's proposals

1. Allow the agency the time it requires.
2. Start by restating the objectives of the activity – or, better still, ask the agency to do so.
3. Use those objectives as your test. Try not to be swayed by the flood of

exciting creative ideas; the important question is, will the ideas achieve your objective?

4. Demand full costings of design, production and placement.
5. Consider asking the agency to accept payment by performance.

This last point refers to a relatively recent development in the world of advertising and promotion: payment by performance. The confident agency should be pleased to work on such a basis, but less than confident suppliers should not use this as an excuse to enter into promotional activities that they think are not going to work! The vitally important issue with such arrangements – and the agency will not be backward in letting you know this – is to have clarity on precisely what the objectives of the promotional activity are, and for them to be quantifiable. Given that this payment method encourages such precision, it has much to recommend it.

When you finally award the work, do so in writing, and repeat the crucial elements of objectives, mechanics, timings and costs.

Some marketing people would encourage the involvement of professional purchasing people in the agreement of contracts, etc. This is fine, provided that your own purchasing people understand the objectives (and especially if you are considering payment by performance), and that you don't allow them to 'steal' the relationship.

Budgets

How much to spend? This is often the toughest question of them all, especially for those is a B2B environment, where there is no doubt what the three sins of promotion are: budget, budget and budget.

On the one hand, we recall Henry Ford's comment on advertising expenditure: 'Half of the money is wasted; unfortunately, you can never be certain which half.' On the other hand, we too often see marketing plans with expansive vision strangled at birth by parsimonious promotional budgets.

There are various ways to arrive at the right sum: a percentage of sales revenue; a percentage of profit; some benchmark based on a competitor's spend; last year's spend plus or minus a percentage dreamed up by the finance department. All are used frequently, but none of them is remotely satisfactory.

Perhaps the percentage of sales or profit approach is OK if you have long experience of the relationship between spend and performance, but times change. Not only that, such measures have a way of self-perpetuating themselves with a deadly circular logic.

There is only one basis on which to determine the budget. Promotion is one of the four P's in the marketing mix. The marketing mix is how you plan to achieve your marketing objectives, and, for you to be certain of success, the elements must be in balance. The promotional spend must be adequate for the job in hand. Expect the costs to be higher for the introduction of something new than they are for a boost to an old favourite, but also recognize that each circumstance is unique; the application of simplistic formulas is unlikely to work.

If after presenting your marketing plan you find that the promotional budget is cut, then you must seriously consider changing the other elements of the mix, or the objectives of the plan.

None of this says that you shouldn't seek creative ways to stretch a budget; we saw in the section on the special-interest press how Kodak made clever use of a tight budget. Nor does it suggest that we shouldn't continually review the impact of our expenditure, with a view to changing it as required.

Tracking

It is important to track the effectiveness of what, for many businesses, will be one of their highest single expenditures. This is not just about looking at the impact on sales; there are often too many competing variables for us to be confident of pinning growth on a promotional campaign. For a £5 million TV campaign it will be worth spending the additional £80,000 to measure the campaign's impact on customer perceptions and attitudes. A typical tracking study would look at levels of awareness (often called the _cut-through_ of the medium): what perceptions are formed of the brand or product, what promises are seen to be made, what level of belief or confidence exists that they will be upheld, and what disposition does the audience have to make a purchase? Only with such information (and the sales statistics!) can you go to your finance director and properly justify your expenditure, as you increasingly, and quite rightly, must.

28

Price

Price is probably the issue that most frightens marketers, and with good reason: get it wrong and you're stuck with it. How can you put a price up if you start too low and find that you're giving it away? Aim too high and you're dead before you start. And what if the price is right, but your costs are wrong? This chapter aims, not to make pricing easy – that would be an error – but to help you avoid the bear traps. It will lay out the options for pricing and show how you can steer a course between the market's demands, your own needs and your competitors' behaviour. But first, why is it so important?

WHY PRICE MATTERS

Because it is the best way to increase profits?

You are the marketing manager of a large manufacturing company and you have just received next year's profit target from the board: a 15 per cent improvement on this year, without any damage to the long-term business. Unfortunately, you have no new products in the pipeline and so your choices are slim: sell more of your existing products, reduce costs or raise prices. Which should it be?

Of course, the three choices are not independent of each other. Sell more – sure, perhaps by dropping the price, but what will that do to profits? Reduce costs – but might that damage quality and so adversely affect the price you can get, or the volume you can sell? Raise prices – but what will happen to volume?

Let's start by understanding the relative effects of changes to prices, volumes or costs – and maybe there will be some surprises in store. For the sake of this exercise we will assume that each choice can be made independently of the others, just to compare them. Figure 28.1 shows the three options, starting from your current position of selling 200,000 units at 1 euro each. Last year's profit was 50,000 euros, so you need to improve that to 57,500 euros.

	Current Business	Option 1 More Volume	Option 2 Raise Price	Option 3 Reduce Cost
Units sold	200,000	230,000	200,000	200,000
Cost per unit	€ 0.75	€ 0.75	€ 0.75	€ 0.7125
Price per unit	€ 1.00	€1.00	€ 1.0375	$1.00
Turnover	€ 200,000	€ 230,000	€ 207,500	€ 200,000
Profit per unit	€ 0.25	€ 0.25	€ 0.2875	€ 0.2875
Gross profit	€ 50,000	€ 57,500	€ 57,500	€ 57,500
% Change		+15%	+3.75%	-5%

Figure 28.1 *Volume, price or costs – the best route to profitability?*

Option 1 is a volume increase, option 2 is the price rise and option 3 is the reduction in costs, each assuming all other things remain the same.

An equation or two...

There is a simple equation that will help you make this same comparison in other cases. If you ask the question 'What price increase will bring the same profit improvement (all else being equal) as a given volume increase', the answer is given by:

$$\frac{\% \text{ gross margin} \times \text{the } \% \text{ volume increase}}{100} = \text{the } \% \text{ price increase required}$$

(Gross margin in this case means the sales price minus raw material costs.)

Ask the question the other way, 'What volume increase will bring the same profit improvement (all else being equal) as a given price increase?', and the equation is:

$$\frac{\% \text{ price increase } 100}{\% \text{ gross margin}} = \text{the } \% \text{ volume increase required}$$

Some comments on the choice

1. *The surprise*. The price rise required is only 3.75%, compared to a 15% increase in volume or a 5% reduction in costs.
2. *The problem with all this*. In the real world we cannot assume that all other things will stay the same.
3. *The danger*. Of all the choices, reducing costs always seems the easiest, but what might it mean in the long term?

Cost reduction may be the easiest option, but what is the *best* option? I am going to suggest the price rise, not only because it is relatively small compared to the volume increase, but because it is the option too often ignored, and it is the option that calls most on the marketer's skills. Raising prices means raising the perceived value, and this is an issue that the marketer should be working with every day.

Because cutting price doesn't always drive enough extra volume...

Let's now link price and volume together in a different scenario: cutting price to drive extra volume. Suppose you choose to drop your price by 5 per cent. What extra volume do you need to sell in order to make the same level of profit? The answer depends on what level of profit margin you were working on before the price cut.

Figure 28.2 shows the volume increase required (in the centre boxes) for any given price cut, across a range of percentage gross margins (assuming there to be no economies of scale from the higher volumes gained).

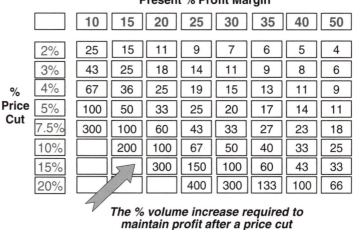

Present % Profit Margin

% Price Cut	10	15	20	25	30	35	40	50
2%	25	15	11	9	7	6	5	4
3%	43	25	18	14	11	9	8	6
4%	67	36	25	19	15	13	11	9
5%	100	50	33	25	20	17	14	11
7.5%	300	100	60	43	33	27	23	18
10%		200	100	67	50	40	33	25
15%			300	150	100	60	43	33
20%				400	300	133	100	66

The % volume increase required to maintain profit after a price cut

Figure 28.2 *The volume increase required in order to match a given price cut*

There is also an equation that will help you calculate the increase in volume required for a given price cut (assuming no economies of scale result):

$$\frac{\% \text{ price cut} \times 100}{\% \text{ gross margin} - \% \text{ price cut}} = \text{the } \% \text{ volume increase required}$$

Perhaps the significant thing here is the surprisingly large volume growth required for relatively small price cuts, and at low profit margins the growth required is huge. The question raised must be: can you achieve such growth? If the answer is no, then don't chase prices down in pursuit of a volume-driven profit. We have a saying in my business: 'The pursuit of volume is vanity, the pursuit of profit is sanity' (and we also add the third part, 'and getting the cash is reality!'). If the answer to the question is 'yes' and, in addition, that greater volume will bring economies of scale and so lower costs, then a price for volume strategy may just work – provided that the competition doesn't follow suit, which of course it almost invariably does!

'Volume is vanity, profit is sanity'

Figure 28.2 raises two other important points: the significance of high margins, and the importance of _knowing_ those margins. Low-margin businesses are very vulnerable to falling prices unless significant economies of scale are gained from resultant higher volumes, if indeed they do result. Price wars can be fatal for such businesses; indeed, price will sometimes be used as a weapon for putting a low-margin competitor out of business. Most markets see price wars at some time, but they hurt the most in low-margin environments such as the petrol pump, or on the shelves of the CTN (confectionery, tobacco and news) retailer. So why do they get started there? Often because the forecasts of volume growth are inflated, or, quite simply, the sums are not properly understood.

Discounting is a dangerous game at the best of times, but a business that does this and yet doesn't know its own margins is flying blind. Most businesses will know their overall gross margin – the annual accounts will tell them that – but what about measuring margins by product, or segment, or customer? If you don't know your margins to this level, and you are involved in discounting or rebates, then this should become a priority action for you to find out.

Knowing your gross margins is one thing, but what about knowing the additional effect of your fixed costs on the profit of particular products? Without such knowledge some very strange decisions may be taken in pursuit of profit...

The business that went bust in pursuit of profit

Unfortunately, most businesses _marmalade_ their fixed costs across products. Table 28.1 shows a typical allocation of costs to a four-product business, with the apparent outcome for net profit by product.

The results suggest that product D is a loss-maker, and so in the pursuit of overall profit the product is deleted. Unfortunately, overheads do not reduce immediately by the 60 that had been allocated to product D, but they do go

Table 28.1   *'Marmalading' of fixed costs*

	Product A	Product B	Product C	Product D	Total
Gross Profit	100	80	60	50	290
Overheads	60	60	60	60	240
Net Profit	40	20	0	–10	50

down by 30, and people give themselves a slap on the back for a smart decision, the results of which are shown in Table 28.2.

Table 28.2   *'Marmalading' of fixed costs*

	Product A	Product B	Product C	Product D	Total
Gross Profit	100	80	60	xxxx	240
Overheads	70	70	70	xxxx	210
Net Profit	30	10	–10	xxxx	30

The company is still in profit, but now product C is apparently a loss-maker. The same lack of knowledge of the true allocation of fixed costs is apparent, and so unfortunately the same error is repeated and product C is deleted, though of course the fixed costs do not reduce in line…

Table 28.3   *'Marmalading' of fixed costs*

	Product A	Product B	Product C	Product D	Total
Gross Profit	100	80	xxxx	xxxx	180
Overheads	90	90	xxxx	xxxx	180
Net Profit	10	–10	xxxx	xxxx	0

I think you can guess what happens next.

Because price is your reward for all your marketing skill

There are four P's, but three of them lead to the fourth. What you do with your product, how you promote it, and how you manage the place – these all result in the price you get to charge. It would be a sin to be thoughtful and professional and clever only three times out of four.

SETTING THE PRICE: FOUR GENERIC METHODS

We will consider four options:

● cost-plus pricing;
● marginal pricing;
● market-based pricing;
● value-based pricing.

Cost-plus pricing

Provided that you know the costs that are involved in providing your product or service, the cost-plus method method of pricing is fairly straight-forward. Take those costs and add the margin you require – instant pricing. The method has three things to recommend it:

● It forces you to examine your costs.
● It is relatively easy (even accountants can do it).
● It ensures that you make the intended profit – _provided you can sell at this price._

After that, the negatives tend to outweigh the positives.

First, who is to say that you can achieve the margin you aim for? If the customer will not pay, do you sacrifice your margin by reducing price, or by improving the offer and so increasing your costs? If so, why use this method in the first place?

Second, who is to say that you couldn't achieve a higher price and margin? The cost-plus method tends to make the supplier lazy; satisfied with meeting their target, they celebrate, and look no further.

Third, cost-plus encourages the supplier to focus on its own costs (the benefit noted above), but sometimes to the exclusion of looking at the market. For a business determined to drive costs down and use price to penetrate the market (see 'Competitive pricing strategies, page 350) this may be less of a problem, but for any business seeking to differentiate its offer this could be a very serious failing.

Fourth, what happens when the customers discover your method? **Buyers in control** Professional buyers are trained to ask for _cost breakdowns_; they want to know your costs, and so your margin. Armed with that, they are in control. They can use the discount table (Figure 28.2) to tell you what price cut you can give them in return for the volume increase they will give to you.

Then it gets worse: they tell you that one of your costs, let's say technical service, is of no relevance to them, so please remove it from the price calculation and reduce the price accordingly. Quite simply, the customer is in control of the price debate and slowly but surely determines *your* pricing strategy.

Customers may even seek to argue that your percentage margin is much greater than theirs, and ask, is that fair? This last point is almost always bogus – comparing apples with pears, as businesses at different points of the market chain will work on very different percentage profit margins, because of their different circumstances and dynamics. A supermarket may make only a few percentage points on a product that the manufacturer makes 30 per cent on, and a raw material supplier might make 50 per cent on its part of the product, but the dynamics of these three businesses are such that all remain happy with their lot. In the end, it should be remembered that you don't bank percentages; you bank money.

Cost breakdowns: the nightmare scenario

A supplier of a prestige range of cosmetics and toiletries to a retail chain is having a hard time with the customer on its price. 'You never do anything for us,' the buyer asserts, 'and you charge a fortune.' Up against the wall, the supplier may be tempted to argue back, 'That's not fair. Don't forget our sales and merchandising force. They call on all your stores, take orders, build displays, offer advice and training, handle problems. Perhaps you don't realize that just that sales force alone costs us over £100,000 a year.'

The customer says nothing until three months later when they sit down to negotiate the next year's terms. 'We understand that your sales team costs you £100,000. Starting next month we no longer need it to call – we will do our own ordering. Instead, we would like the £100,000 as a discount or rebate.'

The nightmare gets worse. The supplier removes its sales force (it has no choice, as it is banned from the store) and increases the customer's 'advertising support'. Three months later it finds that its sales have slumped. Its products are in less attractive parts of the store, there are gaps on the shelves, and complaints and problems are not being resolved, except expensively. The supplier goes back to the customer and asks to be allowed to put its sales force back in. 'Sure,' says the customer, 'but you can't have your advertising support money back…'

The customer 'unbundled' the supplier's package – and worse, it knew the costs involved in that unbundling. In truth, it valued the sales force highly, but in pursuit of a significant financial gain for a short-term loss in service and sales it was prepared to 'forget' that value, at least in conversation with the supplier.

Marginal pricing

For some businesses, marginal pricing is just an occasional tactic rather than a long-term pricing methodology, but for others it is part of their everyday life. Let's return to the business described in Figure 28.1. It buys items for 0.75 euro and sells them for 1.00 euro. It has a gross profit of 0.25 euro per unit, or 25 per cent, the gross profit being what is left after subtracting the *variable costs*. We didn't discuss the other costs of this business, the *fixed costs* that carry on regardless of whether it sells its units or not. Let's say that this business has fixed costs of 30,000 euros, or a further 0.15 euro per unit. This means that its net profit is 0.10 euro per unit, or 10 per cent.

Now let's suppose that it has difficulty with a particular customer in getting its full price of 1.00 euro. The customer offers to pay 0.90 euro, and the supplier accepts, happy with the deal. How can the supplier be happy when we have just seen that after variable and fixed costs are taken into account, it only makes 0.10 euro profit per item at the full price? This deal sees it making no profit at all!

The answer is: marginal pricing. The 0.15 euro per unit fixed costs will exist whether it sells anything or nothing. In fact, if it doesn't sell 200,000 units then the fixed costs per unit will go up, as 30,000 euros has to be divided across the fewer items sold. By accepting a price of 0.90 euro, the supplier is making no profit, but it is *contributing* money towards its costs.

Making a contribution...

There are occasions when such a policy would be very wise indeed. If the supplier were to be left with surplus capacity, it might as well use it and get some revenue in as a contribution towards fixed costs. Airlines and hotels practise this form of pricing with standby tickets or late-arrival offers at reception. If the seat would otherwise be empty, then why not fill it with someone whose ticket price will at least contribute towards some of the airline's fixed costs? Better still, if the bedroom would otherwise be empty, why not fill it with someone who may spend money in the bar or the restaurant? This goes beyond marginal pricing, but shows one of its possible benefits.

Equally, there are circumstances when such a policy can run out of control. Salespeople armed with the contribution theory of marginal pricing can justify discounts that leave you selling everything on this basis! Hotels cope with this problem by having an allocated number of rooms available at marginal prices, to be sold only at the end of the day. Sometimes, however, they will calculate in advance how many such rooms to sell and promote them as special offers. This can work provided that their forecasting systems are good and they do not find themselves discounting rooms that could otherwise have been sold at full price. Airlines do something similar when they sell tickets in bulk at much-reduced prices to travel agents. The critical issue is calculating correctly how many seats will be sold at full price and so how many can be discounted without loss.

Perhaps the worst scenario for marginal pricing is when it is managed so loosely that customers realize that they need never pay the full price again, whatever the circumstances of the purchase. The key to marginal pricing is control, and this is a real issue for the marketer. Don't allow marginal pricing to become a sales tactic used by salespeople to boost volume; it should be a marketing tool used by marketers to manage assets and costs.

... with marketing in control

Market-based pricing

Market-based pricing in its purest form is selling at whatever price the market will accept. Economists will talk of supply and demand and the magic point at which they are in equity so that the perfect price emerges. Rarely are real markets as predictable as the graphs used to depict supply and demand, but the principle is a good place to start the discussion of market-based pricing.

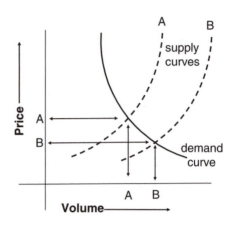

Figure 28.3 *Supply and demand curves*

Figure 28.3 shows a typical supply and demand situation, with supply curve A and the resultant price A. If supply is increased with no increase in demand, as shown by the intersection of supply curve B with the demand curve, the price goes down to B. The amount the price goes down depends on what the economists call the elasticity of demand. If the demand curve is very steep, this means that price changes very little as demand changes; if it is shallow, prices shift a lot as demand goes up or down. What makes a demand curve steep or shallow? Some products are very price sensitive: 10 per cent off house prices might drive demand sky-high (a situation represented by a shallow curve). Others are less so: 10 per cent off bread will not see us rushing to the stores (a situation represented by a steep curve).

Supply and demand curves are only a start; they represent 'perfect' situations with no external complications. In the real world, things are more complex; neither suppliers nor customers can be relied on to behave as the textbooks say they should!

Limiting supply

If there is a market for 100 units of a product, and only one supplier, and that supplier has a capacity to make 80 units, the outcome will be in effect an auction to the highest bidder, and price will move upwards. This is what happens when supply lags behind demand. In such a situation, another company will doubtless see that there is profit to be had and will enter the fray with a capacity of, say, 40 units. All at once, supply is greater than demand, and prices will fall as the two competitors start to slug it out for the customers' business. The first supplier may try to hold out for a higher price on at least 60 units (the volume demanded that cannot be supplied by the competitor) and may even choose to sell only 60, but if it seeks to sell its full capacity then prices will have to come down.

In the sole supplier scenario, there are of course factors that will limit the supplier's ability to charge whatever price it wants to. First of all it will test the 'elasticity' of the demand for its product – just how far it can stretch the price before the demand disappears, either in pursuit of a lower-priced alternative solution or just to do nothing at all.

Some years back on the BBC programme *Troubleshooters*, Sir John Harvey-Jones was famously agitated by Morgan cars' insistence on making only six cars per week, leading to a waiting list as long as six years. Just as famously, he was asked (politely) to leave, on the grounds that such demand versus supply did wonders for prices. Morgan has chosen to increase production in recent times, though, rather ironically, the increase is now against a picture of declining demand. The market has changed, perceptions have altered, and the old Morgan is not the catch it used to be. The economies of supply and demand have shifted, and Morgan must grow its appeal with the launch of a new model, the Aero 8. Only time will tell the outcome.

The rationale of rationing

Taking advantage?

If price is linked too closely to supply and demand, there is a danger that customers will become cynical with regard to your intentions. For years, OPEC has been criticized for maintaining artificially high prices for oil simply by not producing enough of the stuff.

Coca-Cola once trialled a new vending machine in Japan; the machine was sensitive to the outside temperature, and, as the mercury climbed, so did the price of the drink inside the machine! The company had no plan to put the machines on to the market, it said, wary of the reaction to such an economically pure pricing strategy. Market pricing is always working at this edge, and 'getting what you can get' can sometimes tip over into 'taking advantage'.

Taking advantage?

The perils of the protective price umbrella

Stretching the market price to its highest level, especially when done by a dominant supplier, will sometimes provide a protective price *umbrella* beneath which smaller suppliers can enter the market. This was the scenario experienced by IBM in the 1970s and 80s, when its high market price (IBM was of course at one time pretty much the only supplier of any standing) allowed new entrants to gain a toehold by pricing well below that level, perhaps for a product and service that at first might have been inferior, but would soon improve as the toehold became a foothold...

A similar situation occurred in the retail grocery market, where branded goods maintained price levels that allowed the retailers to introduce own-brand alternatives, often at tantalizingly bargain price levels. Short-term profitability for the branded suppliers has come home to haunt them, certainly in the United Kingdom, where own-brand products account for nearly 40 per cent of grocery sales, by value.

Losing the price negotiation

In a B2B environment, where market prices are the norm, buyers always have an advantage. Sellers see one buyer; the buyer sees perhaps a dozen suppliers. Buyers know more, and they can predict better, and in market price markets, prediction is an important capability.

Figure 28.4 shows the peril awaiting the 'innocent' supplier.

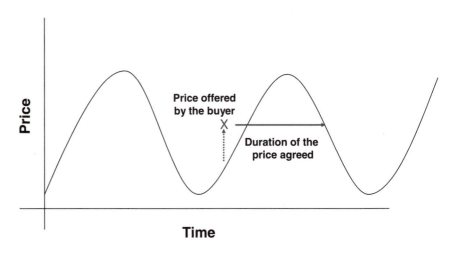

Figure 28.4 *The market price 'game'*

The buyer, knowing full well that prices are about to rise, offers a price well above the current market price. The supplier thinks it is Christmas, and even more so when the customer suggests a one-year fixed-price contract. And then the market price goes up, and up, and before long it is well above the price negotiated by the canny buyer. The buyer sits back and enjoys a handsome discount for the duration...

Value pricing

One way to avoid the accusation of 'taking advantage' is to base your price not simply on what you *can* get, but on what you *should* get. Many marketers regard this as the Holy Grail of pricing: *value pricing*.

Costs in use

Value-pricers must first escape the chains that bind them: an undue focus on the price itself. A price is simply a marker, a point at which you are happy to trade. This is something quite different from costs, and something quite different from value.

Customers incur costs in purchasing and using your product or service. Suppose it is a can of paint. They have to pay for petrol to come and buy it in the DIY store. They have to buy a paintbrush in order to be able to use it. They have to return to the store (more petrol costs) to buy the white spirit to remove the paint that dripped on to the carpet while they were painting. They never quite manage to use all the paint in the can, so they bear the cost of what has been wasted. Finally, being responsible citizens, they spend more money on petrol taking the can to a proper place of disposal. And we haven't yet tried to calculate the cost of the person's time... We will call these costs the customer's *costs in use*. Sometimes they might be so high as to make the original purchase price seem quite insignificant, and here lies the first clue for the budding value-pricer. A customer who cares about those costs in use will gladly pay a higher price for a product that will reduce them, provided that the savings outweigh the premium.

Consider your pricing strategy in the following scenario. You sell heavy-duty electric pumps used by a variety of manufacturing companies in a variety of plants. Your price is $40,000 and has been for some time. One of your customers has just informed you that there is a new kid on the block with a similar pump selling at $36,000. What do you do?

The tale of the pump...

First you ask some questions:

- Is it the same specification as yours? More or less, it seems.
- Is the supplier reputable? Very.
- Does it have similar terms and conditions? Almost exactly.
- Does its pump use the same amount of electricity? I'm afraid it does – no cost in use savings there.

So where does that leave you: cutting your price, or losing the sale?

A little more homework might find you a solution. As a good market-focused supplier, you have of course good relationships with your customers, and a few more questions furnish you with some interesting data. Over a five-year period, the average life of the pump, the costs in use look something like those shown in Table 28.4.

Table 28.4 *Costs in use: the pump*

Item	Total Cost over 5 Years
Purchase price	$40,000
Spares	$5,000
Installation costs	$40,000
Energy consumption	$230,000
Maintenance	$35,000
Disposal	$4,000
Total costs in use	**$354,000**

Armed with this knowledge, what would you do?

Provided you had the capability, wouldn't redesigning your pump to save energy used be of potentially greater value to the customer than a simple price reduction? Sure, it might cost you to do this, and might mean a more expensive pump, but wouldn't a pump selling at $44,000 that reduced energy costs by 10 per cent be a good trade? We recall again that price is simply one of the four P's in the marketing mix, and by varying the mix it is possible to change the price.

Value pricing and the tools of marketing

Here we are getting to the root of value pricing: understanding what the customer expects and wants from the product. This involves us in all the tools of marketing so far discussed, and it is with value pricing that we find the greatest interplay of those tools. The following examples of value pricing examine just some of those many intertwinings.

Value pricing and promotion

Of course, customers don't always realize that they want something – remember the tale of Alexander Graham Bell and his telephone (see Chapter 3) – and so the marketer has a triple task: calculate the value delivered, educate the customers to recognize their need, and influence them to use a means of measuring value that favours your product.

Hoover and the 'dirt per minute'

Let's start with an example from nearly a hundred years ago (there really is very little new in this world): Hoover and its vacuum cleaner, the one that 'BEATS as it Sweeps as it Cleans'. Hoover introduced the notion of the dpm. (dirt per minute) measure, promoting it as 'the accurate measure of electric cleaner efficiency'. The advice to consumers was that they should ask their dealer to explain the dpm and have him demonstrate the Hoover against this measure. And you can be sure that Hoover's training of dealership staff was second to none.

Value pricing and segmentation

Figure 28.5 shows a more recent example of this 'quantified measure of value' approach to value pricing.

Kyocera and the cost per page

On the basis of price alone, the Panasonic will win every time, but Kyocera aims to play a different game. It is not the price of the printer that matters, says Kyocera, but the total costs in use of cartridges, toner, etc. If that is taken into account then the Kyocera wins through. Further than that, if Kyocera can persuade customers to use the cost per page printed as their measure of value then the price of its printer is of much less importance, and charging a premium over the competition is made all the easier. So far this is the same approach as Hoover's from all those years ago, but now there is something to be added: segmentation.

Kyocera's value proposition will not appeal to all; it is of most appeal of course to the heavy user – the insurance company sales office, the hotel chain –

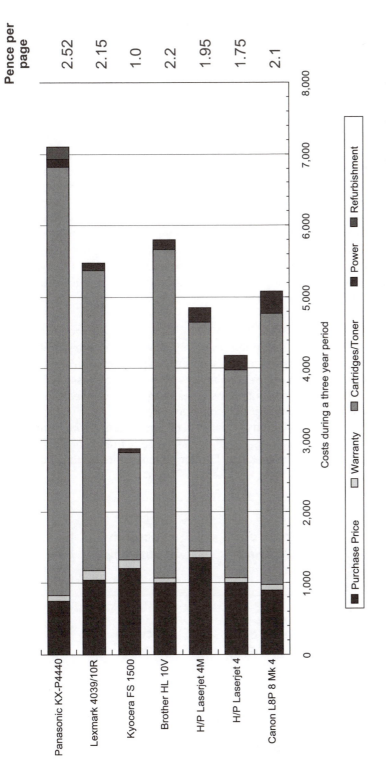

Figure 28.5 *The true cost of printing. Comparisons are based on a three-year period, assuming street purchase prices and an average throughput per day for 8ppm–425, 10ppm–500 in order to reflect the weight of usage expected within different working environments* Source: Cost of ownership of page printers, *Context* (July 1994)

not domestic users who don't know what quantity of toner they use, and don't use the printer enough to care about the cost per page printed. Indeed, we can begin to see here another possible method of segmentation: segmenting the market based on the value you bring to each segment – seeking those segments where you can be seen to present the greatest *intensity of value*.

Value pricing and customer relationship management

The Kyocera strategy and that discussed for the pump manufacturer are based on a complete grasp of the Marketing Model: understanding the customer's needs and matching them with a unique proposition. It also calls on an additional capability: that of being able to communicate the proposition to the right person. Perhaps the buyer of the pump is not responsible for the electricity bill; perhaps the toner for the printer is bought by somebody other than the buyer of the printer. The supplier has to make contact with those people and argue its case. Here we enter the realm of customer relationship management, as discussed in Chapter 19, and again we see how the tools and concepts of marketing must come together if we are in pursuit of true value pricing.

Value pricing and B2B 'supplier positioning'

A B2B customer views its suppliers in different ways. Just as a supplier will distinguish some of its clients as key accounts, so the client will look for key suppliers. The matrix in Figure 28.6 shows how some professional buyers might go about this, positioning their suppliers against two axes: the relative spend with each, and the relative significance of each.

Significance will involve many and varied factors, ranging from technology, geography, the ease of changing supplier, to the use of brands or the financial security of the supplier. For instance; Du Pont increases its significance to the

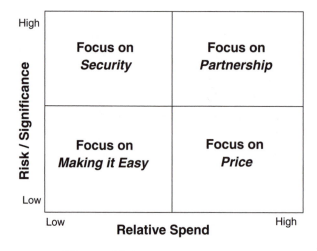

Figure 28.6 *Supplier positioning*

customer through the use of brand names that appear on the customer's product – Teflon and Lycra being two high-profile examples.

So what is the impact on price of such positioning exercises? If a supplier is positioned in the bottom right box then the focus is very much on the price itself; discounts for volume will head the agenda and the ability of a supplier to practise value pricing is greatly restricted. In the other three boxes, the attitude to price may be somewhat different.

In the bottom left box, the ability of a supplier to take on the burden of procurement for the customer – policing itself, managing inventory, managing forecasts, etc – might rank higher in importance than the lowest price. Providing such services will allow a value pricing strategy. It is not uncommon to find a sole-supplier arrangement in such circumstances, perhaps for an item such as stationery, where the task is not worth the professional buyer's time, and a premium is paid to be relieved of the bother. Others within the customer's organization may not understand, pointing out (as they do!) that they can buy pencils more cheaply in their local supermarket – but this misunderstands the purchaser's concern, purpose and definition of value.

In the top right box, such a supplier is of great significance to the customer's future, both financially and operationally; larger concerns than discounting will colour this relationship. Money matters, but it may be discussed more in terms of helping to reduce the customer's costs in use rather than simply reducing price – at least, the wise value-pricing supplier will ensure that is so.

For a supplier positioned in the top left box, let's consider a real case, that of a supplier to Unilever's butter business, the supplier of the butter flavour. The amount of money spent on the flavour, as a percentage of the total Unilever spend, is minuscule – so it is placed well left of centre on the matrix. That the flavour is central to the quality of the final butter product is obvious – so we find it placed well above the centre line for significance. There are expectations put on such suppliers: absolute security of supply, complete consistency of quality, and the like. Provided these expectations are met, those suppliers will be highly valued. Figure 28.7 illustrates the position.

Figure 28.7
The fat man

The fat man represents the total costs of all materials purchased by the Unilever butter business. The heart represents the flavour component – and note that well: it is the heart. Nobody, both sides recognize, nobody is going to have a heart transplant for the sake of a price discount!

Value pricing and the customer's product life cycle

In Chapter 25 we considered the product life cycle, and discussed how price might vary from introduction (high) through growth (falling) to maturity (lowest) and on to decline (rising). Here we are going to consider the customer's product life cycle.

Consider the case of a pharmaceutical company. How does it view its supplier's prices as it moves through the product life cycle of one of its drugs?

Before the introduction of the drug, its focus is very firmly on ensuring that it passes the various stages of regulatory approval. At this point it will certainly not jeopardize the success of a billion-dollar investment for the sake of a sharp discount on a supplier's product. Suppliers are key to its success: they bring expertise, perhaps services that speed the drug through the pre-launch stages or help to ensure the drug's efficacy. The value placed on such a supplier is almost beyond calculation.

Once the drug is launched, the pharmaceutical company's attention shifts from efficacy and regulatory approval towards the supplier's ability to keep pace with volume growth. The supplier that can match the pace without any risk to security and quality will still be valued. It is a different kind of value, and perhaps not quite so incalculable, but price will not yet be a burning issue.

It is only as the drug enters the maturity stage and approaches the date when competing generics can become available that the pharmaceutical company will start to turn its attention towards price. But even here there are opportunities for the value-pricing supplier. If a packaging supplier can come up with a design and style of pack that maintains the drug's position above the clamouring crowd of generic imitators then the wise pharmaceutical company will value that supplier and pay it accordingly.

Value pricing and risk

Training companies, like my own, often get called in to some fairly hairy situations. Sad to say, many clients wait until they have a problem before looking for help and, as any doctor will tell you, prevention is always better and cheaper than cure. A typical situation will be a client planning to launch a new product and realizing as the date approaches that it is far from certain how to go about the whole thing. Chapter 12 showed us, using the Ansoff matrix, that new product development (NPD) is a high-risk growth strategy. Businesses taking such risks need help from good suppliers, help that often marks the difference between success and failure. Putting a price on a training course on NPD at such a moment has little to do with cost breakdowns. Even when the client *does* prepare well in advance, and the training is 'preventive' rather than 'curative', the value of such an intervention is well beyond the question of days spent. A supplier that helps its client reduce risk is a supplier to be valued, and that is another root of value pricing.

Value pricing and the adopters curve

Chapter 15 introduced the idea of the adopters curve, representing the number of people who bought into a new product or idea over time. Consumer products in particular have long made use of this model in their pricing strategies. A product at its introduction is obviously novel, interesting and desirable – to a particular segment of the market: the innovators. Innovators will see value in a product sometimes simply because of its novelty. A good example is the launch of a new car, especially if it is heralded by a blast of publicity and media coverage. Such publicity surrounded the launch of the Jaguar 'S type' in 1999, a car that harked back to the glory days of the 1960s. There was without doubt a group of customers for the 'S type' who would place great value on being seen to drive this car – early. Ego and prestige alongside exclusivity are powerful drivers for value pricing, and the new Jaguar responded to the opportunity.

Jaguar and the early adopter

Another example of the value of newness is found in the world of mobile communications. The rate of technological change makes for a never-ending stream of new products, each eagerly awaited by innovators and early adopters. At the other end of the adopter's curve, the late majority are often buying products that are already well past maturity and about to disappear. This provides fertile ground for pricing policies that distinguish the different segments of the market indicated by the adopters curve. Significant premiums are paid to be the first to have the absolute leading-edge model, as the glass cabinet displays at airport duty-free shops make clear. Value in such markets is definitely denoted by newness.

Summary of the four generic methods of pricing

We have considered the four methods in turn, and in isolation, but in truth, most businesses will be using a mix of methods at any one time. There is no harm in that, provided that it is a managed mix. Marginal pricing can be a useful tactic, if used sparingly and always kept under the control of the marketer, not the salesperson. Market pricing and value pricing have some obvious points of overlap: market pricing imposes a limit on just how far value pricing can go, but also a spur to escape its clutches. Cost-plus pricing received a fairly severe thrashing in this chapter, but let us not forget its main merit: its focus on the desire to make a profit. Perhaps cost-based pricing can be used as an initial target-setting exercise, or as a final sanity check on the profitability of your value-based creativity?

There is one last thing to say in summary of these methods: none of them exists in a vacuum. Unless you have a monopoly (and that is a whole new ballgame for pricing), our discussion on pricing needs to take a further twist of complexity: there is the competitive response to consider.

COMPETITIVE PRICING STRATEGIES

Pricing, as well as being a means of ensuring that you receive your just reward, is a means of determining your competitive advantage – a defensive tool for fighting off aggressive competitors, or even a weapon used in trying to destroy them. This is, as it sounds, a dangerous and complex place of action, reaction and counter-action; we need a means to the right choice. We will look at a two-step process: 1) the price/performance audit; and 2) the competitive pricing strategy matrix.

The price/performance audit

Consider your own current performance and place your product(s) or service(s) on the matrix in Figure 28.8.

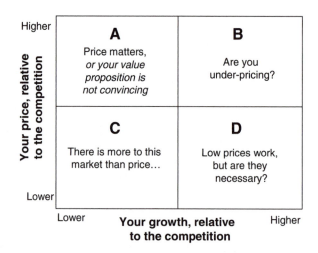

Figure 28.8   *The price/performance audit*

The matrix asks you to consider whether your price is higher or lower than that of the competition (the vertical axis), and whether your business growth is faster or slower than that of the competition (the horizontal axis). We might then reach the following general conclusions depending on where you find yourself on the matrix:

- *Box A*. Whatever value you are claiming for your product or service, either it is not sufficient for the price you are asking, or it isn't wanted by the customers. Your competitors are offering a better price–value fit.
- *Box B*. You appear to be getting it right, but take care that you are not missing an opportunity for more, or perhaps even offering *too much* value.
- *Box C*. There is obviously more to this market than price.
- *Box D*. Low prices seem to work, but are they necessary? Could you charge more?

The analysis is general, and raises more questions than it answers. The second step of this competitive pricing strategy process raises two of them.

The competitive pricing strategy matrix

The matrix in Figure 28.9 shows four possible pricing strategies that result from the consideration of two questions: what opportunity do we have to reduce our own costs, and what opportunity do we have to differentiate our offer?

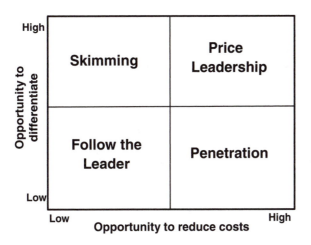

Figure 28.9 _Competitive pricing strategies_

The opportunity to reduce costs may come from a number of factors, including the following:

- You have spare capacity, and filling it with volume would bring unit costs down.
- Your product or service enjoys significant economies of scale from higher volume.
- You are able to invest in improved efficiency.
- A lower price for your product will allow you to reduce quality or service.
- The _experience curve_ is the notion that the longer you are involved in an activity, the better you get at it. A manufacturer should be able to produce at a lower and lower cost (ignoring inflation) as experience increases (see page 353).

Remember that this matrix is about competitive pricing, so the question is not just whether you can reduce costs, but whether you can reduce them faster and further than competitors can.

351

The opportunity to differentiate your product or service may come from a variety of factors, including the following:

- the use of brand names;
- promotional expenditure;
- PR activities;
- service packages;
- product quality;
- the impact of relationships.

Remember again that this matrix is about competitive pricing. It isn't just a question of whether you have good ideas, products or service packages; the question to ask is, will they outpace the competition, and will customers regard them as being worth a premium?

The generic strategies

Four generic competitive pricing strategies emerge from this analysis:

- skimming: pricing above the competition and selecting the 'cream' from the market;
- penetration: pricing below the competition to gain share;
- being price leader – meaning that you can 'direct' the market price, up or down;
- being a price follower – meaning that you must follow the price leader.

Skimming

Skimming is an attractive option when more volume will not drive costs down, or where there is no volume to chase, or when your capacity is full, or if you have such a large share of the market that further volume growth would be difficult, or where economies of scale do not apply to you.

Penetration

Penetration is an attractive option if the market demands a low price and will accept a mass-produced, uniform product or service. It is, however, fraught with problems.

Penetration and the real world

A manufacturer of chemicals for the leather industry in the United States decided upon a penetration strategy, not because it believed it could reduce its own costs, but because it believed it could stand the heat of lower margins longer than its competitors. The competitors would be 'shaken out' of the market. The low prices offered succeeded in winning volume, market share grew, and competitors had to follow prices down, but then a problem was encountered. The manufacturer reached capacity in its factory, and competitors were able to edge prices up again because demand was still ahead of supply. A competitive pricing strategy came up against the twin realities of production capacity and supply and demand. Few pricing strategies can operate in complete independence of these factors.

The success of a penetration pricing strategy as described here depends on a _genuine_ opportunity to reduce costs – through volume, through economies of scale or through the _experience curve_ (see below). Very often, of course, companies will use what looks like a penetration strategy to gain trial for their product – a common phenomena in fmcg markets – but it is not a true penetration strategy in the sense described here; rather, it is a short-term pricing tactic. Where such approaches often come unstuck is that they encourage a response from the competition that can scupper not only the tactic, but also the profitability of the whole market.

Price leadership

Price leadership is great, if you can pull it off – and what it requires, of course, is excellent marketing skills! You have the choice to penetrate, knowing that others cannot keep up with you, or to skim, knowing that you can command a premium, but beware the protective price umbrella discussed earlier in the chapter.

Being a price follower

The position of price follower is an uncomfortable one. Try to avoid it (good marketing), try to escape it (good marketing) – or perhaps you have to leave this market? This last choice can also be good marketing: there is nothing clever about hanging on in a market where you cannot win.

The generic strategies discussed here are of course only a guide to what is possible and 'wise'. In the end, your final choice of price in a competitive environment will be determined by what you intend to achieve in that market: profit growth, market share, high perceived value, trial, etc.

Many people have broken the rules and succeeded – or at least, they appeared to have broken the rules. The no-frills airlines have used penetration strategies that the traditional players didn't think possible. The likes of BA were dismissive, at first, of the ability of easyJet to bring down its costs sufficiently to make its business model work. What easyJet was doing was jumping into the virtuous circle of a pure penetration pricing strategy – not just cutting price to gain share, but cutting price because the volume gained drove costs down. This virtuous circle is shown in Figure 28.10.

Of course, the question now is, how long can this virtuous circle continue, and does the overcrowding of the market by like-minded competitors break the model? We will have to wait and see.

The experience curve

For most business activities, it is true that the longer you are involved in the activity, the better you become at it. Costs should reduce for a manufacturer

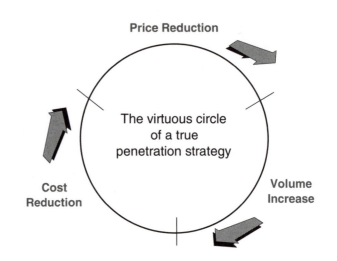

Figure 28.10   *The virtuous circle of true penetration pricing*

as it learns how to make the product, improves its process, grows its volume, gets smarter with suppliers, etc. Customers have been known to use this theory as a means of persuading suppliers to lower their prices.

The 'Lopez factor'

Any supplier to the automotive industry will recognize the scenario, often referred to as the 'Lopez factor'. Ignatius Lopez was a senior manager at General Motors, remembered for demanding price cuts from suppliers on a long-term basis. A supplier that could commit to price reductions this year, the next *and* the next would stand a chance of staying listed. The argument put forward was twofold: more volume would come your way as the number of suppliers able to oblige reduced, and the benefits of the *experience curve* would take effect. The theory was quite workable for some suppliers, but didn't work so well for those that had fewer opportunities for economies of scale.

It is an important notion whether it applies to your own business or not, because it may just apply to your competitor's.

Riding the experience curve...

Back in the 1970s, Kodak had the lion's share of the European film market, and enjoyed healthy prices and margins as a result. Then Fuji entered the market. Fuji came in with a price well below Kodak's, even below Kodak's costs to manufacture, and Kodak regarded this as a very short-term phenomenon; how could Fuji survive at such a price?

Indeed, Fuji was not making a profit at these prices, and, worse, its costs were significantly higher than Kodak's at this point. But this was all deliberate. Fuji was following a penetration strategy closely allied to the theory of the experience curve. As its price gained it volume, and as it became more experienced at operating in these new European markets, so its costs came down. Fuji, like many a Japanese company, was 'playing the long game', and was prepared to wait a long time before its cost curve dipped below its price line. At last it did, and it was clear to Kodak that Fuji was no temporary phenomenon.

At this point Kodak had a choice to make: to chase Fuji down the price route, hoping to gain some of the cost savings for itself as volume came back, or to differentiate its offer. The opportunity to differentiate (in comparison to Fuji's offer) was far greater than the opportunity to reduce costs (in comparison to Fuji's costs), and so Kodak chose the product innovation route – and both, as they say, have lived relatively happily ever after.

... or differentiating through innovation

A final strategy: the zero price or zero margin strategy

This final strategy may seem a rather crazy one – selling for nothing, or selling for no profit – but it demonstrates how price is but one part of the marketing mix, and just one means to profitability. Suppliers will often offer their products for free trial: sachets of shampoo taped to magazines, time-share operators giving trial weekends, agrochemical suppliers providing 'aid' to the Third World. Each has its motive, ranging from encouraging trial, to building desire, to establishing dependency.

Retailers use the 'loss-leader' tactic: offering well-known brands at cost (or less) in order to entice us into their store, where we will doubtless spend our money on other, 'full margin' items. Studies have shown in fact that shoppers who go out in response to these promoted bargains will very often end up spending more than they would on a normal shopping trip. Having said that, I recall the owner of an independent grocery store in East Anglia who took great delight in shopping at his competitors' whenever they made these offers, buying huge quantities of the 'loss-leader' items, and only those, to sell in his own store at the normal rate (the supermarket's sale price was often below the price he could get from the wholesaler). He saw this as a means of striking a blow against the unfair tactics of the big boys, and is doubtless still doing it to this day!

Service providers such as mobile phone network companies use the price of the mobile phone itself (much below its actual cost or even free) as a means to tie us into their service, at which point the real pricing strategies begin. Never was it more truly said that 'you don't get owt for nowt!'.

There are some wholesale cash-and-carry operators that take the zero margin idea to its extreme, making no profit on the sale of items to their customers. The secret is in the cash flow. The cash-and-carry, as its name implies, offers no credit: it takes cash payments only. If it is able to negotiate long credit terms with its suppliers, and if it concentrates on lines with high stock-turns, then it will generate free cash that it can invest for a return elsewhere. This kind of cash-and-carry operation is merely a means to an end: cash. To be in competition with such a business and not understand its use of price would be a frustrating experience indeed!

Where cash is King

355

OPEN BOOK TRADING

Many purchasing organizations have learnt that the supplier's choice of price, despite the theory of cost-plus, market based or value based, is often arbitrary and mysterious. An increasingly common policy in the light of this is to ask for *open book trading*. Suppliers are asked to disclose the make-up of their price, justifying each element and its principle. This may seem just like asking for cost breakdowns (as discussed on page 337 under cost-plus pricing), with all the attendant risks of losing control of the package. In some cases it is, but in others it is a genuine attempt to improve the effectiveness of the customer–supplier relationship. So how should the supplier respond?

One option is to refuse to comply, which generally works until the competition starts to comply – and then the fun starts. Another option is to comply, but with such complexity as to defeat the purpose – effective in the short term, very unpopular in the long term.

Perhaps the only real answer to such requests is to ensure that your price is a value-based price. Examine your own activities and determine which of them *genuinely* provide value to the customer. Make every effort to eliminate those activities that don't. The customer won't ask you to remove an element of your offer that gives it value, and if it does ask you to remove something then this tells you where you are going wrong!

In the end, the only suppliers with anything to fear from this debate are the guilty ones: the cost-plus brigade, those with no true value to offer, and, most importantly, those that don't understand the value they provide.

There is, then, one step further that you should take in responding to requests for open book trading: ask the customer to respond with detail on its own costs in use, and use this information to tailor your offer to ensure that it provides the maximum value possible. This should be the start of another virtuous circle…

A PRICING SELF-ASSESSMENT

Having read this chapter, and before reading the case study in Chapter 29, you might like to take 15 to 20 minutes to consider the following questions. It will be helpful to identify a specific product or service and a specific customer when considering your answers.

Viewed from your perspective:

1. Where and how do you add value to your customer's business? Is it through:
    – the product?
    – the service?
    – the relationship?
    – other?

2. Where and how do you achieve value-based pricing?
3. Where do you incur costs, without adding value?
4. Under what circumstances do you fail to achieve value-based pricing?

Viewed from the customer's perspective:

1. For one of your products or services, identify:
   - its features (tangible characteristics);
   - its benefits (what those features do for the customer);
   - its value (the value the customer derives from those benefits).
2. Identify the customer's definition of value received.
3. Try to quantify that value received. (What would be the cost to the customer's business of not receiving the product or service?)
4. Is your price for this product or service based on its features, its benefits or its value?
5. What are the customer's alternatives to buying your product or service:
   - a competitor's products or services?
   - alternative solutions?
   - to do nothing?
6. What does your answer to question 5 indicate to you about 'price elasticity' (how far your price could go up before the customer chose one of those alternatives)?

29

The Ambient Ltd case study

Ambient started life in the 1970s on the back of the North Sea oil and gas business, supplying pipework sealants to the rigs. Still based in the United Kingdom, but now supplying exploration companies around the world, Ambient has built a reputation for quality, largely through the success of a product introduced in 1997: Ambo 5.

Ambo 5

When Ambo 5 was introduced, its unique properties established it as the clear market leader. The 'secret' was in the hardener, which allowed for a wide variation in setting times (depending on the dose) and in final rigidity. This made Ambo 5 particularly beneficial for use in difficult environments – ideal for the oil and gas exploration market.

The future?

Ambient's forecasts for the coming years show a downturn in oil and gas exploration, at least in Ambient's main territorial markets, and its MD, Martin Doyle, has been keen to look for new markets, with new applications. A lot of time had been spent looking at the European building market, and for the last year a small pack size of Ambo 5 has been on sale through UK builders' merchants, more or less as a market testing exercise. Early reports suggest that the product is regarded as of high quality, but is difficult to use – the instruction leaflet runs to four pages!

The competition

The success of Ambo 5 hit the competition hard, and before long, two of Ambient's competitors were launching copycat products. Lotus 'C' was launched in 1999 and, although the quality of early production was variable, it sold well because demand was greater than could be met by Ambient's limited production capacity at that time. The following year, X-Tec was launched by another competitor.

The market history

The first three years were growth years for all players with Ambo-type products. By 2000, prices were very similar for all three suppliers, and market shares were stable, with Ambo taking half of the market and the rest being shared being between Lotus and X-Tec.

Sales growth started to slow from 2001 and it became clear that the market had not been growing for some time and that the sales growth of previous years had come largely from replacing older technologies. The new, smaller pack size for the building market was a tiny proportion of sales, but at least it was showing growth, unlike Ambo's total sales in 2004.

In January 2004, Ambient had increased its price to £10.00 per kilo from £9.50. Both competitors held their prices at £9.50. In Q1, Q2 and Q3, Ambo 5 sales volume was down by 10 per cent, and both Lotus and X-Tec increased their market shares.

Pricing for 2005

By October 2004 it was clear that neither competitor was going to raise its price (there had been hopes that they would do so in July or, failing that, in September), and Ambient was faced with a difficult pricing decision for 2005. Martin Doyle, Ambient's MD, called a special board meeting to discuss the matter.

The Ambient board

The board members were as follows:

Martin Doyle, Managing Director
Barry Sellers, Sales Director
Walter Plant, Works Manager
Marion Marks, Marketing Director
Faith Mooney, Finance Director

Martin (MD) made it clear that it would be a short meeting because he had a 12.30 lunch appointment, and that each board member should come prepared to argue his or her case. (Martin's 12.30 appointment was with an old friend, the boss of the company that supplied Ambient with its main production equipment.)

Martin asked Marion Marks (Marketing) to circulate details of estimated market size and shares (Table 29.1), and also the quoted prices from 1998 to date (Table 29.2). Faith Mooney (Finance) was asked to circulate the confidential data on Ambo 5's production costs at different volumes (Table 29.3).

Table 29.1 *Estimated market size and sales volumes (kg)*

Year	Total (est)	Ambo 5 (act)	X-Tec (est)	Lotus 'C' (est)
1997	60,000	60,000	–	–
1998	140,000	140,000	–	–
1999	350,000	210,000	–	140,000
2000	610,000	335,000	155,000	120,000
2001	830,000	410,000	210,000	210,000
2002	990,000	515,000	250,000	225,555
2003	1,140,000	630,000	260,000	250,000
2004	1,255,000	565,000	350,000	340,000
2005	*1,330,000*			

Table 29.2 *Quoted prices (£)*

Year	Ambo 5	X-Tec	Lotus 'C'
1998	5.60	–	–
1999	6.00	–	5.60
2000	7.00	7.00	6.80
2001	8.00	8.00	8.00
2002	9.00	9.00	9.00
2003	9.50	9.50	9.50
2004	10.00	9.50	9.50

The meeting

The meeting opened at 11.00 prompt. Barry Sellers (Sales) and Faith Mooney (Finance) had already agreed with each other that they would argue for

Table 29.3 *Confidential production costs*

Volume (kg)	530,000	560,000	590,000	620,000	650,000	680,000	710,000
Direct costs	£/Kg	£/Kg	£/Kg	£/Kg	£/Kg	£/Kg	£/Kg
Materials	2.10	2.10	2.10	2.10	2.10	2.10	2.10
Labour	1.12	1.05	1.00	0.98	1.00	1.06	1.10
Other costs	£/Kg	£/Kg	£/Kg	£/Kg	£/Kg	£/Kg	£/Kg
Manufacture	0.06	0.04	0.04	0.03	0.04	0.05	0.06
Selling	0.06	0.05	0.04	0.03	0.03	0.04	0.05
Admin	0.02	0.01	0.01	0.01	0.02	0.03	0.04
Fixed costs	£/Kg	£/Kg	£/Kg	£/Kg	£/Kg	£/Kg	£/Kg
Manufacture	3.75	3.54	3.36	3.2	2.93	2.80	2.68
Selling	1.58	1.50	1.42	1.35	1.29	1.24	1.18
Admin	1.06	1.00	0.95	0.90	0.86	0.82	0.79
	£/Kg	£/Kg	£/Kg	£/Kg	£/Kg	£/Kg	£/Kg
Total costs	9.75	9.29	8.92	8.60	8.27	8.14	8.00

Ambient to hold its price at £10.00 per kilo. Faith gave their reasons, turning to look at Walter Plant (Works Manager): 'You have said it often enough this summer, Walter, they must be mad to sell at £9.50. They surely must be losing money at that price.' Faith went on to forecast that prices for 2005 would converge at £10.00; it seemed unlikely that the competition could hold prices for three years running, even with low inflation. 'If that is the case, as I'm sure it will be,' she continued, 'we will probably regain a market share of 50–52 per cent.' She turned to Barry (Sales): 'I would suggest a sales target of 680,000 kilos, with a projected profit of over £1.25 million.'

Marion Marks (Marketing) waved a dismissive hand towards the Finance Director and expressed her own view: 'Personally, I would have thought that with our competitors' sales up by around 40 per cent, they are more likely to be earning good profits than losing money.' Walter (Works Manager) nodded awkwardly. He was annoyed that Faith (Finance) had referred to his rather rash remarks from earlier in the summer. Once he had seen the autumn sales projections for Lotus 'C' and X-Tec, he had recognized the improved plant utilization they were getting: both had three production units, each with a 120,000 kg annual capacity.

Barry Sellers (Sales) passed a sheet of paper to the MD and went into presentation mode:

'As you can see, we have looked at the possibility of them holding on to £9.50. If they do that, we still think that a sustained sales push will recapture some lost volume. My estimate would be that a 46–47 per cent market share is quite possible.'

Faith Mooney (Finance) nodded and added that at 620,000 kilos the contribution to overheads was still over £4 million. Barry and Faith smiled at each other: they were pleased with their morning's collaboration.

The MD remembered that he had agreed only a year back to put the Sales team on a volume-related bonus scheme, and now he always felt nervous whenever he heard Barry talking about a 'sales push'. He asked for views on putting the price up to £10.50 per kilo.

'Everything I said,' Barry jumped in quickly, pushing a second sheet of paper towards his boss, 'everything depends on our holding our price' – he paused, and then continued, expecting a howl of disapproval from Marion Marks (Marketing) – 'or dropping it.' The second sheet of paper showed Barry's calculations based on an Ambo 5 price increase: volume down to 530,000 kg, plunging market share, and a slump in profits to £400,000.

As the MD read out the dire predictions, Barry nodded his head furiously and then, looking straight at Marion (Marketing), he almost spat out the words, 'Any further widening of the price differential would be disastrous.'

Barry was surprised by the silence in the room, by the heads nodding around the table, but, most of all, by Marion's response: 'I agree. The growth in the market is levelling off, and in those circumstances market share is vital. Even a fall to 47 per cent – that was your guess, I think, Barry, if we all stay as we are – even that would be disastrous. I think it's time we put the pressure back on the competition.'

To everyone's surprise, and before anyone else could speak, Marion was on her feet, and, taking a pen, she wrote in large, thick letters on a flip chart, **'PRICE REDUCTION TO £9.50.'**

Walter Plant (Works Manager) was the first to comment: he was completely behind Marion, he said. The energy levels in the room were rising fast, and Walter was getting quite excited by the turn of events. Back in 2002, Walter had persuaded the board to approve a sixth production unit (they were standard machines producing 120,000 kg per annum) based on sales projections of 690,000 kg in 2003 and 720,000 kg in 2004. Things had started out well: the sixth machine had come on stream with impressive speed, helping Ambient to record sales in 2003. Walter had been something of a hero, with a handsome performance bonus to show for it. But for most of this year the machine had stood idle. Walter had managed to switch production to it as he took out each of the older machines for overhaul and maintenance, but that had not taken long. Now the additional staff he had taken on were going to be as idle as the machine, unless sales rose again. He faced with dismay the prospect of dismissing staff newly taken on – not least because his nephew was among the newer recruits and would almost certainly be one of the first to go. He liked what he was hearing from Marion.

Marion (Marketing) and Barry (Sales) were now standing side by side at the flip chart, drawing upward-sloping curves with the sort of enthusiasm that the board had not seen since the launch of Ambo 5. At £9.50, market share would go back to 52 per cent, and with a strong sales effort behind the price cut, the market might well grow by more than the projected 6 per cent. The price cut should stimulate growth of just over 8 per cent (to 1,360,000 kg), with Ambo 5 accounting for 710,000 kg.

Faith (Finance) tapped out the new figures on her calculator, and with Marion, Barry and now Walter standing around the flip chart, they barely noticed the MD getting up to leave. 'Thank you for your thoughts,' he said. 'I suggest we meet again at three this afternoon. Is that OK with everyone?'

Just like the boss, they thought. No clue to what he was thinking, and no support for their new-found enthusiasm. They separated, each wondering what would happen when they regathered at 3.00 pm.

Case questions

1. Consider, and comment on, the views of each board member.
2. Comment on the figures provided by the two board members shown in Tables 29.1, 29.2 and 29.3. How useful were these in the pricing decision?
3. Comment on the way in which the board members discussed the issues and prepared their plans for 2005.
4. If you were the MD, going to a meeting with the supplier of the machinery used by you, and your competitors, to manufacture Ambo 5-type products, what would be the questions you would be asking the supplier?
5. If you were employed as a consultant to the board, what proposals would you make for 2005 pricing, and for any other marketing issues?

If you would like to e-mail your answers or any other comments on this case study to INSIGHT at Customer.service@insight-mp.com, we will gladly critique your report and send you our own thoughts.

Part VI

Making it happen

30

The marketing health check

The following questionnaire (also to be found on the CD ROM) is designed to help you and your colleagues self-assess your current level of marketing excellence, and to identify those issues requiring further attention. Throughout, replace 'you' and 'your' with 'we', 'us and 'our', if that is more appropriate.

For each question in the following list, indicate whether you are fully effective, only partially effective or not at all effective in your current activities. Then, scan for the 'not at alls' as first priority for improvement, followed by the 'only partially' answers. (Chapter numbers indicate where you can find more detail on the issue concerned.)

A	The marketing process and plan *(Part I)*	**Fully**	**Only partially**	**Not at all**
A1	Do you follow a clearly structured marketing process? *(Chapter 5)*			
A2	Is that process based on a disciplined market audit designed to help you make the necessary strategic and tactical decisions? *(Chapter 5)*			
A3	Does the process provide a flow from strategic positioning, through development of the value proposition, and into the tactical application of the marketing mix (the 4 P's)? *(Chapter 5)*			

		Fully	**Only partially**	**Not at all**

A4 Does the process result in the creation of future-orientated, formally written marketing plans available to all and capable of easy updating? *(Chapter 6)*

B **The strategic market audit** *(Part II)*

B1 Have you conducted a PESTLE analysis and determined your conclusions? *(Chapter 9)*

B2 Have you drawn out the market map, identifying the main channels to market, through to the end user, showing the shares and volumes by channel, such that you properly understand the dynamics and influences in this market? *(Chapter 9)*

B3 Have you assessed the current and potential impact on your competitive position by using Porter's five forces analysis? *(Chapter 9)*

B4 Have you conducted a full SWOT analysis of your position in the market – in particular, expressing your strengths and weaknesses as they are perceived by your customers? *(Chapter 9)*

B5 Have you used the Directional Policy Matrix (DPM) to determine the priority target markets or segments? *(Chapter 9)*

C **Strategic positioning** *(Part III)*

C1 Do you have a vision that makes clear 'what business we are in', and includes SMART objectives? *(Chapter 11)*

C2 Have you identified your preferred options for growth, assessed the risks involved in those growth strategies, and identified the means of reducing those risks? *(Chapter 12)*

C3 Have you identified your source of competitive advantage: to be the lowest-cost supplier, or to be a differentiated supplier? *(Chapter 13)*

C4 Do you have clearly articulated *value drivers*, agreed by all? *(Chapter 14)*

	Fully	Only partially	Not at all

C5 Have you segmented your market in a way that allows you to position specific and unique marketing mixes by segment? *(Chapter 15)*

C6 Have you determined the role of your brand(s) in your strategic positioning, and constructed the appropriate brand architecture? *(Chapter 16)*

D **Delivering the value (by segment)** *(Part IV)*

D1 Have you conducted a full segment audit – in particular, drawing out the segment/customer value chain and identifying the total business experience required in the segment? *(Chapter 17)*

D2 Have you determined your value proposition by using the customer activity cycle and positive impact analyses? *(Chapter 18)*

D3 Have you classified your customers as key accounts, key development accounts, maintenance accounts and opportunistic accounts? *(Chapter 19)*

D4 Have you drawn up distinct sales and service strategies for each customer classification? *(Chapter 19)*

D5 Have you defined and communicated the value context and emotional charge of your brand(s)? *(Chapter 20)*

D6 Are all relevant functions aligned behind the goals and processes of your marketing plan? *(Chapter 21)*

D7 Have you identified the priorities and the expected returns from the products within your product portfolio? *(Chapter 22)*

E **Tactical application** *(Part V)*

E1 Do you conduct regular tactical audits, including (for instance) market share reports, customer satisfaction ratings, competitor activity reports and tracking studies? *(Chapter 23)*

		Fully	**Only partially**	**Not at all**
E2	Do you manage each product in accordance with its product life cycle, and, in particular, do you look for opportunities to augment products or extend product life? *(Chapter 25)*			
E3	Do you have a robust procedure for new product development? *(Chapter 25)*			
E4	Have you mapped out the different channels to market, and assessed the value added by your partners and customers in those channels *(Chapter 26)*			
E5	Have you maximized the utility and manageability of your channel partners? *(Chapter 26)*			
E6	Do you have a robust process for supply chain management, focused on reducing unnecessary costs and maximizing the positive contribution to customer value? *(Chapter 26)*			
E7	Do you have clear objectives for your promotional plan? *(Chapter 27)*			
E8	Have you developed a clear, single-minded proposition? *(Chapter 27)*			
E9	Have you identified the best choice of media for delivering that proposition? *(Chapter 27)*			
E10	Are you utilizing the sales team as a promotional vehicle? *(Chapter 27)*			
E11	Does your pricing policy aim to maximize the rewards received for a clear value proposition? *(Chapter 28)*			
E12	Are you able to base prices on calculations of the customer's cost in use, or value received? *(Chapter 28)*			

The INSIGHT Performance Map

The Performance Map (Figure 30.1) gives a visual representation of the state of marketing in your business, as perceived by the respondents to this or an expanded version of this self-assessment questionnaire. The map highlights good and poor performance, and indicates where the priorities for improvement should be.

The map recognizes that good marketing results from effective links between all the elements of the process and plan, building from data through positioning, to development of the value proposition, to tactical application. Thus, poor performance at the start of the process can only result in sub-optimal performance at the later stages.

The map is shown here in black and white, while the real thing uses colour to indicate strengths and problem areas. The lines linking the 'elements' of marketing are shown in green where a good performance is leading to the next element, and in red where a poor performance will be damaging the effectiveness of the next activity in line.

For further details on using this Performance Map, please contact INSIGHT: details as shown in Chapter 31.

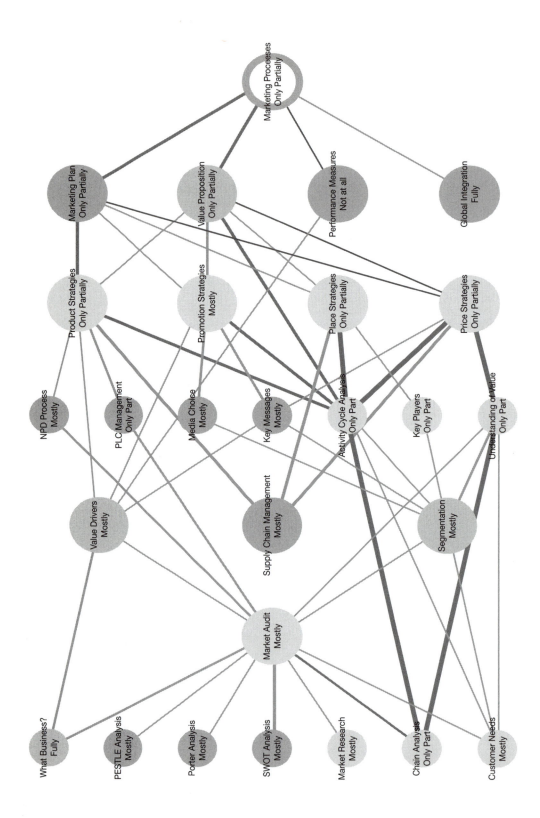

Figure 30.1 *The INSIGHT Marketing Performance Map*

31

Getting further help

The second edition of this book is largely the result of comments and questions from readers, complimentary and otherwise! We welcome questions on all aspects of marketing practice, and will do our best to answer them, or put you in touch with people who can. Please feel free to contact us at:

INSIGHT Marketing and People Ltd
1 Lidstone Court
Uxbridge Road
George Green
Slough SL3 6AG
United Kingdom
Tel: +44 (0)1753 822990
Fax: +44 (0)1753 822992
e-mail: customer.service@insight-mp.com
www.insight-mp.com

I can suggest four further ways of developing your knowledge, understanding and expertise:

- the CD ROM application tools;
- training;
- on-the-job experience;
- further reading.

APPLICATION TOOLS

The CD ROM attached to this book contains a number of tools designed to help you with the application of what you have been reading:

1. *A PowerPoint template for a marketing plan.* This is not a fixed set of rules of what must be in a plan: the final choice is up to you and must suit your circumstances, but please think hard before deleting anything!
2. *The Directional Policy Matrix.* This is a simplified version, limited by the number of markets/segments/products/customers that you are able to compare, but it provides a simple introduction to the use of this hugely valuable tool. (If you want to make use of a more powerful version, allowing a much wider scope of comparisons, please contact INSIGHT as shown above.)
3. *The activity cycle.* This is a beautifully simple means of recording the details of an activity cycle analysis (see Chapter 18) and highlighting the priority actions.
4. *The INSIGHT self-assessment questionnaire.* This will help you focus on where you need to improve your company's marketing performance. The questionnaire can be used as the basis for a company-wide assessment of your capabilities, using the INSIGHT Marketing Performance Map (see Chapter 30). If you would like further details on this, please contact INSIGHT as above.

TRAINING OPPORTUNITIES

There are many hundreds of training opportunities available, provided by training companies large and small, business schools, and professional institutes such as the Chartered Institute of Marketing. Making recommendations is impossible, but I can give four bits of advice:

1. Ask if the course's focus is consumer or manufacturing, fmcg or B2B, or service.
2. If it is a public event, ask what other companies will be attending. Do you want to be in like company, or do you deliberately want to broaden your horizons?
3. It is almost always better to organize training 'in-company', asking the provider to tailor it to meet your own circumstances and challenges. If it won't, or can't, or it is clear that it has only changed the title slides, it is not the provider for you.
4. If you get a provider to work in-company, ask for its experience in tailoring. Most say they will do it; disappointingly few actually will!

Please feel free to contact INSIGHT, as above, for advice on finding the right training solution for you and your business.

ON-THE-JOB EXPERIENCE

The value of on-the-job experience cannot be overestimated. The secret to using your own work experience to develop your expertise is to challenge the status quo. Take care not to make yourself unpopular, or even a genuine nuisance, by unthinking criticism; rather, always ask 'why?'. Get people to explain their decisions (you may even help them to learn something), and be enthusiastic in suggesting alternative approaches. Any marketing professional who doesn't value debate, and shuns alternative views, is to be regarded with sympathy, for the end is near... For your own part, encourage such questioning and debate among your own team, and don't be surprised if you find yourself learning hugely from the experience.

It is often said that the best way to learn is to teach. Where you have opportunities to impart your knowledge to others, formally or informally, seize that opportunity and give the task the time required to do a good job. The reward for your time will be ample.

FURTHER READING

The list of books on marketing is huge, and if your interest is an 'academic' one then the following list will only begin to scratch the surface. It is intended primarily for those wishing to understand further the practical application of the tools and techniques discussed, and includes those titles that my own clients have expressed an interest in as being useful in 'making it happen'.

Bird, D (2000) *Commonsense Direct Marketing*, Kogan Page, London

Cheverton, P (2002) *If You're So Brilliant, How Come Your Brand Isn't Working Hard Enough?*, Kogan Page, London

Cheverton, P (2004) *Key Account Management: The route to profitable key supplier status*, 3rd edn, Kogan Page, London

Haig, M (2004) *Brand Failures*, Kogan Page, London

Kotler, P (1999) *Kotler on Marketing*, Free Press, New York

McDonald, M (1999) *Marketing Plans: How to prepare them, how to use them*, Butterworth-Heinemann, Oxford

Porter, M (1980) *Competitive Strategy*, Free Press, New York

Treacy, M and Wiersema, F (1995) *The Discipline of Market Leaders*, HarperCollins, London

Index

Key Account Management

A complete action kit of tools and techniques for achieving profitable success

"A combination of clarity, enthusiasm, and common sense... reading this is a rewarding experience."

Professor Malcolm McDonald, Cranfield School of Management

"Will help any business focus their sales activities where they matter... on those (customers) that will take your business where you want it to go. All in all, this is the essential guide to global best practice."

Winning Business

Any organization's key accounts are its lifeblood. This highly practical book puts forward a unique yet simple planning methodology for identifying, obtaining, retaining and developing key customers.

Completely updated and revised with lots of new material to reflect the latest best practice, this edition will reinforce its standing as the premier book on the subject. This is one of very few books to take the long-term, team-selling strategic view of Key Account Management (KAM).

Apart from finding great resonance with business practitioners all over the world, *Key Account Management* has established itself on many academic reading lists. Translated into five languages, it was also short-listed for Business Book of the Year in Sweden (2002).

Key Account Management in Financial Services
Peter Cheverton, Bryan Foss, Tim Hughes & Merlin Stone

Key Account Management (KAM) has never been so important in the financial services (FS) industry as it is today. As the FS market becomes more competitive, more global and more mature, effective customer relationship management (CRM) has become a big issue, of which the KAM approach is an essential part.

Key Account Management in Financial Services has been written in response to a demand for a book devoted exclusively to the subject for this market. It offers specific advice on marketing and selling financial products, with real-world examples and case studies from FS companies around the globe.

Compiled from original in-depth research and interviews, it is divided into seven parts and is designed to take the reader through the process of understanding, analysis, planning, implementation and performance monitoring, so it can be used as a 'before, during, and after' guide to practical implementation.

This book is a must-have for anyone working or studying in this field.

Peter Cheverton's *Key Account Management* (3rd edition 2004, Kogan Page) has established itself as the leading book on the subject. The idea for this new book was prompted by the huge up-take for his *KAM Masterclass* workshops from sales and marketing people in FS companies all over the world. It also builds on the success of *CRM in Financial Services* (2002, Kogan Page) by Bryan Foss and Merlin Stone and their work with IBM's FS clients.

Beyond Branding: *How the new values of transparency and integrity are changing the world of brands*
Nicholas Ind

Brand Driven: *The route to integrated branding through great leadership*
F Joseph LePla, Susan Davis and Lynn M Parker

Brand Failures: *The truth about the 100 biggest branding mistakes of all time*
Matt Haig

Brand Management Checklist: *Proven tools and techniques for creating winning brands*
Brad van Auken

Brand New Brand Thinking: *Brought to life by 11 experts who do*
Edited by Merry Basking and Mark Earls

Brand Royalty: *How the world's top 100 brands thrive and survive*
Matt Haig

BRANDchild: *Remarkable insights into the minds of today's global kids and their relationships with brands*
Martin Lindstrom

CRM in Financial Services: *A practical guide to making customer relationship management work*
Bryan Foss and Merlin Stone

The Essential Brand Book: *Over 100 techniques to increase brand value*
2nd edition, Iain Ellwood

Global Brand Strategy: *Unlocking brand potential across countries, cultures and markets*
Sicco van Gelder

If You're So Brilliant…How Come Your Brand isn't Working Hard Enough?: *The Essential Guide to Brand Management*
Peter Cheverton

Integrated Branding: *Becoming brand-driven through company-wide action*
F Joseph LePla and Lynn M Parker

Living the Brand: *How to transform every member of your organization into a brand champion*
2nd edition, Nicholas Ind

Marketing: *Essential principles, new realities*
Jonathan Groucutt, Peter Leadley and Patrick Forsyth

Marketing Communications: *An integrated approach*
4th edition, P R Smith and Jonathan Taylor

Media Monoliths: *How great brands thrive and survive*
Mark Tungate

The Philosophy of Branding: *Great philosophers think brands*
Thom Braun

Reinventing the Brand: *Can top brands survive the new market realities?*
Jean-Noël Kapferer

The above titles are available from all good bookshops. To obtain further information, please contact the publisher at the address below:

Kogan Page Limited
120 Pentonville Road
London N1 9JN
United Kingdom
Tel:+44 (0) 20 7278 0433
Fax:+44 (0) 20 7837 6348

order online at:

www.kogan-page.co.uk